THE ATHLETIC BENCHLEY

105 EXERCISES FROM
THE DETROIT ATHLETIC CLUB NEWS

ROBERT C. BENCHLEY
EDITED BY
THOMAS J. SAUNDERS

WITH DRAWINGS BY GLUYAS WILLIAMS, BURT THOMAS, IRVIN, R. BARTON,
HERB ROTH, R.F. HEINRICH, DON HEROLD

PUBLISHERS
GLENDOWER MEDIA, LLC
WHITMORE LAKE, TORONTO
2010

THE ATHLETIC BENCHLEY
105 EXERCISES FROM THE DETROIT ATHLETIC CLUB NEWS

Copyright 2010, by Glendower Media,LLC
Printed in the United States of America

By arrangement with
The Detroit Athletic Club News
Ken Voyles, Editor

FIRST EDITION

TJS/GM

GDM 0710510101-H

ISBN 9780914303015

GDM 0610510201-P

ISBN 9780914303022

www.glendowermedia.com

THIS book is for Charles Hughes, who had the vision in the first place; for the members of the Detroit Athletic Club, past and present, for whom excellence is a constant pursuit; for Jim and Ellen Saunders, Jim and Barbara Finn and Rita Finn, who taught me the Gospel of Mr. Benchley in the fields of Sunny Las Los; and for my wife, Teri, who puts up with my crazy plots and talks me down.

Charles A. Hughes' Little Known Contributor to American Magazine Publishing

Although he remains an obscure figure in the world of American magazine publishing, Charles A. Hughes was a leader in metro Detroit publishing and printing, launching a magazine that continues to reach an important audience 95 years later. His impact nationally cannot be taken lightly thanks in part to his relationship with people like Robert Benchley.

After a brief, but successful newspaper and advertising career, Hughes went on to found in January of 1916 what is today one of the oldest continuously published monthly magazines in Michigan, the DAC News. The magazine still reaches an audience of more than 10,000 of the most important, powerful and successful leaders in metro Detroit and the state

No simple club "newsletter," the award-winning DAC News was founded by Hughes based on such journalistic principles of fair and objective reporting, well researched stories, an informative product, a singular devotion to being a civic service to the community it covers and a consistency of style and editorial standards. It didn't hurt that he also had a unique appreciation for literary style

Over the years the magazine's content has included feature and sports writing, essays and humor writing - all the hallmarks of America's great magazine tradition that took shape in the early part of the 20th century. It featured the works of numerous American authors, many who are household names today, as well as original art, illustrations and cartoons in a style similar to what one might see in The New Yorker. This combination of journalism and a erudite literary approach, especially during the DAC News' golden years of the 1920s and 1930s, brought Hughes great success, and he went on to own and operate the magazine until his death in 1953.

One of Hughes' collaborators and friends included renowned Detroit sports writers, E.A. "Eddie" Batchelor who wrote for the Detroit Free Press for decades; Edgar Guest, another Free Press journalist and Detroit poet, was a frequent contributor and sometime staff member. A number of other Detroit writers and artists have been connected to the magazine, offering a local flavor to a publication that also included regular essays from such New York notables as Dorothy Parker and, of course, Robert Benchley.

In the magazine's fifth year Hughes announced that he had landed "star writers" Benchley and Ring Lardner for the magazine, beginning a relationship with both that would last for many years. Years before Lardner had been Hughes' first choice for managing editor of his fledgling publication but the young sports writer's career took off so Hughes brought him on as a contributor instead.

Hughes was known as a "fixture" in New York literary circles, especially the Dutch Treat Club, a group of local theater and literary types. Humorist Frank Sullivan, a DAC News contributor for many years, said the publisher was a charter member of "The Table" a sub-group of the Dutch Treat Club, along with New Yorker publisher Harold Ross and Corey Ford.

Through this group, and the fabled Algonquin Club, Hughes got to know many of the literary agents, writers and artists. Eventually he became nearly as well known in New York as in Detroit. His mission, besides a passion for publishing, was to persuade the hot American talent of the day to write for his magazine.

Throughout the magazine's history a number of other important individuals contributed articles, often on a regular basis and often for many years. James Thurber's first published magazine piece ever to appear was in the DAC News (it was his only contribution). Other humorists (and more serious types) included Donald Ogden Stewart, Weare Holbrook, Don Herold, Stephen Leacock, Groucho Marx, Walter Winchell, Paul Gallico, S.S. Van Dine, Arthur C. Clarke (who had several stories rejected), Charles Goren and P.G. Wodehouse.

Within a few years of its founding, the DAC News' was the most significant magazine being published in the Midwest. Today with more than 1,100 issues published it can rightly be called the most significant benchmark for any Michigan magazine (and many national publications to boot).

This wonderful book should help go along way to restoring Charlie Hughes to a place of honor among the pantheon of American magazine publishers.

Kenneth H. Voyles
DAC News Publisher/Editor 2010

CONTENTS

Editor's Note

One day in October 1920, Charles Hughes, publisher of the Detroit Athletic News, wrote a bit that would change the face and content of his house organ forever. He announced the addition of several writers who would contribute from time to time to the pages of this already literary leaning publication. Hughes was a founding member of the DAC, as it was being called, and he wanted only the best for his members and for the reputation of his club. He certainly got it.

For years the DAC News brought to its readers, who were and are the leaders of American industry and commerce, not only Club doings in athletics and the arts, but writers who dominated the scene in plays, novels, news journals and articles. Perhaps the most beloved was Robert Benchley, Drama Critic for LIFE magazine and commentator on the impedimenta of daily life. Benchley's pieces have become the foundation for generations of comics, writers and commentators. Pulitzer Prize winners(Dave Berry), Academy Award winners(Woody Allen), Avery Hopwood winners and television and movie writers all hail Robert Benchley as the Father of Nonsense for its own sake; the inventor of the Rant against all things inanimate, and a man dedicated to letting the air out of the tires of the pompous, while keeping a watchful eye on his martini.

It all started in the lower right hand corner of an innocent magazine.......

Speaking about Ed Wynn he lives here in Goiter and the whole town is a asylum for actors you might say. Some of our neighbors is Geo. Cohan and Jack Hazzard and Ernest Truex and T. Roy Barnes and Oscar Shaw and Frank Craven and Jane Cowl and etc. Joan Sawyer use to live up the hill in back of us, but the Dr. says she must have quiet so she moved to Paris. Jack Hazzard is my favorite amist the actors. The stuff he has got is between 7 and 8 per cent stuff and I wished you could see the gang that calls on him Sunday afternoons to see if he is getting along O. K. Jack is the pitcher of health, but every Sunday they's a rumor around town that he has catched some disease another and everybody is worried and wants to find out for themself if it's true. I suppose they might call up and get the information only it's against the law to transport foam over the telephone wires.

Another citizen of Goiter is Gene Buck that come from Detroit and now he writes the Follies, that is he writes everything but the gags and the music. The gags is by Noah and the music from Memory. I and Gene plays shinny together pretty near every day out to the Goiter golf club. I wished we could get you on that course Chas. The dues is reasonable but they have got a gondolier that you are supposed to give him a dime every time he rescues one of your floaters and I and Gene practically supports him you might say. They's a couple of holes where you don't half to drive acrost Long Island sound. They call one of them a dog's leg, but believe me they didn't never make it out of a dachshund. I win this hole one day from Gene and Jack Wheeler both, and I was down in a eagle 11. The other dry hole use to be where Dan O'Leary the pedestrian done his road work. After he had walked from the tee to the green a couple times, his New York to San Francisco hikes seemed like stepping into the other room a minute. A good drive

takes you to where you can pretty near see the fair way. If you keep whacking them on the nose your 4th brassey crosses the Lincoln highway at Grand Island, Neb., and then 4 or 5 irons will bring you to the Sacramento valley where you can see the green from. They have got easy chairs and divans on the green and pretty near everybody either sets or lays down to putt.

The par for the course is 72. Try and get it.

Maybe some of Gene's Detroit friends would be interested in knowing that he has built himself a house here where him and his Mrs. entertains with a lavish hand. The interior of the house was painted by Urban and you half to wear smoked glasses when you first go inside. He has got a Finnish couple working for him. The husband puts in his time going around Goiter looking for Gene's dog. The wife, Harriet, does the cooking. Gene calls them Finn-and-Hattie.

That's about all I know to write about Chas. only that this is a grand place and I wished you could of seen it and to show how good it is, I haven't been to New York since them exciteing yacht races. The last time I was in I dropped in the Lambs Athletic Club and they was an Englishman there that had brought in a bun from outside and he got talking about the war and he says to Wilton Lackaye "Don't never get it into your head that you win the war." "No," says Wilton, "we didn't win the war, but we stopped it."

Give my regards to the family even if they ain't all boys like mine and also remember me to Mr. Briggs and Mr. Tannahill and Mr. Remick. The last named don't seem to give a d-m about the songs I write, but even Shakespeare wasn't appreciated till his body was moulting in the grave.

Respy,
RING W. LARDNER.

LOONEY WITH US AGAIN

JOHN LOONEY, the first superintendent of service the club ever had, is back on the job, succeeding Harry Martin. Mr. Looney has been in the service of many of the fine resort hotels of the east during the past four years. He is regarded as one of the real head-liners among dining room service men. Few men can see as much in a glance around a crowded dining room as he can. He is a welcome addition to the service.

Mr. Looney did splendid work in organizing the staff of dining room servants when the club opened in 1915. He was quick in getting together a good corps of waiters and captains, and largely through his efforts the D. A. C. standard of service was soon regarded as the best.

STAR WRITERS "SIGNED"

IT IS a pleasure for the D. A. C. NEWS to be able to announce that three of the top-notch humorists of America have been secured to contribute to this magazine from time to time during the coming year.

Mr. Lardner, whose stories are immensely popular everywhere, will send a contribution now and then; Mr. Robert Benchley, dramatic critic of *Life*, will be represented by an article at regular intervals— not on the drama, necessarily, but along the lines which his "Vanity Fair" stories followed. Benchley has no superior among American writers in subtle humor. He has the pulse of the discriminating readers as few others have.

Likewise, that great favorite, Stephen Leacock, will be heard from now and then. He is always a delight.

DAC NEWS

JULY 1922

RULES AND SUGGESTIONS FOR WATCHING AUCTION-BRIDGE

By ROBERT C. BENCHLEY

Drawings by
GLUYAS WILLIAMS

"Thus he may say, 'The lead was over here, George.'"

WITH all the expert advice that is being offered in print these days about how to play games, it seems odd that no one has formulated a set of rules for the spectators. The spectators are much more numerous than the players, and seem to need more regulation. As a spectator of twenty years' standing, versed in watching all sports except six-day bicycle races, I offer the fruit of my experience in the form of suggestions and reminiscences which may tend to clarify the situation, or, in case there is no situation which needs clarifying, to make one.

In the event of a favorable reaction on the part of the public, I shall form an association, to be known as the National Amateur Audience Association (or the N. A. A. A., if you are given to slang) of which I shall be treasurer. That's all I ask, the treasurership.

This being an off-season of the year for outdoor sports (except walking, which is getting to have neither participants nor spectators) it seems best to start with a few remarks on the indoor-sport of watching a bridge game. Bridge watchers are not so numerous as football watchers, for instance, but they are much more in need of co-ordination and it will be the aim of this article to formulate a standardized set of rules for watching bridge which may be taken as a criterion for the whole country.

Number Who May Watch

There should not be more than one watcher for each table. When there are two or more, confusion is apt to result and no one of the watchers can devote his attention to the game as he should. Two watchers are also likely to bump into each other as they make their way around the table looking over the players' shoulders. If there are more watchers than there are tables, two can share one table between them, one being dummy while the other watches. In this event the first one should watch until the hand has been dealt

and six tricks taken, being relieved by the second one for the remaining tricks and the marking down of the score.

Preliminaries

In order to avoid any charge of signalling, it will be well for the following conversational formula to be used before the game begins:

The ring-leader of the game says to the fifth person: "Won't you join the game and make a fourth? I have some work which I really ought to be doing."

The fifth person replies: "Oh, no, thank you! I play a wretched game. I'd much rather sit here and read, if you don't mind."

To which the ring-leader replies: "Pray do."

After the first hand has been dealt, the fifth person, whom we shall now call the "watcher," puts down the book and leans forward in his (or her) chair, craning the neck to see what is in the hand nearest him. The strain becoming too great, he arises and approaches the table, saying: "Do you mind if I watch a bit?"

No answer need be given to this, unless someone at the table has nerve enough to tell the truth.

Procedure

The game is now on. The watcher walks around the table, giving each hand a careful scrutiny, groaning slightly at the sight of a poor one and making noises of joyful anticipation at the good ones. Stopping behind an especially unpromising array of cards, it is well to say: "Well, unlucky at cards, lucky in love, you know." This gives the partner an opportunity to judge his chances on the bid he is about to make, and is perfectly fair to the other side, too, for they are not left entirely in the dark. Thus everyone benefits by the remark.

When the bidding begins, the watcher has considerable opportunity for effective work. Having seen how the cards lie, he is able to stand back and listen with a knowing expression, laughing at unjustified bids and urging on those who should, in his estimation, plunge. At the conclusion of the bidding he should say: "Well, we're off!"

As the hand progresses and the players become intent on the game, the watcher may be the cause of no little innocent diversion. He may ask one of the players for a match, or, standing behind the one who is playing the hand, he may say:

"I'll give you three guesses as to whom I ran into on the street yesterday. Someone you all know. Used to go to school with you, Harry. . . Light hair and blue eyes. . . Medium build . . . Well, sir, it was Lew Milliken. Yessir, Lew Milliken. Hadn't seen him for fifteen years. Asked after you, Harry! . . . and George too. And what do you think he told me about Chick?"

Answers may or may not be returned to these remarks, according to the good nature of the players, but in any event, they serve their purpose of distraction.

Particular care should be taken that no one of the players is allowed to make a mistake. The watcher, having his mind free, is naturally in a better position to keep track of matters of sequence and revoking. Thus, he may say:

"The lead was over here, George." or

"I think that you refused spades a few hands ago, Lillian."

Alternatives

Of course, there are some watchers who have an inherited delicacy about offering advice or talking to the players. Some people are that way. They are interested in the game, and love to watch, but they feel that they ought not to interfere. I had a cousin who just wouldn't talk while a hand was being played, and so, as she had to do something, she hummed. She didn't hum very well, and her program was limited to the first two lines of the chorus of "The Love Nest," but she

"As she had to do something, she hummed"

carried it off very well and often got the players to humming it along with her. She could also drum rather well with her fingers on the back of the chair of one of the players while looking over his shoulder. "The Love Nest" didn't lend itself very well to drumming, so she had a little patrol that she worked up all by herself, beginning soft, like a drum corps in the distance, and getting louder and louder, finally dying away again so that you could barely hear it. It was wonderful how she could do it —and still go on living.

"Stopping behind an especially unpromising array of cards, it is well to say: 'Well, unlucky at cards, lucky in love, you know'"

Those who feel this way about talking while others are playing bridge have a great advantage over my cousin and her class if they can play the piano. They play ever so softly, in order not to disturb, but somehow or other you just know that they are there, and that the next to last note in the coda is going to be very sour.

But, of course, the piano work does not technically come under the head of watching, although when there are two watchers to a table, one may go over to the piano while she is dummy.

But your real watcher will allow nothing to interfere with his conscientious following of the game, and it is for real watchers only that these suggestions have been formulated. The minute you get out of the class of those who have the best interests of the game at heart, you become involved in dilettantism and amateurishness, and the whole sport of bridge-watching falls into disrepute.

The only trouble with the game as it now stands is the risk of personal injury. This can be eliminated by the watcher insisting on each player being frisked for weapons before the game begins, and cultivating a good serviceable defense against ordinary forms of fistic attack.

BEAVERS ENTERTAIN

DIRECTORS of the club were guests of honor at one of the Beavers' Thursday noon luncheons recently. President Larned made a dandy speech to the swimming fans which they thoroughly enjoyed and appreciated.

How to Watch a Chess Match

(After You Find One)

By Robert C. Benchley

Drawings by
Gluyas Williams

"It's not so much to do a nice pair of book ends as to help you along in watching the chess match"

SECOND in the list of games which it is necessary for every sportsman to know how to watch comes chess. If you don't know how to watch chess, the chances are that you will never have any connection with the game whatsoever. You wouldn't, by any chance, be playing it yourself.

I know some very nice people who play chess, mind you, and I wouldn't have it thought that I was in any way spoofing at the game. I would sooner spoof at the people who engineered the Panama canal or who are drawing up plans for the vehicular tunnel under the Hudson river. I am no man to make light of chess and its adherents, although they might very well make light of me. In fact, they have.

But what I say is, that taking society by and large, man and boy, the chances are that chess would be the Farmer-Labor party among the contestants when the final returns were tabulated.

Now, since it is settled that you probably will not want to play chess, unless you should be laid up with a bad knee-pan or something, it follows that, if you want to know anything about the sport at all, you will have to watch it from the side-lines. That is what this series of lessons aims to teach you to do (of course, if you are going to be nasty and say that you don't want even to watch it, why all this time has been wasted on my part as well as on yours).

Search in the Mitten District

The first problem confronting the chess spectator is to find some people who are playing. The bigger the city, the harder it is to find anyone indulging in chess. In a small town you can usually go straight to Wilbur Tatnuck's general store, and be fairly sure of finding a quiet game in progress over behind the stove and the crate of pilot-biscuit, but as you draw away from the mitten district you find the sporting instinct of the population cropping out in other lines and chess becoming more and more restricted to the sheltered corners of Y. M. C. A. club rooms and exclusive social organizations.

However, we shall have to suppose, in order to get any article written at all, that you have found two people

playing chess somewhere. They probably will neither see nor hear you as you come up on them; so you can stand directly behind the one who is defending the south goal without fear of detection.

At first you may think that they are both dead, but a mirror held to the lips of the nearest contestant will probably show moisture (unless, of course, they really should be dead, which would be a horrible ending for a little lark like this. I once heard of a murderer who propped his two victims up against a chess board in sporting attitudes and was able to get as far as Seattle before his crime was discovered).

Soon you will observe a slight twitching of an eye-lid or a moistening of the lips and then, like a greatly retarded moving-picture of a person passing the salt, one of the players will lift a chess-man from one spot on the board and place it on another spot.

Excitement Runs Riot

It would be best not to stand too close to the board at this time as you are likely to be trampled on in the excitement. For this action that you have just witnessed corresponds to a run around right end in a football game or a two-bagger in baseball, and is likely to cause considerable enthusiasm on the one hand and deep depression on the other. They may even forget themselves to the point of shifting their feet or changing the hands on which they are resting their foreheads. Almost anything is liable to happen.

When the commotion has died down a little, it will be safe for you to walk around and stand behind the other player and wait there for the next move. While waiting it would be best to stand with the weight of your body evenly distributed between your feet, for you will probably be standing there a long while, and if you bear down on one foot all of the time, that foot is bound to get tired. A comfortable stance for watching chess is with the feet slightly apart (perhaps a foot or a foot and a half), with a slight bend at the knees to rest the legs and the weight of the body thrown forward on the balls of the feet. A rythmic rising on the toes, holding the hands behind the back, the head well up and the chest out, introduces a note of variety into the position which will be welcome along about dusk.

Not knowing anything about the game, you will perhaps find it difficult at first to keep your attention on the board. This can be accomplished by means of several little optical tricks. For instance, if you look at the black and white squares on the board very hard and for a very long time, they will appear to jump about and change places. The black squares will rise from the board about a quarter of an inch and slightly overlap the white ones. Then, if you change focus suddenly, the white squares will do the same thing to the black ones. And finally, after doing this until someone asks you what you are looking cross-eyed for, if you will shut your eyes tight you will see an exact reproduction of the chess-board, done in pink and green, in your mind's eye. By this time, the players will be almost ready for another move.

This will make two moves that you have watched. It is now time to get a little fancy work into your game. About an hour will have already gone by and you should be so thoroughly grounded in the fundamentals of chess-

"A rythmic rising on the toes, introducing a note of variety into the position"

watching that you can proceed to the next step.

Have some one of your friends bring you a chair, a table and an old pyrography outfit, together with some book-ends on which to burn a design.

Seat yourself at the table in the chair and (if I remember the process correctly) squeeze the bulb attached to the needle until the latter becomes red hot. Then, grasping the book-ends in the left hand, carefully trace around the penciled design with the point of the needle. It probably will be a picture of the Lion of Lucerne, and you will let the needle slip on the way round the lion's face, giving it the appearance of having shaved in a Pullman that morning. But that really won't make any difference, for the whole thing is not so much to do a nice pair of book-ends as to help you along in sticking by the chess-match.

If you have any scruples against burning wood, you may knit something, or paste stamps in an album.

And before you know it, the game will be over and you can put on your things and go home.

"At first you may think that they are both dead"

ORPHANS HAVE GLORIOUS CHRISTMAS AT CLUB

NO happier party ever sat down to a banquet in the D. A. C. than that one which came together in the tank room at noon, December 23. The occasion was the second annual blow-out for the boys from the Protestant Orphan Asylum, given under the direction of the Beavers. The club was functioning at its proudest right at that moment, so the scores of members felt who either participated in the event or were silent spectators to it.

First the boys had a shower, then a swim, the water having been drawn down low enough to provide for the littlest fellows at the shallow end of the tank. After the splash party, came the big feed, with oceans of turkey, cranberry sauce, stuffing, mashed potatoes, mince pie 'n everything. Every boy sat between two Beavers,

who made it their business to see that each guest was properly looked out for. A present of a fifty-cent piece, a league baseball, and a package of candy was given each of the youthful guests.

Most of the directors were present and after the gorge President Larned made a speech to the boys which was one of the best our president ever dashed off on the spur of the moment—and he has a long record of hits.

Ernest Thompson Seton, America's most noted Boy Scout chief, was also present and gave a delightful ten-minute talk to the boys.

The Beavers wanted to pay for the spread out of their pockets, but on account of the club's rule against passing the hat, the bill was paid for out of the receipts from the Midnight Frolic by the Ziegfeld Follies.

"Isn't that a picture of
E. S. Willard hanging
in the lobby?"

DOWN IN FRONT

By ROBERT C. BENCHLEY
Drawings by GLUYAS WILLIAMS

THE reform movement in the theatre is gaining
ground rapidly. Old stables are being turned into
little theatres with the actors creaking across the stage
in the corner where the bran-mash used to be served, and
the audience sitting in the large, open space where they
formerly kept the dust-covered buggy in winter and the
pung in summer. It is grand.

The plays are receiving a thorough overhauling as well.
The old-time maid servant and butler who used to be
discovered dusting off the piano-stool when the curtain
went up, explaining to each other how strange it seems
to have the young Duke back again after four and a half
years in India, have been sent to the reformatory, and
in their places are actors who talk so naturally that you
can't hear them, and whose most significant lines are,
"Please pass me a little more of that preserve," and "It
looks like a fog tonight, Daughter."

Any play which discloses more action than the slamming of a door is discarded as old-fashioned, and soon it
may be so that our theatrical performances will be given
by local families, who will, in rotation, simply get up on
the stage and do the things that they would be doing
anyway at home, that night. Every play will then end
by putting the cat out and setting the alarm.

But why should all the reform be directed at the plays
and players? Is the audience going to get off "scot free"
(as people say who do not know the Scots)?

Audience Retards Drama

For years and years the audience has been the worst
feature of the theatre. Many a good play has failed,
and many a frightful one succeeded, simply because the
audiences in this broad and fertile (it certainly is fertile,
you can't deny that) land of ours, if all assembled in one
large field, would average in a mentality test something
approximating one-half of one per cent, or three grammes

pennyweight, which is the standard set for
the chipmunks before they can become
squirrels. If it weren't for the audiences, the
drama would be miles ahead of where it is now.

Among the many reforms which must be
instituted in the pit of the theatre before the
stage can progress is the ostentatious and
horribly painful execution of all people who
come in late.

What chance has Ibsen if, just as Helma
or Tholwig, or whoever the girl is, begins to
explain why she finds herself at the age of
thirteen with three husbands, you have to
stand up and clutch your overcoat upside
down and drop your program to allow a
theatre-party of five to scrape past you on their way to
the "fourth-fifth-sixth-seventh-and-eighth seats in,
please?" How can you keep your mind on the *nuances*
of Ben-Ami's performance if your shirt-front is constantly
being scratched by the jet beads or the Masonic fob of
some tardy dowager or bon vivant crushing in front of you?

Eclipse of the Star

A lot of good it does for them to say "So sorry!" as
they grind the gloss from your pump. Slight return is a
muttered "I beg your pardon" for the obstructed vision
of Delysia kissing the young Prince. If they are so polite
as all that, they should begin the good work by starting
dinner earlier when they are going to the theatre, or
going without the demi-tasse, or standing up back until
the act is over. Or better yet, hiring the actors to come
to their house and give them a private performance.

So much for them! Lead them away!

We next come to the bronchial buster, or the man (it

"His next seat will be in the electric chair"

is usually a man) who, being in the throes of a terrific throat and tube trouble chooses that night for theatre-going on which the crisis is expected. If he can cough his way back to life on that night, the doctor has said that he will pull through, and so he decides that a good show is what he needs to keep him entertained between paroxysms.

He will soon learn to pick his pauses with finesse. It does no good to cough while there is a great deal of noise going on on the stage. No one can hear. The time is just as the star is about to do a little low speaking to her dying lover or when the hero, alone in his garret, goes silently over to the fireplace and tears up the letter. Then for a good rousing bark, my hearty, followed by a series of short, sharp ones like those of a coxswain! If possible the appearance of apoplexy should be simulated. This will cause consternation among those around you—consternation for fear that you may come out of it alive.

Have a Seat

Before the current has been turned off, let us offer the chair to the person who applauds long after everyone else has settled down to go on with the show. His offense is born of enthusiasm, it is true, and he thinks that he is doing both actors and audience a favor, but that won't get him anywhere if the reform I have in mind is ever instituted. He will look just the same as the late birds and the cougher when they are all stretched, cold and silent, in the tumbril on its return trip.

This one appears to be under the delusion that he is the Prince of Wales or the King of Italy (Italy *has* a king, hasn't it? It is so hard to keep track these days) or some other occupant of the royal box, and that, if he likes a song, all he has to do is clap his palms together and the song shall be repeated until he has had his imperial fill. When his favorite actor or actress comes on the show needs must stop while he lets them know that he is right with them every minute of the time. This is especially satisfying encouragment if the favorite actor's entrance happens to be one in pursuit of a fleeing police-man or a sudden discovery of his wife saying "hello" to the man who came to fix the bell. In the midst of such trying scenes, the favored actor must either stop in his pursuit to bow in acknowledgment, or stand stock still, in awkward tableau, waiting for the applause to die down so that he may cry: "So this is how matters stand, is it?"

Punishment Fits the Crime

It may be claimed that the actors themselves like this, and if they don't mind, who am I to object? Well, I'll tell you who I am. I'm the guy that some night is going to get right up and go across the aisle and untie the neck-tie of the inordinate clapper and, if he says anything back to me, I will tie it up again so that it looks simply terrible. That's who I am.

There isn't much to be said about the reform which must be brought about in the line at the box office.

All people who come in late are to be executed

Everyone recognizes that, but, as most of the victims will have to be women, we men are rather hestitant about proceeding. Even nowadays a man can't step up and kill a woman without feeling just a bit unchivalrous.

But sooner or later it has got to come if the women don't learn how to buy tickets. It makes no difference how good a mother a woman may be, or how lovely in her own home, if she is going to stand at the head of a line of twenty people who are waiting to buy tickets and ask the theatre-treasurer to show her a picture of the stage from the seats he is trying to sell her, and change her mind about the Wednesday and Saturday matinees, and lose her money, and demand to be told if that isn't a picture of E. S. Willard hanging in the lobby, if she is going to do these things, then she must be killed. There are no two ways about it..

And then, when we have made a start with these few drags on the progress of the drama, it will be time enough to pay some attention to the plays themselves.

DIRECTOR MARY APPROACHES

MARY GARDEN is coming to pay us a visit. She was scheduled to give a concert at Orchestra Hall last fall but her pipes were rusty. Then she was just common or plantation Mary. Now she comes as director of the Chicago Grand Opera Company. The difference in the elevation will doubtless be noticed at the box office March 10.

Miss Garden was with her company in New York during the drive carried on by the Detroit Symphony Society. The *Journal* wired her for an expression as to what she would think of a city that wouldn't support its great orchestra (That was before the fund had been all secured). The answer received was just one word—"Incredible."

But that wasn't what Mary wrote on the telegraph form. She wrote two words, but the Western Union wouldn't transmit them. They were: "Damned Shock-ing."

Some girl, that Mary.

How to be a Spectator of Spring Planting

By Robert C. Benchley

Drawings by Gluyas Williams

Nothing is so satisfying as.......to observe the slow, rythmic swing of the digger's back

THE danger in watching gardening, as in watching many other sports, is that you may be drawn into it yourself. This you must fight against. Your sinecure standing depends on a rigid abstinence from any of the work itself. Once you stoop over to hold one end of a string for a groaning planter, once you lift one shovelful of earth or toss out one stone, you become a worker and a worker is an abomination in the eyes of the true garden watcher.

A fence is, therefore, a great help. You may take up your position on the other side of the fence from the garden and lean heavily against it smoking a pipe, or you may even sit on it. Anything so long as you are out of helping distance and yet near enough so that the worker will be within easy range of your voice. You ought to be able to point a great deal, also.

There is much to be watched during the early stages of garden-preparation. Nothing is so satisfying as to lean ruminatively against a fence and observe the slow, rythmic swing of the digger's back or hear the repeated scraping of the shovel-edge against some buried rock. It sometimes is a help to the digger to sing a chanty, just to give him the beat. And then sometimes it is not. He will tell you in case he doesn't need it.

There is always a great deal for the watcher to do in the nature of comment on the soil. This is especially true if it is a new garden or has never been cultivated before by the present owner. The idea is to keep the owner from becoming too sanguine over the prospects.

"That soil looks pretty clayey," is a good thing to say. (It is hard to say, clearly, too. You had better practise it before trying it out on the gardener).

"I don't think that you'll have much luck with potatoes in that kind of earth," is another helpful approach. It is even better to go at it the other way, finding out first what the owner expects to plant. It may be that he isn't going to plant any potatoes, and then there you are, stuck with a perfectly dandy prediction which has no bearing on the case. It is time enough to pull it after he has told you that he expects to plant peas, beans, beets, corn. Then you can interrupt him and say: "Corn?" incredulously." You don't expect to get any corn in that soil, do you? Don't you know that corn requires a large percentage of bi-carbonate of soda in the soil, and I don't think, from the looks, that there is an ounce of soda bi-carb. in your whole plot. Even if the corn does come up, it will be so tough that you can't eat it."

Then you can laugh, and call out to a neighbor, or even to the man's wife:" Hey, what do you know? Steve here thinks he's going to get some corn up in this soil!"

In the Matter of Stones

The watcher will find plenty to do when the time comes to pick the stones out of the freshly turned-over earth. It is his work to get upon a high place where he can survey the whole garden and detect the more obvious rocks.

"Here is a big fella over here, Steve," he may say. Or: "Just run your rake a little over in that corner. I'll bet you'll find a nest of them there."

"Plymouth Rock" is a funny thing to call any particularly offensive boulder, and is sure to get a laugh, especially if you kid the digger good-naturedly about being a Pilgrim and landing on it. He may even give it to you to keep.

Just as a matter of convenience for the worker, watchers have sometimes gone to the trouble of keeping count of the number of stones thrown out. This is done by shouting out the count after each stone has been tossed.

28

It makes a sort of game of the thing, and in this spirit the digger may be urged on to make a record.

"That's forty-eight, old man! Come on now, make her fifty. Attaboy, forty-nine! Only one more to go. We-want-fifty-we-want-fifty-we-want-fifty."

And not only stones will be found, but queer objects which have got themselves buried in the ground during the winter-months and have become metamorphosed, so that they are half way between one thing and another. As the digger holds one of these *objets dirt* gingerly between his thumb and forefinger the watcher has plenty of opportunity to shout out:

"You'd better save that. It may come in handy some day. What is it, Eddie? Your old beard?"

And funny cracks like that.

The idea of running a rake softly over the the susceptible surface is almost too tempting to be withstood

The Ordeal by Raking

Here is where it is going to be difficult to keep to your resolution about not helping. After the digging, and stoning, and turning-over has been done, and the ground is all nice and soft and loamy, the idea of running a rake softly over the susceptible surface and leaving a beautiful even design in its wake, is almost too tempting to be withstood.

The worker himself will do all that he can to make it hard for you. He will rake with evident delight, much longer than is necessary, back and forth, across and back, cocking his head and surveying the pattern and fixing it up along the edges with a care which is nothing short

Attaboy, forty-nine! Only one more to go. We-want-fifty-we-want-fifty-we-want-fifty

of insulting considering the fact that the whole thing has got to be mussed up again when the planting begins.

If you feel that you can no longer stand it without offering to assist, get down from the fence and go into your own house and up to your own room. There pray for strength. By the time you come down, the owner of the garden ought to have stopped raking and got started on the planting.

The Planting

Here the watcher's task is almost entirely advisory. And, for the first part of the planting, he should lie low and say nothing. Wait until the planter has got his rows marked out and has wobbled along on his knees pressing the seeds into perhaps half the length of the first row. Then say:

"Hey there, Charlie! You've got those rows going the wrong way."

Charlie will say no he hasn't. Then he will ask what you mean the wrong way.

"Why, you poor cod, you've got them running north and south. They ought to go east and west. The sun rises over there, doesn't it?" (Charlie will attempt to deny this, but you must go right on.) And it comes on up behind that tree and over my roof and sets over there, doesn't it?" (By this time, Charlie will be crying with rage.) "Well, just as soon as your beans get up an inch or two they are going to cast a shadow right down the whole row and only those in front will ever git any sun. You can't grow things without sun, you know."

If Charlie takes you seriously and starts in to rearrange his rows in the other direction, you might perhaps get down off the fence and go in the house. You have done enough. If he doesn't take you seriously, you surely had better go in.

DAC NEWS

HFH

April, 1920

Watching Baseball

By
ROBERT C.
BENCHLEY

Drawings
by
GLUYAS
WILLIAMS

"Any dissenting opinions may be expressed in a minority report"

EIGHTEEN men play a game of baseball and eighteen thousand watch them, and yet those who play are the only ones who have any official direction in the matter of rules and regulations. The eighteen thousand are allowed to run wild. They don't have even a Spalding's Guide containing group photographs of model organizations of fans in Fall River, Mass., or the Junior Rooters of Lyons, Nebraska. Whatever course of behavior a fan follows at a game he makes up for himself. This is, of course, ridiculous.

The first set of official rulings for spectators at baseball games has been formulated and is herewith reproduced. It is to be hoped that in the general clean-up which the game is undergoing, the grandstand and bleachers will not resent a little dictation from the authorities.

In the first place, there is the question of shouting encouragement, or otherwise, at the players. There must be no more random screaming. It is of course understood that the players are entirely dependent on the advice offered them from the stands for their actions in the game, and how is a batter to know what to do if, for instance, he hears a little man in the bleachers shouting "Wait for 'em, Wally! Wait for 'em," and another little man in the south stand shouting "Take a crack at the first one, Wally!"? What would you do? What would Lincoln have done?

The official advisers in the stands must work together. They must remember that as the batter advances toward the plate he is listening for them to give him his instructions, and if he hears conflicting advice there is no telling what he may do. He may even have to decide for himself.

Therefore, before each player goes to bat, there should be a conference among the fans who have ideas on what his course of action should be, and as soon as a majority have come to a decision, the advice should be shouted to the player in unison under the direction of a cheer-leader. If there are any dissenting opinions, they may be expressed in a minority report.

In the matter of hostile remarks addressed at an unpopular player on the visiting team it would probably be better to leave the wording entirely to the individual fans. Each man has his own talents in this sort of thing and should be allowed to develop them along natural lines. In such crises as these in which it becomes necessary to rattle the opposing pitcher or prevent the visiting catcher from getting a difficult foul, all considerations of good sportsmanship should be discarded. As a matter of fact, it is doubtful if good sportsmanship should ever be allowed to interfere with the fan's participation in a contest. The game must be kept free from all softening influences.

Personal Disputes

One of the chief duties of the fan is to engage in arguments with the man behind him. This department of the game has been allowed to run down fearfully. A great many men go to a ball game today and never speak a word to anyone other than the members of their own party or an occasional word of cheer to a player. This is nothing short of craven.

An ardent supporter of the home-team should go to a game prepared to take offense, no matter what happens. He should be equipped with a stock of ready sallies which can be used regardless of what the argument is about or what has gone before in the exchange of words. Among the more popular nuggets of repartee, effective on all occasions, are the following:

"Oh, is that so?"

"Eah?"

"How do you get that way?"

"Oh, is that so?"

"So are you."

"Aw, go have your hair bobbed."

"Oh, is that so?"

"Well, what are you going to do about it?"

"Who says so?"

"Eah? Well, I'll Cincinnati you."

"Oh, is that so?"

Any one of these, if hurled with sufficient venom, is good for ten points. And it should always be borne in mind that there is no danger of physical harm resulting from even the most ferocious-sounding argument. Statistics gathered by the War Department show that the percentage of actual blows struck in grandstand arguments is one in every 43,000,000.

Explaining Score-Keeping

For those fans who are occasionally obliged to take inexperienced lady-friends to a game, a special set of rules has been drawn up. These include the compulsory purchase of tickets in what is called the "Explaining Section," a block of seats set aside by the management for the purpose. The view of the diamond from this section is not very good, but it doesn't matter, as the men wouldn't see anything of the game anyway and the women can see just enough to give them material for questions and to whet their curiosity. As everyone around you is answering questions and trying to explain score-keeping, there is not the embarrassment which is usually attendant on being overheard by unattached fans in the vicinity. There is also not the distracting sound of breaking pencils and modified cursing to interfere with unattached fans' enjoyment of the game.

Absolutely no gentlemen with uninformed ladies will be admitted to the main stand. In order to enforce this regulation, a short examination on the rudiments of the game will take place at the gate, in which ladies will be expected to answer briefly the following questions:

"A short examination will take place at the gate"

"One of the chief duties of fans is to engage in arguments"

(Women examiners will be in attendance.)

1. What game is it that is being played on this field?

2. How many games have you seen before?

3. What is (a) a pitcher; (b) a base; (c) a bat?

4. What color uniform does the home-team wear?

5. What is the name of the home-team?

6. In the following sentence, cross out the incorrect statements, leaving the correct one: The catcher stands (1) directly behind the pitcher in the pitcher's box; (2) at the gate taking tickets; (3) behind the batter; (4) at the bottom of the main aisle, selling ginger-ale.

7. What again is the name of the game you expect to see played?

8. Do you cry easily?

9. Is there anything else you would rather be doing this afternoon?

10. If so, please go and do it.

It has been decided that the American baseball fan should have a distinctive dress. A choice has been made from among the more popular styles and the following has been designated as regulation, embodying, as it does, the spirit and tone of the great national pastime:

Straw hat, worn well back on the head; one cigar, held between teeth unlighted; coat held across knees; vest worn but unbuttoned and open, displaying both a belt and suspenders, with gold watch-chain connecting the bottom pockets.

The vest may be an added expense to certain fans who do not wear vests during the summer months, but it has been decided that it is absolutely essential to the complete costume, and no true baseball enthusiast will hesitate in complying.

LARGER ASPECTS OF THE COMING DRAMATIC SEASON

By
ROBERT C. BENCHLEY

Drawings by
RALPH BARTON

"There is nothing like a good bachelor apartment for a compromising situation"

IT has finally been decided that there is going to be a coming dramatic season after all. For a while, along back in June and July, it looked as if most of the theatres in New York City would be devoted to roller-skating or Irish meetings of protest during the winter of 1921-22. Managers, when interviewed about their plans for the season, shook their heads and said that they were thinking of going in for bee culture up in Connecticut or catching up on their reading. Things were shaping up very badly for everybody but the public, and the public stood a good chance of saving a little of the money that it has been forcing into the pockets of the ticket-agencies ever since the beginning of the war now popularly known in munition and profiteer circles as "the War of the Roses."

But then all of a sudden the theatre displayed recuperative powers like those of the early season invalids on the Yale football team, and, at the first tinkle of out-of-town money in the offing, droves of plays began to spring up out of nowhere. Some of them went right back to nowhere the next week. But others are still hanging around, speaking of themselves in the advertisements as "hits," and it is from these that we can trace a few of the less important features of the 1921-22 dramatic outlook.

First Call for Hero Squad

In the serious drama, it begins to look as if those actors training for hero parts would have to take a run around the board-track every afternoon and perform Exercise No. 7 in Walter Camp's Daily Dozen (hands on hips, head erect, heels together, squat until flask touches heels and up again, one hundred thousand times) to develop the calves of the legs and upper tibia against the use of knee breeches. For costume plays are upon us again.

This will also mean that a facility for walking around a sword will be necessary. Many a hero who has got along very well of late wearing sack suits and manipulating nothing more unwieldy than a malacca stick and a cigarette-holder, will find himself out of a job unless he can walk across the stage with a sword dangling at his belt without snapping it off short between his shins or tripping against the leading lady. Actors who have risen to fame during the "Jane Clegg" and "Miss Lulu Bett" period of serious drama will have an entirely different proposition to meet from the one to which they are accustomed, in which the most agile feat they have been called upon to accomplish has been the turning-up of a lamp wick or drumming meditatively on the table with their fingers.

Not that this will make any difference in anything. It simply is noted here as a trend, and not a very significant trend either.

The Apartment Shortage

However much easier the housing situation in New York may be this Fall, there is one class of apartment which seems to be taken on five-year leases with no chance of there being a vacancy for a long time yet. The congestion appears to be in stage bachelor apartments. There promises to be a revival of the demand for them this season, in spite of the fact that they went out of date several decades ago, supposedly for good and all.

But after all, there is nothing like a good bachelor apartment, along about eleven-thirty at night, for a compromising situation. If you have a young heroine who finds herself out on the street with a wrap thrown on over her evening gown, there really is no place to have her go but to a bachelor's apartment. There she is sure to find a coal-fire burning cozily in the grate, the Japanese butler laying the table for midnight supper for two (with champagne) and the bachelor in a silk dressing-gown, tapping his cigarette on the brass cover of the box which contains one hundred, waiting expectantly for the sound of the bell. You couldn't do this so well anywhere except in a bachelor's apartment. Neither could you have the husband or the fiancee rush in with such good effect in a scene representing the office of the Eureka Milk Cap Producing Co. or the living room of the Dwights' home on Long Island late afternoon of the next day. It simply has to be in the rooms of a compromising-looking man with grey on his temples, and just so long as there is the demand for such situations there will be overcrowding in such apartments, and any stage hero who is looking for a nice sunny place for himself and Japanese valet this season will probably have to put up with a remodeled fire-barn or a shirtwaist loft.

In musical comedy there seems to be little prospect of change. The joke about blue laws looks good for another season with practically no remodeling at all, unless, perhaps, it is to make it into a verse for a topical song. As a matter of fact, there is some discussion among etymologists and philologists as to which came first, the spoken blue-law joke or the topical verse in which it is averred that if the blue laws go much further it will be illegal for babies to be born on Sunday. The records containing the first quips along these lines are now illegible and there is danger of the controversy never being definitely settled.

At any rate, both joke and verse are with us now and constitute practically the entire libretto of most musical shows. Given any encouragement at all, they are sure to last another three or four seasons.

In the matter of musical comedy songs, the prospects are very bright for the blues. It is doubtful if there will be a score written for the coming season which does not contain at least one song which sets forth the lament that the singer has got the blues of one kind or another.

"Costume plays are upon us again"

This feature, along with the prohibition joke, is a holdover from seasons past, and yet it shows no sign of waning. Seldom has any motif secured such a hold on the imaginations (perhaps "imagination" is too strong a word) of our song writers. Starting with the "Memphis Blues," it has now reached the point where people are suffering from the "Wang-wang Blues" and there is every reason to expect that before the end of the season our local hospitals will be called upon to care for cases of "Hamburg-steak-with-French-fried-potatoes Blues" or perhaps an ultimate case of a man who is borne in screaming " 'Cause I got the dog-gone-tired-of-these-everlasting-blues Blues."

A rather terrifying prospect in musical shows is the threat of more gymnastic dancers. When first these agile couples were included in the line-up of our revues, they weren't so bad. Usually they come on clad in as nearly tub-side form as the width of the orchestra pit will permit and the man generally has smeared himself all over with "3-in-1" to make himself look oriental. There is a great deal of running barefooted about the stage, leaping at each other, snarling and panting, ostensibly symbolic of the Birth of the Pearl or the Vision of Direct Primaries or something, but really nothing more or less than good, old-fashioned Swedish gymnastics done to music.

Now a little of this in a year you don't mind. It makes the modern dances that our young people do seem a little more respectable. But there is every indication that our national life is going to be entirely given over to this impetuous sort of thing. Every musical show that looms up in the distance carries with it at least one complete set of bouncing bodies ready to fling themselves at each other and whirl about at a moment's notice. If, as has happened in the past, the dances done first as stunts on the stage later become the vogue of the country-club and of the drawing-room when the rugs have been rolled back, I don't know what this country is coming to. I have tried to accommodate my wife and learn the various mazurkas and folk-dances as they came along, but if I am soon to be asked to take off my clothes with one exception, grease myself with cocoa-butter, and entertain one of Elsie's friends "who doesn't know many men here" by tossing her about in the air and running out of the room with her flung over my shoulder, then it is high time that a halt was called and the old-fashioned waltz dusted off for use again.

This last is the only really serious trend of the year.

"Then it is high time that a halt was called and the old-fashioned waltz dusted off for use again"

"Nothing amuses a wicked old man so much as to see some poor goof leading a decent life on the stage."

THE MENACE OF THE CLEAN PLAY
By ROBERT C. BENCHLEY—*Drawings by* RALPH BARTON

SOMEONE (I'll bet it was I at some time or other) has said that the theatre of a nation is an accurate gauge as to the nation's proximity to collapse. The nearer to ruin a civilization is, the lower the moral standard of its theatre. Look at Rome. (Everyone always says "Look at Rome," when a point is to be made about national morality. You can prove anything by looking at Rome. As a matter of fact the Roman theatre, just before the fall of the Empire, was probably no worse than it was when Roman consuls were selling at 120. It probably was pretty punk at any period.)

However, if low moral standards on the stage are a sign of impending national collapse, then they had better begin backing the moving-van up to New York City right now.

In the first place, there are too many clean plays in town. Scarcely a week goes by but someone produces a play which can be billed as "wholesome" and which has a scene in "the settin'-room" somewhere before the final curtain. These clean, wholesome plays are a bad sign. A citizenry who were living clean, wholesome lives at home wouldn't have to go to the theatre to see someone act clean and wholesome. As a nation we go to the theatre to be amused, and nothing amuses a wicked old man so much as to see some poor goof leading a decent life on the stage.

But more than that, in most of these rural plays, to which the kiddies are supposed to be brought with

impunity, or even with Grandpa and Grandma, we find a low moral standard prevailing. The hero is usually some smart young guy who wears a cap and who, albeit physically impeccable, would cheat the platinum fillings out of your teeth if you happened to come between him and making Tatnuck Grove the biggest town in the valley. The plot usually centers around the sly young man's getting the franchise for his home-town by pretending to be the gas-meter man and crippling the grouchy old street-railway president of the neighboring town on his way out of his house with the papers and silver. But the young man uses the stolen money to buy a new home for his old mother; so you can see that his heart is in the right place.

In these clean, wholesome plays one also meets more meanness than in any other type of drama. Practically two-thirds of the cast are rustic characters who wear chin whiskers and mufflers and who stand in the doorway saying, "Heh-heh! Wall, I don't reckon I kin let yer have any more time on that there note, Abner." According to the clean, wholesome playwrights, the rural population of this country is made up of Presbyterian Shylocks who loosen up only just enough to stamp the snow off their boots when they come into the house, and anyone can be the hero of the play who is smart enough to cheat them.

Is that the kind of play you want to take your children to? Do you want them to grow up believing that this world is full of trickery and that the only one who gets ahead is the one who knows the most tricks? Do you want them to think that any method of action is justified, so long as it makes a lot of money? The answer is, of course, "Yes, if they are ever going to be able to take care of me in my old age." But, nevertheless, it is a low moral standard.

Now, on the other hand, take the so-called "immoral" plays. There was a time when a play was called "immoral" if, in the third act, the young wife was discovered sewing on tiny garments. Now anything goes so long as it doesn't hurt the advertisers in the theatre program. So far, mayhem has not been committed on the stage in full view of the audience, but that about completes the list.

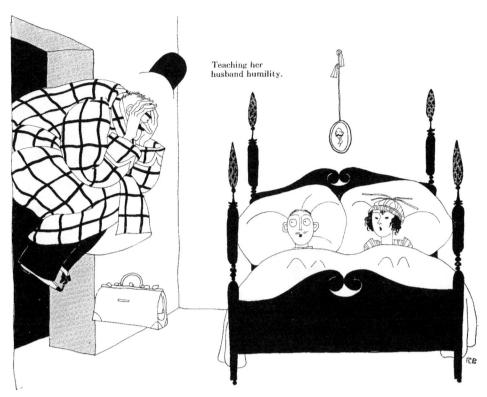

Teaching her husband humility.

Lilies of the Drive

In these "immoral" plays, however, we find a paradoxical high standard of moral conduct on the part of most of the characters. For instance, there are in the neighborhood of six plays now running in New York dealing with the lives of ladies who live in Riverside Drive apartments with no visible means of support, or at least, he is visible only occasionally. They are, in the title-words of one of these plays, "Lilies of the Field." You remember how the rest of the quotation goes. It's from "Twelfth Night," I think.

Now unquestionably loose as the lives of these ladies are, we find them on the stage to be, for the most part, as nice, kind, generous and big-hearted a lot of girls as you would care to see. Sisterly love is not the least of the kinds handed out, and they would as soon cut off their April coupon as to help another lily in distress.

They are always coming into each other's apartment and saying, "Now, dearie, you look tired. Let me get you some aspir'n," or "Here is a basket of fruit Charlie sent up to me.

"I want you should have some."

I want you should have some." They are continually lending each other money and sometimes even sending a check back home to the old folks in Erie every Saturday night. Aside from a slight disregard for the conventions, they seem to be model women.

This is very confusing. Shall we have special children's matinees for "Lilies of the Field," "The Easiest Way," "Back Pay" and the rest, to teach the little ones the homely virtues? In "Bluebeard's Eighth Wife" a young wife induces the juvenile to enter into an apparently very compromising situation with her simply to teach her husband humility. She had a rather discouraging time convincing her husband that it was all for his own good, but, in the end, he is a better man for it. I am sure that there is a lesson in this for each and every one of us.

Bring on the Crooks

It would seem, then, that a crusade should be started in New York against the steadily-rising flood of wholesome plays which teach business chicanery, opportunism, mistrust of one's neighbor and the gospel of the fresh young man. What we need are more plays of the *demi-monde*, where people are genuine, generous and honorable. The old-fashioned crook play, in which the hero was a cracksman and the villain the District Attorney, should be revived. Here we found true-blue boys who would never go back on a pal even in the face of the most treacherous wiles of the law. Men were men in those days, and women were made of sterner stuff than those weak sisters who cringe through the clean plays of today, wiping their eyes on their aprons and beseeching their sons not to let the old town get done out of eleven dollars by them competitors in the valley.

Someone was asking me only the other day, "Bob, what are we coming to?" And I said, "Lew, I don't know."

"There! There stands the man who has never treated me like anything but a sister!"

NEW YEAR'S RESOLUTIONS

By
ROBERT C. BENCHLEY

Drawings by
RALPH BARTON

NOW that no one drinks liquor any more, it is difficult to find things to swear off on for 1922. Actors and actresses are particularly hard hit, for it was a well-known fact that in the old days, they were notoriously fast livers. But things are different now. An actor told me the other noon that no liquor had passed his lips since eleven o'clock that morning. And the poor fellow was a wreck. There is such a thing as breaking off a habit like the drink habit too abruptly.

There are several suggestions, however, that could be made to stage folk in lieu of New Year's resolutions against liquor. As a qualified representative of the theatre-going public, I will list them below, and if the actors and actresses specified under the group headings will try during the coming year to do better in their respective fields, I am sure that the theatrical year of 1922 will stand out in dramatic history as the Year of the Great Reformation instead of as the Year of the Great Raspberry Plague which it is now shaping up to be.

Ever since the advent of realistic drama, our heroines have been growing more and more careless about their honor. There was a time when the minute a young woman came on the stage in a simple country frock with her hair done in the fashion of rustic virgins, you could be pretty safe in laying a bet on her ultimately coming through unscathed, even if she had to slap the villain's face to escape him.

But now you can't trust anyone. The heroines seem to be made of weaker fibre than they used to be. It takes only a very small man to send a great strapping heroine home to her father in hysterics, and when in the first act the girl in the simple frock comes on it is a toss-up whether she has just graduated at the head of her class from the Bedford Reform School for Girls or whether she is just preparing to take her entrance examinations.

Let us urge then, that during the coming year the heroines in our realistic drama watch their false step a little more carefully. There used to be some novelty in being ruined, but at the present rate of exchange, we shall soon be hearing the heroine stamp her foot and, pointing to the cringing man in a silk hat, exclaim, "There, there stands the man who has never treated me like anything but a sister!"

A little less promiscuity, heroines, please!

There ought to be a great deal less bounding among the young men on the stage. The only way to tell a juvenile from a more mature character in a play today is to watch their respective entrances. The mature character walks on, but the juvenile bounds. He has to have a clean fifty-yard straightaway in front of the door at which he is to enter so that he can make it in good form, and then, at his cue, he comes leaping out, with a tennis racquet under his arm and wearing golf clothes, shouting, "Hello, father! Hello, mater! Hello, everybody! Where's Vivian?"

Now this leaping wouldn't be so bad, if he didn't leap right over to the library table and take a cigarette out from the long box holding one hundred, tap it on his thumb-nail and light it. After three puffs he throws it away and in a couple of minutes lights another. Just then *Vivian* comes in and he crushes the second Camel against the ashtray and says hello to her. Then he offers her one and takes one himself. In this way, no less than twenty cigarettes are lighted and thrown away during the course of a scene, which makes an awful mess for the stage hands to clean up afterward, besides being very uneconomical.

In seventy-eight years of theatre going, including the performance when Edwin Booth first appeared as the illegitimate baby in "King Lear," I have never yet seen an actor finish smoking a cigarette on the stage, that is, so that he had to hold it between his thumb and fore finger with his little finger held gingerly away to keep from burning it. I have seen plenty of actors do it in the privacy of their own clubrooms,

"Hello, father! Hello, mater! Hello everybody! Where's Vivian?"

even to the extent of sticking a pin into the butt and throwing it away only when the flaming shingles and soot began to come through into their mouth. If they can do it with their own cigarettes, why can't they with the manager's?

More smoking and fewer cigarettes, then, for the male characters in general, and less bounding for the juveniles.

There is one thing that ought to be stopped by law among the fancy dancers who have now taken possession of our musical comedies. I refer to the inevitable part of the act when the lady puts her hands around the neck of her smiling partner, allows her feet to leave the floor and swings around through the air as he turns in a circle. The dangerous point about this is that some night she is

going to have knuckle trouble or is going to get laughing and will let go, shooting over the footlights and into my lap. I am not speculating on this. I *know* that it is going to happen. Every time that I sit and watch a dancing team perform this charming figure, I crouch instinctively down into my dress shirt, for an instinct which has never yet failed me (it told me that Wilson was going to be elected in 1916) says in words of one syllable that I am some night going to be the lucky man on whom the lady dancer will crash. It will probably be an evening when my wife is not with me, and sooner or later she will get word that I was seen with a sun-kist girlie in my lap mussing my hair up. This will call for an explanation, and I will look fat saying that she landed on me by accident, having flown off from her husband's neck.

Furthermore, I am worried about the etiquette in such cases. Is the man at whom a lady dancer is catapulted supposed to do as a baseball spectator does when a foul enters the stand at his point, and throw her back? The only way out of the situation is for dancers to swear off doing it entirely.

Although liquor drinking has been entirely stopped throughout the country, there is still a great deal of drinking done on the stage, and a particularly vicious kind of drinking it is, too. The beverage is usually cold tea or variously colored waters which give the effect of whiskey or cocktails when seen from across the footlights. Actors who have drunk these concoctions, however, tell me that the effect is really not the same.

Judging from the results, in fact, the effect is a great deal worse than that of ordinary spirituous liquors. A character on the stage pours himself out, let us say, two fingers of cold tea and tosses it off, with a great deal of coughing and clearing the throat to show how powerful it is. Immediately the beast in him rises to the surface. His eyes become heavy and he lurches toward the young lady in the room with menacing gestures, falling in a drunken stupor just before he reaches her.

The stage cocktails are particularly stimulating to maiden aunts. Give *Aunt Lucy* one before dinner and she immediately registers alarming well-being, followed by a desire to dance on the table and a total inability to assemble words. And two of these insidious drinks will send the weak young brother of the heroine out to rob his employer or shoot his rival.

Here, then, is a chance for a real reformation. If stage drinks were abolished, or if actors would swear never to let cold tea pass their lips during the new year, think of the happiness that would result! Of course, the next best thing would be to abolish actors.

"Some night she is going to have knuckle trouble and will let go, shooting over the footlights and into my lap."

"The most popular kind of scenery is the kind which has little electric lights showing through the back drop."

A COURSE IN THE DRAMA
By ROBERT C. BENCHLEY—*Drawings by* RALPH BARTON

WE hear a great deal about Professor Baker's course in the Drama at Harvard. Perhaps we are meant to. At any rate, old timers in the theatrical game, managers who started out in life as professional wrestlers or trainers and who have worked their way up in the stage business from the bottom to the next floor above the bottom, are chagrined to find themselves being elbowed out of the limelight by young upstarts in soft-collared shirts who talk about "technique" and their "greens" and their "blues."

It all shows what a little study in advance will do for a man who wants to put on a show. And for those who haven't got the time or the soft-collared shirts to go to Harvard, a brief course in the construction of popular drama is here offered, free, with a subscription to the D. A. C. News. It can be studied in the privacy of your own room, and your friends need never know that you are training for playwriting until you appear among them some day with a contract signed by a Broadway manager. Not that a contract signed by a Broadway manager *means* anything, but it is a good start. After

you have enough contracts signed by Broadway managers you can paper the guest-room with them.

This course will include only those subjects which have proved to be popular among the theater-goers of New York, as it is the theater-goers of New York who live all over the rest of the country when they are at home. The resident New Yorker gets to the theater about once every Spring, and then goes to the Hippodrome.

Scenery

First will be the course in scenic designing. It has been proved by trained observers that the most popular kind of scenery, the kind which gets a salvo of applause the minute that the audience spots it, is the kind which has little electric lights showing through the back-drop. Sometimes they represent trolley-cars running over the hills in the distance. Sometimes it is the old home that is lighting up for the night, with first the kitchen lights going on, then the dining room and then, with incredible rapidity, the entire upper floor, showing that when the old folks light up they do it right. Or, if the play be a melodrama, it may be the 6:45 express coming through the cut. In this event it will be heard signalling for the crossing with a whistle such as used to come with little boys' sailor-suits. Whatever the little electric lights may connote, it will be found that to the American public they are the last word in popular scenic effects.

Another point for designers, who would make a setting after the hearts of the public, is the efficacy of glass chandeliers. Any scene which has large blobs of sparkling chandeliers hanging from the flies, on which the lights are made to play, is considered Hot Potage among the susceptible ones in the audience. (And who, in an audience, is *not* susceptible, excepting, of course, the dramatic critics?)

In the class with glass chandeliers come Japanese lanterns. Any house will applaud frantically the very

"Tiny children are practically spontaneous combustion."

raising of the curtain on a scene across which Japanese lanterns are strung, just as they will applaud artificial roses over a trellis. It is a strange and even discouraging thing, that people will sit undemonstrative and cold through Ibsen and go into paroxysms of delight at the sight of an imitation garden, consisting of cloth lilacs growing side by side on the ground with crepe golden-rod in a scene supposed to be taking place in mid-July.

And for the climax of emotion, if it is desired to bring the house down in a frenzy of artistic appreciation, a magic-lantern should be employed to throw an effect of clouds rushing across the backdrop, if possible across the face of a moon. Beyond this the American public asks for nothing in visual delights.

Construction

We now come to certain dramatic features which should be injected into every effort to please the average theater-goer. Without them your play may possibly succeed, but with them, success is certain.

In the first place, America must be referred to as often as possible as "God's country." It might be well to have some of the other characters champion a foreign country or make slurring remarks against America. This will give the hero a chance to make his "God's country" speech, ending with a fake clout on the side of the head for the Englishman (it usually is an Englishman, one

who says, "Ah, bah Jove!"). You can't go wrong if you include this bit of dramatic action in your play.

If you possibly can work it, have something let down from above on wires. The public loves it. Many a musical show, which has shown signs of being a flop, has been saved in the last act by having the comedian come down from the flies as if he had fallen out of an airplane. If you can't get the comedian to risk it, try a dog.

And speaking of dogs, any one who wants to put on a sure-fire hit should introduce an animal of one kind or another into it. A dog is usually very effective, especially if he is a puppy, but there is always the danger that puppies will suddenly develop a too-active interest in the plot and refuse to leave the stage at their exit cue. They either affect a scornful indifference to the whole thing and yawn loudly when presented, or else become offensively enthusiastic and try to kiss the actors. It is therefore better, if the story will permit, to use pigeons or even tiny children.

Tiny children are practically spontaneous combustion. All that is necessary is to lead them across the stage in a song-number and half a dozen extra encores will be the reward. There is a law against small children dancing in evening performances, but they may walk around in a circle or even run, and the murmur of delight which runs through an audience at the sight of small children dressed up like South Sea Islanders or Scots will warm the cockles of the manager's box-office.

These are just a few of the features which a playwright should be familiar with if he is to fashion a play which is to make money. They are probably not taught in Professor Baker's course at Harvard, in fact, they are probably frowned upon, but the authors who have made money by using them could get up a team that would tear through Professor Baker's money-makers like a dog through a strange town.

"The hero may then make his 'God's Country' speech, ending with a clout on the side of the head for the Englishman."

The stage furnishes us Spring models in love-making

THE SPRING FRET IN THE DRAMA

By ROBERT C. BENCHLEY—*Drawings by* BURT THOMAS

THERE seems to be a well-defined rumor abroad that Spring and love-making go hand in hand, or neck and neck, or whatever it is they call it now. This is doubtless due to the superior press-agenting that Spring has had throughout the ages, but whatever the reason, whenever you mention Spring to the average man, he rolls his eyes, straightens his tie, and makes a try at looking seductive.

Naturally, we turn to the stage for Spring models in love-making, for it is on the stage that we find people doing things as we feel that we could do them if we only had the build and the clothes. There probably isn't a man in the civilized world, when he clears his throat to propose marriage (or walk in the park, for that matter) who doesn't indulge in a flash-back to some doggy swain he has seen on the stage, and who doesn't for the minute kid himself into believing that he is on the verge of carrying the thing off with the aplomb of a John Barrymore or a Conway Tearle. Just as soon as his voice starts on the first bar he realizes that it isn't so, but for one second he is consciously striving after the manner of someone he has seen doing the same thing on the stage. The 1922 line-up is only fair, judging by standards in

past years. Love-making, in our modern plays, seems to be becoming less an emotional experience and more in the nature of small-talk to pass the time away while the butler is showing someone up from downstairs. There was a time when a hero, in order to do the thing up right, had to take a stance about two feet away from his inamorata, crouch down as in Figure 5 of Walter Camp's Daily Dozen, breathe heavily through the nose for a full minute, and then spring. If he made a good landing, he carried the lady with him half-way across the stage, and by the time they had regained their balance, she knew in a general way that he was in love with her.

Hold Back, Boys

But this season repression is the thing. The idea is to give the girl no idea that you think anything more of her than you would of your room-mate's sister from Canton, until just as she is about to call it an evening and put on her clothes to go to bed. Then spring it, somewhat in the manner in which you would spring an announcement of the fact that you had cracked your watch-crystal. Many new plays are modeling their love scenes on the one in "The Circle," and their passionate trend is something like this:

JACK CARROWAY (*to the girl*): "It is perfectly ripping of you to sit out here listening to me run on like this, when really I have nothing to say. But if you could only see that little motor-boat! Up and down the lake all summer and only one blow-out! And Aunt Virginia makes the best lettuce sandwiches! Just the right thickness. I've never known two people to be more congenial than Mother and Aunt Virginia. They are just like sisters. In fact, they *are* sisters. And—by the way—did you know that I'm frightfully in love with you?"

At this, the young lady nods and says, "Yes," and they shake hands.

* * *

Another method of stage love-making which seems to be coming into vogue this Spring is that in which two hearts beat as one-step. Playwrights have begun to wax evangelical and are now directing their attention to the menace of jazz, showing right on the stage just how far our young people are going under the head of "dancing." In dramas of this sort, such as "The National Anthem," "Up The Ladder," etc., the entire cast spend most of their time toddling back and forth from left to right, speaking whatever lines the author may have given them down the neck of their partner. While waiting for their cues they toss off a few cocktails made of colored water.

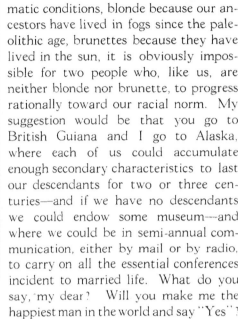

And, after all, what better way is there?

Everybody Listens In

The courtship in these cases is never particularly subtle. The beau is usually what is known in temperance circles as "pie-eyed" and delivers himself of his tender sentiments without the aid of make-up. In order to make himself heard above the saxophones he has to shout it, so that for every girl who is proposed to, eight or ten others are able to listen in, as if it were being done by radio all over the United States. These dramas are, of course, supposed to teach a lesson and are considered pretty gosh-darned stark, but the effects seem to be about the same as those of the more refined courtship in the light comedies.

* * *

The various Shaw revivals and the marathon production of his "Back to Methuselah" have raised the tone but lowered the temperature of dramatic loving considerably. In Shaw love-affairs, and especially in his latest opus, the agitation is almost entirely confined to the brain-pan. In "Back to Methuselah" for instance, one gentleman complains that the chief trouble with the idyllic position, unanimously praised by all poets, in which the lady reclines in the young man's arms, is that it stops the

circulation just below the elbows and becomes very tiring after a time. You can't work up much of a love-scene when the author feels like that about it. If the Shaw influence creeps any farther in our drama, the police may be called upon to stop something like this during the sentimental passages of some new play:

RUPERT (*to Kay, who is sitting in the next room*): "My dear girl, we can't go on this way. The whole thing is too rudimentary. If, as you say, we humans are the result of centuries and centuries of varying climatic conditions, blonde because our ancestors have lived in fogs since the paleolithic age, brunettes because they have lived in the sun, it is obviously impossible for two people who, like us, are neither blonde nor brunette, to progress rationally toward our racial norm. My suggestion would be that you go to British Guiana and I go to Alaska, where each of us could accumulate enough secondary characteristics to last our descendants for two or three centuries—and if we have no descendants we could endow some museum—and where we could be in semi-annual communication, either by mail or by radio, to carry on all the essential conferences incident to married life. What do you say, my dear? Will you make me the happiest man in the world and say "Yes"?

* * *

About the only place in the theatre in which you can count on seeing an old-fashioned courtship this Spring is in musical comedy. Things don't change much there. The industry has been thoroughly standardized. The juvenile's pockets may slant up or they may slant down, there may be a back-drop showing the Bay of Naples off the Jersey Coast or nothing but a white John Murray Anderson drapery, but whatever the scenic effects, the young lover always holds his straw hat up against his chest, places one foot daintily to the right and slightly to the rear, and, watching apprehensively for the amber spot-light, proceeds to tell his little girl that he has wandered from England to sunny Sevilla, from Aix-la-Chapelle to Cathay, that he's traveled o'er France and to far Cascadilla, and ridden from Rome to Bombay, but although he had searched he had never discovered the maiden he wanted to find, till he opened her heart and they two ne'er will part, and that's the message of the columbine.

The song ended, he says to her: "Why, Betty, haven't you seen? Haven't you known that I loved you? I have loved you since the very first time I saw you that day down on the pier when you were dancing with that other fellow, and now all I need is your father's consent to make you my very own, to make your dreams and my dreams come true." (Song: "When Your Dreams and My Dreams Come True.")

And, after all, what better way is there to do it?

D'AC NEWS

DRAWING BY R. F. HEINRICH

September - 1921

"In the reign of Henri IV, it was boasted that there were more tennis players in Paris than drunkards in England."

"ROLL YOUR OWN"

Inside Points on Building and Maintaining a Private Tennis Court

By ROBERT C. BENCHLEY
Drawings by RALPH BARTON

NOW that the Great War is practically over, and until the next one begins, there isn't very much that you can do with that large plot of ground which used to be your war-garden. It is too small for a running-track and too large for nasturtiums. Obviously, the only thing left is a tennis-court.

One really ought to have a tennis-court of one's own. Those at the Club are always so full that on Saturdays and Sundays the people waiting to play look like the gallery at a Davis Cup match, and even when you do get located you have two sets of balls to chase, yours and those of the people in the next court.

The first thing is to decide among yourselves just what kind of court it is to be. There are three kinds: grass, clay, and corn-meal. In Maine, gravel courts are also very popular. Father will usually hold out for a grass court because it gives a slower bounce to the ball and Father isn't so quick on the bounce as he used to be. All

Mother insists on is plenty of headroom. Junior and Myrtis will want a clay one because you can dance on a clay one in the evening. The court as finished will be a combination grass and dirt, with a little golden-rod late in August.

A little study will be necessary before laying out the court. I mean you can't just go out and mark a court by guess-work. You must first learn what the dimensions are supposed to be and get as near to them as is humanly possible. Whereas there might be a slight margin for error in some measurements, it is absolutely essential that both sides are the same length, otherwise you might end up by lobbing back to yourself if you got very excited.

The worst place to get the dope on how to arrange a tennis-court is in the Encyclopedia Britannica. The article on TENNIS was evidently written by the Archbishop of Canterbury. It begins by explaining that in

America tennis is called "court tennis." The only answer to that is, "You're a cock-eyed liar!" The whole article is like this.

The name "tennis," it says, probably comes from the French "*Tenez!*" meaning "Take it! Play!" More likely, in my opinion, it is derived from the Polish "*Tinith!*" meaning "Go on, that was *not* outside!"

During the Fourteenth Century the game was played by the highest people in France. Louis X died from a chill contracted after playing. Charles V was devoted to it, although he tried in vain to stop it as a pastime for the lower classes (the origin of the country-club); Charles VI watched it being played from the room where he was confined during his attack of insanity and Du Guesclin amused himself with it during the siege of Dinan. And, although it doesn't say so in the Encyclopedia, Robert C. Benchley, after playing for the first time in the season of 1922, was so lame under the right shoulder-blade that he couldn't lift a glass to his mouth.

This fascinating historical survey of tennis goes on to say that in the reign of Henri IV the game was so popular that it was said that "there were more tennis-players in Paris than drunkards in England." The drunkards of England were so upset by this boast that they immediately started a drive for membership with the slogan, "Five thousand more drunkards by April 15, and to Hell with France!" One thing led to another until war was declared.

The net does not appear until the 17th century. Up until that time a rope, either fringed or tasseled, was stretched across the court. This probably had to be abandoned because it was so easy to crawl under it and chase your opponent. There might also have been ample opportunity for the person playing at the net, or at the "rope," to catch the eye of the player directly opposite by waving his racquet high in the air and then to kick him under the rope, knocking him for a loop while the ball was being put into play in his territory. You have to watch these Frenchmen every minute.

The Encyclopedia Britannica gives fifteen lines to "Tennis in America." It says that "few tennis courts existed in America before 1880, but that now there are courts in Boston, New York, Chicago, Tuxedo and Lakewood and several other places." Everyone try hard to think now just where those other places are!

Which reminds us that one of them is going to be in your side yard where the garden used to be. After you have got the dimensions from the Encyclopedia, call up a professional tennis-court maker and get him to do the job for you. Just tell him that you want "a tennis-court."

Once it is built the fun begins. According to the arrangement, each member of the family is to have certain hours during which it belongs to them and no one else. Thus the children can play before breakfast and after breakfast until the sun gets around so that the west court is shady. Then Daddy and Mother and their little friends may take it over. Later in the afternoon the children have it again, and if there is any light left after dinner Daddy can take a whirl at the ball.

"Daddy will stick around in the offing all dressed up in his tennis clothes."

What actually will happen is this: Right after breakfast Roger Beeman, who lives across the street and who is home for the summer with a couple of college friends who are just dandy-looking, will come over and ask if they may use the court until someone wants it. They will let Myrtis play with them and perhaps Myrtis' girl-chum from Westover. They will play five sets, running into scores like 19-17, and at lunch time will make plans for a ride into the country for the afternoon. Daddy will stick around in the offing all dressed up in his tennis-clothes waiting to play with Uncle Ted, but somehow or other every time he approaches the court the young people will be in the middle of a set.

After lunch, Lillian Nieman, who lives three houses down the street, will come up and ask if she may bring her cousin (just on from the West) to play a set until someone wants the court. Lillian's cousin has never played tennis before but she has done a lot of croquet and thinks she ought to pick tennis up rather easily. For three hours there is a great deal of screaming, with Lillian and her cousin hitting the ball an aggregate of eleven times, while Daddy patters up and down the side-lines, all dressed up in white, practising shots against the netting.

Finally, the girls will ask him to play with them, and he will thank them and say that he has to go in the house now as he is all perspiration and is afraid of catching cold.

After dinner there is dancing on the court by the young people. Anyway, Daddy is getting pretty old for tennis.

"For three hours there is a great deal of screaming, with Lillian and her cousin hitting the ball an aggregate of eleven times."

COPYRIGHT, 1922, BY DETROIT ATHLETIC CLUB

"She must not see him until he has come right up behind her and placed his hands over her eyes"

GRADUATION DAY IN THE THEATRE

By Robert C. Benchley   *Drawings by* Herb Roth

THIS being the time of year when the young people of our land are waddling up to the platform to receive diplomas (which they will tuck away in a desk-drawer for safe-keeping and eventually forget), it seems only fair to arrange a little something for the young people of our theatre. They have had a hard season, along with the old people of the theatre and the middle-aged people of the theatre, and something ought to be done to make this June a happy one for them. They ought to be graduated into something, preferably a detention camp, but in any event, the thing should be given the recognition of some sort of ceremony.

First there are the stage kiddies. They may be divided into two groups: dumb and piping. The dumb ones are those that are led across the stage in the big song numbers, usually wearing wisps of straw or kilts, causing low murmurs of, "Oh, aren't they

"The young man will have to enter a room at one bound"

cute!" to sweep over the theatre. The member of the cast who leads them across the stage registers kindly interest in the little tots' progress, probably muttering to herself, "A fine job this is for a grown woman!" and hoping that the kiddies will get slivers in their feet so that they won't be at the next show to hog the act.

The dumb ones are, however, unobjectionable, unless they take it into their heads to do pantomime. Any child precocious enough for pantomime, is precocious enough to be at work. The minute a stage kiddie starts making faces to indicate cuteness, it places itself in the class with the "pipers."

The "pipers" are the ones that are always piping up with cunning lines, musically intoned and carefully enunciated, such as "My daddy's never been home since Pres-i-dent Taft's in-aug-u-ra-tion, and I'm *so* lonely!" or "*Please* don't take me away from my mummy, Mr. Children's-Relief-Society-Man, I'll be dood!" Sometimes they are very, very bright little children, in which case the little boys shove their hands very deep into their pockets, place their feet wide apart and say "Aw, shucks!" just like a regular boy.

Well, sir, the graduation exercises for this junior department of stage kiddies is to be as follows:

Assembling in front of the Belasco Theatre they will all pile into a waiting van, decorated with banners and just full of all kinds of goodies. All the little girls who have yellow hair done in long, spiral curls hanging down their backs will be placed near the tail-board where there will be a possibility of their falling off on the trip down town. Once they have arrived at the Battery the van will be driven right on board a big, big steamer, and before anyone knows it, someone (probably the writer of this article) will give the boat a shove and it will start off on a dandy long cruise around the world. When it has been around the world once, it won't stop, even to take on water, but will keep right on going until the kiddies are all grown up and can come back to the stage and not act cute.

The next class to graduate will be the juveniles. They will receive diplomas in bounding, love-making, and in tucking the bow-tie under the collar. In order to pass in bounding, the young man will have to enter a room at one bound, fling a hat on the table, and throw himself into an easy chair with his legs stretched out, sighing: "Some party last night, I'll tell the world!" The nature of the other two courses will be evident. In the love-making course they will have to make love in front of the Board of Overseers and the Faculty, with special reference to concealing the powder left by the ingénue on the coat-sleeve, and in the course devoted to tucking the tuxedo tie-ends under the collar they will have to tuck the ends of a tuxedo tie under a collar.

The graduation of the ingénues should be impressive pictorially, but you can't expect much from above the ear-rings. They must know how to sit down at the piano and thumb out three or four chords to wile away the time until the juvenile bounds in. Those who can play the piano and look wistful at the same time get a *cum laude*

Edna Gerrish doesn't believe in the old alibi and her sheepskin will be made out of goat hide

Nothing less than an LL. D. for Milton Brown, who refused to play in a show by Avery Hopwood

degree, but if the little missy finds that she can't do both it is much better to stop trying to look wistful and watch the keyboard. A wistful look and a slightly underdone note just detract from the desired effect. And, incidentally, when the juvenile has bounded in, she must not see him until he has come right up behind her and placed his hands over her eyes. Then she must say: "Oh, Jack, you naughty boy, how you frightened me!" If she can really look frightened, and not just plain stupid, she rates a lavender ribbon around her diploma.

Another difficult thing for the ingénues is to be able to blush and look downward and slightly to the left when the juvenile suggests that after they are married perhaps they will have "something running about the house besides the hedge." When the young man has pulled this line once a performance over a run of six months, it becomes actual physical pain for *Miss Elsie* to look coy, but she must learn to do it if she is ever going to get ahead as an ingénue. This about disposes of all the young folks who are to graduate. All that now remains is the awarding of the honorary degrees to those stage-folk who have been out of school for some time but who have rendered conspicuous service to the drama during the past year.

GEORGE SPELVIN, who played the part of a detective from Police Headquarters and who not only took off his hat when he came into the house but *didn't* shoot a revolver off when the lights went out.

EDNA GERRISH, who played the part of a woman of the streets and who didn't have a single good excuse to offer for having taken her initial false step.

LUCIEN DUBAL and MIMI DULAC, who were husband and wife in a French comedy and had no outside interests.

MILTON BROWN, who refused to play in an Avery Hopwood show.

MARY RITTING, who played a part calling for seductive gestures and never once rolled her eyes or pushed up close to her victim with her hands on her hips.

FELIX ROGERS, who, as a young husband, said "Damn" when his wife showed him the tiny garments in the work-basket.

"A wicked old fairy clouts them and they see a procession of beautiful women."

WHAT THE SUMMER SHOWS TEACH US

By ROBERT C. BENCHLEY — Drawings by REA IRVIN

THERE is a type of mind which, on a good hot night, suddenly becomes possessed with the idea of going to the theatre. Whether this is due to the accidental loss during youth of certain sections of the brain, or whether the person was just born cuckoo, has never been determined by science. Whatever the cause, it is a bad sign.

These people will be sitting around after a dinner of jellied soup and shaved ice, gasping and mopping with the heat, when all of a sudden one will say: "I'll tell you what! Let's go to a show!" Immediately some wicked old fairy flies down and clouts them with a magic wand, so that they see a vision of a nice, cool theatre with the seats all in white shirts and the ushers floating up and down the aisle, spraying gin-rickeys over the audience. They think they see the stage, cool and dark, with a procession of beautiful women wearing no clothes and comical comedians cracking brand-new jokes all over the place, while the sweet harmony of beautiful music fills the air. And they all hop up and put on their collars and stagger out to an agency to get seats.

They never remember that the last time they went to the theatre on a hot night they lost an aggregate of forty pounds in a party of four people. On that occasion they

entered the theatre, beaming and expectant, and took their seats, just as they will do this time, and settled back confident that their minds were going to be taken off the heat. Then the show began and the fans stopped, and gradually they became conscious that they were slowly melting up into their original ore formation. A perspiring orchestra leader was bringing himself to a quick stroke of apoplexy by waving a baton at four very cross violinists and a disintegrating cornetist, while on the stage a comedian with the lower half of his face washed clear of make-up was trying to keep an acrobatic lady dancer from dying until he could drag her into the wings. From all over the house came the sounds of fanning programs and of people pulling themselves away from the backs of their seats. Every now and then there would be a dull thud and the ushers would slide out a casualty. At the end of the first act they went out on the sidewalk and took a plebescite, voting not to go back again, not even to get their hats.

Barnum Right Again

But all this is forgotten in the enthusiasm of the present scheme, and once more the continually merry spirit of Phineas T. Barnum shakes with triumphant laughter.

It is for such as these that the summer shows are

designed, so you can't expect too much. All that the audience on a hot night wants to see is someone who is cooler than they are. "The Follies" is the place to go for this, without any question. A cooler crew of young ladies you couldn't ask for. They look as if they wouldn't give you a smile if you were drowning and came up to them on bended knees and begged them for one. One of Mr. Ziegfeld's directions for his show girls must be: "Look bored, now, girls! Give them a nasty, fifty thousand dollar eye-brow elevation and under no circumstances let them see the whites of your eyes!" No sadder sight can be seen in New York than a Hot-Dog buyer, accustomed to taking his pick from the chorus of an Oliver Morosco show, sitting in the front row at the Follies and trying to inject personality into a flash at a haughty dame dressed to represent Frigidity in the Ballet of the Emotions. It is like my little boy trying to tell something to Nauen, Germany, over his Woolworth radio outfit.

Of course, I am not saying that the ladies in the Follies can't be made to smile. That would be like saying that you couldn't build a railroad from New York to San Francisco. It has been done. It took good money, but it has been done. A smile from one of those tall, willowy ones would be worth on the market today about the equivalent of fifty shares of Eskimo Pie, Ltd. During the course of a season the girls probably get about six hearty laughs apiece. Sometimes the guy who is paying for it knows they are laughing. Sometimes they wait until they get home alone before they do it.

This, however, has nothing really to do with the main idea of this article which, it has just been decided, deals with summer styles as shown in the summer shows. Every big opening of a musical revue is covered by representatives of various fashion papers and scouts from dressmaking establishments, who take notes on skirt lengths, guimpes, and all the other thousand and one things that women are interested in. These notes are then given to designers who work the ideas over into something practical for every-day use. Readers of this paper will now be able to get in touch with these styles at least a month ahead of the rest of the country.

A nice model that seems to be very popular among the girls consists of a strap. It is a pretty long strap and is made of something that looks like black velvet. Beginning at the neck, where it is wound once and fastened with a diamond, it is brought down around the waist, where it disappears. There is a little diamond clasp at

"A large picture hat will keep the hips from getting sun-burned."

one hip from which to hang a handkerchief or a shopping list, or knitting, in case the wearer is going on a long trolley trip. A large picture hat will keep the hips from getting sun-burned.

Another popular misses' model is called the Half Dollar. This is made up of a brand-new half dollar worn around the waist on a banjo string. This gives a very pretty effect out-of-doors when the sun strikes the shiny coin just right. Open overshoes may or may not be worn with this rig.

Allegory seems to be playing a large part in the costuming of the current shows. You don't just dress up like a lady any more; you dress up to represent Ginger Ale, or Muscular Rheumatism, or the Fordney Tariff. These big allegorical numbers, in which twenty girls symbolizing the twenty different ways in which minced ham can be served, or the twenty counties in the State of Massachusetts, file one by one down a long flight of steps, have brought dressmaking to a condition where a dress is no dress at all unless it has some allegorical significance.

Don't Get Signs Mixed

This effect carried into frocks for home wear will be at once unique and spectacular. For example, we are getting out a model now, green with yellow slashes running criss-cross down the front, which represents Bad Headache. When you come down to breakfast in the morning and see your wife wearing this, you will know enough not to suggest having folks out to dinner and will lay off asking about that extra household money that you gave her last week. Another nice effect is in red crepe, symbolizing the Spirit of Lady Whose Husband is in Toronto on Business for the Rest of the Week. The possibilities in this method of dressing are enormous, the only drawback being the absolute necessity for understanding the symbolism and not getting the code mixed. A careless thinker in this respect might very easily get involved in some rather nasty shooting.

Oh, and for the well-dressed summer-man! What do the summer shows offer for him? There is something nice being worn by several male dancers, consisting of a coat of gold leaf rubbed well into the body, with a breech cloth thrown in for good measure. This has the advantage of requiring no trousers-pressing and I myself tried it out at the June convention of Rotary Clubs with conspicuous success.

WHAT TO DO WHILE *the* FAMILY IS AWAY

By
ROBERT C. BENCHLEY

Drawings by
REA IRVIN

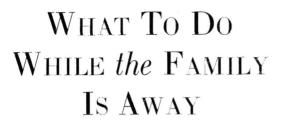

"Even the waiters seem unfamiliar"

SOMEWHERE or other the legend has sprung up that, as soon as the family goes away for the summer, Daddy brushes the hair over his bald spot, ties up his shoes. and goes out on a whirlwind trip through the hellish districts of town. The funny papers are responsible for this, just as they are responsible for the idea that all millionaires are fat and that Negroes are inordinately fond of watermelons.

I will not deny that for just about four minutes after the train has left, bearing Mother, Sister, Junior, Ingabog, and the mechanical walrus on their way to Anybunkport, Daddy is suffused with a certain queer feeling of being eleven years old and down-town alone for the first time with fifteen cents to spend on anything he wants. The city seems to spread itself out before him just ablaze with lights and his feet rise lightly from the ground as if attached to toy balloons. I do not deny that his first move is to straighten his tie.

But five minutes would be a generous allowance for the duration of this foot-loose elation. As he leaves the station he suddenly becomes aware of the fact that no one else has heard about his being fancy-free. Everyone seems to be going somewhere in a very important manner. A great many people, oddly enough, seem to be going home. Ordinarily he would be going home, too. But there wouldn't be much sense in going home now, without— But come, come, this is no way to feel. Buck up, man! How about a wild oat or two?

Gets the Icy Stare

Around at the club the doorman says that Mr. McNartly hasn't been in all afternoon and that Mr. Freem was in at about four-thirty but went out again with a bag. There is no one in the lounge whom he ever saw before. A lot of new members must have been taken in at the last meeting. The club is running down fast. He calls up Eddie Mastayer's office but he has gone for the day. Oh, well, someone will probably come in for dinner. He hasn't eaten dinner at the club for a long time and there will be just time for a swim before settling down to a nice piece of salmon steak.

All the new members seem to be congregated now in the pool and they look him over as if he were a fresh-air child being given a day's outing. He becomes self-conscious and slips on the marble floor, falling and hurting his shin quite badly. Who the hell are these people anyway? And where is the old bunch? He emerges from the locker-room much hotter than he was before and, in addition, boiling with rage.

Dinner is one of the most depressing rituals he has ever gone through with. Even the waiters seem unfamiliar. Once he even gets up and goes out to the front of the building to see if he hasn't got into the wrong club-house by mistake. Pretty soon a terrible person whose name is either Riegle or Ropple comes and sits down with him, offering as his share of the conversation the dogmatic announcement that it has been hotter today than it was yesterday. This is denied with some feeling, although it is known to be true. Dessert is dispensed with for the sake of getting away from Riegle or Ropple or whatever his name is.

Ah! The Night Life

Then the first gay evening looms up ahead. What to do? There is nothing to prevent his drawing all the money out of the bank and tearing the town wide open from the City Hall to the Soldiers' Monument. There is nothing to prevent his formally introducing himself to some nice blonde and watching her get the meat out of a lobster claw. There is nothing to prevent his hiring some bootlegger to anoint him with synthetic gin until he glows like a fire-fly and imagines that he has just been elected Mayor on a Free Ice-Cream ticket. Absolutely nothing stands in his way, except a despairing vision of crepe letters before his eyes reading: "And For What?"

He ends up by going to the movies where he falls asleep. Rather than go home to the empty house he stays at the club. In the morning he is at the office at a quarter to seven.

Now there ought to be several things that a man could do at home to relieve the tedium of his existence while the family is away. Once you get accustomed to the sound of your footsteps on the floors and reach a state of self-control where you don't break down and sob every time you run into a toy which has been left standing around, there are lots of ways of keeping yourself amused in an empty house.

You can set the victrola going and dance. You may never have had an opportunity to get off by yourself and practice those new steps without someone's coming suddenly into the room and making you look foolish. (That's one big advantage about being absolutely alone in a house. You can't *look* foolish, no matter what you do. You may *be* foolish, but no one except you and your God knows about it and God probably has a great deal too much to do to go around telling people how foolish you were.)

Tackle Some Nifties

So roll back the rugs and put on "Kalua" and, holding out one arm in as fancy a manner as you wish, slip the other daintily about the waist of an imaginary partner and step out. You'd be surprised to see how graceful you are.

Pretty soon you will get confidence to try a few

"It makes no difference if you fall on the whirl."

"—while the house is still burning."

tricks. A very nice one is to stop in the middle of a step, point the left toe delicately twice in time to the music, dip and whirl. It makes no difference if you fall on the whirl. Who cares? And when you are through dancing you can go out to the faucet and get yourself a drink—provided the water hasn't been turned off.

Lots of fun may also be had by going out into the kitchen and making things with whatever is left in the pantry. There will probably be plenty of salt and nutmegs with boxes of cooking soda, tapioca, corn-starch and maybe, if you are lucky, an old bottle of olives. Get out a cook-book and choose something that looks nice in the picture. In place of the ingredients which you do not have, substitute those which you do have, thus: nutmegs for eggs, tapioca for truffles, corn-starch and water for milk, and so forth and so forth. Then go in and set the table according to the instructions in the cook-book for a Washington's Birthday party, light the candles and with one of them set fire to the house.

There is probably a night-train for Anybunkport which you can catch while the place is still burning.

To those male readers whose families are away for the summer: Tear the above story out along dotted line and mail it to the folks, writing in pencil across the top: "This guy has struck it about right." Then drop around tonight at seven-thirty to Eddie's apartment. Joe Reddish, John Liftwich, Harry Thibault and three others will be there and the limit will be fifty cents. Game will absolutely break up at one-thirty. No fooling. One-thirty and not a minute longer.

WELCOME HOME

By
ROBERT C. BENCHLEY

THE next few weeks bid fair to be pretty trying ones in our national life. They will mark the return of thousands and thousands of vacationists to the city after two months or two weeks of feverish recuperation, and there is probably no more obnoxious class of citizen, taken end for end, *than the returning vaca-tionist.*

In the first place, they are all so offensively healthy. They come crashing through the train-shed, all brown and peeling, as if their health were something they had acquired through some particular credit to themselves. If it were possible, some of them would wear their sunburned noses on their watch-chains, like Phi Beta Kappa keys.

They have got so used to going about all summer in bathing suits and shirts open at the neck that they look like professional wrestlers in stiff collars and seem to be on the point of bursting out at any minute. And they always make a great deal of noise getting off the train.

Drat That Bessie!

"Where's Bessie?" they scream, "Ned, where's Bessie? . . . . Have you got the thermos bottles? . . . . Well, here's the old station just as it was when we left it (hysterical laughter). . . . . Wallace, you simply must carry your pail and shovel. Mamma can't carry *everything,* you know. . . . . Mamma told you that if you wanted to bring your pail and shovel home you would have to carry it yourself, don't you remember Mamma told you that, Wallace? . . . . Wallace, listen! . . . . Edna, have you got Bessie? . . . . Harry's *gone after the trunks.* . . . . At least, he *said* that was where he was going. . . . . Look, there's the Dexter Building, looking just the same. Big as life and twice as natural. . . . . I know, Wallace, Mamma's just as hot as you are. But you don't hear Mamma crying, do you? . . . . I wonder where Bert is. . . . . He said he'd be down to meet us, sure. . . . . Here, give me that cape, Lillian . . . . you're dragging it all over the ground. . . . . *Here's*

There is probably no more obnoxious class of citizen than the returning vacationist.

—and Shut Up!

Drawings by
REA IRVIN

Bert! . . . . Whoo-hoo, Bert! . . . . Here we are! . . . . Spencer, there's Daddy! . . . . Whoo-hoo, Daddy! . . . . Junior, wipe that gum off your shoe this minute. . . . . Where's Bessie?"

Daddy Gets in Bad

And so they go, all the way out into the street and the cab and home, millions of them. It's terrible.

And when they get home things are just about as bad, except there aren't so many people to see them. At the sight of eight Sunday and sixty-two daily papers strewn over the front porch and lawn, there are loud screams of imprecation at Daddy for having forgotten to order them stopped. Daddy insists that he did order them stopped and that it is that damn-fool boy.

"I guess you weren't home much during July," says Mamma bitterly, "or you would have noticed that something was wrong." (Daddy didn't join the family until August.)

Sure, There's a Burglar

"There were no papers delivered during July," says Daddy very firmly and quietly, "at least, I didn't see any" (stepping on one dated July 19).

The inside of the house resembles some place you might bet a man a hundred dollars he daren't spend the night in. Dead men's feet seem to be protruding from behind sofas and there is a damp smell as if the rooms had been closed pending the arrival of the coroner.

Junior runs upstairs to see if his switching engine is where he left it and comes falling downstairs panting with terror, announcing that there is Something in the guest-room. At that moment there is the sound of someone leaving the house by the back door. Daddy is elected by popular vote to go upstairs and see what has happened, although he insists that he has to wait downstairs as the man with the trunks will be there at any minute. After five minutes of cagey maneuvering around in the hall outside the guest-room door, he returns looking for

Junior, saying that it was simply a pile of things left on the bed covered with a sheet, "Aha-ha-ha-ha-ha!"

Then comes the unpacking. It has been estimated that in the trunks of returning vacationists, taking this section of the country as a whole, the following articles will be pulled out during the next few weeks:

25,685 pairs of sneakers, full of sand which will be shaken out on the floor.

20,478 bathing suits, still damp from the "one last swim" taken just before departure.

4,674 dead tennis balls.

26,498 last month's magazines, bought for reading in the grove and never thrown away.

Good for Ballast

126,175 shells and pretty stones picked up on the beach for decoration purposes, for which there has suddenly become no use at all.

4,567 horse-shoe crabs, salvaged by children who refused to leave them behind.

1,689 lace scarfs and shawls, bought from itinerant Armenians.

1,784 remnants of tubes formerly containing sunburn ointment, half-filled bottles of citronella and white shoe-dressing.

2,174 pairs of white flannel trousers, ready for the cleaners.

26,375,308 snap-shots, showing Ed and Mollie on the beach in their bathing suits.

5,267,264 snap-shots which show nothing at all.

3,365,125 faded flowers, dance-cards, and assorted sentimental objects, calculated to bring up tender memories of summer evenings.

34,167 uncompleted knit-sweaters, half of them being the initial efforts of ambitious children.

87,432 pairs of white shoes that probably never can be restored to their glory of an earlier day.

Snapshot showing Ed and Mollie on the beach in their bathing suits.

They stop perfect strangers on the streets.

4,637 receipts for money paid out to teachers of esthetic dancing, who find the money not hard to take while enjoying a rest from their terrific labors in town.

You Can't Stop Them

Then begins the tour of the neighborhood, comparing summer vacation experiences. To each returning vacationist it seems as if everyone in town must be interested in what he or she did during the summer. They stop perfect strangers on the streets and say: "Well, a week ago today at this time we were all walking up to the Post Office for the mail. Right in front of the Post Office were the fish-houses, and you ought to have seen Billy one night leading a lobster home on a string. That was the night we all went swimming by moonlight."

"Yeah?" says the stranger, and pushes his way past.

Then two people get together who have been to different places. Neither wants to hear about the other's summer—and neither does. Both talk at once and pull snap-shots out of their pockets.

"Here's where we used to take our lunch—"

"That's nothing. Steve had a rich friend up the lake who had a launch—"

"—and every day there was something doing over at the Casino—"

"—and you ought to have seen Miriam, she was a sight—"

Never Fatal, Unfortunately

Pretty soon they come to blows trying to make each other listen. The only trouble is that they never quite kill each other. If only one could be killed it would be a big help.

The next ban on immigration should be on returning vacationists. Have government officials stationed in each city and keep everyone out who won't give a bond to shut up and go right to work.

Tired mothers have begun hiding their bonds behind the clock where they
can be stolen by wayward sons to buy fur underclothes for chorus girls.

JUST ABOUT THE SAME, THANK YOU

By
ROBERT C. BENCHLEY

Drawings by
REA IRVIN

THE early stages of the new dramatic season shape up just about as the early stages of every dramatic season have shaped up since 1895, with the possible exception of the property grass. There doesn't seem to be so much property grass being used in the rural sets. This may be due to the shortage of light blue-green dye stuffs, or to the influence of the *Wiener Kartoffle Schauspielhaus* on the new theatre movement. Whatever the reason, the situation exists, and we must face it.

Aside from the grass crop, things look about the same. The old heart strings seem to be in for a heavy winter of being strummed on, for already tired mothers have begun hiding their bonds behind the clock where they can be stolen by wayward sons to buy fur underclothes for chorus girls, little New England seamstresses have started bakin' pies in the kitchen and fixin' up the settin'-room real neat for the long-lost lover, pale young girls in hall bedrooms have begun coughing for the open country and the birds and trees, and so many sad heroines are devoting their evenings to choking down sobs that Broadway sounds like the old frog pond on a summer's evening.

As in former years, it is going to be inadvisable for a young girl to take a position as secretary to a rich man if she doesn't want to have someone writing home to her folks that she has taken the step which is so often de-scribed as "worse than death." (You notice that it is called "worse than death" only by those who have never taken it. The rest come on wearing ermine wraps and dia-monds and don't seem to be having a half bad time. However, that's none of my business.) The fact remains that, on the stage today, as soon as a rich man engages a girl as his secretary and has her sit beside his carved mahogany desk, taking dictation, the only decent thing he can do for her next is to marry her.

Things are also looking pretty black for extravagant wives. Some day there is going to be a play about a wife who spent all her husband's money on doggy clothes and Elizabeth Arden face education, and, as a result, hooked a rich old promoter into a big business deal, netting a profit for the family of about 175% on the capital invested. But just now dramatists are bound that the thing won't work. Just as soon as the rich old promoter has paid the wife's car-fare in the subway, he begins to rub his hands together and play satyr, and the race is off. The only thing for stage wives to do this season is pull down the shades at half-past seven and get into a kimono for an evening of parchesi with the children.

The only novelty that the stage has had to offer so far, is in the line of complete and nasty murdering. There have already been more cute ways devised for killing people than the Medici bunch had in their entire catalogue.

One man is killed by merely placing a telephone receiver to his ear, with his assailant miles away in a pay-station. Another lies down on a couch and is immediately snatched down into the cellar where he and his girl friend are prepared for vivisection. It is getting so that a decent citizen won't dare to get up out of bed in the morning for fear that his slippers will jump up and bite him to death, and yet won't dare to lie in bed for fear that someone will have thought up a way to push the headboard over on him by pressing a button in the next town.

This race for novelty in murder is a development of the old mystery play of past seasons in which you were supposed to remain in ignorance of the culprit until the final curtain. After six or seven of these, in which the person least suspected always turned out to be the guilty boy, the audience began to look around during the first act for the one character who did nothing but bring in the egg sandwiches or pull the portieres together, and before the show was a third over he was as good as arrested by every amateur detective in the house. No one has yet thought of writing a murder mystery in which it is finally shown that the man, discovered with the smoking revolver in his hand in the first act, committed the crime.

But the writers of these melodramas are a more forward-looking crew than their confrères who write the emotional dramas. They have seen that audiences can no longer be mystified over *who* did it, but must be tantalized by a desire to know *what* it was done with. The others will probably always go on writing plays, oblivious of the fact that the audience knows at the start that *Vivian* is going to marry *Mr. Montgomery* in the end and that *Tom Nesbit* wasn't really lost at sea but will turn up in the last act with the proof that *Doris* is the daughter

Symbolic motions calculated to placate the God of Green Corn on the Cob.

of *Earl Beamish* and the rightful owner of Dampwood Manor. And incidentally, they will probably go right on making money, which is what makes me so damn mad.

We come now to the field of musical shows, where novelty long ago ceased to put up a struggle for existence.

The Hawaiian idea, for example. Certainly, we got all through with Hawaiian songs and dances in 1920 after several good long seasons of them. And yet this year, with the air of producing something to knock you cold with novelty, they are bringing on hula-hula numbers and ukeleles. Soon some manager will be flashing an Apache dance on us and we shall all be back again in the days when Woodrow Wilson was known as the Scholar Governor of New Jersey.

There is, however, one feature of these native Hawaiian dances which seems to be gaining ground, and which I don't remember ever having seen before this year, certainly not in my own home. It is a strange movement participated in by the chorus as they sing, a sort of spasmodic gripping of the various joints of the body, as if the victim were being seized by a series of pains in the knees, hips, elbows and stations on the Fitchburg line. This probably has some social significance which has never been explained to me because I am not old enough. It may be a survival of an old native dance in which the young men and women of the tribe went through certain symbolic motions calculated to placate the God of Green Corn on the Cob to the point of endowing them with a good crop of Yellow Bantam or Country Gentleman.

Whatever it may mean, it has got a terrible hold on the choruses of our musical shows, and until the thing is explained to me, I shall make it a point to go right straight home after the show and take no chances on getting my knees sprained.

The rich old promoter begins to rub his hands together and play satyr.

DAC NEWS

DRAWING BY R. F. HEINRICH

October - 1921

Hand in hand with old Grandpa Sandman as the whistle blows.

HOW TO WATCH FOOTBALL

By ROBERT C. BENCHLEY
Drawings by REA IRVIN

PERCY HAUGHTON has written a book on "How to Watch Football." Mr. Haughton ought to know what he is writing about, as he, perhaps more than any one man, has made football worth watching—for the Harvard side of the field, at any rate. There was a time when any book on watching football should have contained a chapter in the back for the Harvard readers, giving six good clean ways to commit suicide after the game. Percy Haughton changed all that, and is certainly entitled to write a book.

But there are several things which Mr. Haughton, in the flush of his success, has neglected to include in his volume. There are other pointers necessary for us poor sons-of-guns who sit shivering in the stands besides knowing how to tell who is carrying the ball. In an attempt to supplement the information in this book by the founder of Harvard college, we have drawn up the following suggestions for spectators to help them to see and understand the game better.

From Outside the Field

As almost everyone is late in arriving at a football game, there is a period of perhaps twenty-five minutes after the kick-off when you are milling around outside the gate in the crowd, looking for your proper entrance. This is perhaps the most trying period of all for the spectator. He hears occasional barkings from the quarterback, followed by terrible silence, and then a roar from one side or the other, he can't tell which. Almost anything may have happened. The visiting half-back may be racing down the field for a touchdown, or good old Grimsey of the home-team may have caught a forward pass on the enemy's three-yard line. Alternate waves of apprehension and elation sweep up and down the fur-clad back of the tardy partisan. What to do? What to do?

The first impulse is to jump up on the shoulders of the people standing next you. This would, however, get you nowhere, as they would probably move away after a while and leave you flat. The next idea is to ask someone if he knows what has just happened. This is equally silly, as he is just about to ask you.

The best way is simply to turn around and push your way through the crowd back to the street, where, in a few minutes, newsboys will be selling extras giving the score as far as the first quarter, and, in addition, you will then be able to see how Ursinus and Pratt University stand at the end of their first quarter. Then you can go back into the crowd and wait until another extra is out.

The "Full-Back in Front" Play

For those who finally do get into their seats, there are several points to be noted before a successful following of the game can be accomplished. In order to see the plays as they are pulled off, there is one thing that is essential. *The man in front of you must be sitting down.* I cannot emphasize this point too strongly. No matter how conversant you may be with the technical side of the game, you simply cannot watch it intelligently if your range of vision is blocked by six square feet of raccoon coat and a pair of waving arms.

You are pretty sure to have one of these Mexican jumping beans in front of you. So it is well to be prepared. He will sit quietly until just as the quarterback begins to give the signals. Then he comes up and yells: "Let's go!" It does no good to call "Down in front!" He thinks you are shouting at someone in front of him, and perhaps joins in the demand himself. There is just one way out. It is the way that all honorable men have taken since the beginning of history whenever the good of the state has demanded that they act and act quickly.

We are getting out a special folding pocket dagger this season (with sheepskin case, $7.00). It will go through any fur coat, no matter how heavy, and will inflict a dangerous if not fatal wound.

Rules Are Just a Handicap

A very serious mistake to which prospective members of a football crowd are prone is trying to learn the rules. One cannot be too emphatic in condemning this happily diminishing practice. It is likely to spoil the entire afternoon for a loyal alumnus, because of its tendency to undermine his belief that all penalties called against the dear old 'varsity are unjust. Then where is the sweet consolation of knowing that we would have won if the referee had not been on parole from the penal institution to which he was committed for robbing a child's bank?

It is well, too, for the football enthusiast of maturer years to make no attempt to learn all the Alma Mater yells. Most of them are so complicated that the words can be learned only by years of constant study and so difficult of articulation that they threaten permanent injury to the aging larynx. A better plan is to content yourself with chanting "Touchdown!" or "Hold 'em!" as the case may be. Alumni of some of our leading universities have found "Hold 'em!" alone a complete cheering equipment for years at a time.

Faulty Vision

In recent years there has arisen a great deal of complaint about not being able to see the players distinctly. This trouble has been traced to the pocket-flask. Perhaps you have been bothered by this. The symptoms follow:

For the first period, everything goes along nicely. The numbers on the players are clearly visible and you can even distinguish their features, so long as their features remain distinguishable to anyone.

Shortly after the beginning of the second period, you discover that there are six men playing in the back-field, in three groups of two each. The quarter also has a friend with him. Their team work impresses you as being remarkable, as each group of two is perfectly co-ordinated in its movements. When one man stoops over, his mate stoops at exactly the same angle. You call your friend's attention to this evidence of perfectly bully coaching. He says: "By George, thas' ri'."

But as soon as the ball is put into play, the thing is not so pretty. The men seem to have no idea of what they are doing. Some go one way, some another. Others vanish entirely into thin air. Several of them seem to be smoking, which hides one whole section of the scrimmage line in a sort of haze. This smoking is, of course, strictly against training regulations and should be punished.

Shut off by six square feet of raccoon coat.

Faulty vision has been traced to the pocket-flask, the game degenerating into a Maypole dance.

Then the affair degenerates into a sort of Maypole dance, in which all the second-string men and the Freshman team seem to have been invited to join, and you just give the whole thing up in disgust. You won't even look at it. Neither will your buddy. The afternoon is spoiled, just because a lot of selfish boys got silly when they should have been playing football.

These are the symptoms of the faulty vision resulting from pocket-flasks. It is difficult to think up ways to overcome it. Of course, one could always leave the pocket-flask at home, but that seems impractical. It gets so cold along about four o'clock that to be without a flask would be nothing short of foolhardy. A thermos full of coffee might do, but if you have coffee you have to have things to go with it, like apple pie and cheese and crackers, and that would make too big a package.

The only other suggestion is this. Start drinking from the flask at, let us say, ten o'clock on the morning of the game. If necessary, or rather *as soon as* necessary, re-fill the flask. Be within calling-distance of a good, soft couch, with an easy pillow for the head. Don't eat any lunch. Turn the heat on in the room and shut the windows.

Then, when it comes time to start for the game, you will already have started, hand-in-hand with Old Grandpa Sandman, on the road to Never-Never Land, and it won't make any difference whether or not the man in front of you stands up, or the wind blows under the seats, or Yale wins, or anything. For you, my little man, will be safe and warm at home, where, after all, is the place to be on the afternoon of a football game.

HERE COME THE CHILDREN

By
ROBERT C. BENCHLEY

Drawings by
REA IRVIN

No old-style party for the children of today. They want red meat—and a Paul Jones party.

MANY parents are confronted this month by the problem of homing children. Just as you have got the house picked up after Thanksgiving, the private schools and colleges let their charges loose again for two or three weeks because of Christmas or some such pretext, and before you know it Spencer and Beth and eight or ten of their little playmates land on you, palpitating for entertainment. What, as the question runs, to do?

There was a time when all you had to do to entertain the kiddies was to string some festoons of red paper from the chandelier to the corners of the table and cry "Surprise, surprise!" when they came into the room. Then perhaps some of those godawful snapping arrangements with paper hats and mottoes concealed inside a percussion cap would throw the young folks into such a state of excitement that they couldn't eat for a week afterward. Those who were able to stand up after this enervating sport were allowed to indulge their sex appetites in a game of "Post-Office." And when their parents came for them at a quarter to nine, it was voted that a delirious time had been had and thank you, Mrs. Hosmer.

But if you want to hear the merry sound of children's mocking laughter, just try one of those parties on them today. The chances are that they will start throwing rolls and olive pits at you and leave the house with curses on their lips. The children who are coming home from school today for the holidays are built of sterner stuff. They want red meat. The holidays mean to them something like what King Manuel of Portugal used to go off on when he would disappear from home and not show up for ten days.

In view of this change in standards of entertainment, it would perhaps be well to line up a few ways of keeping the young folks happy while they are in our midst celebrating the Nativity. For, after all, we must keep in touch with the children, because some day they will get all of Grandma's money.

A Paul Jones Party

This is one of the most successful entertainments for boys and girls just home from the exacting confinement of school. It is called a "Paul Jones" party, because Paul Jones was a notorious souse. It was even whispered at one time that he was the father of the American navy, but no one was ever able to prove it.

In order to prepare the house for this party, it will be necessary to take down all the pictures and draperies and move all the furniture out. The corners in every room should be banked and a tarpaulin stretched over the floors.

A lemonade should be prepared, consisting of lemon juice, gin, vermouth, bitters, and a little crushed mint. For the older children something with bacardi is nice, or perhaps, if they are children from the neighborhood whom you know very well, just straight Scotch.

Begin the party at 11:30, which will give them time to go to the theatre first. Do not be discouraged at their scornful air as they enter the house. They are that way to everybody. The lemonade will soon fix that, and before the evening is over they may warm up to the extent of coming over and speaking to you personally.

Paul Whiteman's orchestra should have been imported from New York for the occasion and should be made to play continuously. Nothing short of Paul Whiteman's will do, and if even they aren't playing their best, considerable comment will be elicited from the tiny guests.

After sufficient dancing has been indulged in, the big game of the evening may be suggested. The company is divided into couples and each couple is provided with a high-powered roadster. Starting in relays from the porte-cochère, they should be sent off in different directions. The idea of the game is to see which couple can stay out the longest. The winners will be presented with a marriage license and their flat silver.

Keeping Tabs

The chief trouble that parents have in keeping their children entertained during vacation time is in keeping them in sight. In a three-weeks' vacation, a father may see his son perhaps four times, two of which will be at the station as he comes and goes. A good way to get a look at him is to go up to his room when you come home for lunch and see him as he sleeps.

If, however, you have a lot of things that you want to talk over with him the following is about the only course to adopt. Buy a pair of roller skates and follow on behind as he goes to and from his various social engagements. You can do your work at the office in the morning and reach home about noon when he is starting out for the country club. You will have time for several sentences on the way from the house to the machine and, if he has all the seats filled with his playmates, you can spin along behind until they get outside the city limits. Then there isn't much use in your trying to keep up.

He must come home to dress for his dinner party, however, so there you have him. While he is in the tub and putting the studs in his shirt, you can get in a lot of good fatherly conversation, which you can finish on roller-skates if his party is in town. In this way, during the course of the three weeks, you may manage to find out how he likes his school, what courses he is taking, if any, and how it happened that he had to have money for laboratory fees twice in the same term. And then again, you may not.

In case, however, you cannot spare the time from your

Buy a pair of roller skates and follow on behind as he goes to and from his social engagements.

business to follow him to and from his parties, we have compiled a list of questions which parents always ask their children and have indicated the answers which they get. Our statistician has figured out that these answers vary in general only by about 0.45% throughout the country, so if you don't get a chance to ask yours, you may accept these answers as essentially correct:

Q. How do you like it there?

A. *Oh, all right, I guess.*

Q. How are the teachers?

A. *Oh, all right, I guess.*

Q. Have you been well?

A. *Sure.*

Q. Do they give you hot cereal for breakfast?

A. *Sure.*

Q. Is your room-mate nice?

A. *Sure.*

Q. What do you do for a bathrobe these cold mornings. Is your old one warm enough?

A. *It's all right.*

Q. You don't smoke too much, do you?

A. *No.*

Q. Do you ever see anything of the Head Master?

A. *No.*

Q. Is he nice?

A. *Sure, I guess so.*

Q. How are your socks holding out?

A. *Oh, all right, I guess.*

Q. Do you need any more money?

A. *Well, I'll tell you. A lot of the fellows get extra books and things to help them in their work and it might be a good thing if I had some extra money to buy maps and things that you have to have, and then a lot of times we are supposed to buy charts and things, etc., etc., etc.*

With these questions all answered for you, and the certainty that you won't see the kiddies for more than six minutes in all anyway, it might be just as well to write to the school authorities and ask them to keep Norman there during vacation. It would save his carfare home and he might get some sleep.

While he is in the tub you can get in a lot of good fatherly conversation.

A CHEERY GLANCE BACKWARD

*Showing 1922
in Retrospect*

By
ROBERT C. BENCHLEY

*Drawings
by*
REA IRVIN

THERE is nothing so invigorating at the beginning of a new year as to turn around and look at the plans that were made at the beginning of the year past. They shape up like something you find on a butter plate in the back of the ice-box on Friday which the cook hated to throw away after Sunday dinner.

For those who had thought of starting off 1923 with a light heart, let us review a few of the big features which one finds in glancing back over the newspaper files for the first weeks of 1922.

In the first place, there was a dandy big conference being held in Washington with the avowed purpose of preventing another war. All the boys were there, sitting around in a circle, and saying "Yes, yes." Photographs were taken showing the delegate from Portugal going up the steps to the Pan-American Building and the delegate from Oblatz coming down the steps of the Pan-American Building, and the Chinese delegates sweeping off the steps of the Pan-American Building. President Harding was quoted as saying that it was a "most significant occasion" and Secretary Hughes threw discretion to the winds and said that, in his mind, it was "an occasion of the highest significance."

It is true that along about the middle of January most of the delegates had begun to look at their watches and say that they had to meet a man, but still, there was an air of quiet accomplishment.

Since that time, as we all know, the nations of the earth have been just about as friendly as a cageful of pumas. The only wars that we have had have been between Turkey and Greece, with side-fights by England and France, Roumania and Gravia, Hydrangia and Czecho-

Droptalia, and the Yankees and St. Louis. Aside from that, the world has been just like one great big family. Just exactly.

There was a great deal of mention made of a conference to be held later at Cannes, which was to fix everything up that was left unfixed at Washington. Can any bright little boy or girl tell Teacher now what happened at Cannes? The name is Cannes, C-a-n-n-e-s. A picture in the papers showed Premier Briand starting out for Cannes after saying that he hoped to arrange there an alliance with England. As I remember it, nothing more was ever heard of Briand, although some natives said that they saw a man with a heavy black moustache roaming along the beach in his undershirt and a pair of knickers, saying that he was looking for an alliance that he had lost somewhere. Unless an "alliance" is something where two men stand up in a ring and bite each other until one passes out cold, I guess he never got his wish.

Then there was a great deal of rejoicing that the Irish situation had been fixed up so neatly with the ratification of the treaty. King George congratulated Queen Mary and Queen Mary congratulated King George, and all the papers had cartoons showing Ireland resting on a harp with a rising sun behind her and the caption: "At Last." President Harding said that it was a very significant event. Just then the roof fell in.

Domestic

In our own dear land, Republican Leader Mondell was predicting the passage before June 1st of the Bonus Bill, and energetic steps looking toward a refunding of the allied debts to the United States and the establishment of a permanent merchant marine. Heigh-ho! Mr. Mondell is a lot of fun, once you get him going. He'll say anything for a laugh.

At about the same time, Henry Ford let it be known that seventy-five miles was going to be the length of the city he was about to build at Muscle Shoals. Seventy-five miles as the bull flies, that is. There were a lot of pictures and diagrams in the papers showing how by developing Muscle Shoals he was going to make it possible to do without cows in the production of milk, and perhaps even get a lot of fun out of little odds and ends that you had put away in the attic as being of no use. There still may be plans afoot for Muscle Shoals, but afoot is about all they are.

Chinese delegates sweeping off the steps of the Pan-American Building.

Another good giggle may be squeezed from the big story which filled the papers during the first week in January, 1922, concerning the indicting by a Grand Jury of an ex-Prohibition commissioner of New York and sixteen others, charged with conspiring to defraud the United States by issuing false liquor permits. There was considerable talk of jail sentences, electrocution, or even of taking away their baseball passes, and it was rumored that the resulting inquiry would unearth culprits even "higher up" than the Commissioner. If the "resulting inquiry" was ever held, it was held in the bulkhead of an abandoned farm-house on Long Island and all the participants were gagged and thrown into a swamp immediately afterward. Certainly no one ever told me anything about it, and I could swear that I saw that Prohibition Commissioner trying to get out of the rough at Siwanoy only last month. A great little thing, the Majesty of the Law.

The Big Murder Mystery

And speaking of the Majesty of the Law, the early weeks of 1922 broke out with one of the bulliest murders in movie history, when Mr. Taylor (you remember the name), the handsome director, was found dead in his study at Hollywood. The police gave out statements every six minutes, saying that they expected an arrest within twenty-four hours. Then it was "forty-eight hours," and then "ninety-

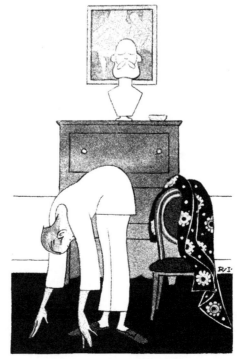
On January first I did every one of Walter Camp's Daily Dozen.

six hours." All kinds of suspects were "grilled" and there were inside stories of mysterious women in white, green, blue, and maroon. Special story writers for the newspapers ran pictures of Mable Normand and Mary Miles Minter and Will Hays, together with charts of Taylor's study, with dotted lines showing where the murderer escaped. The dotted lines, however, stopped at the threshold, and up until a late hour last night, had not been traced any further. The police report that they are watching a certain party, but are waiting for him to get a little older before they arrest him.

Personal

The above about completes the summary of questions which were agitating the nation just a year ago, and we note with satisfaction that they have all been satisfactorily cleared up. Much the same may be said of my personal schedule.

As I remember it, I was to begin in January and do exercises every morning, with a view to eliminating a large belt of adipose tissue which manifested itself every time I leaned forward to tie up my shoes. Don't think that I was getting fat. I was simply being on the safe side.

On January first I did every one of Walter Camp's Daily Dozen. Also on January second. That night I had to sit up late (just a bunch of fellows, nothing much) and all I had time for on the morning of the third was the first half dozen. Then came a cold spell, and I had to get dressed in the bath-room where it was warm, but where there wasn't room to do the windmill figures without banging my knuckles against the medicine chest. So I just did the squatting ones and the deep breathing. After a while (the cold spell lasted a long time) I forgot how to do the windmill ones, and, as there wasn't much sense in doing some and not the rest and run the danger of becoming overdeveloped on one side and not enough on the other, I gradually cut them down to the deep breathing, which I did on the way to the train.

I had other items on my list of things to do in 1922, but I am ashamed to mention them. Anyway, things will be different in 1923.

Beginning *today!*

A MID-WINTER SPORT CARNIVAL

By
ROBERT C. BENCHLEY

Drawings by
REA IRVIN

Bear-hunting has lost its flavor since the supply of bears ran out.

ALONG about this time of year, we sportsmen find ourselves rather up against it for something to do to keep the circulation pounding even sluggishly along. Golf, tennis, and paddling about on water-wings are out of season, and somehow bear-hunting has lost its flavor. Bear-hunting has never been the same since the supply of bears ran out. There really is nothing much to do except sit behind the stove in the club-house and whittle. And even then you are likely to cut your thumb.

In an attempt to solve this mid-winter problem for red-blooded men, a postal ballot has been taken to see what others of our sort are doing during the long evenings to keep themselves fit for the coming open season. Some of the replies are strictly confidential and cannot be reprinted here. You would certainly be surprised if you knew. Send a dollar and a plain, self-addressed envelope and maybe we can make an exception in your case. The address is Box 25, Bostwick, Kansas.

Following, however, are some excerpts from letters concerning which the writers have no pride:

Parchesi

"I keep in training during the winter months," writes one man, "by playing parchesi with my little boy. The procedure of this only fairly interesting game is as follows:

"I am reading my paper after dinner. My son says: 'Dad, play parchesi with me?' And I say: 'No.' Then my wife says: 'I don't think it would hurt you to pay a little attention to your children now and then.' 'Oh, is that so?' I reply.

"The parchesi board is then brought out and I am given my choice of colors. It is a good rule to pick a bright-colored set of buttons (the technical name for parchesi men escapes me at the moment) because as the game progresses and you get sleepier and sleepier, a good bright color, like red, will help you focus on the board.

"As you probably know, the way in which parchesi is played is a combination of that man's game—'crap,' and the first six pages of Wentworth's Elementary Arithmetic. Unless you had played it, you wouldn't believe that rolling the bones could be transformed into anything so tepid. One evening when my wife was out getting a drink of water I gave the boy a few pointers on what could really be done with the dice by going about it in the right spirit, and before she came back I had got the fifteen cents he had been saving up to buy a pair of shoes with. I had to give it back to him, however, as he cried so hard she asked him what was the matter.

"As the evening wears on, I get so that I can roll and make my move without being more than one-third conscious. The only danger is that I will lean too heavily on the board in the middle and close it up, throwing the men in all directions. This, of course, has the advantage of stopping the game, but you can't work it very often."

Carving

"You ask what I do for exercise during the winter," writes another. "Well, I am quite a carver. During the summer and spring (and autumn, too, if you like) when there are other things to do, we have chops and meat-balls and fish for dinner, things which do not have to be carved. But as soon as the weather gets bad, I just shut the doors and light a good fire, and give up my time to hacking roasts to pieces for a family of five.

"In this I am aided immeasurably by my wife. Let us say that we have for dinner a leg of lamb. My first move is to prop it up on its side against a potato and drive the fork deep into the ridge. I may take three shots for this, owing to the tendency of the potato to slip, letting the roast turn heavily over into the dish-gravy. A little time is necessary also to cover up the spots on the table-cloth before the Little Woman notices, of doing which there is a fat chance.

"Then it begins.

" 'Why don't you carve it down the other way?'

" 'What other way?'

" 'Why straight across, of course. You'll never get anywhere hacking at it that way.'

" 'Where did you ever see anyone carve meat straight across?'

" 'Everyone carves it that way. You're the only man I ever saw who tried to gouge it out like that.'

" 'Gouge it out? Who's gouging it out? What's the matter with that slice?' (*Holding up a slab on the fork and dropping it into the cauliflower*).

" 'What's the matter with it? It's in the cauliflower!' (*Shrill, irritating laughter*).

"I then turn the roast over and slice along the side as requested, doing it badly on purpose to show that that is *not* the way to carve meat. In messing it up, I overdo

Hacking roasts to pieces for a family of five is a fine winter sport.

the thing and slip with the knife, cutting my wrist.

" 'Now you see? God never meant Man to cut that way. I've hurt myself.'

" 'I never said that God did mean Man to cut that way, the way you were cutting. All God meant Man to do was to use his brain—if any. Here, give me that knife, and you go and dish out the beans.'

"And so it goes, every time we have a roast, and double the strength when we have chicken. It keeps the winter months from becoming dull and works up quite a good forearm development."

Snow-Shoeing

An advocate of outdoor sports is the writer of the following:

"As for me, give me the invigorating fun of snow-shoeing when Mother Nature has thrown her mantle over golf-course and tennis-court. Just as soon as the first snow comes, I get out all the picture books in the house, showing people plunging around in the drifts, cheeks aglow and ears a-tingle. Then to the sporting-goods store, where I buy a pair of snow-shoes.

"Trying on snow-shoes in a store is not so easy as trying on a pair of regular shoes. The clerk straps them on your feet and says: 'Now just walk up and down a bit to see how they feel. There's a mirror over there.'

"Just try walking up and down a bit on a board floor with snow-shoes on, and you will see why so few people bother to get the right size when buying them. Owing to this carelessness, however, arises much of the flat feet among snow-shoers. Their snow-shoes don't fit them.

"Then one has to have a stocking-cap, preferably red, and a good stout stick. The stick is for clouting people who make fun of you. In case there is too much ridicule, you can pull the stocking-cap down over your face and then they won't know who it is. They won't dare kid anyone whose face is hidden, for fear it might turn out to be Charles Evans Hughes or someone like that.

"Then, when I have made all my purchases, I take them home with me and order a fire lighted in the fire-place. Next some nails and good strong cord. Standing on a step-ladder (just an ordinary step-ladder will do) I take the snow-shoes, cross them, and hang them up over the fireplace, with the stick as a cross-bar. By this time a merry fire is crackling, and by standing across the room you will get as pretty a picture as you could wish to see, with the crossed snow-shoes fairly dancing in the glimmer of the fire-light. A Scotch and soda helps make this sport one of the most stimulating in the world."

Write in and tell us what *you* do in the winter months to keep fit.

You will get as pretty a picture as you could wish.

SHAKESPEARE GOOD FOR ONLY 1000 YEARS MORE

By
ROBERT C. BENCHLEY

Drawings by
REA IRVIN

The whole trouble with Shakespeare is that too many people have taken him up.

AT the end of the current theatrical season, the trustees of the Shakespeare estate will probably get together at the Stratford House and get pie-eyed. It has been a banner year for "the Immortal Bard," as his wife used to call him. Whatever the royalties are that revert to the estate, there will be enough to buy a couple of rounds anyway, and maybe enough left over to hire an entertainer.

There was a time during the winter in New York when you couldn't walk a block without stepping on some actor or actress playing Shakespeare. They didn't all make money, but it got the author's name into the papers, and publicity never hurt anyone, let alone a writer who has been dead three hundred years and whose stuff isn't adaptable for the movies.

The only trouble with acting Shakespeare is the actors. It brings out the worst that is in them. A desire to read aloud the soliloquy (you know the one I mean) is one of the first symptoms a man has that he is going to be an actor. If ever I catch any of my little boys going out behind the barn to recite this speech, I will take them right away to a throat specialist and have their palates removed. One failure is enough in a family.

And then, too, the stuff that Will wrote, while all right to sit at home and read, does *not* lend itself to really snappy entertainment on the modern stage. It takes just about the best actor in the world to make it sound like anything more than a declamation by the Spirit of Holly-Berries in a Christmas pageant. I know that I run coun-

ter to many cultured minds in this matter, but I think that, if the truth were known, there are a whole lot more of us who twitch through two-thirds of a Shakespearean performance than the 1920 census would lead one to believe. With a company consisting of one or two stars and the rest hams (which is a good liberal estimate) what can you expect? Even Shakespeare himself couldn't sit through it without reading the ads on the program a little.

But you can't blame the actor entirely. According to present standards of what constitutes dramatic action, most of Will's little dramas have about as much punch as a reading of a treasurer's report. To be expected to thrill over the dramatic situations incident to a large lady's dressing up as a boy and fooling her own husband, or to follow breathlessly a succession of scenes strung together like magic-lantern slides and each ending with a perfectly corking rhymed couplet, is more than ought to be asked of anyone who has, in the same season, seen "Loyalties" or any one of the real plays now running on Broadway.

It is hard to ask an actor to make an exit on a line like:

"I am glad on't: I desire no more delight
    Than to be under sail and gone tonight"

without sounding like one of the characters in Palmer Cox's Brownies saying:

"And thus it was the Brownie Band,
    Came tumbling into Slumberland."

That is why they always have to exit laughingly in a

Shakespearean production. The author has provided them with such rotten exits. If they don't do something—laugh, cry, turn a handspring, or something—they are left flat in the middle of the stage with nothing to do but say: "Well, I must be going." In "The Merchant of Venice," as produced by Mr. Belasco, the characters were forced to keep up a running fire of false-sounding laughter to cover up the artificial nature of what they had just said:

"At the park gate, and therefore haste away
For we must measure twenty miles today. A-ha-ha-ha-ha-ha!" (*Off l. c.*)

To hear *Lorenzo* and *Gratiano* walking off together, you would have thought that *Lorenzo* had the finest line of funny stories in all Venice, so loud and constantly did they laugh, whereas, if the truth were known, it was simply done to save their own and Shakespeare's face. Now my contention is that any author who can't get his stuff over on the stage without making the actors do contortions, is not so good a playwright technically as Eugene Walters is. And as for comedy—

An actor, in order to get Shakespeare's comedy across, has got to roll his eyes, rub his stomach, kick his father in the seat, make his voice crack, and place his finger against the side of his nose. There is a great deal of talk about the vulgarity and slap-stick humor of the movies. If the movies ever tried to put anything over as horsy and crass as the scene in which young *Gobbo* kids his blind father, or *Falstaff* hides in the laundry hamper, there would be sermons preached on it in pulpits all over the country. It is impossible for a good actor, as we know good actors today, to handle a Shakespearean low comedy part, for it demands mugging and tricks which no good actor would permit himself to do. If Shakes-

I will have their palates removed.

peare were alive today and writing comedy for the movies, he would be the head-liner in the Mack Sennett studios. What he couldn't do with a cross-eyed man!

Another thing which has made the enjoyment of Shakespeare on the stage a precarious venture for this section of the theatre-going public at least, is the thoroughness with which the schools have desiccated his works. In "The Merchant of Venice," for example, there was hardly a line spoken which had not been so diagnosed by English teachers from the third grade up that it had lost every vestige of freshness and grace which it may once have had. Every time I changed schools, I ran into a class which was just taking up "The Merchant of Venice." Consequently, I learned to hate every word of the play. When *Bassanio* said:

"Which makes her seat of Belmont Colchos' strand,
And many Jasons come in quest of her"

in my mind there followed a chorus of memories of questions asked by Miss Mergatroid, Miss O'Shea, Miss Twitchell, Mr. Henby, and Professor Greenally, such as: "Now what did Shakespeare mean by 'Colchos strand'?" "Can anyone in the room tell me why Portia's lovers were referred to as 'Jasons'? Robert Benchley, I wonder if you can leave off whispering to Harold Bemis long enough to tell me what other Portia in history is mentioned in this passage?" And so forth, throughout the whole darned show.

Perhaps that is the whole trouble with Shakespeare anyway. Too many people have taken him up. If they would let you alone, to read snatches from his plays now and then when you wanted to, and *stop* reading when you wanted to, it might not be so bad. But no! They must ask you what he meant by this, and where the inflection should come on that, and they must stand up in front of scenery and let a lot of hams declaim at you while you are supposed to murmur "Gorgeous!" and "How well he knew human nature!" as if you couldn't go to Bartlett's "Quotations" and get the meat of it in half the time. I wouldn't be surprised, if things keep on as they are, if Shakespeare began to lose his hold on people. I give him ten centuries more at the outside.

Even Shakespeare couldn't sit through one of his shows without reading the ads on the program.

"HOWDY, NEIGHBOR!"

By
ROBERT C. BENCHLEY

Drawings by
REA IRVIN

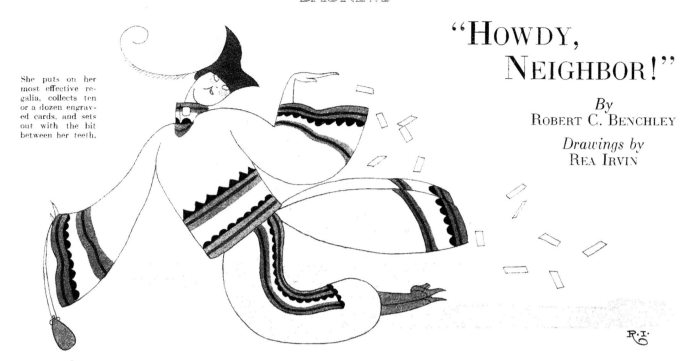

She puts on her most effective regalia, collects ten or a dozen engraved cards, and sets out with the bit between her teeth.

AMONG the inhabitants of North America there is a queer tribal custom which persists in spite of being universally unpopular. Its technical name is "paying a call." The women of the tribe are its chief priests, but once in a while the men are roped in on it and it is then that the lamentations and groans may be heard even in the surrounding villages.

Among the women-folk the procedure is as follows: The one who is to "pay a call" puts on what she considers her most effective regalia, collects ten or a dozen engraved cards bearing her name and twice that number bearing her husband's (he doesn't even know that he *has* any cards, let alone that they are being thrown around the neighborhood every Wednesday afternoon), and sets out with the bit between her teeth.

The idea is to call on as many other women as she thinks will not be at home. Ringing the door-bell at each house on her list, she inquires of the maid if her mistress is in. On receiving a favorable answer ("No") she drops the required number of cards and runs down the street to her car or bicycle or whatever she came in, and rushes off at top speed lest the maid should suddenly discover that her mistress is at home after all. The chances are, however, that the maid has had instructions to say "no" from the lady of the house herself, who is at that moment standing at the head of the stairs waiting for the door to shut.

Par for the Course

The social amenities having been satisfied in this manner at perhaps ten other houses, the caller returns home, where she sinks into a chair, pulls off her gloves, and sighs: "Thank Heaven, *that's* done!"

It is on those rare occasions when the men of the tribe are impressed into service in this paying of calls that the thing assumes its most horrible aspect. Let us take a peek into a typical celebration of the rite.

The man returns home from the office at night, all set for an evening with a motor-boat catalog in front of the fire.

"I thought we might run up and call on the Grimsers tonight. We've owed them a call for a long time now."

"The Grimsers?" queries the husband.

"Yes, you know them. He's the little short man we saw in the drug-store the other night. She is quite pleasant, but rather fast, I understand. She told me that her husband was very anxious to know you better."

"What is he—in the insurance business?"

"No, he isn't. He's a very nice man. And *she* is just mad about you. 'Mrs. Tomlin,' she said to me, 'you don't mean to tell me that that nice-looking husband of yours is forty years old! He looks about twenty-five. And such nice hair!'"

"Well," says the husband, not unmoved by this bit of strategy, "I suppose if we must, we must. Do I have to get dressed up?"

Welcome as the Measles

And so they start out for a call on the Grimsers, with whom they have no more in common than the same milk-man

Their reception is more or less formal in tone, as the Grimsers had planned on going to bed early, Mr. Grimser even having gone so far as his dressing-gown.

"Do sit over here," urges Mrs. Grimser, indicating her husband's favorite cavity in the corner of the divan, "that rocker is so uncomfortable."

"It just suits me," lies Mrs. Tomlin. "Ed says that he is glad that I like chairs like this, as it leaves all the comfortable ones in the house for him."

Everyone looks at Ed as the author of this pleasantry, and there is general, albeit extremely moderate, laughter.

"Well, did you ever see such weather?" This might come from anybody. In fact, two or three are likely to say it at once. This leads to an account on the part of

Mr. Tomlin leads off with one he heard at the club but receives a warning from his wife—a tapping of her right foot.

old scout," or "Yes, sir, Nick is a great old scout." Everyone possible having been classified as a great old scout, they just sit and puff in silence, frankly talked out.

The ladies, in the meantime, have been carrying on much the same sort of line, except that each has her eye out for details outside the conversation. Mrs. Grimser is trying to make out just how Mrs. Tomlin's transformation is tied on, and Mrs. Tomlin is making mental notes of the material in Mrs. Grimser's under-

Mrs. Grimser of what the dampness has done to her jelly in the cellar, and a story by Mrs. Tomlin illustrating how hard it is to keep a maid contented during a rainy spell. Mr. Tomlin leads off with one he heard at the club about the farmer who prayed for rain, but noticing a sudden tightening of his wife's lips accompanied by a warning tapping of her right foot, he gathers that probably Mrs. Grimser's father was a clergyman or something, and trails his story off into a miserable series of noises.

This is a signal for Mrs. Grimser to say: "I just know that you men are dying to get off in a corner and talk to each other. Harry, why don't you show Mr. Grimser the plans for the new garage?"

The two men are then isolated on a window-seat, where they smoke and try to think up something to say next. Mr. Tomlin, knowing nothing about blue-prints and caring less about the Grimsers' garage, is forced to bend over the sheets and ask unintelligent questions, cooing appreciatively now and then to show that he is getting it. They finally are reduced to checking up on mutual acquaintances in the automobile business, summarizing each new find with: "Yes, sir, George is a great

curtains. Given nothing to talk about, women can make a much more convincing stab at it than men. To hear them from a distance, you might almost think that they were really saying something.

When all the contestants are completely worn out and the two men reduced to a state of mental inertia bordering on death, Mrs. Tomlin brightens up and says that they must be going. This throws a great wave of relief over the company, and Mr. Tomlin jumps to his feet and says that he'll run ahead and see if the engine is working all right. The Grimsers very cautiously suggest that it is early yet, but unless the Tomlins are listening very carefully (which they are not) they will not hear it.

"Fine Story You Told!"

Then, all the way home, Mrs. Tomlin suggests that Mr. T. might be a little more agreeable to her friends when they go out of an evening, and Mr. Tomlin wants to know what the hell he did that was wrong.

"You know very well what you did that was wrong, and besides, what a story to start telling in front of Mrs. Grimser!"

"What story?"

"The one about the farmer who prayed for rain."

"What's the matter with that story?"

"You know very well what's the matter with it. You seem to think when you are out with my friends that you are down in the locker-room with George Herbert."

"I wish to God I *was* down in the locker-room with George Herbert."

"Oh, you make me sick."

The rest of the ride home is given over to a stolid listening to the chains clanking on the pavement as the wheels go 'round.

This is known in the tribe life of North America as being "neighborly," and a whole system has been built up on the tradition. Some day a prophet is going to arise out of some humble family and say, "What's the use?" and the whole thing is going to topple over with a crash and everyone is going to be a lot happier.

The Grimsers had planned on going to bed early, Mr. Grimser even having put on his dressing gown.

D'AC NEWS

COVER DESIGN FROM A PAINTING BY
ANTON OTTO FISCHER

JULY · 1924

Next comes the fish

THE LURE OF THE ROD

By
ROBERT C. BENCHLEY

Drawings by
REA IRVIN

FISHING is one of my favorite sports, and one of these days I expect to catch a fish. I have been at it fourteen years now and have caught everything else, including hell from the wife, a cold in the head, and up on my drinking. Next comes the fish. Immediately after that I'll take up something else.

Along about the time when the first crocuses are getting frozen for having popped out too soon (and, by the way, you might think that after thousands of years of coming up too soon and getting frozen, the crocus family would have had a little sense knocked into it) the old lure of the rubber-boot begins to stir, and Fred and I begin to say, "remember that time——?" From then on the *decensus* is extremely *facilis*, unless you know what I mean.

Out come the rods from the attic, and several evenings are spent in fingering over the cards bearing the remnants of last season's Silver Doctors, Jolly Rogers, Golden Bantams, or whatever they are called. Inveterate fisherman that I am, I have never been able to take seriously the technical names for flies. It is much simpler to refer to them as "this one" and "that one" and is less embarrassing if you happen to be self-conscious. The

man who made up the names for flies must have been thwarted in a life-long desire to have children, and at last found that outlet for his suppressed baby-talk.

"Well, I'll tell you," says Fred, "I could get off for about ten days and perhaps we could run up to Rippling Creek, or Bubbling Brook."

"If you can get off as easy as that for ten days to run up to any place," says Mrs. Fred, "you can run up to the attic and put up that partition around the trunk-room. The boards have been lying up there ready since last October."

"Who said I could get off for ten days?" replies Fred, hotly. "I said I *might* be able to get off for a day or two. I don't know. I doubt very much if I could make it."

So Fred doesn't go on the trip.

But there are three or four of us who do, and we start to leave about four weeks before the train is ready. George has to buy some new flannel shirts. These are tricky things to buy, and you have to get them far enough ahead so that if they don't fit right around the neck you can change them. It is important that they fit right around the neck, because you'd hate to have Jo

Rapusi, the Pollack who takes care of the shack, see you with a badly-fitting shirt. George buys half a dozen shirts and wears one the whole time he is away.

Eddie needs rubber-boots. His old ones have no feet to them and can be used only as leggings. So we all have to go with Eddie while he tries on a new pair. We sit around in the boot-ery and watch him galumph up and down the strip of carpet, giving him advice on the various styles which the clerk brings out.

"How are these?" asks Eddie, a little proudly, stepping off in a pair into which he has not quite got his right foot, with the result that he is thrown heavily to one side as it buckles under his weight.

"They're fine, Eddie," we say, "only watch out for that right one. It's got a nasty canter."

"The fish will hear you coming in those, Eddie," is another hot one. "You ought to wear them on your hands."

"The fish will hear you coming in those, Eddie"

This sort of thing takes quite a time, because it has to be done well if you are doing it at all. There is just enough time left to go and see about the liquid bait which Mac is getting from the door-man at the club in three portable cases, and to sample it, and then it is almost midnight, and we are due to leave on the trip in four days.

These days are spent in making enemies among our friends by talking about what we are going to do.

"Well, you poor sons-of-guns can think of us a week from today, wading down the stream after a nice big baby with round blue eyes," we say. "And when we get him all nice and slit up and fried in butter, we'll stop and think of you before we eat him and maybe drink a silent toast to the goofs at home."

"'At's fine!" say our friends. And then they start a petition around among the other members of the club to have us locked up in the steam-room until August.

The day for the Big Departure comes around and Eddie finds that, at the last minute, he can't make the grade. He uses his new rubber-boots to plant bay-trees in, one at each corner of his drive-way. The rest of us get started, loaded down with rods and baskets, blankets and flasks, and seven knives to cut fish with. (On reaching the camp next day, it is found that no one in the party has a knife.)

There is a great deal of singing on the way up. The line-up consists of five tenors and one voice to carry the air. This gives a rich, fruity effect which necessitates each song's being sung through twenty-five times, exclusive of the number of times we sing it after we have returned to town, to remind one another of what a good time we had singing it on the trip.

There is also considerable talk about what we are going to do with the extra fish. Roberts is going to send his home to his brother's family. They love fish. It turns out, oddly enough, that Mac's father (who lives in Wisconsin) also loves fish, and Mac is going to send his surplus to him. He has always sent his father fish, every Spring, and it seems to be the only thing that has kept the old man alive. Mac says that he has never known such a grand old man as his father, eighty-nine and reads the papers every Sunday, especially the funnies. If anyone takes the funnies out of the paper before his father gets them, he raises a terrible row. At this, Mac starts to cry slightly, just at the thought of his poor old father's having to go without his funnies, even for one Sunday.

Skinner, to whom Mac is confiding, also starts to cry a little, but he never lets on that it is at the thought of his own father, thirty years dead, that he is crying. Skinner is too much of a man for that. He lets Mac think that he is affected by the tragedy of Old Mr. Mac. This brings the two men together to a touching degree and they decide not to go on with the fishing trip at all, but to stop at the next town they go through and start in business together for themselves, and when they have made enough money they will have Mac's father come and live with them. The conversation ends in a disgusting fight between Mac and Skinner over the kind of business they are going into.

Once in a while someone catches a fish. As I said in the beginning, I, personally, never have, but that is because once I get out in the open air I get so sleepy that I don't move off my cot, except to eat, from one day to the next. I am going to try to finish Guedalla's "The Second Empire" this trip.

The only thing that has kept the old man alive

"Look at Mr. Dow!"
they cry. "Some good-
looking girl you make,
Mr. Dow."

THE CHURCH SUPPER

By
ROBERT C. BENCHLEY

Drawings by
REA IRVIN

THE social season in our city ends up with a bang for the summer when the Strawberry Festival at the Second Congregational Church is over. After that you might as well die. Several people have, in fact.

The Big Event is announced several weeks in advance in that racy sheet known as the "church calendar," which is slipped into the pews by the sexton before anyone has a chance to stop him. There, among such items as a quotation from a recent letter from Mr. and Mrs. Wheelock (the church's missionaries in China who are doing a really splendid work in the face of a shortage of flannel goods), and the promise that Elmer Divvit will lead the Intermediate Christian Endeavor that afternoon, rain or shine, on the subject of "What Can I Do to Increase the Number of Stars in My Crown?" we find the announcement that on Friday night, June the 8th, the Ladies of the Church will unbelt with a Strawberry Festival to be held in the vestry and that, furthermore, Mrs. William Horton MacInting will be at the head of the Committee in Charge. Surely enough good news for one day!

The Committee is then divided into commissary groups, one to provide the short-cake, another to furnish the juice, another the salad, and so on, until everyone has something to do except Mrs. MacInting, the chairman. She agrees to furnish the paper napkins and to send her car around after the contributions which the others are making. Then, too, there is the use of her name.

The day of the festival arrives, bright and rainy. All preparations are made for a cozy evening in defiance of the elements; so when, along about four in the afternoon, it clears and turns into a nice hot day, everyone is caught with rubbers and steamy mackintoshes, to add to the fun. For, by four o'clock in the afternoon, practically everyone in the parish is at the vestry "helping out," as they call it.

"Helping out" consists of putting on an apron over your good clothes, tucking up the real lace cuffs, and dropping plates. The scene in the kitchen of the church at about five-thirty in the afternoon is one to make a prospective convert to Christianity stop and think. Between four and nine thousand women, all wearing aprons over black silk dresses, rush back and forth carrying platters of food, bumping into each other, hysterical with laughter, filling pitchers with hot coffee from a shiny urn, and poking good-natured fun at Mr. Numaly and Mr. Dow, husbands who have been drafted into service and who, amid screams of delight from the ladies, have also donned aprons and are doing the dropping of the heavier plates and ice-cream freezers.

"Look at Mr. Dow!" they cry. "Some good-looking girl you make, Mr. Dow!"

"Come up to my house, Mr. Numaly, and I'll hire you to do our cooking."

"Alice says for Mr. Numaly to come up to her house and she'll hire him as a cook! Alice, you're a caution!"

And so it goes, back and forth, good church-members all, which means that their banter contains nothing off-color and, by the same token, nothing that was coined later than the first batch of buffalo nickels.

In the meantime, the paying guests are arriving out in the vestry and are sniffing avidly at the coffee aroma, which by now has won its fight with the smell of musty hymn books which usually dominates the place. They leave their hats and coats in the kindergarten room on the dwarfed chairs and wander about looking with week-day detachment at the wall-charts showing the startling progress of the Children of Israel across the Red Sea and the list of gold-star pupils for the month of May. Occasionally they take a peek in at the kitchen and remark on the odd appearance of Messrs. Numaly and Dow, who by this time are just a little fed up on being the center of the taunting and have stopped answering back.

The kiddies, who have been brought in to gorge themselves on indigestible strawberry concoctions, are having a gay time tearing up and down the vestry for the purpose of tagging each other. They manage to reach the door just as Mrs. Camack is entering with a platter full of cabbage salad, and later she explains to Mrs. Reddy while the latter is sponging off her dress that this is the last time she is going to have anything to do with a church supper at which those Basnett children are allowed. The Basnett children, in the meantime, oblivious of this threat, are giving all their attention to slipping pieces of colored chalk from the black-board into the hot rolls which have just been placed on the tables. And, considering what small children they are, they are doing remarkably well at it.

Only a few of the adolescent element show up at the beginning of the meal

At last everyone is ready to sit down. In fact, several invited guests do sit down and have to be reminded that Dr. Murney has yet to arrange the final details of the supper with Heaven before the chairs can be pulled out. This ceremony, with the gentle fragrance of strawberries and salad rising from the table, is one of the longest in the whole list of church rites; and when it is finally over there is a frantic scraping of chairs and clatter of cutlery and babble of voices which means that the hosts of the Lord have completed another day's work in the vineyard and are ready, nay, willing, to toy with several tons of food-stuffs.

The adolescent element in the church has been recruited to do the serving, but only a few of them show up at the beginning of the meal. The others may be found by any member of the committee frantic enough to search them out, sitting in little groups of two on the stairs leading up to the organ loft or indulging in such forms of young love as tie-snatching and braid-pulling up in the study.

The unattached youths and maidens who are induced to take up the work of pouring coffee do it with a vim but very little skill. Pouring coffee over the shoulder of a person sitting at a long table with dozens of other people is a thing that you ought to practice weeks in advance for, and these young people step right in on the job without so much as a dress rehearsal. The procedure is, or should be, as follows:

Standing directly behind the person about to be served, say in a loud but pleasant voice: "Coffee?" If the victim wishes it, he or she will lift the cup from the table and hold it to be filled, with the left forefinger through the handle and bracing the cup against the right upper-arm. The pourer will then have nothing to do but see to it that the coffee goes from the pitcher to the cup.

Where the inexperienced often make a mistake is in reaching for the cup themselves and starting to pour before finding out if the victim wants coffee. This results in nine cases out of six in the victim's turning suddenly and saying: "No coffee, thank you, please!", jarring the arm of the pourer and getting the coffee on the cuff.

For a long time nothing is heard but the din of religious eating and then gradually, one by one, forks slip from nerveless fingers, chairs are scraped back, and the zealots stir heavily to their feet. All that remains is for the committee to gather up the remains and congratulate themselves on their success.

The next event in the calendar will not be until October, when the Men's Club of the church will prepare and serve a supper of escalloped oysters and hot rolls. Join now and be enrolled for the social season of 1923-24!

These young people pour coffee without a dress rehearsal

SOMETHING NEW IN SUMMER-WEAR

By
ROBERT C. BENCHLEY

Drawings by
REA IRVIN

THE dramatic year of 1922-23, like the biblical tree, brought forth many fruits in its season. "Fruits" is right.

Probably at no time in the history of the drama has the cuckoo been abroad in the land with so great a wing-spread. There was a time when people whose minds were beginning to get spongy and take the impressions of their hatbands, were led into a big cool building and given papers to cut up for the rest of their lives. Now, so long as they don't try to chew their friends, they are let alone and told to write plays. And they do.

The past season has produced something like the following assortment of choice nut-meats:

Four plays in which the hero's eyes are never uncrossed.

Two plays in which the hero keeps saying "Nir-r-r-r!"

Eleven plays in which the scenery consists of an old shawl hung over a screen to indicate that the hero is going through a period of great mental confusion.

Three plays in which there is no scenery at all and no characters except an occasional body hurtling across the stage to show what a mysterious thing Life is.

Now all of this cannot help but have an effect on the nature of the summer shows which are coming to town. We may look for a gradual diminution in the number of old-fashioned revues in which the audience can clearly distinguish the characters on the stage and can hear the notes of the songs which are being played. No more scenes showing the ballroom of the Grand Duke Sergius, with a flight of real steps in the background and honest-to-God glass chandeliers hanging from the flies. No more realistic backdrops showing the Bay of Naples on fire, or the sunken gardens on the Long Island estate of Horace L. Panickle.

What we must look for are musical shows in which we are carried along in a semi-darkened house through the various stages of paranoia of a wracked soul. The opening chorus will consist of a stage full of things in Wamsutta sheeting which glide back and forth on wires, singing "No, no, no, no, no, no, no, no!" This will

mean that no matter how hard a man may try, he can't. This will be followed by a specialty number in which three spirits of troubled babies will do a little dance to the tune of "Why Was I Born, Daddy, Tell Me Why?" Then a big spectacular number showing different ways of committing suicide, with a refrain: "And This Is How They Killed Themselves When Grandma Was a Girl." There will be a good chance for pretty costumes in this scene and, with a catchy tune made up of minor discords and sour eighths, it ought to be the song-hit of the piece. All the way through the revue will run a steady blast of cold, damp air with little cinders flying about in it. This will represent the general cussedness of Man's Existence.

The scenery will probably be one of the big features of this summer show, and will consist of big, smashing effects done in gunny-sack and beaverboard. The big set, showing the interior of the Courtyard of the Soul, will be composed of heavy strips of linoleum hanging straight down from the flies, on which yellow lights will be played to indicate the different stages of disintegration through which the poor chap is passing. Four slabs of plain, soiled canvas, can be arranged in diverse formations in the middle of the stage, like a tent to show the hero's worries about his liver, like a little house when he is driving himself mad with a milk-diet, or in the shape of a diamond when he finally decides that Life is, after all, a great hoax and that he might as well marry the Princess and sing a song.

As members of the audience gradually succumb to the influence of this mental chaos and one by one crawl mumbling up the aisle on their hands and knees, the ushers will hand out hand-embroidered straight-jackets to be taken home as souvenirs of the occasion with a little tag on the sleeve of each one reading: "I Have Been to the Cuckoo Follies."

Next to the New Theatre Movement, under which head comes the bla-bla effect just outlined, no other influence during the past season has been so great as that of the visiting Russians. The summer shows will undoubtedly reflect this.

Some time during July we may look for "The Droshkies of 1923." All the words will be Russian, which will be a big advantage over the other summer shows, as you won't be able to understand them. The big song-hit will probably be done by a chorus of idiot boys and girls. dressed in the inconspicuous costume of the village poorhouse, and will be called, "My Uncle Samovar Girl," running something like this.

CHORUS

Nutch lubvey shouisky moon-light
Chekovska kostilyoff spoon-light
Krivoy zob
Kvashnya nob
Miedviedieff Bubnoff love
Aloyoshka vaska stars above
Pepel kleshtch dear old U. S. A.

For the dance, a pony ballet can come on and, in the place of the ribbon reins used in the old-time shows, each girl can hang onto a long beard growing from the chin of her chorus-man, driving him off the stage like a little horse. In the finale, these beards can be entwined around a large May-pole in the center of the stage, leaving their owners hanging dead as the curtain descends.

That is one good thing about the Russian musical show. All the characters will have to die in the end in order to conform with the best traditions of the Russian drama. This is a feature which should have been intro-

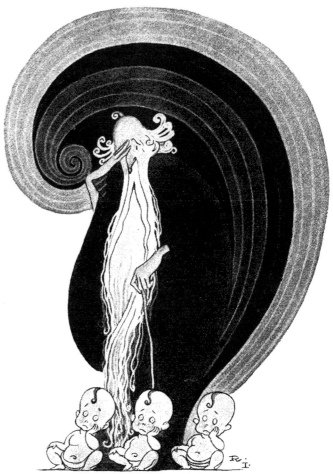

"Why Was I Born, Daddy?"

duced into our own native musical comedy years ago. True, some of them, in the past, have been dead before the curtain went up at all, but the thing has never been officially recognized. They have been allowed to go on and sing and dance just as if nothing had happened. Now that we have learned our lesson from the Slavic boys, we know that it is no disgrace to admit that you are dead. In fact, it gives quite a tone to the show.

It is not going to be so easy to discuss one phase of the new drama without knowing just who is going to read about it. There are a lot of older people who won't understand what you mean when you say that after "The God of Vengeance" and several other of the more advanced treatises on sex, we may look for something a little queer in the musical comedies of tomorrow. The younger generation, who have cut their teeth on Havelock Ellis and Freud, will know what we mean, and we trust that this magazine will not be allowed to fall into the hands of their parents.

As a matter of fact, the foregoing speculations have been entirely imaginary, evolved in an attempt to say something about summer shows that hasn't been said every summer for the past thirty years. Except for the joke about King Tut and Coué, you might be listening to the show that you got up and left last August because you couldn't stand hearing all the old ones again. Maybe the ones about King Tut and Coué *were* in last year's show. We certainly have heard them *somewhere* before.

The paranoia of a wracked soul

The news-boy waits to yell until he sees signs of slumber on the child's face

KIDDIE-KAR TRAVEL

By
ROBERT C. BENCHLEY

Drawings by
REA IRVIN

IN America there are two classes of travel—first class, and with children. Traveling with children corresponds roughly to traveling third-class in Bulgaria. They tell me there is nothing lower in the world than third-class Bulgarian travel.

The actual physical discomfort of traveling with the Kiddies is not so great, although you do emerge from it looking as if you had just moved the piano upstairs single-handed. It is the mental wear-and-tear that tells and for a sensitive man there is only one thing worse, and that is a church wedding in which he is playing the leading comedy role.

There are several branches of the ordeal of Going on Choo-Choo, and it is difficult to tell which is roughest. Those who have taken a very small baby on a train maintain that this ranks as pleasure along with having a nerve killed. On the other hand, those whose wee companions are in the romping stage, simply laugh at the claims of the first group. Sometimes you will find a man who has both an infant *and* a romper with him. Such a citizen should receive a salute of twenty-one guns every time he enters the city and should be allowed to wear the insignia of the Pater Dolorosa, giving him the right to solicit alms on the cathedral steps.

There is much to be said for those who maintain that rather should the race be allowed to die out than that babies should be taken from place to place along our national arteries of traffic. On the other hand, there *are* moments when babies are asleep. (Oh yes, there are. There *must* be.) But it is practically a straight run of ten or a dozen hours for your child of four. You may have a little trouble in getting the infant to doze off, especially as the train newsboy waits crouching in the vestibule until he sees signs of slumber on the child's

face and then rushes in to yell, "Copy of *Life*, out today!" right by its pink, shell-like ear. But after it *is* asleep, your troubles are over except for wondering how you can shift your ossifying arm to a new position without disturbing its precious burden.

If the child is of an age which denies the existence of sleep, however, preferring to run up and down the aisle of the car rather than sit in its chair (at least a baby can't get out of its chair unless it falls out and even then it can't go far), then every minute of the trip is full of fun. On the whole, having traveled with children of all the popular ages, I would be inclined to award the Hair-Shirt to the man who successfully completes the ride with a boy of, let us say, three.

In the first place, you start with the pronounced ill-will of two-thirds of the rest of the occupants of the car. You see them as they come in, before the train starts, glancing at you and yours with little or no attempt to conceal the fact that they wish they had waited for the four o'clock. Across from you is perhaps a large man who, in his home town, has a reputation for eating little children. He wears a heavy gold watch chain and wants to read through a lot of reports on the trip. He is just about as glad to be opposite a small boy as he would be if it were a hurdy-gurdy.

In back of you is a lady in a black silk dress who doesn't like the porter. Ladies in black silk dresses always seem to board the train with an aversion to the porter. The fact that the porter has to be in the same car with her makes her fussy to start with, and when she discovers that in front of her is a child of three who is already eating (you simply have to give him a lemon-drop to keep him quiet at least until the train starts) she decides that the best thing to do is simply to ignore him and not give him the slightest encouragement to become friendly. The child therefore picks her out immediately to be his buddy.

For a time after things get to going, all you have to do is answer questions about the scenery. This is only what you must expect when you have children, and it happens no matter where you are. You can always say that you don't know who lives in that house or what that cow is doing. Sometimes you don't even have to look up when you say that you don't know. This part is comparatively easy.

It is when the migratory fit comes on that you will be put to the test. Suddenly you look and find the boy staggering down the aisle, peering into the faces of people as he passes them. "Here! Come back here, Roger!" you cry, lurching after him and landing across the knees of the young lady two seats down. Roger takes this as a signal for a game and starts to run, screaming with laughter. After four steps he falls and starts to cry.

On being carried kicking back to his seat, he is told that he mustn't run down the aisle again. This strikes even Roger as funny, because it is such a flat thing to say. Of course he is going to run down the aisle again and he knows it as well as you do. In the meantime, however, he is perfectly willing to spend a little time with the lady in the black silk dress.

"Here, Roger," you say, "don't bother the lady."

"Hello, little boy," the lady says, nervously, and tries to go back to her book. The interview is over as far as she is concerned. Roger, however, thinks that it would be just dandy to get up in her lap. This has to be

You march down the car, attracting wide attention to your very obvious excursion

stopped, and Roger has to be whispered to.

He then announces that it is about time that he went to the wash room. You march down the car, steering him by the shoulders and both lurching together as the train takes the curves and attracting wide attention to your very obvious excursion. Several kindly people smile knowingly at you as you pass and try to pat the boy on the head, but their advances are repelled, it being a rule of all children to look with disfavor on any attentions from strangers. The only people they want to play with are those who hate children.

On reaching the wash-room you discover that the porter has just locked it and taken the key with him, simply to be nasty. This raises quite a problem. You explain the situation as well as possible, which turns out to be not well enough. There is every indication of loud crying and perhaps worse. You call attention to the Burrows Rustless Screen sign which you are just passing and stand in the passage-way by the drinking-cups, feverishly trying to find things in the landscape as it whirls by which will serve to take the mind off the tragedy of the moment. You become so engrossed in this important task that it is some time before you discover that you are completely blocking the passage-way and the progress of some fifteen people who want to get off at Utica. There is nothing for you to do but head the procession and get off first.

Once out in the open, the pride and prop of your old age decides that the thing to do is pay the engineer a visit, and starts off up the platform at a terrific rate. This amuses the onlookers and gives you a little exercise after being cramped up in that old car all the morning.

(Continued on page 52)

He is just about as glad to be opposite a small child as he would be if it were a hurdy-gurdy

KIDDIE-KAR TRAVEL

(Continued from page 50)

The imminent danger of the train's starting without you only adds to the fun. At that, there might be worse things than being left in Utica. One of them is getting back on the train again to face the old gentleman with the large watch chain.

The final phase of the ordeal, however, is still in store for you when you make your way (and Roger's way) into the diner. Here the plunging march down the aisle of the car is multiplied by six (the diner is never any nearer than six cars and usually is part of another train). On the way, Roger sees a box of animal crackers belonging to a little girl and commandeers it. The little girl, putting up a fight, is promptly pushed over, starting what promises to be a free-for-all fight between the two families. Lurching along after the apologies have been made, it is just a series of unwarranted attacks by Roger on sleeping travelers and equally unwarranted evasions by Roger of the kindly advances of very nice people who love children.

In the diner, it turns out that the nearest thing they have suited to Roger's customary diet is veal cutlets, and you hardly think that his mother would approve of those. Everything else has peppers or sardines in it. A curry of lamb across the way strikes the boy's fancy and he demands some of that. On being told that he has not the slightest chance in the world of getting it but how

would he like a little crackers-and-milk, he becomes quite upset and threatens to throw a fork at the Episcopal clergyman sitting opposite. Pieces of toast are waved alluringly in front of him and he is asked to consider the advantages of preserved figs and cream, but it is curry of lamb or he gets off the train. He doesn't act like this at home. In fact, he is noted for his tractability. There seems to be something about the train that brings out all the worst that is in him, all the hidden traits that he has inherited from his mother's side of the family. There is nothing else to do but say firmly: "Very well, then, Roger. We'll go back *without* any nice dinner," and carry him protesting from the diner, apologizing to the head steward for the scene and considering dropping him overboard as you pass through each vestibule.

In fact, I had a cousin once who had to take three of his little ones on an all-day trip from Philadelphia to Boston. It was the hottest day of the year and my cousin had on a woolen suit. By the time he reached Hartford, people in the car noticed that he had only two children with him. At Worcester he had only one. No one knew what had become of the others and no one asked. It seemed better not to ask. He reached Boston alone and never explained what had become of the tiny tots. Anyone who has ever traveled with tiny tots of his own, however, can guess.

WE NOMINATE
for
OUR OWN HALL
OF FAME

ROBERT C. BENCHLEY—Because he has just shown an interested smart set that always reads every story he writes, as well as his dramatic page in "Life," that he is a star on the stage. Benchley has been headlining as an after-dinner speaker in New York, and taking the laurels from Will Rogers and other famous wits. So the "Music Box Revue" reached out and snared him for its new show which has just opened. To the wise ones in the audience, Benchley is the best thing in the show.

THE EARL OF BIRKENHEAD—Because he has been the most interesting figure in recent British politics, next to Lloyd George. He is coming to Detroit, October 23, under the auspices of the Women's City Club, to tell about "My Twenty Years in Parliament." When last here he was plain Frederick E. Smith. After Mr. Smith's cyclonic war speech at the Board of Commerce, Ted Reed, the Liberty Loan yell master, rushed over to him and shouted: "Smithy, Old Boy, we are now going to slip you the damndest cheer you ever heard." Since then Mr. Smith became Attorney General of Great Britain, and later, the Lord High Chancellor of England, the highest lay dignitary of the realm, next to a prince of the blood.

VLADIMIR DePACHMANN—Because he admits that he is the greatest pianist in the world. He was quite matter of fact about placing himself at the head of the piano stars when he arrived in America a few weeks ago to begin his concert tour. He will be in Detroit before long, and here display his new style of playing with a stiff wrist, contrary to all orthodox technique. DePachmann is a master interpreter of Chopin. He talks to his audience all the time he plays. "Listen to this now. Isn't that wonderful?" he says as he plays along. On account of all those monkeyshines, a Boston critic referred to him as a Chopinzee.

HELEN WILLS—Because she is the new queen of American tennis courts, having defeated Mrs. Mallory and ended her reign as champion, which lasted for seven years. Miss Wills is only eighteen years old. Leading critics hold high hopes that some day she will be able to win the world's championship by defeating Mlle. Suzanne Lenglen.

PRIZE BREEDING
Getting a Head-Start on the Literary Judges
By Robert C. Benchley — Drawings by Rea Irvin

EVERY year a lot of judges get together and decide on the best novels and plays of the season. Nobody asks them to. They just do it to be funny. And then, after they have made their decision, the fight starts, thus reversing the procedure of prize-fighting.

In order to avoid all this unpleasantness this year, I am going to write both the prize novel and the prize play now and get them out of the way. All I have to work with is a set of trends noted in the novels and plays of the past season, a remarkable knowledge of the working of the human mind, inherited from my grandfather, Immanuel Kant, and a small mirror.

Judging from the batch of extremely personal, introspective novels which were turned out in 1922-23, something like this one will do very nicely. We will call it:

COFFEE-GROUNDS
Chapter 1

The boyhood of Elmer Razz. His father is a fire-bug and his mother hates children. Elmer is kept locked up in the trunk-room until he is eleven years old and is never told anything about walking. He doesn't know that there is such a thing. All he has ever done is hitch himself along on his hips from one end of the trunk-room to the other. At the age of eleven, Elmer is visited by a neighbor's son who has climbed up on the roof and in at the attic window. The neighbor's son tells him that everybody is walking now, and teaches him some of the simpler steps. This so excites Elmer that he lies awake all night wondering what to do about it. At about three in the morning he climbs out on the roof and drops to the ground, walking to the corner of the street as a climax.

Chapter 2

Drunk with his new-found power, Elmer keeps on walking until he comes to the railroad tracks. Here he meets Bessie. Bessie's last name is 14,214, her father and mother having been inmates of the State Institution and numbered 7,310 and 6,904, respectively. (Add them up for yourself.) Bessie is just learning how to cross-stitch and is as nervously wrought-up over it as Elmer is about walking. They sit down on the track to talk it over and compare enthusiasms. The 7:52 comes along, and about Friday they wake up in Emporia, Kansas.

Chapter 3

The Great War breaks out and Elmer is drafted as a horse-shoer. He is forced to live on a mud-scow in the middle of the Seine. His buddie is a Chinaman, and one night Elmer wakes up and finds him trying to saw off his (Elmer's) foot. Elmer kills the Chinaman and is court-martialed for eating candy during parade. He is sent to prison, and the Germans win the war.

Chapter 4

In the meantime, Bessie has taken up peddling dope in front of the Public Library in New York City. She has a little stand right by the crossest-looking lion, and has a yellow banner draped across the front of it, reading: "Please Buy a Deck for Auld Time's Sake." Business is bad, however, and she is forced to solicit subscriptions for the *Saturday Evening Post* in her spare time. Elmer, released from jail, meets her one night going from house to house with her little canvas bag of *Posts* and asks her what she is doing. She lies to him and says that she is peddling dope, but he sees through her deception. He tells her that he has a nice little cottage down at Atlantic City and suggests a week-end there. When they get on the train he tells her that he has no cottage at all. They get off at Manhattan Transfer.

THE END

So much for the novel. Unless I am mistaken, it will be hailed as one of the really Big Things of the year.

A game of Bean Porridge Hot with a tight-rope walker interrupted by the Spirit of Intercostal Neuralgia

The play will be even Bigger. When a thing is called Big, it means that it has shaken off the conventions of form and structure and just sits down and lets 'er ride. There won't be more than two things in my play that the audience can understand. One of them will be the Final Curtain. The play will be entitled:

THE POOR GOOF
Act 1

Scene: Interior of John Goof's House.

John is discovered sitting by himself, thinking of what a rotten deal he has had. A large part of the ceiling falls on him. He lies under the debris and plaster, counting, "One-two-three, one-two-three." This shows that one day is much the same as the next with him.

Twenty-five policemen, all dressed alike and all muttering "A, B, C," over and over again in a monotone, file across the stage, each kicking John as they pass him. This indicates the hold which the Law has on the average man.

John pulls himself out from under the plaster and crawls back to his chair again, where he starts in again to think of what a rotten deal he has had. The curtain falls on him saying, "One-two-three, one-two-three."

Act 2

Scene: The business-office of John's employer.

Twenty-five clerks all sit in a row saying, "Mi-my-mo, mi-my-mo," in high falsetto. From this you are able to realize the horrid condition of the modern business establishment, where hundreds of people sit all day without once being allowed to write poetry or dance a folk-dance.

John enters, dragging behind him a chain composed of fifteen moaning women. They represent Marriage. The Boss, who is sitting in a large Morris chair, hands out a bundle of nickels to John, who takes them and gives them, one by one, to the women. The women swallow them.

Elmer is a horse-shoer on a mud-scow in the middle of the Seine.
His buddie is a Chinaman

John then sits down at a desk and the ceiling falls on him.

Act 3

Scene: The top of the world.

John, after years of work, has at last reached the top of the world. He sits there, playing "Bean Porridge Hot, Bean Porridge Cold" with Luella, a tight-rope walker. The Spirit of Intercostal Neuralgia flies up and has the following dialogue with John:

Spirit of I. N.— Who was that lady I seen you on the street with the other day?

*John—*That warn't no lady, that was my Nemesis, and a hot sketch she is, too. (*They both laugh and the Spirit of Intercostal Neuralgia pushes John playfully so that he topples over backward and falls off the world into space.*)

Act 4

Scene: Space.

John is seen falling through the air. As he passes them, the following malign spirits take a crack at him: *Hay Fever, Integral Calculus, Dish-Washing, Sunburn, and French Coffee.*

Under each blow from these evil fairies, John cringes and cries, "Oi." There is a tremendous crashing of glass as he finally lands in East Hell.

Act 5

Scene: East Hell.

John is discovered sitting alone, thinking over what a rotten deal he has had. He starts to play on a mandolin and the E string breaks. He flings it aside and starts to cry, just as the ceiling falls on him. As the curtain descends slowly, he is heard saying from under the pile of plaster: "One-two-three, one-two-three."

FINAL CURTAIN

And here you have, for the price of one issue of this magazine, the leading novel and the leading play of the coming season. Don't thank me. It's really nothing.

At a time like this a man should be alone with his own soul

IN THE BEGINNING

Thoughts on Starting up the Furnace

By ROBERT C. BENCHLEY

Drawings by REA IRVIN

ALONG about now is the time when there falls upon the ears of the Old Man one of the most ominous of all household phrases: "Well, Sam, I guess we'll have to get the furnace-fire started today."

No matter what Daddy is doing at the moment, no matter how light-hearted he may be, gathering autumn leaves or romping on the terrace, at the sound of these words a shadow passes across his handsome face and into his eyes there comes that far-away look of a man who is about to go down into the Valley. He drops his golf-clubs or balloon or whatever it is he is playing with when the news comes, and protests softly: "The paper says warmer tomorrow."

But in his heart he knows that it is no use. The family has been talking it over behind his back and has decided that it is time to have the furnace started, and he might as well tell the back wall of the Michigan Central Terminal that the paper says it will be warmer tomorrow and expect it to soften up. So there is nothing for him to do but get ready to build the fire.

Building the furnace-fire for the first time of the season is a ritual which demands considerable prayer and fasting in preparation. I would suggest that the thing be considered far enough in advance to get it done right, and to this end have outlined a course of preliminary training.

For a man who is about to build a furnace-fire, good physical condition and mental poise are absolutely essential. I knew a man once who had been up late every night during the week preceding his ordeal in the cellar and as a result was tired and nervous when the day came. Furthermore, he had neglected his diet in the matter of proteids, so that his system was in rather poor shape. When confronted with the strain of getting the kindling going and putting the coal on, he simply went all to pieces and when they found him he was kicking and screaming in the bins, trying to burrow his way through the pile of pea-coal in the corner of the cellar. They caught him just in time, otherwise he might have succeeded and would probably never have been found.

It would be wise, therefore, along about the first of September, for the prospective father of the bouncing fire to pack up and leave home for a few weeks, taking a complete rest in the wilds somewhere and eating nothing but the plainest and most healthful foods. Ten hours' sleep a night would not be too much, and during the day he should be careful to let his mind dwell on nothing but the most peaceful thoughts. He should say to himself every afternoon at three o'clock: "I am Love. Love is All. I reflect no disturbance. I am Being." For exercise, he should go out and chop down several good-sized trees. This will help him when the time comes to break up the kindling.

After several weeks of this kind of training he will be in fair shape to face what he has to face. If it is possible, he should stay in his retreat until it is time to build the fire, coming home on the day of the event. If this cannot be arranged, he should be most careful not to lose the good effect of his rest, and should refuse all invitations for the week previous. Above all, he should take no alcohol into his system. (An alternative to this prescription would be to take all the alcohol that he can get just before going down cellar, so that he is in a state of extreme intoxication during the procedure, thereby deadening the unpleasant features of what he has to do and lending a certain gaiety and enthusiasm to the affair which could not possibly be stimulated otherwise. The danger of this method is, of course, that he might become so interested and excited in what he was doing that he would set the house on fire, too.)

At last the day comes. Kissing his family all around and leaving his papers and insurance documents where they can easily be found in case of the worst, he descends into the cellar. It is better to have no one accompany him to witness his shame, or to hear what he has to say. At times like these, a man should be alone with his own soul.

There will be no kindling ready. This is a certainty. This means that he will have to break up some boxes. It will be found that these boxes, while seemingly constructed of wood like other boxes, are in reality made of a sort of marble composition which was originally put together to resist the blows of an axe. (In case there is no axe in the cellar, which is more than likely, the shaker to the furnace will do nicely. Place the box or board against the wall and strike it heavily with the iron shaker, saying, "You.... ....!" at each blow. Your chances are at least even that it will not bounce under the blow and fly up and strike you in some vital spot. If it doesn't do this, it may split.)

After breaking up a sufficient number of sticks, you will take them over to the furnace. The furnace has been standing there all this time, laughing.

A quantity of newspaper is necessary, and while crumpling it up preparatory to filling the bottom of the

Hurrah! Hurrah! The fire is out!

fire-box with it, you will probably discover several old funny sections which you have never seen before and will have to sit down and read over. This will rest you after the chopping and will take your mind off the furnace. If your wife inquires from the top of the cellar stairs how the fire is coming on, you can reply that you are waiting for it to catch.

The papers once placed in the fire-box, the time has come to pile the sticks in on top of it. Now is also the time to discover that the sticks are too long and won't fit. Back to the axe or the furnace-shaker and a little more fun, smashing and talking to yourself. And now for the big moment!

Placing the wood on the paper, you apply the match. The first match. Follow thirty other matches. Then discover that the draughts aren't open. A good joke on you, at which you laugh heartily.

And now a merry blaze! Up goes the paper in a burst of flame and you feel that the job is about done. After all, not such a hard task, once the wood is split. You shut the door, in order to give the wood a better chance to catch, and hear the cheery roar as the flames rush up the flue. Gradually the roar dies down and you strain your ears to catch the sound of crackling wood. Now the roar is gone, but there is no crackle. Carefully you open the door, afraid to learn the worst, and there, in a nice, black fire-box, is your wood, safe and sound, with one or two pink wisps of paper blowing coyly underneath. The rest is silence.

Pick the wood out carefully, piece by piece, and start again. Oh, the joy of starting again! Think of what it means, this glorious privilege which Nature gives us of making a fresh start after each one of our little failures! In with more paper! In with more wood! Now the match! And again the roar! Is it not splendid, Little Father? This time certain sections of the wood catch and flicker sadly.

The wood started, we now come to the real test of the fire-builder. Sneak quietly to the bin and get a shovelful of coal. Stand with it by the door of the fire-box, behind which the wood is blazing. Quick! Open door! Quicker! In with the coal! Back for another shovelful! In with it! That's right! It may look for a minute as if you were smothering the bright blaze with the black coal, but don't waver. Another shovelful to cover the last tongue of flame from the burning wood. Hurrah! Hurrah! The fire is out!

The next thing to do is go upstairs and telephone for Jimmie, the Italian who makes a business of starting furnace-fires and keeping them going throughout the winter. This requires no more practice than knowing how to use the telephone. And it is the only sure way of getting your furnace going.

He kisses his family all around and leaves his papers and insurance documents where they can be found in case of the worst

DECEMBER 1923

EDITHA'S CHRISTMAS BURGLAR

By
ROBERT C. BENCHLEY

Drawings by
REA IRVIN

IT was the night before Christmas, and Editha was all agog. It was all so exciting, so exciting! From her little bed up in the nursery she could hear Mumsey and Daddy down-stairs putting the things on the tree and jamming her stocking full of broken candy and oranges. She cocked her curly little head on one side and wondered how much longer that couple of goofs would go on thinking that they were kidding her.

"Hush!" Daddy was speaking. "Eva," he was saying to Mumsey, "it seems kind of silly to put this ten-dollar gold-piece that Aunt Issac sent to Editha into her stocking. She is too young to know the value of money. It would just be a bauble to her. How about putting it in with the household money for this month? Editha would then get some of the food that was bought with it and we would be ten dollars in."

Dear old Daddy! Always thinking of someone else! Editha wanted to jump out of bed right then and there and run down and throw her arms about his neck, perhaps shutting off his wind.

"You are right, as usual, Hal," said Mumsey. "Give me the gold-piece and I will put it in with the house funds."

"In a pig's eye I will give you the gold-piece," replied Daddy. "You would nest it away somewhere until after Christmas and then go out and buy yourself a muff with it. I know you, you old grafter." And from the sound which followed, Editha knew that Mumsey was kissing Daddy. Did ever a little girl have two such darling parents? And, hugging her Teddy-bear close to her, Editha rolled over and went to sleep.

* * *

She awoke suddenly with the feeling that someone was down-stairs. It was quite dark and the radiolite traveling-clock which stood by her bedside said eight o'clock,

but, as the radiolite traveling-clock hadn't been running since Easter, she knew that that couldn't be the right time. She knew that it must be somewhere between three and four in the morning, however, because the blanket had slipped off her bed, and the blanket always slipped off her bed between three and four in the morning.

And now to take up the question of who it was down-stairs. At first she thought it might be Daddy. Often Daddy sat up very late working on a case of Scotch and at such times she would hear him down-stairs counting to himself. But whoever was there now was being very quiet. It was only when he jammed against the china-cabinet or joggled the dinner-gong that she could tell that anyone was there at all. It was evidently a stranger.

Of course, it might be that the old folks had been right all along and that there really was a Santa Claus after all, but Editha dismissed this supposition at once. The old folks had never been right before and what chance was there of their starting in to be right now, at their age? None at all. It couldn't be Santa, the jolly old soul!

It must be a burglar then! Why, to be sure! Burglars always come around on Christmas Eve and little yellow-haired girls always get up and go down in their nighties and convert them. Of course! How silly of Editha not to have thought of it before!

With a bound the child was out on the cold floor, and with another bound she was back in bed again. It was too cold to be fooling around without slippers on. Reaching down by the bedside, she pulled in her little fur foot-pieces which Cousin Mable had left behind by mistake the last time she visited Editha, and drew them on her tiny feet. Then out she got and started on tip-toe for the stairway.

She did hope that he would be a good-looking burglar and easily converted, because it was pretty gosh-darned

Burglars always come around on Christmas Eve and little yellow-haired girls always get up and go down in their nighties and convert them.

cold, even with slippers on, and she wished to save time.

As she reached the head of the stairs, she could look down into the living room where the shadow of the tree stood out black against the gray light outside. In the doorway leading into the dining room stood a man's figure, silhouetted against the glare of an old-fashioned burglar's lantern which was on the floor. He was rattling silverware. Very quietly, Editha descended the stairs until she stood quite close to him.

"Hello, Mr. Man!" she said.

The burglar looked up quickly and reached for his gun. "Who the hell do you think you are?" he asked.

"I'se Editha," replied the little girl in the sweetest voice she could summon, which wasn't particularly sweet at that as Editha hadn't a very pretty voice.

"You'se Editha, is youse?" replied the burglar. "Well, come on down here. Grandpa wants to speak to you."

"Youse is not my Drandpa," said the tot, getting her baby and tough talk slightly mixed. "Youse is a dreat, bid burglar."

"All right, kiddy," replied the man. "Have it your own way. But come on down. I want ter show yer how yer kin make smoke come outer yer eyes. It's a Christmas game."

"This guy is as good as converted already," thought Editha to herself. "Right away he starts wanting to teach me games. Next he'll be telling me I remind him of his little girl at home."

"This guy is as good as converted already," thought Editha to herself.

So with a light heart she came the rest of the way down stairs, and stood facing the burly stranger.

"Sit down, Editha," he said, and gave her a hearty push which sent her down heavily on the floor. "And stay there, or I'll mash you one on that baby nose of yours."

This was not in the schedule as Editha had read it in the books, but it doubtless was this particular burglar's way of having a little fun. He *did* have nice eyes, too.

"Dat's naughty to do," she said, scoldingly.

"Yeah?" said the burglar, and sent her spinning against the wall. "I guess you need attention, kid. You can't be trusted." Whereupon he slapped the little girl. Then he took a piece of rope out of his bag and tied her up good and tight, with a nice bright bandana handkerchief around her mouth, and trussed her up on the chandelier.

"Now hang there," he said, "and make believe you're a Christmas present, and if you open yer yap I'll set fire to yer."

Then, filling his bag with the silverware and Daddy's imitation sherry, Editha's burglar tip-toed out by the door. As he left, he turned and smiled. "A Merry Christmas to all! and to all a Good Night," he whispered, and was gone.

And when Mumsey and Daddy came down in the morning, there was Editha upon the chandelier, sore as a crab. So they took her down and spanked her for getting out of bed without permission.

The HOME BOYS' PROTECTIVE ASSOCIATION

By
ROBERT C. BENCHLEY

Drawings
by
REA IRVIN

Post-card used by members to "sell" the delights of northern winter life to friends in the south.

IF there is ever a revolution in this country (and, begging the State Department's pardon, I certainly hope that there is) it will be led by a delegation in red shirts consisting of the poor suckers who aren't able to make Palm Beach in the winter. And right up with the drum-major will be the author of this interesting article.

For ten winters now I have been sitting out in the children's snow fort in the back yard and reading post-cards and letters from wealthy friends ("friends," ha! ha! *very raucous*) who were whiling away the months of January, February, and March at Miami or "on board the house-boat, *Idle-Hour*," and whose only worry has been keeping the sun off the back of the neck. At first, I used to be glad for them. (Yes, I did, really. I used to be queer that way. In fact, there was some talk in my youth about my being of divine origin, but my father soon put a stop to that rumor.)

I really did, however, feel very glad that good old Bill was having a chance to get rested up at Palm Beach, and that George was getting so nice and brown at Miami. I wrote them letters telling how cold it was in New York and how badly the snow was leaking in at our house, and ended up by calling them "lucky old stiffs."

Then, gradually, I began to turn sour. It wasn't entirely my fault. It was the way they took advantage of my humility. "Well, you poor old bum, you," they would write. "Take a look at this stretch of beach and then go out and slip on the ice," or, "A good joke on you, you slush-hound. We just played eighteen holes and are sitting in the shade to cool off."

Then they started sending cocoanuts. One winter I got seventeen cocoanuts, each bearing a taunt, such as "How would you like to be here picking these with us?" It got so that the postman would come in each morning and say: "Your cocoanut is out on the porch, Mr. Benchley. What shall I do with it?" Then I started

sending them back. This was my first actual gesture of revolt. I sent the cocoanuts back and stuck a label on each one reading: "Not wanted," or, "Not at this address." Later I got vicious and had labels reading, "Go to hell!" and, "You know what you can do with this."

From then on, I have thrown all pretense of altruism to the winds. Sometimes, I don't even open letters marked "Palm Beach." I use them in the fireplace to keep myself warm. I have forbidden any Sunday rotogravure sections in my house, because I become so infuriated at the sight of the thousands and thousands of photographs of "Mrs. Blackstone Leeding and her daughter Muriel emerging from a dip at Palm Beach," and "Harry Ewart Pendle basking on the sands at Palm Beach," and "Far from the sleet and snow of New York, those merry-makers indulge in fishing in the limpid waters off Miami. Reading from left to right, etc."

The rotogravure sections cause more unrest than any other single feature of modern journalism. For an honest man to pick one of them up just as he is trying to get the bottom draft on the furnace to function so that at least the front of his house may be warmed up, and to see pictures of totally unknown people frisking about in bathing-suits in sun so hot that they have to blink when they face the camera, this, my friends, is the emotion of which revolts are born.

Not content with ignoring the pleasant features of life in the Sunny Southland, I have this season taken up lying on my own hook. I lie about the weather in New York; I send telegrams saying: "Just like spring here. Why don't you come to New York and get some real weather?" or "Have just picked a crocus. Tie that if you can." I have an arrangement with the American News Company, whereby all New York papers telling of blizzards, cold snaps, sleet storms and such are to be lost in transit to Florida, so that the folks there won't have the satisfaction of reading about them and saying: "Look what it's doing up North, will you! We got away just in time." If I could only raise a little more money I might be able to get out spurious editions of the papers, telling about the phenomenal spring weather that obtains all over the North Atlantic states and quoting old inhabitants to say that never have they known anything like it.

And here is where you can help. If we can only get together, we shut-ins, and organize, we can make that Florida bunch look pretty silly. In the first place, we can get up a publicity campaign, to meet the publicity campaign of the Florida hotels and railroads. Each and every one of us, in his letters to the South, can lie about the weather up North. We can have pictures made showing us sitting in bathing-suits on Jefferson Avenue or lolling about the sheep-meadow in Central Park in flannels and sport costumes. Any good photographer can fake a summer backdrop and we can lie down on some property grass in front of it and squint at the camera. I, personally, would be willing to get into a bathing suit and paddle around in the icy waters at Coney Island if I could cause any heartache among the Palm Beachers when they saw the pictures of me.

All that we have to do is get together and work as a unit. We can do nothing so long as some of us are cutting loose and writing South about the terrible weather we are having up here. One letter like that will ruin the whole campaign, for a vacationist who receives one letter from home complaining about home conditions will pass that letter around hotel lobbies and club verandas until the whole resort knows about it.

The whole thing ought to be put on a war basis. If we were at war, we could bring the population around to a definite program of propaganda, so that every citizen would become an official propagandist. How much more important than war is the present crisis!

The National Headquarters of the Stay-At-Home Campaign will be, for convenience sake, in New York, but we will be in touch with local chapters in every large

"Here's your cocoanut!
What shall I do with it?"

city in the country. The publicity department will furnish members with post-cards to be sent to Florida, showing how much fun we are having up North—boating and fishing scenes, swimming in the North Atlantic and Great Lakes, and tennis. Form letters will be composed suitable for personal use, and these will be distributed to all those who are not very skillful at lying by mail.

A special feature of the campaign will be the sending of apples and wheat cakes to friends in the South. Each wheat cake will have a label so that it can be sent through the mail, and on the reverse side it will say: "Picked today. Come up and get some real food."

Just as soon as we get the thing in running order, we can begin getting fancy. There are years and years of suffering to be made up for, and I would like to suggest to the National Council some method whereby these insufferable, un-American Palm Beachers can be tweaked for all that they have handed out in the past.

My idea would be this: Let the Stay-at-Homes adopt a uniform something like that of the Ku Klux Klan, only instead of a sheet, we could wear the typical ulster and overshoes of the Home-Bird, with a fur hat pulled down over a pair of ear-muffs to render the wearer unrecognizable. Then, as the publicity campaign begins to work and the loafers from Miami begin to decide that they are missing something good by cooping themselves up on a house-boat or on the beach way down South, they will start to migrate northward. Scouts along the road will keep us in touch with their movements, and when we learn that they are due, a delegation will meet them at the station, force them to unpack their bags right there in the waiting-room and don the summer togs we have heard so much about. Then, in their white knickers and sport sweaters, they will be dragged out through the snow and the slush to the public square, where they will be laughed at until dead.

Plans for this part of the program are to be held up temporarily until I see whether or not I am going to get a bid to go down on Irvin Berlin's house-boat next week. If I get it, the plans are off entirely.

Some striking outdoor advertising would help the publicity campaign.

Spend the
WINTER
IN
NEW
YORK
LAND
OF
MOONSHINE
&
NUTS

GAY LIFE BACK-STAGE

By
ROBERT C. BENCHLEY

Drawings by
REA IRVIN

AT the very mention of the word "back-stage," especially back-stage at a musical show, your Wise Boy murmurs "slicky-slicky" and begins shuffling his feet. There is a fairly prevalent notion that if you have been behind the scenes where the chorus girls are, you ought to go to confession right away, but that it is worth it.

In my long career on the stage (five months now) I have found that the only danger back-stage is that of having something drop on you. I went into the thing rather hoping that I was going to be tempted. Not only have I not been tempted; I have been stepped on, and anyone hanging around with other things on his mind than getting out of the way as soon as possible will get stepped on too.

Right at the stage door, you get your first big set-back. The doorman has been chosen for the job because, when he was quite young, he had his heart taken out. He is also quite likely to be hard of hearing. It is only after you have been working with a show for two weeks that he will let you in at all. Until then, you have to bring your mother or your pastor along.

Furthermore, the space between the stage door and the next portal is just large enough for a medium-sized rabbit to turn around in, and while you are standing there, fourteen people have to get past you on their way downstairs under the stage. Some of these are beautiful young ladies dressed as mackerel or bunches of figs, but there is a certain businesslike manner in the way in which they brush past you that makes you sure you are not being tempted; not right at that minute, anyway.

The next division of floor space that you step into is a little larger. A father-rabbit would have it pretty comfortable here, provided he didn't try to do any tricks. A flight of stairs leads from here up to the dressing rooms and these stairs are crowded at all hours of the day and night with people in a great hurry to get dressed or undressed. If you want to go up, the best way is to cling to the outside of the banisters. You will find that everyone is very pleasant, so long as you let them get to

The only danger is that of having something drop on you.

where they are going. Otherwise, you are out of luck. If any organization of tired businessmen worked as hard or as fast on their jobs as the chorus girls in a big musical show, they would die of apoplexy.

Let us turn from the stairway leading to the dressing rooms and go into the region which is directly behind the scenes. First we step through a doorway, where we are hit on the head by a large boat which is being hauled up into the roof. Everything except the actors is hauled up into the roof when not in use. So when you walk across any space between the back walls of the theatre, you stand a good chance of having the top of your head crashed in with almost anything from a table to a jolly old replica of the Sphinx.

The only thing that saves you from this is the fact that you aren't in one place long enough to have anything drop clean on you. From one direction comes a couch being pushed by four union men; from another, a gondola being dragged by four more union men; while the floor beneath you starts to heave as a trap opens to let eight union men shoot up some orange trees in full bloom. Anything that is going to hit you on the head has got to move fast to keep up with you.

And now for the gay life back-stage and the girls! How about a little revelry! Here comes a bevy of them now, dressed as several of the warmer months of the year. They look promising, and seem to be laughing at something. What do you suppose it is? Well, it turns out to be you. You discover this after they have walked over you on their way to their entrance. Heigh ho! A good laugh never hurt anyone.

And who is this pretty little miss sitting all alone on the top of a bookcase? A peek over her shoulder discloses the fact that she is reading "Political Parties and Party Problems in the United States," waiting for the signal which is to start her up on a plunger as the Spirit of the Open Fireplace in the big Home-Building number. It would be best to tip-toe away before you get "Political

Parties and Party Problems in the United States" thrown at your head, my little man.

With the prevalence of trick numbers in our musical revues, in which young ladies and vegetables and small buildings are shot up through the stage on plungers, there is the increasing danger to the visitor or casual actor of stepping on a trap and either dropping down into the cellar or being elevated up into the middle of a scene.

A young man once came for the laundry to the "Music Box" while the performance was in progress and, in order not to disturb the show, he went down and under the stage to get to the dressing rooms on the other side of the theatre. While under the stage, he tried to engage in familiar conversation with one of the girls and was encouraged to a point where he became engrossed in his task and not a little pleased with his prowess as a man-about-town. Suddenly some one shouted, "Right!" and there was a grinding of machinery, and the young man, dressed in a natty sack suit and derby, was projected with his lady friend up through the stage floor and into the big Fish number. She was supposed to be a goldfish. The audience couldn't quite figure out what his rôle was, but they sized him up as a pickerel in a derby hat and gave him a big hand. The success of his first appearance went to his head and he decided that the stage was the

They seemed to be laughing.

career for him, and that, my friends, is how James K. Hackett got his start.

The people back-stage who really have the gay time are the stage-hands. All being good union men, there are ten of each on hand for every job calling for one, and so they have plenty of time for gaiety, and a dandy crowd of congenial boys to make merry with.

Consider the life of the carefree members of the stage crew of a big show. Arrive at the theatre at 7:45 and have a good smoke, just to start the evening off right. A good smoke never hurt anyone. Then, if you happen to be third assistant curtain man, you walk with the first and second assistant curtain men across the stage at 8:15 and shake the corner of a big portier three times. After the overture you pull your end of it halfway across the stage and then go out and take another smoke. Then you go down beneath the stage and help a young lady stand on a plunger and ask her a couple of snappy questions about her health. You may, if you know her well enough, or even if you don't, pull a couple of wise cracks about life in general.

Then for another good smoke and a cozy half hour around the circle with fifteen or twenty others of the boys who haven't anything in particular to be doing at that moment. And many a good story will come out then in the course of conversation. Perhaps a smoke will top off the evening, after you have given the curtain another good tug at the conclusion of the performance.

So when you hear about the carefree, bohemian life of theatrical people behind the scenes, dismiss the picture of romping chorus girls and visiting Johnnies in full-dress suits from your imagination, and drink a toast to the man in overalls with the gay smile, for he is the Pet of the Theatre at a handsome consideration per hour, and a handsome consideration-and-a-half for overtime.

When he was young he had his heart cut out.

THE FLOPS OF 1924

By ROBERT C. BENCHLEY

Drawings by REA IRVIN

Hundreds of taxicabs
occupied only by
dummies.

THUS far, the theatrical summer of 1924 has turned out to be Nothing At All. And Mamma and Papa had such high hopes for it, too!

In the first place, there was to have been the Big Strike. When the first of June came around, all the actors were going to roll up their cutaways and toupees and walk out, leaving New York showless. This was contingent, of course, on the managers' holding to their announced intention of selling their beautiful white bodies in the market place rather than give in to the demands of the Actors' Equity Association.

For a while it looked as if the thing had a chance to be pulled off. Arrangements were made by the managers to rush in a whole new supply of scab labor, and for this purpose members of the junior class in manual training in the local high schools were being warmed up to pinch hit for the striking leading juveniles, and had almost all the lines learned. Then it was discovered that they hadn't enough blue-collared shirts to go around, and there was no sense in trying to fill the juveniles' places without blue-collared shirts; and so the whole thing was called off, and one by one the managers capitulated.

It is true, several of them held out and there was a baby strike in several of the theatres, but there are still some forty playhouses open and running, and that's just awful. And with all the poor families that there are who would be only too glad to have those papier mâché turkeys and rubber celery, to say nothing of the heavy portieres which stage butlers are always yanking backward and forward across French windows. If the strike had only been pulled off as it should have been, think of the amount of "Stay-Kombed" hair-fixative alone which would have been released for use in other fields, such as stickum for envelopes

and sizing. It is estimated that by keeping these forty leading men at work all summer, the August quotations on envelopes have been kept up forty or fifty cents per gross. Figure it out for yourself what this amounts to in a year in your own business budget.

But, you may argue, "I myself cannot write, and so have no use for envelopes. I should concern myself with whether or not the shows are kept running." Very well, granted that this particular item does not affect you. How about tennis racquets? How about those thirty-odd summer shows in which the juveniles come bounding in with a tennis racquet and announce that everything is all right and that the Mater and Dad have agreed to their marriage with Betty? Those tennis racquets are never used for tennis. In fact, they *couldn't* be used for tennis, even if the juveniles knew how to play, for they are built on the model of the one which used to be carried by the girl in the Huyler's bon-bon advertisements in *Munsey's Magazine* back in 1897. But they are using up good material and sending up the cost of the racquet which you have to buy for your daughter to strain her back with. It is you who pays, Mr. Tennis-Racquet-Consumer!

Here, then, was the first big disappointment of the 1924 summer theatrical season; the strike didn't come off as planned. The managers spoiled it by eating crow, and, as a result, hundreds of actors who might otherwise have spent the summer renting row-boats, were forced into acting; which, in itself, is enough to spoil any summer.

Then there was the Democratic convention in New York. This was counted on to keep many a dying production alive until July. When, along in May, a show began to pick at the coverlet and turn green around the box-office, the management said: "If we can use the old

31

hypodermics until June and keep her gasping until the convention, the poor simps who come on here to nominate a runner-up will have to spend their money somehow, and we may clean up."

So many a house in which the business was so poor that they ought to have been using the time to paint the woodwork for the fall season, kept open to the tune of a thousand smackers gross deficit per night, all in the hope that when the convention came along, the boys would flock in and effect a turn-over, with perhaps something to spare for pop-corn.

This will always be known as one of the Big Laughs of 1924, for the delegates evidently had Something Else to do with their pennies. True, they did take a peek into the "Follies" and one or two others of the Broadway institutions, just so that they could go back home and tell Mother where she got off, but, for the most part, the managers who postponed their May closings until July, were left high and dry on the beach, hugging dead star-fish to their bosoms. Either the delegates spent all their money on post cards on the train before they got to New York, or else they were saving it for canoe rides and the roller-coaster at Coney Island. Whatever the reason, all the money that the theatrical managers culled out of the convention wouldn't have bought a new Catholic collar for Rabbi David Belasco.

That makes two features of the early summer which flopped. The other was the weather. It rained so steadily during May and June that a lot of theatres couldn't close at all because the audiences couldn't get out to go home. One show was planning to ring down for the season on a Saturday night late in May, but along about eleven, just as the performance was over, it began to rain and the people hung around in the lobby waiting for it to stop, or trying to get taxicabs. They didn't know that there had been a new rule made by the Taxi Drivers' Association of New York City never to take any new fares on a rainy night. They didn't know that the hundreds of cabs which they saw slewing past with what looked like people inside were occupied only by dummies, placed there to prevent human beings from getting a ride. Of course, this vow of the drivers never to let anyone ride

Skulking about in the corners and growling whenever rescue parties came in.

in their cabs in the rain is well known now, and a citizens committee has been formed to try and argue with the drivers' representatives, but at that time it was just beginning to dawn on the public that they would either have to walk in the rain or stay wherever the rain caught 'em.

So these poor people in the theatre lobby just hung around, making fools of themselves whistling at passing cabs, and waiting for the rain to let up. They stayed there all night, some of them sleeping across the seats, others curling up under the lobby signs. In the morning it was still raining, and the actors, who had been waiting at the stage-door all night trying to get away, went back on the bare stage and began doing the show over again just to keep warm. The audience caught on to the idea of the thing and went back and sat down and applauded.

This was quite a lot of fun for the first two or three days, but as the week wore on and the dampness from the outside began to seep in and mushrooms started to spring up between the seats, the people grew restive and demanded at least a change in the bill.

By this time the audience was pretty well bored and several died. All the candy which had been on sale in the lobby was devoured and you know how cross a diet of nothing but candy-bars and "Oh Henrys" will make you.

Little fights were always starting among theatre parties and these usually ended in killings. What with one thing and another, the house dwindled down to a bare dozen or two. When it finally stopped raining long enough for them to get out and go home, they had become so accustomed to the dark theatre and their primitive way of living that they were more like wild mountain animals than human beings, and refused to go out into the bright sunlight, skulking about in the corners and growling whenever rescue parties came in from the outside world. As this goes to press, they are still in the theatre but it is expected that they will be captured any day now and taken to the Smithsonian Institute. Then a new show will open there.

A type of picketing that the collapse of the actors' strike forestalled.

UNFAIR HOUSE

HOW TO TRAVEL IN PEACE

The Uncommercial Traveler and His Problems

By
ROBERT C. BENCHLEY

Drawings by
REA IRVIN

WHAT with the advertising convention in London, and the Olympic Games in Paris, the summer of 1924 has probably seen the passage back and forth across the Atlantic Ocean of more tiresome talkers than ever before in its history—and you know what the history of the Atlantic Ocean has been. It has been figured out (right here on this page) that if it had been possible to harness the jaw motion in the smoking rooms of the various liners between June and September, they could have shut down the engines and run the boats on talk-power.

Even in an off year, the conversational voltage is very high on the trans-Atlantic greyhounds (ocean liners). There is something in the sea air which seems to bring a sort of kelp to the surface even in the most reticent of passengers, and before the ship has passed Fire Island you will have heard as much dull talk as you would get at a dozen Kiwanis meetings at home. And the chances are that you, yourself, will have done nothing that you can be particularly proud of as a raconteur. They tell me that there is something that comes up from the bilge which makes people like that on shipboard.

But when you add to this normal production of apple sauce the extra-heavy grade produced by advertising men and athletes in their hours of ease, you will realize what the smoking-room stewards had to stand for during the summer trips. One of the employes told me that what with having to listen to plans for nation-wide campaigns using nothing but full pages in magazines with a class circulation, and alibis as to why the spikes in running-shoes were too long, and what the high-hurdles could have been run in if the track had been in better shape, he hid down in the hold on the third day out from Southampton and didn't come out again until the boat had docked.

I myself solved the problem of shipboard conversation by traveling alone and pretending to be a deaf-mute. I recommend this ruse to other irritable souls.

There is no sense in trying to effect it if you have the family along. There is no sense in trying to effect *any-thing* if you have the family along. I needn't go into that. But there is something about a family man which seems to attract prospective talkers. Either the Little Woman scrapes up acquaintances who have to have their chairs moved next to yours and tell you all about how rainy it was all spring in Montclair, or the children stop people on the deck and drag them up to you to have you show them how to make four squares out of six matches, and once you have established these contacts, you might as well stay in your stateroom for the rest of the voyage.

It is agreed then that you must be a Lone Traveler if you hope to avoid having your good ear talked off. If, by any chance, you find yourself on board ship *with* the family, it is a very easy matter to take them up on the boat deck after dark and push them overboard under the pretext of having them peer over the side at the phosphorous. It is pitiful how unsuspectingly they will peer over the side to look at the phosphorous.

Once you are alone, you can then start in on the deaf-mute game. When you go down to dinner, write out your order to the steward and pretty soon the rest of the people at your table will catch on to the fact that something is wrong. You can do a few pleasant passes of sign language if the thing seems to be getting over too slowly. As a matter of fact, once you have taken your seat without remarking on the condition of the ocean to your right-hand neighbor, you will have established yourself as sufficiently queer to be known as "that man at our table who can't talk." Then you probably will be left severely alone.

Once you are out on deck, stand against the rail and look off at the horizon. This is an invitation which few ocean-talkers can resist. Once they see anyone who looks as if he wanted to be alone, they immediately are rarin' to go. One of them will come up to you and look at the horizon with you for a minute, and then will say:

"Isn't that a porpoise off there?"

If you are not very careful you will slip and say: "Where?" This is fatal. What you should do is turn and smile very sweetly and nod your head as if to say: "Don't waste you time, neighbor. I can't hear a word you say." Of course, there is no porpoise and the man never thought there was; so he will immediately drop that subject and ask you if you are deaf. Here is where you may pull another bone. You may answer: "Yes, very." That will get you nowhere, for if he thinks that he can make you hear by shouting, he will shout. It doesn't make any difference to him what he has to do to engage you in conversation. He will do it. He would spell words out to you with alphabet blocks if he thought he could get you to pay any attention to his story of why he left Dallas and what he is going to do when he gets to Paris.

So keep your wits about you and be just the deafest man that ever stepped foot on a ship. Pretty soon he will get discouraged and will pass on to the next person he sees leaning over the rail and ask *him* if that isn't a "porpoise 'way off there." You will hear the poor sucker say, "Where?" and then the dam will break. As they walk off together you will hear them telling each other how many miles they get to a gallon and checking up on the comparative sizes of the big department stores in their respective towns.

After a tour of the smoking room and writing room making deaf-and-dumb signs to the various stewards, you will have pretty well advertised yourself as a hopeless prospect conversationally. You may then do very much as you like.

Perhaps not quite as you like. There may be one or two slight disadvantages to this plan. There may be one or two people on board to whom you *want* to speak. Suppose, for instance, that you are sitting at one of those chummy writing desks where you look right into the eyes of the person using the other half. And suppose that those eyes turn out to be something elegant; suppose they

"That man at our table who can't talk."

In the general laughter and confusion, you could grab her and carry her up on deck.

turn out to be very elegant indeed. What price being dumb then?

Your first inclination, of course, is to lean across the top of the desk and say: "I beg your pardon, but is this your pen that I am using?" or even more exciting: "I beg your pardon, but is this your letter that I am writing?" Having been posing as a deaf-mute up until now, this recourse is denied you, and you will have to use some other artifice.

There is always the old Roman method of writing notes. If you decide on this, just scribble out the following on a bit of ship's stationery: "I may be deaf and I may be dumb, but if you think that makes any difference in the long run, you're crazy." This is sure to attract the lady's attention and give her some indication that you are favorably impressed with her. She may write a note back to you. She may even write a note to the management of the steamship line.

Another good way to call yourself to her attention would be to upset the writing desk. In the general laughter and confusion which would follow, you could grab her and carry her up on deck where you could tell her confidentially that you really were not deaf and dumb but that you were just pretending to be that way in order to avoid talking to people who did not interest you. The fact that you were talking to her, you could point out, was a sure sign that she, alone, among all the people on the ship, *did* interest you; a rather pretty compliment to her, in a way. You could then say that, as it was essential that none of the other passengers should know that you could talk, it would be necessary for her to hold conversations with you clandestinely, up on the boat deck, or better yet, in one of the boats. The excitement of this would be sure to appeal to her, and you would unquestionably become fast friends.

There is one other method by which you could catch her favor as you sat looking at her over the top of the desk, a method which is the right of every man whether he be deaf, dumb or bow-legged. You might wink one eye very slowly at her. It wouldn't be long then before you could tell whether or not it would be worth your while to talk.

However it worked out, you would have had a comparatively peaceful voyage, and no price is too high to pay for escaping the horrors that usually attend commuting across the Atlantic Ocean.

How funny Daddy looks
in his straw hat!

THE LAST DAY

By
ROBERT C. BENCHLEY

Drawings by
REA IRVIN

WHEN, during the long winter evenings, you sit around the snap-shot album and recall the merry, merry times you had on your vacation, there is one day which your memory mercifully overlooks. It is the day you packed up and left the summer resort to go home.

This Ultimate Day really begins the night before, when you sit up until one o'clock trying to get things into the trunks and bags. This is when you discover the well-known fact that summer air swells articles to twice or three times their original size; so that the sneakers which in June fitted in between the phonograph and the book (which you have never opened), in September are found to require a whole tray for themselves and even then one of them will probably have to be carried in the hand.

Along about midnight, the discouraging process begins to get on your nerves and you snap at your wife and she snaps at you every time it is found that something won't fit in the suitcase. As you have both gradually dispensed with the more attractive articles of clothing under stress of the heat and the excitement, these little word passages take on the sordid nature of a squabble in an East Side tenement, and all that is needed is for one of the children to wake up and start whimpering. This it does.

It is finally decided that there is no sense in trying to finish the job that night. General nervousness, combined with a specific fear of oversleeping, results in a troubled tossing of perhaps three hours in bed, and ushers in the dawn of the last day on just about as irritable and bleary-eyed a little family as you will find outside an institution.

The trouble starts right away with the process of getting dressed in traveling clothes which haven't been worn since the trip up. Junior's shoulders are still tender, and he decides that it will be impossible for him to wear his starched blouse. One of Philip's good shoes, finding that there has been no call for it during the summer, has become hurt and has disappeared; so Philip has to wear a pair of Daddy's old bathing shoes which had been thrown away. (After everything has been locked and taken out of the room, the good shoe is found in the closet and left for dead.)

You, yourself, aren't any too successful in reverting to city clothes. Several weeks of soft collars and rubber-soled shoes have softened you to a point where the old "Deroy-14½" feels like a napkin-ring around your neck, and your natty brogans are so heavy that you lose your balance and topple over forward if you step out suddenly. The whole effect of your civilian costume when surveyed in a mirror is that of a Maine guide all dressed up for an outing "up to Bangor."

Incidentally, it shapes up as one of the hottest days of the season—or any other season.

"Oh, look how funny Daddy looks in his straw hat!"

"I never realized before, Fred, how much too high the crown is for the length of your face. Are you sure it's your hat?"

"It's my hat, all right," is the proper reply, "but maybe the face belongs to somebody else."

This silences them for a while, but on and off during the day a lot of good-natured fun is had in calling the attention of outsiders to the spectacle presented by Daddy in his "store" clothes.

Once everyone is dressed, there must be an excursion to take one last look at the ocean, or lake, or whatever particular prank of Nature it may have been which has served as an inducement to you to leave the city. This must be done before breakfast. So down to the beach you go, getting your shoes full of sand, and wait while Sister, in a sentimental attempt to feel the water for the last time, has tripped and fallen in, soaking herself to the garters. There being no dry clothes left out, she has to go in the kitchen and stand in front of the stove until at least one side of her is dry.

Breakfast bears no resemblance to any other meal eaten in the place. There is a poorly-suppressed feeling that you must hurry, coupled with the stiff collar and tight clothes, which makes it practically impossible to get any food down past the upper chest.

Then follows one of the worst features of the worst of all vacation days—the goodbyes. It isn't that you hate to part company with these people. They too, as they stand there in their summer clothes, seem to have undergone some process whereby you see them as they really are and not as they seemed when you were all together up to your necks in water or worrying a tennis ball back and forth over a net. And you may be sure that you, in your town clothes, seem doubly unattractive to them.

Here is Mrs. Tremble, who lives in Montclair, N. J., in the winter. (There is a resident of Montclair, N. J., in every summer resort east of the Rockies.) That really is a terrible hat of hers, now that you get a good look at it. "Well, goodbye, Mrs. Tremble. Be sure to look us up if you ever get out our way. We are right in the telephone book, and we'll have a regular get-together meeting. . . . Goodbye, Marian. Think of us tonight in the hot city, and be sure to let us know when you are going

Soaking herself to the garters.

through . . . Well, so long, Mr. Prothero; look out for those girls up at the post office. Don't let any of them marry you . . . Well, we're off, Mrs. Rostetter. Yes, we're leaving today. On the 10:45. We have to be back for Junior's school. It begins on the 11th. Goodbye!"

It is then found that there is about an hour to wait before the machine comes to take you to the station; so all these goodbyes have been wasted and have to be gone through with again.

In the meantime, Mother decides that she must run over to the Bide-a-Wee cottage and say goodbye to the Sisbys. The children feel that they are about due for another last look at the ocean. And Daddy remembers that he hasn't been able to shut the big suitcase yet. So the family disperses in various directions and each unit gets lost. Mother, rushing out from the Sisbys' in a panic thinking that she hears the automobile, is unable to find the others. Little Mildred, having taken it upon herself to look out for the other children while they are gazing on the ocean, has felt it incumbent on her to spank Philip for trying to build one last tunnel in the sand, resulting in a bitter physical encounter in which Philip easily batters his sister into a state of hysteria. Daddy, having wilted his collar and put his knee through his

straw hat in an attempt to jam the suitcase together, finds that the thing can't be done and takes out the box of sea-shells that Junior had planned to take home for his cabinet, and hides them under the bed.

The suitcase at last having been squeezed shut and placed with the rest of the bags in the hall, the maid comes running up with five damp bathing suits which she has found hanging on the line and wants to know if they belong here. Daddy looks cautiously down the hall and whispers: "No!"

At last the automobile arrives and stands honking by the roadside. "Come, Junior, quick, put your coat on! . . . Have you got the bag with the thermos? . . . Hurry, Philip! . . . Where's Sister? . . . Come, Sister! . . . Well, it's too late now. You'll have to wait till we get on the train . . . Goodbye, Mrs. Tremble . . . Be sure to look us up . . . Goodbye, everybody! . . . Here, Junior! Put that down! You can't take that with you. No, no! That belongs to that other little boy . . . Junior! . . . Goodbye, Marian! . . . Goodbye, Mrs. McNerdle! . . . Philip, say goodbye to Mrs. McNerdle, she's been so good to you, don't you remember? . . . Goodbye, Mrs. McNerdle, that's right . . . Goodbye!"

And with that the automobile starts, the friends on the porch wave and call out indistinguishable pleasantries, Junior begins to cry, and it is found that Ed has no hat.

The trip home in the heat and cinders is enlivened by longing reminiscences: "Well, it's eleven o'clock. I suppose they're all getting into their bathing suits now. How'd you like to jump into that old ocean right this minute, eh?" (As a matter of fact, the speaker has probably not been induced to go into "that old ocean" more than three times during the whole summer.)

The fact that they reach home too late to get a regular dinner and have to go to bed hungry, and the more poignant impressions in the process of opening a house which has been closed all summer, have all been treated of before in an article called "The Entrance Into the Tomb." And so we will leave our buoyant little family, their vacation ended, all ready to jump into the swing of their work, refreshed, invigorated, and clear-eyed.

Refreshed, invigorated, and clear-eyed.

OLD PLAYS FOR OLD

A Look Into the New Season

Three wise men bringing
a message.

By
ROBERT C. BENCHLEY

Drawings by
REA IRVIN

THERE has long been a silly habit among dramatic reviewers of attending at least one act of the show they are reviewing. This is doubtless due to the old-fashioned superstition held by some of them that they are going to see something new when the curtain goes up. "Go to a show—see something no (new)" was the way the old proverb ran when it was taught to our forefathers by the gypsies, and a great many of us still look for novelty in the theatre, just as we look for sailors' delight to follow whatever the old rhyme says "at night."

I, for at least one, am through with all this superstitious poppycock and am going to trust to my knowledge of scientific theatrical laws, based on years of professional theatre-going, and this season expect to review all plays without so much as entering the gentlemen's smoking room of the theatre. If I don't know what the plays are going to be before I see them, then my little gray-blue eyes have been tight shut all these years.

As a matter of fact, I may just write the plays here and now and get them out of the way. I know that there are going to be just so many plays of one kind and just so many of another, and I can save the producers and public a lot of time by coming through clean with what I know and turning state's evidence.

There will undoubtedly be a dozen little plays about the goings-on of the younger generation. Here they are:

"MAMMA'S BAD SPELLS"
A Comedy by George Lillian Lift

ACT I

The scene is in the living-room of the Whamers' home in a middle-western city. The furnishings are in good taste,

except for a circular iron stairway leading up from the middle of the room into what is evidently a lighthouse. The piano (left) reeks of tobacco.

(Enter Mrs. Whamer and Duffy)

MRS. W.: Standish, I wish you wouldn't slap me so when guests are present. What will they think?

ROGER: What will they think if I *don't* slap you, Mrs. Whamer?

MRS. W.: That is neither here and certainly not there, Marvin. My children will be home from school at any minute now and I must have *something* ready to show them for my whole day in the creamery. What would you suggest?

THURLOW: You can't fool me, Madame. I knew your husband when he didn't have a Sioux, or a Mohican either, for that matter.

MRS. W.: It pleases you to jest, Ralph. It is a serious matter with me. Here I am barely nineteen and the mother of four children, all boys and girls. What will the duke say when he finds out?

PETER: You may rest easy on that point, Ethel—may I call you Mrs. Whamer? For I am the duke and I shall say nothing.

(Upsets the boat as the CURTAIN FALLS)

ACT II

The scene is in the divot room of the Golf Club. A dance of the younger members is in progress and there are several people lying about on the floor looking for pennies.

(Enter RALPH and JUDITH)

RALPH (*coolly*): Heigh-ho!

JUDITH: Just think, dear, every minute brings us just that much nearer home—our home.

RALPH: Whose home? What minute? (*Signals to a man who brings in a tray.*) Can you do tricks with oatmeal, Judith? If not, watch me.

(*Does several tricks with oatmeal which seem to amuse Judith only moderately.*)

RALPH: And now we come to the big surprise of the evening. You remember Paul Berrk, of whom you have often heard me speak?

JUDITH: No, of course not.

RALPH (*eagerly*): Good! . . . And now what shall we do?

JUDITH: Take that (*pulls his tie out*) and that (*tucks it back in again*).

RALPH: And that, my children, is how I came to marry your dear grandmother.

CURTAIN

Then it is a pretty safe bet that there will be another super-spectacle to compete with "The Miracle." It will be advertised that 500,000 yards of rubber-sheeting went into making the big picnic scene and that the three Queens of Bosnia have all been brought over to compete for the rôle of the *Matron in the Jail.*

Here is your spectacle:

"RAMADIN, or THE WONDERFUL TIME"

The first scene is in the courtyard of the palace of Old King Cole, the notorious Merry Old Soul. There has been a big festival at which the King has bought a dozen elephants, none of which he likes but all of which

I am the duke and I shall say nothing.

like him. He has appealed to Alice Walker, a native princess who is versed in mystic lore, to tell him what to do. She has advised him to leave town at once and begin all over again in another country. As the curtain rises the king is seen opening tins of anchovies in preparation for the birthday party of the Infanta, who will be forty-three on Wednesday.

Three wise men come in bringing a message from the mayor of Rochester to the mayor of Utica. They tell the king that the way the tides are running now he will be lucky if he makes Fall River before dark and then only if he uses his motor. This is just enough to make the king pretty sore, and he decides that he will win the princess or know the reason why. At the end of the show he knows the reason why.

The second scene is in the public market-place, where a large number of old people are gathered together to see who is the oldest. This is a national fête of the country, and is called High, Low, Jack, and the Game. The king enters and asks the man who takes tickets if he has seen anyone named Harry. The man asks him if he means Harry Ape, and dies laughing. The native girls then join in a dance around the pump, which is supposed to propitiate the gods and bring rainy crops. It has never worked yet, according to one of the hangers-on, but that doesn't keep the dance from lasting twenty-five minutes.

Then there is a specialty dance, in which the newest team of European disciples of Terpsichore (or is it Hercules?) interprets the opening of the first crocus, or the closing of the last rose of summer, or something having to do with the death throes of the mourning dove.

The last scene shows the king as an old man sitting in front of the fire, smoking his pipe, while all the girls that he has loved pass before him in the smoke. There is the Tennis Girl, the Outdoor Girl, the Big Girl, the Dog-faced Girl, and the Girl who was seen leaving the Metropole Hotel on the night of the Rosenthal murder. As the last girl passes by, the king folds up his toys and says: "And now for the best little girl of them all—my mother." (*His aunt enters.*)

CURTAIN

The king has bought a dozen elephants, none of which he likes, but all of which like him.

D'AC NEWS

THANKSGIVING

DRAWING BY R. F. HEINRICH

November - 1921

ENTERTAINMENT PROGRAM LISTS MANY STARS

ENTERTAINMENTS at the D. A. C. during the winter season having become such an important feature of club life, a determined effort has been made to give the members an even better "course" of Saturday evening attractions than has ever been attempted before. To accomplish this, a slight change in the system has been approved by the board of directors.

Instead of making all the entertainments free, a nominal admission fee is to be charged for some of the super-attractions. That fact has been mentioned before in this magazine and met with instant approval by practically all members interested. It pleased them because, as intimated, it will do away with overcrowding the auditorium and likewise assure a seat to everyone that purchases a ticket.

More than half of the entertainments will be complimentary to the members and for the balance tickets of admission will be required. Within the next few days season tickets will be offered for sale to the members. These course tickets will place a number of the finest attractions available before the members at a price of about one-third of what it would cost to see such performances in a public auditorium. The underlying thought in charging an admission price for the entertainments is not to make money. As a matter of fact, the season's entertainments will cost the club more than ever. At least $10,000 will be spent on the winter's attractions and not more than half of that will be taken in from the sale of tickets. The club is willing and glad to take a loss of $5,000 for the good times it can provide for the members and their families.

The new scheme of things will enable the club to present many of the world's foremost artists in these Saturday night affairs. There will be more musical evenings the coming season than the club has ever booked in the past. Included in the number are Ossip Gabrilowitsch (in his only Detroit recital, barring a series of

OSSIP GABRILOWITSCH
Whose piano recital at the D. A. C. will be one of the treats of a season that promises many delightful events.

historical lectures and concerts he is billed to give at Memorial Hall); Claire Dux, the noted soprano of the Metropolitan Opera Company; Reinald Werrenrath, the ever-popular baritone; Hulda Lashanska, who has scored many notable hits with Detroit concert-goers; John Barnes Wells, tenor, and Fillmore Ohman, pianist, in joint recital; Irene Franklin, who turned away at least 500 persons when she gave her evening of fun at the club one terribly stormy night last winter.

The other attractions on the list are just as meritorious in their special field and serve to round out a program so diversified that it will appeal to all tastes. One number that is sure to make a special appeal comes early in the season. It will bring to Detroit Robert C. Benchley, whose humorous stories have been running in the D. A. C. NEWS for many years. Mr. Benchley, as nearly every club member knows, is *Life's* dramatic critic, and, to many, he stands out as the best dramatic critic in America. Last year Irving Berlin persuaded him to do a stunt in the Music Box Revue. It was called "The Treasurer's Report" and was one of the outstanding hits of that brilliant show.

Stage life interfered too much with Mr. Benchley's writing and he declined to go back into the Music Box this season, although Mr. Berlin was anxious to have him do his monologue on "The Sex Life of the Polyp," a delicious bit of fooling that Mr. Benchley was persuaded to get up for a dinner of celebrities in New York. At the D. A. C., Mr. Benchley will give "The Treasurer's Report," "The Sex Life of the Polyp" and another new one, though, of course, all of his stunts are new to Detroit audiences. Sharing the stage with Mr. Benchley on this occasion will be another Music Box favorite, Phil Baker, who makes so much fun with his accordion and stories. It just happens that the Music Box Revue will be playing in Detroit early in December, and Mr. Berlin has permitted Mr. Baker to be booked with his

PROGRAM OF D. A. C. ENTERTAINMENTS FOR 1924-25

November 25—Annual Keno Party.
November 29—Metropolitan Swimming Meet.
December 6—Col. J. H. Patterson, D. S. O., in a lecture on "The Man-Eaters of Tsavo."
December 13—Robert C. Benchley (monologues) and Phil Baker (and his accordion).
December 26 (Children's Matinee)—Tony Sarg's Marionettes in "Treasure Island."
December 27—Tony Sarg's Marionettes in "The Pied Piper of Hamelin."
January 3—Ossip Gabrilowitsch in piano recital.
January 10—Michigan A. A. U. Swimming Meet.
January 17—Mme. Claire Dux in song recital.
January 20—Annual Club Meeting (Members Only).

January 24—Norman Angell in a lecture on "The British Labor Government."
January 31—John Barnes Wells (tenor) and Fillmore Ohman (pianist) in joint recital.
February 7—Dr. Marion LeRoy Burton in a lecture on "The Fighter."
February 14—Mme. Hulda Lashanska in song recital.
February 21—Horace D. Ashton in illustrated lecture on "The Garden of Allah."
February 28—Aquatic Meet.
March 7—Beatrice Herford and Eugene Lockhart in recital.
March 14—Reinald Werrenrath in song recital.
March 21—National A. A. U. Aquatic Meet.
March 28—Irene Franklin in "An Effort to Entertain."

former colleague for his D. A. C. appearance. This will make a decidedly "different" show.

Another novelty as far as the club is concerned will be two performances by Tony Sarg's marionettes. A children's matinee will be given on the afternoon of December 26. "Treasure Island" will be the offering on that occasion. On the following evening, "The Pied Piper of Hamelin" will be given.

Two other novelties are bound to make a wide appeal to D. A. C. folk. One is the joint recital of John Barnes Wells and Fillmore Ohman. Wells is a great artist and popular here, but Ohman is known only to comparatively few. But he will be known once you hear his piano playing. It is a sort of classical jazz, and competent authorities say he is the best in the world at that line. At any rate, his success in the East has been most emphatic. Make no mistake about that team. They will be one of the outstanding hits of the winter.

Another team that will "go big" is composed of Beatrice Herford and Eugene Lockhart. Miss Herford is on the same general line as Ruth Draper, which is saying a great deal. Mr. Lockhart does pianologues in a manner that delights an audience of the D. A. C. type.

There has been a quite insistent demand for another lecture this season by Dr. Marion LeRoy Burton, and consequently the popular president of the University of Michigan will return for his third D. A. C. appearance. His subject on February 7 will be "The Fighter."

The first number on the course will be Col. J. H. Patterson's lecture on his experiences with the man-eaters of Tsavo. Col. Patterson is the man sent to build a bridge on the Uganda Railway in British East Africa. His account of the troubles he had with bloodthirsty lions near the towns of Tsavo and Voi is bound to keep his hearers on the edges of their chairs.

Norman Angell, though no stranger to Detroiters that enjoy hearing the spoken word of leading students of world affairs, will tell an extremely interesting story when he comes in January. His topic will be "The British Labor Government." That is something which Americans want to know more about from someone well

qualified to tell them. Mr. Angell has that gift and no doubt will be closely listened to when he tells of the Ramsay MacDonald ministry.

Not many moving pictures will figure in this year's entertainments. Lecturers with good movies are getting scarcer every day. Dr. Ditmars, who has appeared on practically every season's program at the club since they were started, will not be back this season. He was invited to return but was forced to decline on account of not having prepared a new lecture.

One movie lecture which is quite sure to interest a large audience will be Horace D. Ashton's "The Garden of Allah." Mr. Ashton covers the ground mentioned in Robert Hichens' well-known novel. The pictures that go with his lecture are considered to be the finest ever made of that interesting country in northern Africa.

One splendid entertainer that will be missed this season is Ruth Draper. When the D. A. C. program was made up it was understood by Miss Draper's manager that she would remain in Europe this season. Afterwards she decided to try vaudeville with a few recital bookings. It was then too late to engage her for the D. A. C., despite a "99-year contract" the club has with her. However, Detroiters will have a chance to hear her at Orchestra Hall, December 1. She will appear in a public recital at that time under the auspices of the Dobbs Ferry alumnae.

There will be general gratification among music lovers to know that Reinald Werrenrath will be back for another recital at the club. His singing last winter was one of the high-spots of a delightful season. There were hundreds of requests to have him re-engaged for another concert.

The Gabrilowitsch followers are naturally in high spirits with the announcement that he will give a recital at the club. He scheduled no concert for himself at Orchestra Hall this winter, but planned a course of lectures on music, to be illustrated by piano selections.

Claire Dux's appearance will be a big event. She made one of the biggest hits in years at the May Festival in Ann Arbor last spring. She has taken her place as one of the great sopranos of the age and no doubt will be greeted by a capacity audience at the club.

THE POLITICAL PROSPECT

By ROBERT C. BENCHLEY
Drawings by REA IRVIN

THIS political article (No, no! *This political article right here, that you are reading now*) is being written several days before election, which is the only reason that I can't use the name of the next president. I can guess, however. And to anyone sending me a stamped, self-addressed case of Scotch I will send the name of the man I think is going to win. Don't ask me how I know. It wouldn't be fair to the campaign managers for me to tell.

However, I can say this. Mr. Coolidge's manager told me that Coolidge would win and Mr. Davis' manager told me that Davis would win. The LaFollette manager told me that not only would LaFollette win but that both Coolidge and Davis would be struck by lightning during the first thunder-storm of 1925. That's all I can tell now, but, by the time this appears, you will be able to check up on my dope and see just how near the ground-floor I was in my exclusive forecast.

As near as I can figure out from reading the pre-election statements of the various committees, anyone stands a good chance of being elected. If I were to run my little boy for president all that would be necessary would be a good, literate campaign committee to give out statements. I could handle the publicity myself. "MIDDLE WEST SOLID FOR BOBBY BENCHLEY, SAYS FATHER"; "BOBBY BENCHLEY WILL SWEEP STATE AND NATION"; "COOLIDGE WORRIED BY BOBBY BENCHLEY TIDE." These would be a few of the headlines. In the body of the story I could give out a reluctant statement:

"I have just returned from a trip through the North-West and Texas" said R. C. Benchley, Sr., in his room at the Bide-a-Wee Home today, "and, while I don't want to appear oversanguine, I must say that it looks like a land-slide for my son, Bobby, for president. Within the past few weeks there has been a definite swing away from Coolidge and Davis and into the Benchley camp. His candidacy has made a particular appeal to the women voters who, having little boys themselves, are naturally in sympathy with the aims and purposes of a little boy. Mrs. Benchley and I look for Bobby's election on Tuesday by at least 800,000."

And then on Tuesday, when Bobby didn't get more than about 300,000 in all, we would just laugh and say: "Oh well! It's all in the game. We knew all along that he probably wouldn't be elected, but he put up a good fight and wishes to congratulate the winner."

I don't see how campaign managers ever are able to get any other jobs after elections are over, when they have proved themselves liars, idiots, and slanderers during the Fall, but they seem to come out of it all right. Suppose I were to hire a manager for my business (pipe-cleaners) who came out with a statement for the press saying: "The Mignonette Pipe-Cleaner Co. announces the discovery in its laboratories of a process whereby pipe-cleaners can be used as a substitute for gasoline. This will save automobilists anywhere from eighty cents to four dollars a mile on their fuel. This remarkable discovery will be put on the market on Wednesday, December 1, and can be bought at all news stands."

And then, when December 1 came around and nothing happened, if my manager (let us say his name was Donald O. Stewart), Mr. Stewart, on being questioned, said: "Well, I guess we made a mistake, that's all," that would be the end of Mr. Stewart as a manager, or as a respected citizen of the republic. I guess it would. But campaign managers do just as untrustworthy things as anything Donald Ogden Stewart has ever done (and that is saying a lot, for I have lived with Mr. Stewart), and yet did you ever hear of a campaign manager suffering for having made such a spectacle of himself during a campaign? I said, did you ever hear of a campaign manager suffering in his other activities from having made such a spectacle of himself during a campaign? . . . Oh, never mind!

And whoever wins (or won), it is the province of this article to predict the next four years of the new administration. Since I was born, seven administrations have flowed under the bridge and I have observed them all with no little interest, in fact, with no interest at all. So I ought to be able to judge what one administration is going to do from what the others have done. So ought anyone, for that matter, but most people seem to be easier fooled than I am about political matters. At any rate, most people keep on voting.

The first administration that I saw much of was the one in office when I was from one to four years of age, and I followed that one through the cartoons in *Puck*. I don't remember who was president, but there was a man with a white beard who was always represented as wearing a large, gray top hat. The name was something like Henderson or Harrison. Maybe he wasn't president. Was there ever a president named Harrison or Henderson? Whoever he was, he figured prominently in the *Puck* cartoons along with a bald-headed man who rode a peanut, or had a peanut or peanuts about him somehow. Hill, his name was. Then there was a Full Dinner-Pail and Labor with a paper cap on. So you see, I *do* remember. You thought I wouldn't.

Backed by this knowledge of the first administration in my political career, I have steadily built up contacts and kept in touch with the workings of this great Ship of

Defeated campaign managers never seem to come to this—though some of them ought to.

State of ours (anyone who wants to take that phrase of mine "Ship of State" and use it, is welcome to it) until now I am able to give you, under my signature, an outline of just what will happen in the next four years no matter which party wins the election.

First there will be a president's message, in which he will outline what he intends to do and what he hopes that congress will do. This will include: (1) Kindness to old people and invalids; (2) increases in the number of rambler rose bushes throughout the country; (3) an arrangement whereby everyone will have lots more money; (4) an arrangement whereby everyone will have lots more fun; (5) no more hangnails; (6) shorter and earlier wars, if any.

Nothing will be heard from the government from then on, except the occasional sound of an arrest when some official gets caught or when a couple of senators stage a little bout in the coat-room or on the Chevy Chase golf course. We may have another war, or have the income tax increased to meet "current expenses," and a bill certainly will be passed widening Mink Creek so that the Fall River boats can run up as far as Colep Landing, but aside from that you won't know that the government is being run.

And then it will be four years again and you'll hear all about it for the first time, just as you've heard this fall.

Just wait and see.

The occasional sound of an arrest when some official gets caught

A CHRISTMAS PANTOMIME
For Kiddies and Grown-Ups, or Neither

By ROBERT C. BENCHLEY
Drawings by REA IRVIN

THE scene is on a snowy plain just outside Wilkes-Barre. Seven stars are seen shining through the back-drop, representing the six sins of Man, the seventh being a moth-hole. A moon is also visible but it doesn't amount to much.

The characters in this pantomime are:

PIERROT . . . . A pierrot
COLUMBINE . . . . A pierrot
CIBOULETTE . . . . A pierrot
RINTINTIN . . . . A pierrot
LITTLE HENRY W. TAFT . . . . . *who dreams the dream.*

As the curtain rises, something goes wrong; so it has to be lowered again. Twenty-five minute wait while it is fixed.

As the curtain rises, PIERROT *is discovered sneaking a drink out of a bottle. He puts the bottle down quickly when he finds out that he has been discovered.*

⊢ Enter COLUMBINE, *awkwardly. She dances over to* PIERROT *and makes as if to kiss him, but he hits her a terrific one under the eye and knocks her cold. Three thousand gnomes enter and drag her off. One gnome (Alaska) stays behind and dances a little.*

END OF THE SHOW: EVERYBODY OUT!

On thinking it over, a Christmas pantomime doesn't seem to be just what is needed. You can get a Christmas pantomime anywhere. In fact, *don't* you? So let's not do a Christmas pantomime. Let's just have some fun and get to bed early.

Let's tell some Yuletide stories!

I know a good Christmas story. It seems there was a man who came to a farmer's house late on Christmas Eve and asked if the farmer could put him up for the night.

"*Ich habe kein Zimmern,*" *sagte der Farmer,* "*aber Sie können mit Baby schlafen.*" ("I have no rooms," said the farmer, "but you may sleep with the baby if you wish.") So the man—

I guess that isn't about Christmas, though. You can tell it as if it were about Christmas, however, by putting that in about it's being Christmas Eve when the man came to the farm-house. But it really wasn't Christmas Eve in the original story and I couldn't deceive you.

Games are good on Christmas Eve. I know some good games. One that we used to play when I was a boy was called "Bobbing for Grandpa." All you need is a big tub full of water, or gin, and a grandfather. Grandpa gets into the tub and ducks his head under the water. Then everyone steals softly out of the room and goes to the movies. You ought to be back by eleven-fifteen at the latest. Then you all rush into the room, pell-mell, and surprise the old gentleman.

Oh, I don't know but what the pantomime was best, after all. You can get more of the spirit of Christmas into a pantomime. Let's go back and do some more of that jolly old pantomime.

CIBOULETTE *enters carrying a transparency which reads*: "This is Christmas and You Are Going to Be Merry, and Like It, Too. . . . Toyland Chamber of Commerce." *She dances around a bit and finally finds a good place to exit, which she does, thank God!*

PIERROT *awakes and sees his image in the pool. He goes right back to sleep again.*

This brings every character on except RINTINTIN *and there doesn't seem to be any good reason for bringing him on at all. However, he insists and comes on, dancing very badly across the stage to where* PIERROT *is sitting. This cleans up the entire cast and after* PIERROT *has danced around the sleeping* COLUMBINE *once or twice, something in the manner of a dying rose-bud, which he claims to represent, the curtains come together again and we are left flat, with only about half of our Christmas Eve over and nothing more to do before bedtime.*

Heigh ho! Perhaps we can get Mr. Rodney to tell us some ghost stories. Mr. Rodney, please!

MR. RODNEY: Well, children. Here it is Christmas Eve and no one has pulled the Christmas Carol yet. If you will all draw up close and stop your necking, I will at least start . . . Stop, there is someone at the door. You answer, Alfred, it's probably for you.

ALFRED: No, Mr. Rodney, it's a little old man in a red coat and a white beard who says he's Santa Claus.

MR. RODNEY: Send for the police. I'll Santa Claus him.

At this moment, SANTA CLAUS *himself enters. He is a tall, thin man, with black side-whiskers, and wears a raincoat and a derby.*

SANTA CLAUS: My name is Mortimer, George Pearson Mortimer. A lot of silly people call me "Santa Claus" and it makes me pretty mad, I can tell you. Santa Claus, indeed! Just because one year, a long time ago, I got a little stewed and hired a sleigh and some reindeer and drove around town dropping presents down chimneys. I was arrested at the corner of State and Market streets and when they took me to the station-house I didn't

Everyone steals softly out of the room.

want to give my right name; so I gave "Santa Claus" and thought it very funny. The trouble *that* got me into!

MR. RODNEY: Do you mean to tell us that there is no such person as Santa Claus?

SANTA CLAUS: I'm telling you and the cock-eyed world in the same breath.

(MR. RODNEY *bursts into tears.*)

MR. RODNEY stops crying to listen. "Hark, what is that?" he says.

"It's the sun on the marshes, Mr. Rodney," they all say in unison and the curtain comes down on the final scene of the pantomime.

In this scene, PIERROT comes to life again and revisits the old haunts of his boyhood where he used to spend Christmas years and years ago. First he comes to the old Christmas turkey, which is much too old by now for any fun. Then he sees the Little Girl That He Used to Play With in His Holidays. She is now the mother of three children and engaged to be married. But still PIERROT seems dissatisfied. He is very evidently looking for something, searching high and low. First he looks in his vest pockets, then in his coat pockets. Finally he looks in his trousers pockets. But whatever it is, he can not find it.

"What are you looking for?" asks CIBOULETTE, voicing the sentiments of the entire gathering.

"I can't seem to remember where I put the check the coat room girl gave me for my hat and coat," he answers. "I could swear that I put it right in here with my old theatre-ticket stubs."

"I didn't give you any check," says the coat room girl. "I know your face."

PIERROT *laughs at his mistake as*
THE CURTAIN FALLS

"I didn't give you any check; I know your face."

STAR ENTERTAINERS SCHEDULED FOR DEC. 13

AS LONG as Robert C. Benchley stayed in New York and sent his stories regularly to the D. A. C. NEWS it wasn't necessary to tell the story of his life. But now that he is going to appear in person before a club audience all the dirt has to be told. Since we have a wholesome respect for the libel laws, we shall quote from Mr. Benchley's authentic biography of himself, in order that everyone who turns out to hear him in his original monologues, December 13, may have the story as it really is:

> Born Isle of Wight, September 15, 1807.
> Shipped as cabin boy on Florence J. Marble, 1815.
> Arrested for bigamy and murder in Port Said, 1817.
> Released 1820. Wrote "Tale of Two Cities."
> Married Princess Anastasie of Portugal, 1831.
> Children: Prince Rupprecht and several little girls.
> Wrote "Uncle Tom's Cabin," 1850.
> Editor "Godey's Lady's Book," 1851-56.
> Began "Les Miserables," 1870 (finished by Victor Hugo).
> Died, 1871. Buried in Westminster Abbey.

ROBERT C. BENCHLEY
Famous humorist, who will appear at the D. A. C.
in a series of monologues on December 13.

It was not from a copy of "Who's Who" that the foregoing was taken, but from Thomas L. Masson's book, "Our American Humorists." That, of course, gives the Benchley autobiography much more weight.

Members of the D. A. C. who saw Benchley in "The Music Box Revue" last season in New York will jump at the chance to hear "The Treasurer's Report" again.

Mr. Benchley will have as a running mate on this occasion Phil Baker, of "The Music Box Revue." Mr. Baker is one of the best entertainers on the stage and is one of the big hits of the famous revue by Irving Berlin. His specialty acts with his familiar piano-accordion have been applauded to the echo on almost every vaudeville stage of any importance in this country. His clowning has also been just as highly appreciated by the patrons of the big musical shows. The reason for the Baker popularity is that he keeps his line of theatrical goods fresh—and original. You'll like this team.

It would be a lot of fun to stand on the
corner and watch the confusion.

PLANS FOR ECLIPSE DAY

What To Do When It Gets Dark

By
ROBERT C. BENCHLEY

Drawings by
REA IRVIN

THE big social event of January, 1925, should be the complete eclipse of the sun on the twenty-fourth. There hasn't been a complete eclipse of the sun in the memory of anyone living now and, if you will figure it out on the back of an envelope, you will find that there won't be another for approximately a long time; so we must make the most of this.

Incidentally, if you really do want to figure out just when and where there will be a complete eclipse of the sun, it is a pretty simple matter. All you have to do is think of a number. The only specification is that it has to be a number of twelve digits. You must know lots of good numbers of twelve digits. When you have found one, you write it on a piece of paper and hand it to an usher. Then you take the circumference of the earth and draw a line from it parallel to the sun's orbit. (You may have a little trouble in finding the sun's orbit, but don't be discouraged. Look everywhere.) Now this line represents the earth's shadow. It isn't a very good representation, it is true, but it will do, unless you are an artist and can draw a good shadow.

The Calendar Will Help

Now put a calendar under this piece of paper (what piece of paper?) and trace the line representing the earth's shadow onto the calendar. When you take off the tracing sheet you will find that the line points to the exact day of the month when the next eclipse will take place. And in some strange way, as yet unexplained by science, you will also find written in a clear, round hand, the exact hour and locations from which the eclipse will be visible. This is the most interesting phase of the whole thing. Where does that writing come from? And yet there are people who deny that there are supernatural forces at work in the world! I forgot to add that if you

want to know how long the eclipse will last, you must add seven to the total, one for each of the days in the week.

Now that we have found out that there is surely going to be an eclipse, the next thing to do is to plan how to take advantage of it. It isn't often that right in the middle of the day you get complete darkness, and there is no sense in just sitting around looking blank while the thing is going on. At such times there is a man's work to be done, and "England expects every man," etc.

Everybody Will Do, Doing It

In the first place, you can count on practically everyone else being out in the street gaping up at the sky or paying fifty cents to look through a telescope at nothing. You will have the run of the town. This is no small advantage. The only thing is that you will have to work fast, for the eclipse lasts only a few minutes. This will make it necessary for you to decide just what it is you want to do, map out your route, and be ready to start the second that darkness sets in.

For instance, supposing that for years you have been repressing a wild desire to insult somebody—Calvin Coolidge; the president of your local board of aldermen; your wife's father—anybody. Find out where he is going to be at the time of the eclipse, station yourself within ten feet of him, and just as soon as it gets good and dark, rush up and pull his hat down over his ears, untie his necktie and then run. By the time the lights are on, or the sun is out again, you can be back at your desk, breathing heavily but very happy.

Perhaps you have always wanted to violate the law against smoking in the Art Museum, or, if you are a woman, in the D. A. C. Very well, now is your chance. Get your pipe or cigarette all lighted and, at the proper moment, rush into the *verboten* territory, take a dozen

31

good drags, and fill the place with smoke. You might even knock a lot of ashes on the floor. You won't have to run after this, for when it grows light you can hide the apparatus and help the authorities look for the culprit.

Another good game would be to hire some accomplices and change all the street signs. This would be more in the nature of a prank and would call for the release of no malicious repressions. It would be a lot of fun that afternoon to stand on the corner and watch the confusion of traffic, with people and cars going up the wrong streets, family men rushing about trying to find their homes (giving up after two or three minutes and staying down town all night), postmen crying softly to themselves and roaming through Elizabeth street looking for 114 South Division street with a lot of undelivered mail, and the whole town in general facing a complete tie-up. It might be necessary to re-district the whole city or perhaps build an entire new one ten miles up the river. Then, a few years later, at the Board of Commerce dinner, you could get up and tell everybody of the joke you played back in 1925 and get a good laugh.

Personally, I intend to devote myself to a more harmless experiment. For years I have wanted to wear a silk hat, a batwing collar, and a spotted bow tie. I tried it once and was told that I looked terrible. It wasn't just a few friends who told me. Perfect strangers wrote letters to the papers about it and said that it was a disgrace to the city that such things should be allowed. A lot of people got up a round robin and sent it to me, reminding me of my wife and children. The thing created such a stir that I bowed to public opinion and put the hat away in a box on the top shelf of my closet and went back to the old fedora. But in my heart I knew that I was in the right and resolved to wear that outfit once more before the Grim Reaper got in his dirty work—in the daytime, too.

Figuring out when and where there will be a complete eclipse is a pretty simple matter.

He is paid to take people up and down, and it's none of his business what they look like.

So on January twenty-fourth, I will stay at home in the morning and have a simple breakfast of fruit and one dropped egg on toast. Then I will put on my Appellate Division coat, with perhaps a gardenia in the buttonhole, a pair of trousers with a modest stripe, patent-leather shoes and gray spats, a white duck waistcoat, and a batwing collar with a spotted bow tie. Then I will have my man ready at the door to hand me my silk hat and stick when the time comes. At the very first sign of darkness, I will start out on a brisk trot up the street, covering the block bounded by Madison avenue, Forty-fourth street, Fifth Avenue, and Forty-fifth street. If I see that things are working out all right and that I have plenty of time, I may slow down to a walk, or even saunter, swinging my stick when I get on Fifth Avenue. I have paced the distance out in my regular clothes and find that I can do it in about five minutes, or under, if the track is fast. This will bring me back to the house just in time to escape the full light of day and yet I guess enough people will see me to give the thing that spice which danger lends to an exploit of this kind. I don't care about the elevator man. He is paid to take people up and down in the elevator and it is none of his business what they look like. He's used to masqueraders anyhow.

The only trouble with these plans for Eclipse Day is that it may not be entirely dark during the event. I can't find anyone who knows exactly about that. It may work out to be merely like a very cloudy day. And in some sections of the country, of course, there won't be a complete eclipse visible at all. This would make it rather difficult to get away with anything spectacular, like kissing Peggy Hopkins Joyce. And, at any rate, the very fact that there is an eclipse going on at all, will give you an excuse for knocking off work for a few minutes.

A self-raising back seat makes motoring more enjoyable.

ECHOES FROM THE SHOW

By
ROBERT C. BENCHLEY

Drawings by
REA IRVIN

LAST month (or was it last year?) saw the Somethingth Annual Automobile Show in New York City. It also saw the complete collapse of my system of cold morning baths, owing to the impossibility of heating our bathroom. I can't, and won't, take a cold bath in a cold bathroom, for anybody.

Which brings us right back to the Automobile Show. Most of the technical features of this exposition have been reported in full, and, even if they hadn't been, I doubt if it would be the province of this article to do it. As I see it, the province of this article is to combine reportorial accuracy and conciseness of statement with a certain moral lift; a spiritual tonic which will make every man, woman, and child who reads it, or has it read to them, just a little better men, women, and children for the experience. I may be wrong, but that's the way it seems to me. At any rate, while it is being read, the reader isn't up to any mischief, and that's a great deal to be said for any ten minutes these days. Old Mischief Days, I call them.

There were several things about the show which I didn't see reported in any of the trade papers, however. The fact that I didn't see any of the trade papers may have had something to do with it, but if you have heard any of these before, just skip this page. Perhaps you have already. If so, never mind.

There were several accessories on exhibition at the show which seemed to have quite a lot of sense back of them. The seat-cooler put out by the Rintex people, for example. This little device is made for drivers of roadsters and others who have occasion to leave their cars standing in the hot sun in summer until the leather cushions acquire a heat sufficient to toast bread. A friend of my father's was so badly burned once, hopping suddenly into a seat with hot cushions, that he had to drive to work for a week on his little boy's scooter. All this would have been avoided if he had had one of these seat refrigerating plants. This accessory is very simple. Two pipes run under the cushion carrying ammonia and whatever other flavor you like best, and no matter how hot the sun may be (and scientists tell us that it is pretty hot) the cooling effect of the artificial ice counteracts the heat so that the temperature of the cushion is practically always seventy or eighty degrees F. That is cool enough for anyone, isn't it?

Another device was the vestibule attachment which depends on a pretty general use for its efficacy, for if the other fellow doesn't have one, yours will be no good. The vestibule attachment is for Sunday driving along crowded postroads, when hundreds of automobile parties spend the afternoon running along in line at maybe ten miles an hour, with no chance of getting ahead or of dropping back. If enough cars in the line have the vestibule attachment they can all be thrown together like Pullmans on a train, and the occupants can get up and move around from one car to another instead of crowding their spines lolling along in the same old car all the way. The last car in the vestibule-line could be made into a sort of club car, with magazines and White Rock, and there might even be a sleeper for those who were tired of looking at the scenery. There might even be eight or ten sleepers. The scenery isn't so good these days.

One of the best little arrangements on display was called the "Dumpo" rear seat trap. By means of this, a button pushed by the driver tilts the entire rear seat upward, leaving an open space plenty large enough for the occupants to be dumped quickly out onto the road-bed. The advantages of this attachment are obvious. You are out driving with your wife, or anybody else who happens to bother you by telling you which road you should have taken instead of the one you took. Zip! Out she goes! You have a couple of gentlemen friends in the back seat who have taken advantage of your being busy at the wheel to slip down a few snifters from the old silver pocket-jug. They start a three-part arrangement of "And She Lives Down in Our Alley." A slight pressure on the button and there they are, back there by the hydrant! You have a nervous aunt who was mixed up in a runaway when she was young and has been fidgety ever since whenever fifteen miles an hour is reached. She leans over the back of the seat and grabs your shoulder: "Please go more carefully, Bert," she says, "you know my—" Smack! Away we go, and Aunt Mildred walks home like the timid girl she is.

The only trouble with this accessory is that it is going to clutter up the highways so. There won't be room for motorists what with the little groups of back-seaters walking home. Running them down might help, but that, too, cuts in on your making any kind of time.

Several automobile manufacturing and selling problems were covered at the show, especially the problem of the used car. As is well known, the biggest job that the dealer has to face is that of disposing of the second-hand cars that have been loaded on him by customers frantic to exchange an old car for a new. Sometimes a dealer will have the back of his garage so loaded up with used cars that it looks like the parking space at a race track. What is he to do with them?

A solution to this problem was offered by a loam firm in Milwaukee which suggested that these old cars be filled with loam and that the dealer plant geraniums or vegetables in them. If this were done, quite a respectable truck garden could be made to take the place of the area

A friend of my
father's was badly
burned.

before given over to idle machines and the dealer might clean up quite a bit on the side in this way.

Another suggestion was that the dealer bring his household furniture down to the garage and have his family live in the cars, thereby releasing his own home for sale or rent. Quite a cozy little nest could be fixed up in the tonneaus of the closed cars, with pictures hung on the walls and cooking apparatus installed, along with a radio and the other appurtenances which go to make the modern home what it is today. The only trouble with this plan would be that, if the dealer had small children, there might be some trouble with their falling out of the cars while playing, and scratching the paint. This could be overcome by telling the children to be very careful and not to fall out unless absolutely necessary.

There were many other accessories which the show brought out, but it seems to me that these were far and away the most practical. Some of the others had good ideas back of them, but I doubt if they would work when you came right down to it. That is the trouble with these inventors. They get so enthusiastic about their schemes that they seem to forget that unless they work they are no good. An inventor is, after all, a kind of a mechanical poet; or you might even go so far as to say, an unmanicured poet. He often turns out something pretty nifty, but most of the time he can't explain just what it's all about, or make it function.

Now all that is necessary is for someone to come along and fix up something that will keep my bathroom nice and hot. I had an electric heater installed, but I leaned against it, and so that's out. The heat has got to come from some outside source and be generally diffused throughout the room. Please everyone think this thing over, will you? And write me about it.

I can't, and won't, take a cold
bath in a cold bathroom.

SPECIAL WASHINGTON CORRESPONDENCE

By
ROBERT C. BENCHLEY

Drawings by
REA IRVIN

THE D. A. C. NEWS, like all the other big magazines, goes to press so far in advance of publication date (in order, so they tell me, to reach subscribers in the Orient on the same day that it is issued in Detroit) that we correspondents have to write our copy up about six months in advance. Sometimes we get it down to six *days*, but that rushes the printers pretty badly and doesn't give Maxwell Parrish much time to do the illustrations.

This article, for example, on the inauguration of President Coolidge on March 4, 1925, is being written for the March issue of the D. A. C. NEWS at Siasconset, Massachusetts, in August, 1924, before President Coolidge has even been elected. Before this comes out, almost anything may happen. Mr. Coolidge may run off with the wife of the Serbian Ambassador, which would automatically debar him from the presidency, under the Federal law which forbids a citizen of the United States to accept a title from any foreign government. Or they might move the capitol from Washington to Old Point Comfort, or the British might burn the White House again. They did once, I remember, and I have never forgiven them for it, either.

By the way, what a thing that was for the British to do, to burn the White House! I don't think that nearly enough has been made of that. It doesn't seem as if they should be allowed to get off so easily as they have. What were they doing in Washington, anyway? They were up to no good, I'll be bound. What are we coming to when a foreign nation can land troops in this country, march to Washington, upset tables and chairs, and finally end up by burning down the president's home? Have we no national pride, or have we? That's what we get for letting all these foreigners in here with matches. All matches should be taken away from foreigners the minute they land in this country. The fact that this outrage was committed a while back doesn't make it any better. It makes it worse, if anything. I will be one of any ten citizens to raise a fund to establish a press-bureau and disseminate the facts in this case throughout the country. We can have a British-Burned-the-White-House Week and get the school children excited about it. Let us find out what the British Ambassador has to say about it. What excuse can he offer? Why should we as a nation continue to give teas and things to the British Ambassador when his people, maybe his own great-grandfather, for all we know, deliberately set fire to one of our most beautiful buildings? I don't think that even the most biased Anglophile will deny that the White House *is* a beautiful building. I would like to hear from readers of the D. A. C. NEWS on how they feel about this thing.

However, we can let that slide for a minute, perhaps, and take up the matter of President Coolidge's inauguration, which, if all goes well (or as well as one can expect with things as they are in the world today), will have taken place shortly before this issue comes off the presses.

It was a very successful affair and President Coolidge

is very happy over it. I understand that there was enough chicken salad left over for three or four days' luncheons at the White House, and that the newspapers and programs left lying about by guests can be bundled together and sold back to the pulp mills for six or seven hundred dollars. This will make it possible to pay the postmen even less than they are getting now, and still keep within the budget.

The weather was probably pretty bad for the ceremonies. This is quite a long journalistic chance to be taking, writing as far ahead as December, 1924 (I couldn't quite finish this article in 'Sconset last August, and so am cleaning it up in New York in December), but it is a pretty safe bet that the weather for the inauguration will be bad. It is estimated that during the last ten inaugurations enough slush has fallen to bury the City of Washington to a depth of seventeen feet, Fahrenheit. May I call attention to the fact that I deliberately passed up a chance in that last sentence to play on the word "slush" and work it around into something about "slush funds." It would have been easy to do, and there might not have been much criticism of it, but we Benchleys have our pride, indeed we have.

Since the weather was so bad, it was decided that it would be better not to go out of doors in all that rain and sleet; so the ceremonies were held up in the attic where it was nice and dry and warm, and everybody had a good, informal time. I sometimes think that you can have more fun on a bad day up in the attic than you can when the weather is fine and everyone feels that he has to go out of doors. Certainly no one could have had a better time than the Coolidges did being inaugurated up in the attic, and several of the older ambassadors dressed up as ghosts and scared the younger ones by jumping out from behind trunks and things, and, after it was all over, the

Reaching subscribers in the Orient the same day that the magazine is issued in Detroit.

I have never forgiven the British

Coolidges' cook, whom they brought on from Northampton, served baked beans and fish-cakes, and everyone voted it a very happy afternoon.

If, by some chance, Nature should have played me a dirty trick and the day should have been fine (writing as far in advance as February, 1925, as I am, it is difficult to predict the weather accurately), then the foregoing paragraph should be discounted.

It is not so difficult, however, to write a notice in advance of the inaugural address. It was a very nice address. Brief, concise, and couched in Yankee terseness of phraseology, the whole thing summed up in a nutshell the policy of the administration for the coming four years. Economy is to be the watchword. "Take care of the pennies," said the President, "and the dollars will take care of themselves—and two others." To this end the inaugural parade was cut right down to the bone. There was no steam calliope at the end and they had only one cage of animals. A lot of people seemed to feel that it wasn't anywhere near so good a parade as they had four years ago, because, say what you will, a good calliope does help round out a procession and sends folks home feeling that they have seen something. But when you figure out how much the taxpayers were saved by the simplification of the parade, and how little the individual taxpayer will notice the saving when his tax bill comes due, you will thank Mr. Coolidge for looking out for your pennies and letting your dollars take care of themselves.

But here it is March 3, 1925, and this article isn't finished yet, and so I must go now and mail it or the printers will never be able to get it out in time for the inauguration. If they don't, it means a wait of four years for another inauguration, unless President Coolidge gets mad at the extravagance of the Navy Department in building another dinghy and resigns.

"BICYCLING," THE NEW CRAZE

By
ROBERT C. BENCHLEY

Drawings by
REA IRVIN

AS SPRING draws near, those of us who are interested in sports (and who is not?) begin to ask ourselves the question: "What sport shall I go in for this year?" Last year perhaps it was badminton, the year before lawn tennis, the year before that punting. Always something. Always the search for the game which will send the blood coursing through the veins and bring the roses back into those cheeks after the long inertia of winter.

There is a new sport this season which bids fair to have great popularity among the younger sets, a sport imported, as are so many of our outdoor games, from England, where it has had a great vogue for several years now. This sport is called "bicycling," and derives its name from the instrument on which it is practiced—the "bicycle." You will see that this word is made up of two words: "bi," meaning "two," and "cycle," meaning wheel—"two wheels." And such indeed it is, a veritable two-wheeled contraption, on which the rider sits and balances himself until he is able, by pushing two pedals arranged for the purpose, to propel the whole thing along the roadway at a great rate. And what a lark it is, too!

We show a picture of a bicycle here, and you may figure out for yourself just how it works. You will see that the pedals are so fixed that when one foot is up the other is down, thus giving the feet an equal chance at the rousing exercise and doing away with any chance of the rider's becoming one-sided, as might well result from a position where one foot was up all the time and one foot down.

You will also observe that the saddle is placed at just the right height from the pedals, so that the rider sits on it easily without having to stretch his legs out beyond their natural length—or, on the other hand, without having to contract them. When experiments were being made on the first bicycle by Philip G. Bicycle, the inventor, it was thought that it would be necessary for anyone who was going to ride one of the things to stretch his legs out anywhere from one to four feet beyond their natural length in order to reach the pedals. Mr. Bicycle was very much discouraged when he realized this, "for," as he said to his partner, "there won't be enough people in the world who *can* stretch their legs out from one to four feet to make any decent kind of sale for my machine at all."

So broken was he at the realization of this fact that he put this invention aside, and for the next three years he worked on the invention of the apple.

Then one day, as he was sitting in a swing on his lawn, he said to himself: "If the force of gravity is sufficient to swing this swing when I push with my feet, why can't I overcome that difficulty in my bicycle by placing the pedals just a leg's length from the saddle?" He rushed out to his workshop, where the discarded model of his bicycle had lain for so long, and proceeded to reconstruct it so that he could sit in the saddle and still reach the pedals without the necessity of stretching his legs.

Another novel feature of the bicycle is the wire rack for carrying books and luncheons. This is fastened right on the front, or "handlebars," of the machine, and with it one is enabled to go out on picnics or reading parties in the woods, the only things then necessary being some luncheon or books to put into the rack, and woods to go to.

Now comes the technical part of this article—an explanation of how to ride the bicycle. For surely one must know how to ride a bicycle if one is to own one. And it is getting so that one must own a bicycle if one hopes to be anyone at all socially. Even a casual visitor at Newport, Rhode Island, will tell you how the craze has caught hold of the fast set there, until one is constantly in danger of being run down by millionaire bicyclists as one walks through the streets. It is even said that at some of the exclusive parties given in the villas there, the guests bring their bicycles right in with them and keep the clips on their trousers all during dinner. It is a mark of distinction to be seen with bicycle-clips on your trousers, for it indicates that you are "up with the times."

The first thing that the prospective rider has to do is take position No. 1, as indicated in the accompanying sketch. This involves standing upright with the bicycle leaning against the right hip, the right hand on the saddle, and the left hand on the left handlebar. The left foot is then placed on the left pedal and the rider waits. At a signal from the bugle ("Boots and Saddles" is usually played), the command "Mount!" is given. At this command the rider leans heavily against the bicycle, swings the right leg up, striking the saddle a smart blow with it, and crashing over on top of the machine, which will fall heavily at the same time in the same direction as the rider. (Fig. 2.) Both rider and bicycle will lie in a heap until picked up by the attendant. Many riders will prefer to go home right then and there.

If you really want to be an expert bicyclist, however, you will try again. Take the same position as the one you took in the first place (Fig. 1) and practice swinging the right leg up over the saddle until you are finally able to clear it clean. This will land you in a sitting position, square on the saddle. Be sure that you are facing the right way (*towards* the handlebars), otherwise you will

FIG. 2

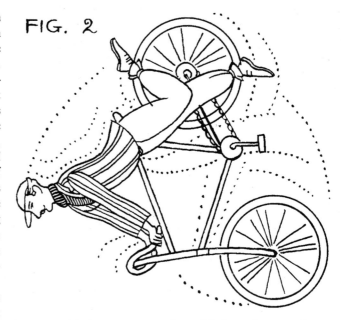

have trouble in steering and are likely to become dizzy.

Now here you are, seated in the saddle, with your right hand on the right handlebar and your left hand on the left handlebar, your right foot on the left pedal and your left foot on the right pedal. You must then bring yourself into a state of mind where you realize the necessity for pushing ahead. That is one thing about riding a bicycle. You can't stand still once you are seated and ready to go. There are three ways for you to go—forward, over to the right, or over to the left. Let us say that at first you go over to the right side. This is the most popular side for beginners, as it carries out the arc begun in the process of mounting. Once you have fallen over to the right side, try the left. This will even things up and make you less lame the next day, or, at any rate, lame in nicely-balanced areas.

Once you have found the knack of going *ahead*, the thing is easy. Push with the feet against the pedals, bringing one up as the other goes down and vice versa. If you do this, you will suddenly perceive that the whole machine is moving forward as if by magic, carrying you with it. Oh, the exhilaration of feeling yourself pushing forward through the air, like, or something like, a bird! No one who has experienced this thrill can conceive of its madness, its tang, its verve, and its *élan*.

When you have ridden as far as you want to ride, the next thing to do is to stop. This is accomplished by heading for something firm, like a post or a large white house, and crashing into it head-on. You will then find that you have not only stopped, but that you are *off*, all in one continuous uninterrupted process.

This concludes our first lesson in bicycling. People may poke fun at you for taking up with the first crazy fad that comes along, and you may not like it at first, but remember that no one ever does anything who is not willing to lead the way and take a chance, and I am sure that the results in improved circulation and general health will more than repay you for the embarrassment of being a pioneer and a cripple.

FIG. 1

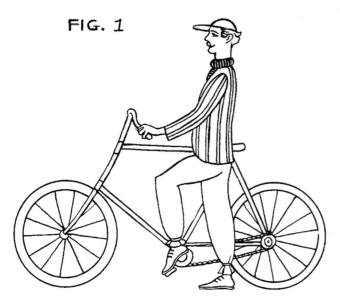

DRAMA CLEANSING AND PRESSING

By ROBERT C. BENCHLEY—*Drawings by* REA IRVIN

SOMETHING has got to be done about the sex-play market in New York. It is all shot to pieces, owing to the fact that a manufacturer can't tell whether he has turned out an obscene play or a work of art. He doesn't know in advance whether his show is going to be found guilty of corrupting public morals or put on President Eliot's list of the Fourteen Most Ennobling Plays on the Atlantic Seaboard. Each opening night there is an equal chance that the next week will find him having an audience with either a judge or the Pope.

This uncertainty has made the managers rather jumpy, as well it might, and if we don't look out they will give up producing sex plays entirely, and then where would we be?

A pretty good way to judge in advance about the intrinsic art of a sex play is to see whether the characters have a good time at it or not. If they get fun out of the thing, then it's a harmful play. If they hate it, it's a work of art. So long as someone dies in the last act, making the show a tragedy, the sky's the limit in the dialogue up to that point. You can have your heroine as indiscreet as you like, so long as you make her protest, with a dour expression, that, so help her Pete, she never had a worse time in her life.

For example, here are two plays, with exactly the same idea back of each, one of which would be suppressed, the other of which would be endorsed by clergymen and Benny Leonard. See if you can tell which is the sincere work of art and which the disgrace to the American stage:

A Farce in One Act

entitled

"WRONG NUMBER, PLEASE"

SCENE: *The boudoir of Mertisse LaFrage in her home on Long Island, furnished in pink and Quelque Fleurs.*

Mertisse is discovered in a single-handed tussle with Elizabeth Arden. She has just cleaned up the Epidermis Cream and is about to begin on the Tissue-Building Lotion, when Ronald enters.

RONALD: Hello, Mertisse, old girl! Where's your husband?

MERTISSE: Oh, Freddie is out whippet-racing.

RONALD: That's fine. Perhaps that will give me a chance to tell you how much I love you.

MERTISSE: It will give you a chance all right, but what guarantee have I that you will take it?

RONALD: I'll take that, and a pound of your best coffee, and you can send them, please. I'll take this along with me. (*Kisses her.*)

(*Freddie enters.*)

FREDDIE: What, what?

RONALD: Did you want to see someone?

FREDDIE: No, I just happened to be passing by and thought I'd drop in and see how far along the plasterers were. They promised to have the job done by Thursday.

RONALD: Well, this is only Friday. Drop in again to-morrow and I'll see if I can place you.

MERTISSE: Oh, and Freddie, on your way out tell Harvey to serve the creamed fish in ramekins tonight.

FREDDIE: Right-o! Well, toodle-oo! Don't do anything I wouldn't do.

RONALD: See you at third base, old bean. So long!

(*Exit Freddie.*)

RONALD: Let's see, where was I?

CURTAIN

"SUNK"

A Drama in One Act

Scene: *A bedroom in a cold New England farmhouse. The only light comes from the ice in the wash-pitcher.*

Hilda is discovered pulling her hair down over her eyes and moaning softly to herself.

(*Eben enters.*)

EBEN: Cold, ain't it?

HILDA: Cold.

EBEN: Whar's Ezra?

HILDA: Out in the barn, torturing the horses.

EBEN: That's good. Mebbe I kin tell yer now, Hilda, how much I love yer.

HILDA: That'd be fine, Eben. (*Punches herself on the jaw. Eben kisses her and they both cry.*)

(*Ezra enters.*)

EZRA: Cold, ain't it?

EBEN: Cold.

HILDA: Cold.

EBEN: Want anything, Ezra?

EZRA: Nothin' Eben. Nothin' but the wind across the hills.

EBEN: You'll get that outside, Ezra.

HILDA: Outside.

EZRA: Wall, I'll be goin'.

(*Exit Ezra.*)

EBEN: Well, Hilda?

HILDA: Well, Eben?

A shot is heard outside, indicating that Ezra has killed himself or one of the horses. Eben and Hilda embrace, moaning with despair.

CURTAIN

It wouldn't take a play jury long to decide which of these plays was harmful to public morality and which was a genuine piece of creative work. And the public discussion of the subject would probably make a big hit out of the second play. The first would have been a hit from the start. But there ought to be some better way of rendering a frank play innocuous and fit to be witnessed by the tenderer and

The bad play

more susceptible section of the theatre-going public. Since the trouble lies in the dialogue, why not utilize those little ruses which are used in family conversations to hide words which should not be spoken? Who could object to the following scene?

The play is called "FREIGHT ON BOARD." The hero has been discovered bringing the morning papers up to the room of his employer's wife. There has been a scene in which the employer accuses the hero of looking at the sporting section of the paper before delivering it. The hero has denied doing this, but does admit that he opened the paper slightly to peek in and see what the weather was going to be. This so enrages the employer that he calls his wife into the room to see what kind of man her lover is.

HUSBAND: Look, Martha, I want you to see just what kind of man your you-know is.

WIFE: My you-know? You are crazy, Paul. I am true to you.

HUSBAND: Don't lie to me, you whad-ye-call it, you! You're no better than a common so-and-so.

WIFE: So that's all the gratitude I get for all that I have been to you.

HUSBAND: What can you expect when you Number 14?

WIFE: I have *not* Number 14ed.

HUSBAND: You lie! My spies have kept me posted.

WIFE: You thingamabob!

HUSBAND: Thingamabob, perhaps, but at any rate not a how-now.

WIFE: Well, Paul, you are forcing me to tell you something that I had not planned on telling for a while yet. But to win back your love and confidence, I see that I must do it now.

HUSBAND: What are you driving at?

WIFE: It is something that I had hoped to keep as a surprise for you; something that would have served as a birthday gift or Easter offering.

HUSBAND: Nothing would surprise me after what I have learned about you. So spring it, and end this awful suspense. I get enough mental exercise doing cross-word puzzles.

WIFE: Can't you guess?

HUSBAND: You mystify me. What is it?

WIFE: We are—going—to—have—a—whatziz.

CURTAIN (*as they embrace*)

The good play

27

J U N E   1 9 2 5

THE BIG BRIDEGROOM REVOLT
All Honor to Hershey, The Emancipator

By
ROBERT C. BENCHLEY

Drawings by
REA IRVIN

JUNE, nineteen hundred and twenty-five, was the year of the Revolt of the June Bridegrooms. It marked the beginning of the independence of the male member of the nuptial team who, hitherto, had been kept in absolute subjection until after the ceremony was over. In the days before the revolt, the first official act of the groom that had any legal standing at all was the signing of the check for the first month's rent. Up until the time when he was allowed to do this he was kept in chains in the cellar with the caterer's men.

From the old records and letters of prospective bridegrooms to their men friends which have recently come to light we are able to reconstruct the process by which the groom was reduced to a condition of servility equalled only by that of the captives who were led through the streets in ancient Rome.

During the courtship there was evidently some semblance of equality between the young man and the young woman. He suggested things which were sometimes carried out and, if he protested against certain courses of action, they were occasionally abandoned. This, however, we now know to have been simply expediency on the part of the young lady. She was saving up for a better day.

Once the engagement was announced and the date set for the wedding, the young man suddenly found himself with a gunny-sack over his head, locked in the trunk-room. Occasionally, when they opened the door to hand him in his meals, he heard plans being made by the girl and her mother for the wedding, plans which made him break out into a cold sweat with apprehension. One time in 1923, a young man in St. Louis dashed out of the closet on overhearing the line of march down the aisle as it was being drawn up, and yelled: "Here, there! I've got something to say about this!" But he was unarmed and was easily overcome by the Praetorian Guard and thrown into a dungeon, where he was given fifty lashes with the whip.

From Lackey, in his "Slavery in the United States after 1865", we have an account of what it must have been like to be a bridegroom before the Revolution. "Church weddings," writes Lackey (p. 458), "were the particular form of torture inflicted on the helpless grooms. The larger the church wedding, the more the young man suffered and, as large church weddings were the delight of the young ladies of the day, the suffering among the men was almost universal and terribly intense. There was the initial embarrassment of appearing at the little door beside the pulpit in full view of the hundreds of critical friends of the bride. It was argued by slave-owners that no one paid any attention to the groom anyway, and that there was no need for him to suffer, but the fact remained that he *was* on public view for those who happened to glance his way and that he was a highly ridiculous figure at best. Then there was the ordeal of the ring, the cracking of the voice in the responses, the itch in the middle of the back during the ceremony and, finally, the ghastly march down the aisle on the bride's arm (technically the bride was on *his* arm, but that fooled

21

no one), under the searching stare of hundreds of curious women, all pitying the bride and wondering what on earth she saw in *him*."

Another phase of the degradation inflicted on early Twentieth Century bridegrooms was the wedding reception. This took place after the ceremony, usually at the home of the bride. Here the groom, already in a weakened condition after his nightmare in the church, was propped up in a reception line consisting of the bride, her father and mother, an aunt or two, the groom's father and mother (the bars were let down for this occasion and the groom's relatives given passes), and the groom.

We have an excerpt from a letter written by one of these grooms to his former room-mate in college, which shows the mental state induced by an affair of this kind. We reprint the letter herewith, with acknowledgment to the Congressional Library in Washington where it is preserved on the "special" shelves.

"Well, Joe, following the ceremony came the reception at Alice's. My God, Joe, what an hour! I stood up with a potted palm sticking into my neck and the boys brought up the customers one by one to Alice and me. All the old bucks took a kiss at Alice and so it was considered a good prank for the gals to take a kiss at me. Once or twice I tried to bite them, but they just thought I was kidding. Kidding! I'd have chewed them to bits if I had had my way. I told Alice before the thing that I didn't want to stand up there in line and be made a cuckoo of, but she just laughed."

That seems to have been the fate of any protests on the part of the grooms in those days—laughter. The groom

He heard plans for the wedding.

was essentially such a sappy figure that any attempt on his part to assert himself was greeted with shrieks of merriment by the bride and her mother. There are several cases on record where the groom made attempts on the life of the bride's mother following laughter of this nature, but we can find nothing to indicate that the groom ever socked the bride, or even hinted that perhaps, since it was so funny, she had better marry someone who could play up to her and wear a red wig and whiskers.

Finally, in 1925, a young groom named Arthur Hershey, of

Hershey monument,
Cleveland, Ohio.

Cleveland, Ohio (1903-1958), touched the spark to the revolt which had been smouldering for decades. Hershey had been engaged to be married to a young lady named Wabton. They had been engaged for two years and in that time Hershey had spent some three thousand dollars on gifts, suppers, taxis, etc., all in the nature of upkeep. When finally the date was set for the wedding (June 4, 1925) the young man got tacit notice that now would be a good time for him to build that boat he had always wanted, or to go into some other form of personal retirement, as nothing would be needed of him until the day of the wedding when they would tell him what to do at the church.

"At the church?" asked the young rebel.

"Yes, it is going to be a big church wedding," explained the girl. "We are going to have Uncle John come on and read the service, little Dorothy and little George are going to be flower-girls, and invitations are going to be sent out to about fifteen hundred. You can come in and help address the envelopes if you want to."

"To answer your statements in the reverse order," said Arthur Hershey, who was a lawyer: "(a) I address no envelopes, (b) if five people attend our wedding they will be lucky, (c) little Dorothy and little George will be fifty miles away at the time of the nuptials, probably drugged, (d) Uncle John reads nothing at my wedding, and (e) it is *not* going to be held in a church. You and I are going to the city clerk's office and take hold of hands and the whole thing is going to be over in five minutes, including the time consumed in sobering me up so that I can stand. Is that clear?"

Miss Wabton and her mother started to laugh, as was

(Continued on page 136)

THE BIG BRIDEGROOM REVOLT

(Continued from page 22)

the custom of the country at that time, but the fun got no farther, for young Mr. Hershey held up his hand.

"We'll have no silly business, please," he said, in a voice that rang 'round the world. "Either you meet my terms, or you marry someone else. Take them or leave them. And do it quickly."

At first the bride-to-be attempted the old bluff of flouncing out of the room and saying that very well she *would* marry someone else, but young Hershey had done his work well. For months he had been planning this *coup* and had pledged young men all over Cleveland and throughout the State of Ohio to rally to his standard when the time came. At Miss Wabton's gesture he called up Henry Mills, who was to have been his best man (Henry Mills was born in 1902 and died in 1946), and said:

"Well, Henry, the blow has fallen. Tomorrow will see whether we are a nation of free men or a galley-full of slaves. Have the boys ready to march at three-thirty."

And at three-thirty that afternoon every eligible young man in Cleveland marched simultaneously with parades of eligible young men all over Ohio, bearing standards reading: "NO BIG CHURCH WEDDINGS," "WE FURNISH THE MONEY—WE WANT FAIR PLAY," "NO WEDDINGS WITHOUT REPRESENTATION," "DOWN WITH RECEPTIONS," "WHOM ARE YOU MARRYING, US OR THE CATERER?" "THE FLORISTS MUST GO," etc., etc.

The revolt spread like wildfire all over the country. Branches of the Bridegrooms' International sprang up in Boston, San Francisco, St. Louis, Detroit, and in every small town. There was a slight attempt at struggle on the part of June brides who had their trousseaux all made with big church weddings in view, but it didn't amount to anything. The young men had the upper hand and they knew it. For years the tradition had been built up by the women folk of the country that it was the men who were anxious to get married and that the girls were doing them a favor. Hershey enunciated the principle that it was fifty-fifty to a man whether he got married or not, and that if the women didn't want to be married they didn't have to. Out of three million prospective brides, two million, nine hundred and eight thousand gave in. The battle was won and the young men of the country held their heads up again. That is why June fourth is now known as Hershey Day.

WOULD ATTRACT ABILITY

A country minister was talking to one of his flock who ventured the opinion that ministers should be better paid.

"I am glad to hear you say that," said the minister. "I am pleased that you think so much of the clergy. And so you think we should have bigger stipends?"

"Yes," said the old man. "Ye see, we'd get a better class of men than we now have."

OUR MONTHLY MARKET LETTER

By Robert C. Benchley

(By Courtesy of The Theatre Guild Program)

IN THE reaction following the election (the 1924 election, that is) the market has shown decided tendencies. So much we can be certain of.

Take bank clearings. (And wouldn't you like to!) Bank clearings have shown tendencies which can not be ignored. In 1907, during the hot spell, Owagena Zinc and Bicarb went off forty points, leaving thousands of investors looking into space. This lesson was hardly learned, before it went off again, this time to Atlantic City. Nobody was to blame. It was just one of those things. But it gave the market a terrible shock.

In June, 1917, both production and consumption picked up. It was late on the evening of June 19 that credit became inflated. The inflation was first noticed by a passer-by who, in turn, notified the police.

This much is history. What is not generally known is that the Federal Reserve Board (then known as the State Boxing Commission), in an attempt to stabilize the situation and bring chaos out of order, threw onto the market three hundred thousand (450,000) shares of U. S. Whistle with a view to breaking the deadlock. The result was an influx of gold and another panic.

Now if we can learn anything at all from this, it is that during periods of great national excitement, such as the Six-Day Bicycle Race or Presidential Election, stocks which are safe are likely to be affected in one of three ways. The readers of this department know very well what those three ways are; so it would be just stupid to re-state them. Suffice it to say that one of them begins with a "W" and the second letter is vertical.

This brings us up to the present condition of the market and an analysis of its significance. According to the tabulation of the *Commercial and Financial Chronicle* (in its special St. Valentine's Day number), bank clearings registered an increase of 18.7% over the same period a year ago. This does not take into consideration the naturally depressing effect of those factors stated above. Europe's plight has not been without its great influence either. Europe's plight is never without significance. No matter what you are figuring on doing, you must count on Europe's plight to furnish at least fifty per cent of the significance and ten per cent of the gross. That makes sixty per cent to be divided among eleven people.

Bringing the whole thing down to cold facts, it becomes obvious that the wise investor will put his money in some good, safe mortgage bonds paying a cool 3% and then take up his music again. Never neglect your music, and bring your children up to be musical.

INSIDE DOPE

If the Declaration of Independence had been Handled in Modern Fashion

By ROBERT C. BENCHLEY—*Drawings by* REA IRVIN

SOLONS IN PHILLY RAP KING IN TAX WAR

Lee, Urging Split, Flays Crown—Offers Bill to End Union

BY ROGER BRODNEY

Special Philadelphia Correspondent for Detroit Athletic Club News

(Copyright, 1776, D. A. C. NEWS and D. A. C. Feature Service)

PHILADELPHIA, June 7, 1776—Official Philadelphia was startled today by the introduction in the Continental Congress by Representative Richard Henry Lee of Virginia, of a resolution calling for the separation of the American Colonies from Great Britain.

The resolution came in the nature of a bombshell in the midst of a debate on the Germantown Creek Widening Bill, sponsored by Representative George Ross of Pennsylvania and opposed by Representative Gerry of Massachusetts. Representative Gerry had just read a poem into the record in which he made fun of the plan to widen Germantown Creek, and Representative Ross was replying to this by saying that Representative Gerry needed a shave, when Representative Lee asked permission to take the floor. The Chair, being out playing quoits in the courtyard at the time, did not object. So Representative Lee arose and read his resolution.

As there were no members of the Congress in the chamber at the time (with the exception of Representatives Ross and Gerry, who were not listening) Repre-

sentative Lee's resolution was not heard by anyone except the clerk, who recorded it.

On being informed by your correspondent of its contents, representatives located on the Brandywine golf course made the following comments:

Representative Wolcott (Conn.) Whig—Representative Lee has said only what I have been saying to the Congress for months. I am glad that he agrees with me.

Representative Nevins (New York) Tory—The whole thing is too absurd to discuss.

Representative Lilly (Conn.) Tory—Perhaps Mr. Lee has forgotten that we get all our hats from London. Sever relations with London, and what shall we do for hats? It is preposterous.

The resolution was referred to the committee on inland waterways for discussion.

* * *

PHILADELPHIA PERSONALITIES—No. 16

A Series of Intimate Side-Lights on the Unofficial Side of our Legislators

BY "SPOT"

Special Personality Writer for the D. A. C. NEWS

(Copyright, 1776, D. A. C. NEWS and D. A. C. Feature Service)

Philadelphia, June 11, 1776—Several weeks ago few people in Philadelphia knew of a quiet representative from Virginia named Richard Henry Lee. Today he has become one of the most talked-of figures in the nation's capital. For it was he who introduced the resolution last week favoring the severing of relations between the colonies and the mother government, a resolution now on the docket for discussion by the committee on inland waterways.

Mr. Lee is a man of few words but decisive action. He has a merry twinkle in his eye which belies the austerity of his manner when dealing with strangers, and I was able to get a few minutes alone with him as he sat at his desk in the Chamber making cat's cradles with a piece of string salvaged from the wastebasket.

"How does it feel to have introduced a bill recommending the severing of relations with the mother country, Mr. Lee?" I asked him, hoping by this indirect means to draw him out and find how it felt to have introduced a bill recommending the severing of relations with the mother country.

The young man who has set all Philadelphia by the ears smiled enigmatically. "How does it feel to *talk* to a man who has introduced a bill recommending severing relations with the mother country?" he asked.

And there the interview ended.

* * *

WOMAN'S WORK AND WILL

Sketches of Interest to our Women Readers

By Ruth Hornsby

(Copyright, 1776, D. A. C. News and D. A. C. Feature Service)

Philadelphia, June 30, 1776—Since the spotlight of notoriety has been turned on Representative Richard Henry Lee of Virginia, author of the resolution now before the committee on inland waterways for the independence of the American Colonies, all eyes of Philadelphia matrons have been focused on the mistress of the Lee household, Mrs. Richard Henry Lee. What manner of housewife is she? Can she cook? What does she wear? What are her hobbies? These are questions of vital interest to all of the women of the nation.

Well, Mrs. Lee is quite like many another American wife. She is devoted to her husband. In fact, it is whispered around that she was not exactly in ignorance of the wording of the resolution as it was being framed in the cozy Lee study at Chestnut and Walnut streets. Not that she wrote it exactly. The soft-

A busy day in the Continental Congress.

spoken little Southern woman would be the first to deny that. But she helped. Indeed she did.

Mrs. Lee, in addition to helping her husband frame resolutions, is an expert cook, and loves nothing so much of a morning as to fuss around in the big Dutch oven weaving corn pone for company. And such corn pone! Ships have been sunk with less, and wars won.

"Whacko" carrying "Mars' Richard" to school.

When she has finished cooking, Mrs. Lee loves to go for a frisk with "Whacko," the pet Great Dane of the Lee household. "Whacko" is fourteen years old and used to carry young "Mars' Richard" to school in his mouth when he was a puppy.

"Will your husband's resolution result in a war with England?" Mrs. Lee was asked.

"Oh, dear me, I certainly hope not," replied the brave little woman. "And anyway, it isn't out of the committee yet. It's too early to begin worrying."

So, you see, Mrs. Richard Henry Lee knows the science of government as well as the science of home-making.

* * *

LEE TOOK HUSH MONEY, AVERS NEVINS

Opponent of Break with Crown Hints at Slush Fund

Philadelphia, August 7, 1776—That Representative Lee of Virginia, sponsor of the resolution favoring a break with England, was involved in the expenditure of large sums of money during the Indian Wars was the claim of Representative Nevins before the committee on inland waterways yesterday. The committee has had the Lee resolution under consideration for three months now and yesterday's charges mark the culmination of a heated debate in opposition to the idea.

According to Representative Nevins, several hundred pounds were expended in the purchase of beads with which to buy the Mississippi River from the Indians, and Representative Lee, having part interest in a bead factory, came in for a share of the profits. An investigation was demanded by Representative Nevins, and, pending this investigation, the Lee resolution was laid on the table, to be taken up at the next session of the Congress.

* * *

TORY FILIBUSTER THREATENS LEE BREACH BILL

"No Hope to Pass," Says Sponsor

Philadelphia, November 7, 1776—The resolution to break relations with England, introduced last spring by Representative Lee of Virginia, and debated in committee for three months, has at last reached the floor of the Continental Congress, where it stands small chance of

(Continued on page 109)

INSIDE DOPE

(Continued from page 29)

passage owing to the filibuster managed by Representatives Nevins, Meeker, and Rodney, the three Tory members. When interviewed tonight at his home Mr. Lee said: "I have small hope that the resolution will be allowed to pass. I am going up to Maine snow-shoeing."

The resolution will, in all probability, be reported back to the committee on inland waterways.

* * *

FROM THE CONTINENTAL CONGRESSIONAL RECORD

Close of 1778 Session

Among the bills passed by the Congress during its 1778 session were the following:

No. 476945—A Bill to Prohibit the Use of Nail Polish.

No. 4768574—A Bill to Build Steps up to the Post Office at Danvers, Mass.

No. 4756356—A Bill to Prevent Screen Doors from Slamming.

No. 4756948—A Bill to Regulate the Expenditure of Money on Eggs.

Among the bills and resolutions put over until the 1779 session were the following:

A Bill to Widen Chestnut Street, Philadelphia.

A Resolution Recommending a Breach with Great Britain.

A Bill Prohibiting Whistling after 7 p. m.

THE BATTLE OF BABY'S LOOKS

THE Battle of Whom Baby Looks Like began as soon after the birth of the infant as members of the family could inspect it. Mother won a slight advantage in the preliminary skirmish, largely technical, it being secretly conceded by all that as yet Baby didn't look like anything.

The first overt act was an attack by Aunt Araminta on the pretense Baby had *her* nose. She was repulsed by Allies, who yielded ground at first and then counterattacked with the declaration that maybe Baby had her nose now, but there was a chance of his getting over it.

Grandfather entered the fray with a verbal volley to the effect that Baby was the living image of *him*, and any fool would grant it who looked at those lines at the corners of the little fellow's eyes. Grandfather swore he would fight it out on those lines if it took all summer, but he was routed by relatives who could talk louder.

It was the general opinion that Uncle Oscar was waging uncivilized warfare when he dug in with a claim to the child's resembling him. Uncle Oscar, you see, was liberally provided with the sinews of war. But it was decided at an armistice council that it was enough to name a kid after a rich uncle without more handicaps.

By that time, however, Baby had developed sufficiently to assure all he was going to be no beauty. So peace was declared on the unanimously accepted terms that Baby looked just like Father, and no mistake.

MUSEUM FEET

A Complaint Contracted by Over-Zealous Parents

By
ROBERT C. BENCHLEY

Drawings by
REA IRVIN

All the breaks are against the pottery.

THERE is one big danger in the approach of autumn, and that is that the cooler weather may excite us into making plans for doing things we ought to have done long ago. Those of us who are parents are likely to decide that we haven't been paying enough attention to the children, that we ought to take them out more to places of interest and instruction. More of a pal than a father, is what we feel we ought to be, and yet withal an instructor, steering them into enlightening byways and taking them on educational trips to fisheries and jute manufactures, etc.

Now this is just a manifestation of fall fever, and will die down; so don't give in to it. Let the children educate themselves. You haven't done such a swell job with yourself that you should undertake to show someone else how to do it. And above all, never take the kiddies to a natural history museum. Taking them to a natural history museum is one of the things a parent first feels coming on when the first autumn days send the blood tingling through his veins, and it's one of the last things he should do.

I, myself, in a burst of parental obligation last fall, decided to take the boys through the Smithsonian Institution in Washington. I would have picked a *bigger* place if there had been one in the country, but the Smithsonian was the biggest I could get. As a result I contracted a bad case of what is known in medical circles as "Smithsonian feet," that is, a complete paralysis of the feet from the ankles down, due to standing on first one foot and then the other in front of exhibition cases and walking miles upon miles up and down the tessellated corridors of the museum. The boys suffered no ill effects from the trip at all.

The sad thing about a trip through a museum with the children is that you start out with so much vigor and zip. On entering the main entrance lobby, you call back little Herbert who takes a running slide across the smooth floor, and tell him that he must stay close to

Daddy and that Daddy will show him everything and explain everything. And what a sap that makes of Daddy before the day is done!

In your care not to miss anything, you stop and examine carefully the very first tablet in the entrance lobby, deciding to work to the left and look at everything on the left side of the building, and then take up the right.

"Look, boys," you say, "it says here that this building was built by the Natural History Society of America in 1876——Oh, well, I guess that isn't very important." And you ask the attendant at the door which is the best way to see the museum, a foolish question at best. He tells you to begin with the Glacier Hall over there at the right. This upsets your plans a little, but what difference does it make whether you see the right or left side first?

"Come on, boys," you call to both of them, who are now sliding back and forth on the floor. "Here is the room where the glaciers are. Come on and look at the glaciers."

The boys by this time are very hot and sweaty, and probably less interested in glaciers than in anything else in the world. You, yourself, find nothing particularly thrilling about the rocks which are lined up for inspection in the room as you enter. However, it is a pretty important thing, this matter of glacial deposits and both you and the boys would be better off for knowing a little something about them.

"Look, Herbert," you say. "Look, Arthur! See here where the glacier went right over this rock and left these big marks."

But Herbert is already in the next hall, which for some mysterious reason is devoted to stuffed rats demonstrating the Malthusian Doctrine,—and Arthur has disappeared entirely.

"Where's Arthur, Herbert?" you yell.

"Look, Daddy," replies Herbert from across the hall. "Come here quick! Quick, Daddy!" There evidently is some danger that the stuffed rats are going to get away

26

"Drive quickly to 168 Elm avenue."

before you arrive, and you have to run to hush Herbert up, although you had much rather not look at stuffed rats, Malthusian Doctrine or no Malthusian Doctrine.

Arthur has, by this time, appeared several miles down the building in the Early American Indian room and screams:

"Come quick, Daddy! Look! Indians!"

So you and Herbert set off on a dog trot to the Indian room.

"You boys *must not* yell so in here," you warn. "And stop running, Arthur! We've got all day. (God forbid!)"

"Where did these Indians live, Daddy?" asks Herbert.

"Oh, around Massachusetts," you explain. "They fought the Pilgrims."

"It says here they lived in Arizona," reads Arthur. (Whoever taught that boy to read, anyway?)

"Well, Arizona, *too*," you crawl. "They lived all over."

"What are these, Daddy?"

"Those? Those are hatchet heads. They used them for heads to their hatchets."

"It says here they are flint stones that they struck fire on."

"Flint stones, eh? Well, they're funny-looking flint stones. They must have used them for hatchet heads, too. The Indians were very versatile."

"What did they use these for, Daddy?"

"If you can read so well, why don't you read what it says and not ask me so much? Where's Herbert?"

Herbert is now on the point of pushing over a little case of Etruscan bowls in an attempt to get at the figure of a Boeotian horse in the case behind it.

"Here, Herbert, don't push that like that! Do you want to break it?"

"Yes," replies Herbert, giving you a short answer.

"Well, we'll go right straight home if you are going to act that way." (Here a good idea strikes you. Why *not* go right straight home and blame it on Herbert?)

The first evidences of "Smithsonian feet" are beginning to make themselves felt. You try walking on your ankles to favor the soles of your feet, but that doesn't help. And you haven't even struck the second floor yet.

By actual count, the word "look" has been called out eighty-two times, and each time you have looked. Forty-three questions have been asked, forty of which you have answered incorrectly and thirty-four of which you have been caught answering incorrectly. It is high time that you did go home.

But the boys are just beginning. They spot another room at the end of the wing and rush to it. You trail after them, all your old fire gone. It turns out to be Glacier Hall again.

"We've been in here before," you say, hoping that this will discourage them.

"There's the door to the street over there. How about going home and coming again tomorrow?"

This suggestion is not even heard, for the boys are on their way up the big flight of stairs leading to the second floor. If you can make half the flight you will be doing well. By the time you reach the first landing, you are in a state of collapse.

"Look, Daddy!" you hear the little voices calling from above. "Come quick, Daddy! Skeletons!"

And skeletons they are, sure enough. Mastodon skeletons. Herbert, turning the corner hurriedly, comes suddenly on one and is thrown into a panic. Not a bad idea! Perhaps they might both be frightened into wanting to go home. But Nature, herself, comes to your rescue. At the end of the mastodon room Herbert comes and whispers to you.

"I don't know," you reply, hopefully. "Perhaps we had better go home."

"No," screams Herbert. "I want to stay here."

"Well, come along with me, then, and we'll see if we can find it. Come on, Arthur. Come with Herbert and Daddy."

So, on the pretext of locating the section of the building in question, you lead the boys downstairs and out the back way.

"Over here, I guess," you say. "No, I guess over there."

By this time, you are at the street and within hailing distance of a taxi. It is but the work of a minute to hit Herbert over the head until he is quiet and to yank Arthur into the cab along with you and throw him over in one corner. To make sure that neither of the boys is going to escape, you decide to sit on Herbert and hold Arthur on the floor.

"Drive quickly to 468 Elm avenue," you say to the driver.

That would be your home address.

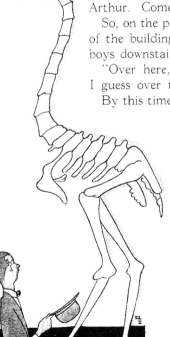

The Great Auk—or something.

27

Où est Papa?

Drawings
by
REA
IRVIN

FRENCH *for* AMERICANS
A Handy Compendium for Visitors to Paris
By ROBERT C. BENCHLEY

THE following lessons and exercises are designed for the exclusive use of Americans traveling in France. They are based on the needs and behavior of Americans, as figured from the needs and behavior of 14,000 Americans last summer. We wish to acknowledge our indebtedness to American Express Co., 11 Rue Scribe, for some of our material.

The French Language

1. *Pronunciation*

Vowels	Pronounced
a	ong
e	ong
i	ong
o	ong
u	ong

2. *Accents*

The French language has three accents, the acute *e*, the grave *e*, and the circumflex *e*, all of which are omitted.

3. *Phrases most in demand by Americans*

English	French
Haven't you got any griddle-cakes?	*N'avez-vous pas des griddle-cakes?*
What kind of a dump is this, anyhow?	*Quelle espece de dump is this, anyhow?*
Do you call that coffee?	*Appellez-vous cela coffee?*
Where can I get a copy of the N. Y. Times?	*Où est le N. Y. Times?*
What's the matter? Don't you understand English?	*What's the matter? Don't you understand English?*
Of all the godam countries I ever saw.	*De tous les pays godams que j'ai vu.*
Hey there, driver, go slow!	*Hey there, chauffeur, allez lentement!*
Where's Sister?	*Où est Sister?*
How do I get to the Louvre from here?	*Où est le Louvre?*
Two hundred francs? In your hat.	*Deux cents francs? Dans votre chapeau.*
Where's Brother?	*Où est Brother?*
I haven't seen a good-looking woman yet.	*Je n'ai pas vu une belle femme jusqu'a présent.*
Where can I get laundry done by six tonight?	*Où est le laundry?*
Here is where we used to come when I was here during the war.	*Ici est ou nous used to come quand j'etais ici pendant la guerre.*
Say, this is real beer all right!	*Say, ceci est de la bierre vrai!*
Oh boy!	*O boy!*
Two weeks from tomorrow we sail for home.	*Deux semaines from tomorrow nous sail for home.*
Then when we land I'll go straight to Childs and get a cup of coffee and a glass of ice-water.	*Sogleich wir zu hause sind, geh ich zum Childs und eine tasse kaffee und ein glass eiswasser kaufen.*

Why haven't you any pie?	*Pourquoi n'avez-vous pas la pie?*	
It's a cold day.	*Il ne fait pas chaud.*	
It's a warm day.	*Il ne fait pas froid.*	
Where is the American Bar?	*Ou est la Bar Americaine?*	
There's no kick in this booze.	*Il n'y a pas le coup de pied dans cet vin.*	
Very well.	*Tres bien.*	
Leave it in my room.	*Tres bien.*	
Good night!	*Tres bien.*	
Where did Father go to?	*Où est Papa?*	

Places in Paris for Americans to Visit

The Lobby of the Ritz

This is one of the most interesting places in Paris for the American tourist, for it is there that he meets a great many people from America. If he will stand by the potted palms in the corner he will surely find someone whom he knows before long and can enter into a conversation on how things are going at home.

The American Express Co., 11 Rue Scribe

Here again the American traveler will find surcease from the irritating French quality of most of the rest of Paris. If he comes here for his mail, he will hear the latest news of the baseball leagues, how the bathing is on the Maine Coast, what the chances are for the Big Fight in September at the Polo Grounds, and whom Nora Bayes has married in August. There will be none of this unintelligible *French* jabber with which Paris has become so infested of late years. He will hear language spoken as it should be spoken, whether he come from Massachusetts or Iowa.

Where to Eat in Paris

Hartford Lunch

There has been a Hartford Lunch opened at 115 Rue Lord Byron where the American epicure can get fried-egg sandwiches, Boston baked beans, coffee rings, and crullers almost as good as those he can get at home. The place is run by Martin Keefe, formerly of the Hartford Lunch in Fall River, Massachusetts, and is a mecca for those tourists who want good food well cooked.

United States Drug Store

At the corner of Rue Bonsard and the Boulevard de Parteuille there is an excellent American drug store where are served frosted chocolates, ice-cream sodas, Coca-Cola, and pimento cheese sandwiches. A special feature which will recall the beloved homeland to Americans is the buying of soda checks *before* ordering.

French Currency

Here is something which is likely to give the American traveler no little trouble. In view of the fluctuating value of the franc, the following table should be memorized in order to insure against mistakes:

Day of Week	American Value of Franc
Monday	5 cents
Tuesday	5.1 cents
Wednesday	4.9 cents
Thursday	1 lb. chestnuts
Friday	2½ yds. linoleum
Saturday	What-have-you

The proper procedure for Americans in making purchases is as follows:

1. Ascertain the value of the franc.
2. Make the purchase of whatever it is you want.
3. Ask "*Combien?*" (How much?)
4. Say "*Trop cher.*" (What the hell')
5. Try to understand the answer.
6. Pay the asking price and leave the shop swearing in English, American, or other mother tongue.

Side Trips From Paris

There are many fascinating trips which may be made by the American sojourning in Paris which will relieve him of the tedium of his stay.

TRIP A.—Take the train at Paris for Havre and from there go by steamer to New York. The State of Maine Express leaves New York (Grand Central Station) at 7:30 p. m. and in the morning the traveler finds himself in Portland, Maine, from which many delightful excursions may be made up and down the rock-ribbed Atlantic coast.

TRIP B.—Entrain at Paris for Cherbourg, where there are frequent sailings westward. By the payment of a slight *pourboire* (outrage) the ship's captain will

(Continued on page 152)

L'Entente Cordiale.

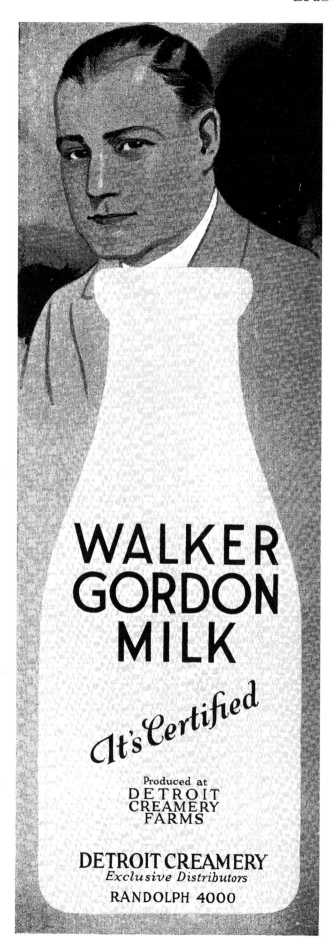

Do you call that coffee?

FRENCH FOR AMERICANS

(Continued from page 27)

put her in at the island of Nantucket, a quaint whaling center of olden times. Here you may roam among the moors and swim to your heart's content, unconscious of the fact that you are within a six-day's run of the great city of Paris.

Ordinal Numbers and their Pronunciation

Numbers		Pronounced
1st.	le premier	leh premyai
2nd.	le second	leh zeggong
3rd.	le troisieme	leh trouazzeame
4th.	le quatrieme	leh kattreame
8th.	le huitieme	leh wheeteeame

Oh, well, you won't have occasion to use these much, anyway. Never mind them.

Other Words You Will Have Little Use For

Vernisser—to varnish, glaze.
Nuque—nape (of the neck).
Egriser—to grind diamonds.
Dromer—to make one's neck stiff from working at a sewing machine.
Rossignol—nightingale, picklock.
Ganache—lower jaw of a horse.
Serin—canary bird.
Pardon—I beg your pardon.

On Arriving Back Home in America

Phrases You Will Need

When I was in Paris—.
Say, you ought to see that place I was telling you about.
Did you get my postcard?
I never want to live anywhere else but Paris.
I got so I really *think* in French.
When I was in Paris—.

A view of the Lawrence, Massachusetts, disaster of 1919.

WATER FOOTBALL
Suggestions to the Rules Committee for Making Use of Rain
By Robert C. Benchley—*Drawings by* Rea Irvin

WHATEVER it is that the football rules committee does during that week in the spring that it spends in New York (and you can't tell me that a group of healthy men can stay in a New York hotel room all the time and think of nothing but football, football, football) it certainly makes no provision for rain on the day of a big game. And anyone who has sat through four two-hour periods in a downpour will tell you that football, as it is played today, is essentially a fair-weather sport.

I had a cousin who went to the Harvard-Yale game last year and contracted gelatin-trouble, owing to the sizing in his fur coat having soaked through into his spine and gone the rounds of his entire system. He sat in a large puddle (one of the largest in the Yale Bowl, he tells me, and you know what a big place the Yale Bowl is) and along about six o'clock, on the way home in the machine, he felt a queer sort of spinal disintegration. "As if I were going to pieces," is the way he expressed it. He thought nothing of it until his arms and legs began to come off and then he went somewhere and lay down. Whatever it was that finally became of him, the point is that watching football in the rain is no darned fun and the least that the rules committee can do is to make some regulations covering a situation that so frequently exists.

For instance, when it is found that the field is going to be knee-deep in mud and water, there ought to be some way of changing the nature of the game entirely, so that the very elements which would, under the old rules, work toward a spoiling of the game, might be turned into favorable factors for all concerned.

Thus we might have a play (to be called "left half around the sandbar") in which, at the signal, the left halfback takes the ball from the quarter, tosses it into a dory, shoves off, and rows around right end. His interference, also in dories, could ward off tacklers by splashing water in their faces, use of the oars as clubs to be called illegal. To meet this play, it would be the function of the defensive backs to row through and, if possible, force the man with the ball in his boat to row onto a sandbar or else create such a wash that it upsets him.

Or, there might be an entirely different ball used during a rain storm—a large, red rubber ball such as some nuisance always has at the beach in the summer. This could be tossed back and forth, the players screaming with excitement the while, until one side or the other gets tired. With this type of ball, a very neat trick play could be utilized, the "U-56, or concealed ball play" in which the quarterback, immediately on receiving the pass, would shove the ball under the surface of the water, sit on it, and paddle himself around left end or through left tackle, if a hole could be opened up for him. The fun here would be for the defense to drown the runner.

Of course, the rain is not always sufficiently heavy to make the water deep enough for the two plays outlined above. Sometimes it merely drizzles and there is nothing but mud on the field. This would call for an entirely new list of plays. Under these conditions, the old Carlisle Indian trick could be revived, each of the backs scooping up an armful of mud and running with it, the defense being unable to tell in which armful the ball is hidden. Or, as an alternate play, the backfield could daub their faces with mud to look like a negro quartette and could start humming old plantation melodies. Then, while the defense stopped and listened, enchanted, the right end could pick up the leather and slide down the field with it.

The big spectacular play, however, for a muddy day is the "sappers' wedge" or "East Side subway." In this trick, the linemen throw up breastworks of mud in front of the line of scrimmage. When the ball is put into play, the backs burrow down into the soft ground and tunnel themselves under the line, digging out on the other side for a gain of perhaps five yards. This play can be used effectively when within five yards of the goal, as the back carrying the ball has made, *ipso facto*, a touchdown.

This outline of aquatic football has, however, not taken the spectators into account. Who ever does? But there they are, millions and millions of them, and something must be done for *them* on a rainy day.

Since there is always someone in front of you who has an umbrella up, you might as well give up any idea you may have had of watching the game. Don't torture yourself by trying to peek around the umbrella, catching sight of the beginning of a play and never knowing until you hear the cheering whether or not it succeeded. In this way lies madness. Just give up trying to spy on the field maneuvers and get your neighbors to enter into a few little games with you to pass the time away.

There is, for example, the game of "Neck Cisterns." In this game, all the people sitting in a row open out the collars of their coats in the back, sitting hunched forward so as to make the opening as big as possible. The idea is to see who can catch the most rain water down the back of the neck. Drippings from an umbrella are not allowed. The water must come directly down and into the collar. The winner is the one whose collar runs over first.

This may seem like a very simple game to play, and one dependent entirely on the capacity of the coat of the contestant. This is not so. A great deal of skill can be brought into playing it by adjusting the angle of the body to meet the angle of the rain at a point where the maximum amount of water will drive into the collar. An old hand at "Neck Cisterns" can fill his coat up to overflowing before a beginner has got even his shoulder blades wet.

Another similar game is that of "Brimming." The players in this turn the brims of their hats up so as to catch the rain water. At a given signal, the brims are suddenly turned down and the heads thrust forward, the idea being to project the deluge of water as far out as possible. The one hitting the person farthest in front wins and is the champion "brimmer" of the section. During the final period of the football game, the champion "brimmers" from each section meet and play off the finals.

Of course, one of the chief features of watching a contest in the rain is the wet seat. You hop up in your excitement at seeing the boys pull off a forward pass (which is grounded) and, by the time you have got around to sitting down again, the place which you have been keeping dry up until the forward pass is now a tiny lily

Left half around the sandbar.

pond with swan boats in it. Into this you sink back exhausted from your cheering, and in it you sit for the rest of the game while, starting from the pond as a base, a series of chills race up your spine to a spot directly behind your ears, where they break ranks.

One of the most interesting by-products of watching a football game in the rain occurred in Lawrence, Massachusetts, in 1919. It had rained all during the first three periods of the game and everyone was sitting in individual pools, giving the matter no more thought. Several hundred of them had been fighting a brave fight against the cold and damp by means of that greatest little cold and damp fighter of them all, the pocket flask, and these brothers didn't even *know* that they were sitting in water. They knew that they were sitting pretty and it didn't make any difference to them where. Suddenly, at the beginning of the fourth period, the weather changed and grew much colder. There was a great deal of time out and dull playing, and no one felt called upon to hop up for quite sime time. As a matter of fact, the game ended with the ball in mid-field and a lot of substitutes running in to get their letter. When the whistle blew, the fans started to get up to go home, but found that they were

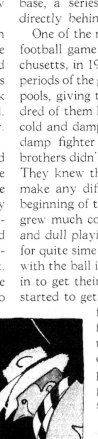
During the final period, the champion "brimmers" from each section meet and play off the finals.

frozen to the stands. The entire Lawrence fire department came with axes and worked until eleven that night chopping the people out. A couple of old grads, who had very poor seats down in the corner behind the goal posts, were overlooked and had to stay there until spring.

In order to avoid a recurrence of this unfortunate accident, and in general to keep the seats dry, it has been suggested that the rules committee make it illegal for any spectator to jump to his feet during a game. This would apply even when two rival rooters started a fist fight in the stand. Coincident with the passage of this rule, similar prohibitions might be put on a man's falling when dropped out of a window, and on the earth's rotating on its axis.

FAMOUS ILLUSTRATORS EXPOSE KRISS KRINGLE

IN response to a request from the editor, some of the well-known illustrators whose work appears regularly in the D. A. C. NEWS have drawn the kinds of Christmas greeting cards that they really wanted to draw—instead of the kinds that are more readily salable to Christmas shoppers.

On page 21, John Held, Jr., hands us something very *chic* and Parisian. On the page opposite, Russell H. Legge shows what is in danger of happening it Mr. Benchley's dire predictions are realized. The top picture on this page indicates Ralph Barton's idea of the modern child's reaction to the Santa Claus idea. Below Rea Irvin, Burt Thomas, and Herb Roth give us a refreshing change from the bromidic "art" that is characteristic of the glad Yuletide.

DAC NEWS
COPYRIGHT, 1925, DETROIT ATHLETIC CLUB

DECEMBER, 1925

The
RISE AND FALL OF THE CHRISTMAS CARD

By
ROBERT C. BENCHLEY

TWENTY-FIVE years ago (December 21, 1885, to be exact) a man named Ferderber awoke after a week's business trip and realized that he hadn't bought any Christmas presents for his relatives and friends. Furthermore, all he had left from the business trip was 80 cents, two theatre-ticket stubs, and a right shoe.

So he cut up some cardboard to fit envelopes and on each card wrote some little thought for the season. Being still a trifle groggy, he thought that it would be nice to make them rhyme although, as he expressed it, with a modest smile, "I am no poet."

The one to his aunt read as follows:

"*Just a little thought of cheer,*
A Merry Christmas and a Happy New Year."

He liked this one so well that he just copied it on all the others. Then he got excited about the thing and drew a sprig of holly on each card. He mailed them on Christmas Eve and discovered that he still had 28 cents left.

This man Ferderber is now wanted in 32 states on the same charge: Starting the Christmas Card Menace. His idea immediately took hold of the public imagination and the next Christmas all his friends and relatives sent cards to their friends and relatives, for, taking the old lie that "it isn't so much the gift as the spirit i.w.i.i.g." at its face value, they felt

A Christmas card from the French.

that people would be much better pleased with a friendly greeting than with a nasty old gift. And, for a while, the custom really was quite a relief.

Then the thing began to get out of hand. Big Christmas card manufacturing concerns sprang up all over the country and factory sites adjacent to freight sidings were at a premium. Millions and millions of cards were printed and millions and millions of people began sending them to each other. Along about December 15, the blight began and, like locusts, the envelopes started drifting in from the mail. Seventy-five thousand extra mail carriers were drafted into service and finally the Government was forced to commandeer all males under 25 who did not have flat feet. Even at that, all the Christmas cards couldn't be delivered until the first of the year, and by that time the flood of New Year's cards had begun, for everyone who received Christmas cards from people to whom they had sent none rushed out and bought New Year's cards to send them the next week just as if that was what they had intended to do all along.

It became impossible to read all these cards, and finally even to open them. Great stacks of unopened envelopes covered desks and hall tables throughout the country. Some of the wealthier citizens had chutes built on the outside of their houses into which the postmen dumped the cards and by means of which they were conveyed direct to the furnace. The poorer people, unable to convert their mail matter into fuel in this manner, unable sometimes to clear away a path from their front door to the street, often starved to death before their provisions could be got to them. The winter of 1927 was known as the Winter of the Red Death, for all over the country families were snowed in with envelopes and perished before help could be brought to them. In some towns fires were accidentally started with results too horrible to relate.

Unearth Valuable Scientific Data

Excavators who have recently been at work in the Middle West digging through mounds of petrified envelopes have furnished valuable data on the nature of these *objets d'art*. The most popular design seems to have been that involving a fireplace with stockings hanging from it, with the slogan, evidently satirical, "A Merry Christmas and a Happy New Year." Candles were also highly considered as decoration; candles and bells. When human figures were introduced, they were of the most unpleasant types: short, fat, bearded men dressed in red, offensively gay little children in pajamas carrying lighted candles, stagecoaches filled with steaming travelers, sleigh rides and coasting parties, and street musicians annoying householders with Christmas carols. The text was usually in Old English type, so that fortunately it was difficult, if not impossible, to read.

Evidently the tide began to turn when some one, perhaps a descendant of the very Ferderber who had brought all this distress on the land, thought of the idea of venting his personal spleen in his Christmas cards. He thought that, since no one read them anyway, he might as well say what he really felt, so long as he said it in Old English type. It would be a satisfaction to him, anyway. So near the top of these mounds of Early Twentieth Century cards we find some on this order:

A picture of a holly wreath with a large hammer stuck through it and the following legend:

"*Just to Wish You the Measles.
Christmas 1931.*"

Another showed a little cottage on the brow of a snow-covered hill with the sun setting behind it. On the cottage was a sign: "For Sale." The sentiment underneath was:

"*Peace on Earth, Good Will Toward Men;
So's Your Old Man.*"

A New Year's card, with "Greetings" embossed at the top, read:

"*If I don't see you in 1933
1934 will be soon enough for me.*"

As soon as this fad caught on, the pendulum swung the other way. The sentiments, beginning with the mildly abusive, gradually became actually vicious.
We find one, dated 1938, which says:

"*This Christmas Eve I want you to know,
That if you don't leave $50,000 in Box 115 before
New Year's, I'll sell your letters, you crook, you.*"

Another, in a wreath of mistletoe bore the following explicit legend:

"*Watch Your Wife.*"

It was naturally but a step from these to downright obscene vituperation, and at this point, the reform societies stepped in. A campaign was carried on throughout the country, which, unlike other reform campaigns, had the backing of a majority of the public. It was but the work of a year or so to induce the necessary two-thirds of the state legislatures to consent to an amendment to the constitution forbidding the manufacture and sale of Christmas cards. Naturally this was followed by a period of widespread bootlegging but it was half-heartedly supported and soon collapsed.

All of which is merely a historical summary of what has been done in the past, preliminary to launching a campaign against the sale and manufacture of all Christmas presents, with the exception of toys. What our fathers did, we can do.

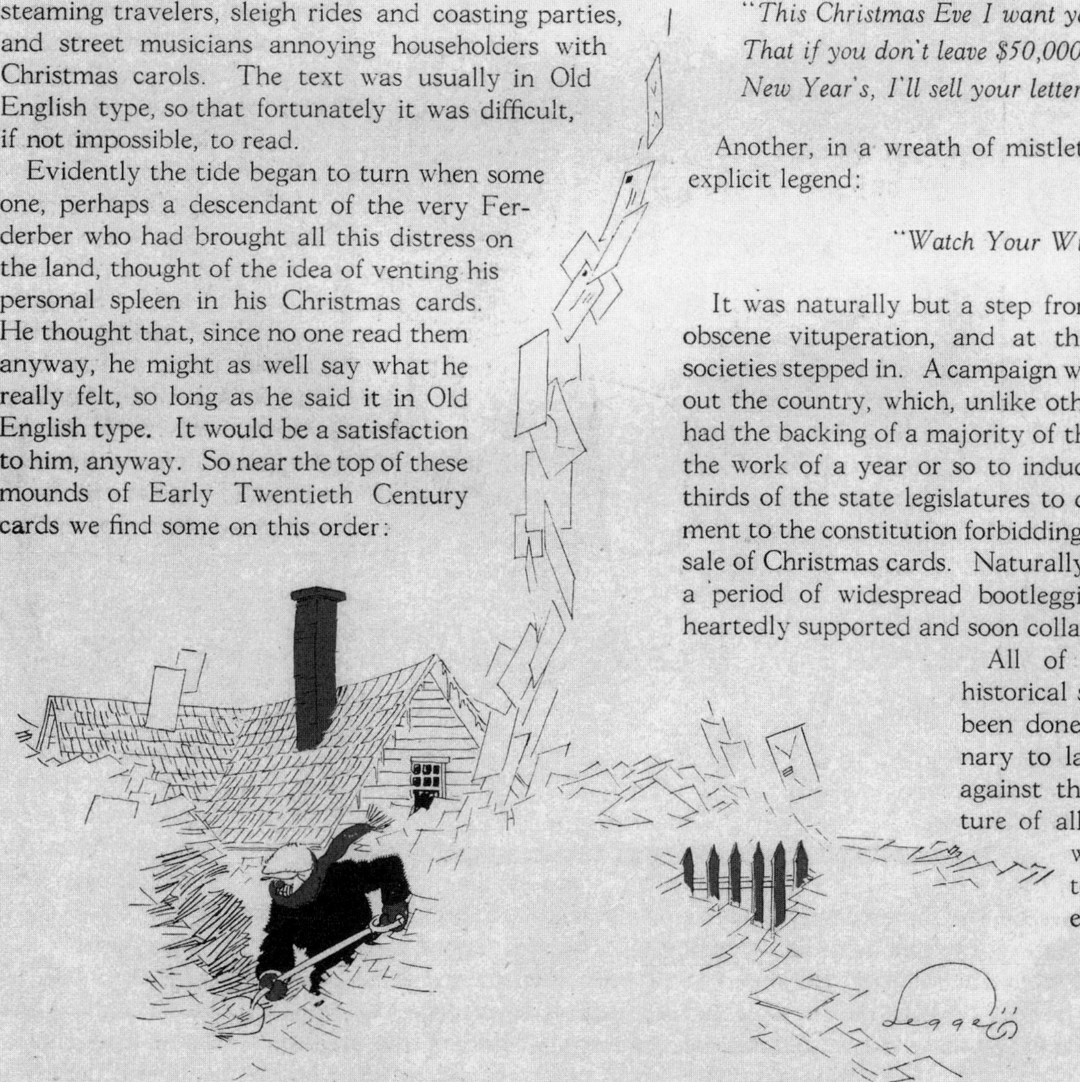

Along about 9 o'clock, things
begin to rough up.

TIME-OFF FROM THE SHOW
New York Sights Which the Visitor Should Not Miss
By ROBERT C. BENCHLEY

YOU can't expect the visitor to New York during the automobile show to stand in front of automobiles all day and all night. He's got to look at something else *once* in a while, just so that he can see the automobiles better when he goes back to look at them. That's only common sense

Now comes the big question—what to look at? New York is a big city now, and unless you are careful you will look at the wrong things and before you know it, it will be time to go back and you will have seen nothing. Or practically nothing. Or next to nothing.

Let us say (Oh, go on! Be a good sport! *Let* us!), let us say that you are to be in New York four days and six nights. Here is a schedule which you may follow or not, but, at any rate, look it over. It suggests something for you to do every evening and, in case you have any spare time during the day, there are one or two extra hints.

Monday Evening

Of course, the very first night that you have free you will want to see the new Reinach collection of tapestries at the Metropolitan Art Museum. This collection is one of the most valuable in the world, and one of the hardest to hide under. The tapestries hang some four feet off the ground, so the minute you try to hide under one of them you are quite exposed up to at least your chest, maybe oftener than that

Most of the tapestries in the exhibit are French, and consequently are kept in a little room off the main hall, to which admission is obtained only by conference with the curator. Of the others, the most interesting is that which depicts the hunting of a stag in the Middle Ages.

In the lower left-hand corner you see the huntsmen starting out after the stag, carrying hauberks and falcons. As you work up through the tapestry, from left to right, it gets even less interesting, until, by the time they have caught the stag in the upper right-hand corner, you aren't looking at it at all and have passed on to the next tapestry which shows huntsmen of the Middle Ages chasing a fox.

It has just occurred to us that the Art Museum is not open evenings; so this plan for Monday night is out. You will have to find something else to do. There is a good place on West 56th street

Tuesday Evening

The Public Library, at 42nd street and Fifth Avenue, is open until 11 o'clock. You will surely want to see this. Enter by the side door on the 42nd street side, as there are two of the nastiest lions you ever saw guarding the front entrance. Ring the little bell by the side entrance and when the man comes ask for Joe Delaney. He will ask who wants to see him and you say that Bob Benchley sent you. He will then let you in to the downstairs lobby, where there is an elevator to take you up to the reading room. This elevator is not running; so you will have to walk up three flights of marble stairs, and a pretty tough pull it is, too.

You will find the reading room brilliantly lighted and practically full of books. Go straight to the case marked "Biography M-TO." Beginning at the top shelf, left-hand corner, pull all the books out, from left to right, and throw them in a pile on the floor Pretty soon you will have quite a big pile and can begin on the case marked "History-Renaissance." This will make another

If your feet drag, you can tuck them in under the saddle or else let them drag.

big pile. By this time, you will have several attendants helping you and you can work faster. If you stick to it until 11 o'clock you will be able to pull out all the books on that side of the room and scuffle through them. Then you can go back to your hotel, tired but happy.

Wednesday Evening

By this time, you will be perhaps ready to see a little of the so-called "night life" of the metropolis. There is no better place to do this than at the Woman's Exchange, on Madison avenue between 54th and 55th streets. The specialty here is breads and cakes, and if you can get a table by the window you can eat your fill while watching the Madison avenue trolley cars go thundering by. It would be well to wear your old clothes to this place, as along about 9 o'clock in the evening things begin to rough up quite a bit, and, by the time the fresh batch of cup cakes is ready at 10, the joint is a regular bedlam. It was here that Harry Thaw had been dining the night he shot Stanford White.

Thursday Evening

We have saved until your last night in New York the big thrill of the week—riding on the Shetland ponies in Central Park. They usually put the ponies to bed at sundown, but by slipping the pony-man a dollar bill you can get him to leave as many of the little fellows out as you may require.

Get to the park at about 8 p. m., wearing red coat and riding breeches. You might as well take along a good, big whip, too, in case your pony gets fresh. Carrying children about all day as they do, they are quite apt to think that they can do anything they like, and you must be ready to show them that they can't. They will respect you all the more after a couple of good belts.

Once aboard the ponies, the best course is around the reservoir. Five times around at a brisk canter makes a nice ride. In case your feet drag on the ground (the ponies are pretty small) you can tuck them in under the

saddle or else let them drag. For steeplechase racing it will be better to let them drag, as it makes it harder for the little animals to get over the hurdles. If you have lots of money to spend on the thing, you can give a hunt breakfast at the Central Park Casino.

Alternate Entertainment

Although you may have seen something of the automobile at the show you will get a better idea of what the automobile really means to our civilization by coming with me to a little private exhibition which I will be glad to stage any afternoon between the hours of 4 and 6:30. I wish that every automobile manufacturer and salesman could join in, because I want them to see just what it is that they have done. If I had my way, I would get them all reservations on a train leaving the Pennsylvania station at 5:30 p. m. Then, at 4:45, I would start them from 44th street in taxicabs or private cars and say "Now, you big automobile men, you have got 45 minutes to go half a mile in. And there isn't another train until tomorrow morning."

I would follow behind on foot, and when they were held up by the jam of automobiles at 42nd street for five minutes, I would jeer. When they were held up at 40th street, I would hoot. During their five-minute holdup at 39th street, I would taunt them with: "What price automobiles, now?" and while they were chafing at the tieup at 38th street, I would call out: "Get a horse!" I would make them so sore at the automobile as an institution they they would swear never to make another

Beginning at the top shelf, left-hand corner, pull all the books out

.... no drinks should be served to that table until it has been definitely ascertained that the men are "all right."

HOW TO START A SUPPER CLUB

By ROBERT C. BENCHLEY
Drawings by REA IRVIN

YOU think that the housing problem in New York is pretty critical, don't you? Well, that just shows how much you know about it. The problem isn't how to take care of all the people who live in New York; it's how to take care of all the people who dance there. Night clubs are springing up like mushrooms (not exactly like mushrooms but near enough) and still there is a shortage. A lot of people have to go home every night without dancing. And you know what that leads to.

A man can't turn his back on a block between Fiftieth and Fifty-ninth streets without three new supper clubs appearing before he looks back again. I left my house in Fifty-fifth street one Wednesday morning (it was the Wednesday morning I left my house in Fifty-fifth street) and after a hard day at the office returned Friday night to find that four stables on our block (I am a horse writing this; "Black Beauty") had been transformed into "La Vache Noire," "Sally Sobel's Cellar," "The Old Oaken Bucket," and "Club O'Hara." It has got so that you can't leave your ice box out on the back porch without someone coming along and turning it into a night club.

The process of transforming a stable or an ice box or a fair-sized umbrella closet into a supper club is pretty simple, once you get the hang of it.

First comes the coat room. This has to be the first feature on the way in, in order to be the last one on the way out, so that the coat room girl can get that last 50-cent piece that the patron has been holding out for taxi fare. You wouldn't believe the number of cheap

skates that try to sneak out with 50 cents or a dollar hidden away in their clothes. It kind of makes you lose your faith in human nature.

From the coat room you arrange a hidden step so that the guest stumbles down into what used to be the place where they kept the mops and brooms and into the arms of the head waiter. This gives the head waiter the chance to accuse the patron of being drunk and refuse him admission.

The choice of a head waiter is very important. Go down to the wharves when a fruit steamer is docking and pick out a stevedore who is less polite than his fellows. Take him uptown and teach him how to put studs into a dress shirt and station him at the entrance to your club. Tell him that he has just been unanimously chosen governor of the State of New York and that it is up to him to maintain the prestige of the office. Also tell him that any patron is a bum until he proves himself otherwise. Show him what you mean by proof and then put it back into the cash drawer.

The interior of your club need cause you no worry—or expense. Hang some old awnings from the ceiling—good and low so as to shut off the air—and paint the walls red and yellow, with perhaps a figure or two in Russian costume, if you can draw—or even if you can't. In the center of the room build a dance floor just big enough for a medium-sized man to lie down on and roll over three times. Not that any medium-sized man is going to do it, but those are the standard measurements for night club dance floors. Fill the rest of the room

Pick out a stevedore who is less polite than his fellows and station him at the entrance to your club.

with small tables which wabble, erect a platform for your jazz band, and you are set.

Now comes your big problem—the entertainment. There was a time when the patrons were satisfied to mill around on the dance floor and bump each other's hips. Then some foolish proprietor started in giving them a little show in between dances and they got spoiled. Now they all want a show for their money. This injustice to proprietors is somewhat mitigated by the fact that the patrons don't care what kind of show it is, so long as they don't have to dance.

There has to be some sort of master of ceremonies, and the proprietor can save a salary right there by doing this himself. All that he has to do is wear a dinner coat and act as if he believes that he has a good line.

"Ladies and gentlemen—and Gentiles. I have the very great honor to present to you to-night two of America's foremost ballroom dancers, two very charming and very talented young people who are filling an engagement at this club before beginning in the new Ziegfeld 'Follies.' They come fresh from a very successful season on the Riviera and I am sure that you will find them very very delightful. So's your old man! . . . Come on, now, give these charming young people a good hand! . . . (Lead the applause) Delacroix and Feeney, ladies and gentlemen!"

For Delacroix and Feeney it will be necessary to procure a young man and a young woman named Hyman and Gatz, respectively, who can waltz holding each other at arms' length. The young man must look at the young lady while they are waltzing and smile as if he really liked her, and the young lady must smile modestly back at him, just as if she were not thinking: "You big bum, I hope you trip and fall and break your shirt front." At the end of the waltz she curtsies so low that she has a good chance of not getting up again—which would be small loss. The master of ceremonies should then lead the applause again, what there is.

It will be necessary then to offer the good, kind patrons a little singing to keep them from dancing some more. What they want in the line of singing is to hear some new songs that they can go home and pick out on the organ. Consequently the ones to give them are "Always," "Yes, Sir, That's My Baby," and "A Cottage Small by a Waterfall," all of which everyone present knows by heart.

The entertainment over, you can turn the patrons lose again, with instructions to the orchestra to play so long that the dancers will fall exhausted by their tables and have to order refreshments. For food a 40-cent chop suey can be served for two dollars and a half and a 10-cent lemonade for a dollar. This will help you to clear expenses and maybe make a little profit.

Now in the matter of dispensing alcoholic drinks a great deal of caution must be used. It is, as many of you know, against the law to sell liquor, a fact which complicates its sale and makes for considerable inconvenience. The authorities are more and more on the alert and consequently the risk of getting caught remains about the same. A night club proprietor cannot be too careful to whom he sells strong drinks. For instance, if a man in the uniform of chief of police, with gold braid and a sword, comes in with a friend who has a flag in his hand on which is written "U. S. Revenue Service," no drinks should be served to that table until it has been definitely ascertained that the men are "all right." As for regular patrons, always wait until they ask for liquor before serving it, as a lot of people have their own with them and don't like to be bothered by representatives of the house standing at their elbows every minute trying to get them to buy. The chief thing to find out about a man before you sell him any illicit beverage is whether or not he has got $12. Once this is made sure, the thing is not so foolhardy.

With these few suggestions to those of you who might be in a position to start a night club, it is to be hoped that more and more citizens will lend a hand to help solve New York's big problem.

You wouldn't believe the number of cheap skates that try to sneak out with 50 cents or a dollar hidden away in their clothes.

However, they think they
are having a good time.

A TALK TO YOUNG MEN

Graduation Address on
"The Decline of Sex"
By ROBERT C. BENCHLEY
Drawings by REA IRVIN

TO YOU young men who only last month were graduated from our various institutions of learning
(laughter), I would bring a message, a message of warning and yet, at the same time, a message of good cheer.
Having been out in the world a whole month, it is high
time that you learned something about the Facts of Life,
something about how wonderfully Nature takes care of
the thousand and one things which go to make up what
some people jokingly call our "sex" life. I hardly know
how to begin. Perhaps "Dear Harry" would be as good
a way as any.

You all have doubtless seen, during your walks in the
country, how the butterflies and bees carry pollen from
one flower to another? It is very dull and you should
be very glad that you are not a bee or a butterfly, for
where the fun comes in *that* I can't see. However, they
think that they are having a good time, which is all that
is necessary, I suppose. Some day a bee is going to get
hold of a real book on the subject, and from then on there
will be mighty little pollen toting
done or I don't know my bees.

Well, anyway, if you have noticed
carefully how the bees carry pollen
from one flower to another (and there
is no reason why you should have
noticed carefully as there is nothing to
see), you will have wondered what
connection there is between this
process and that of animal reproduction. I may as well tell you right now
that there is no connection at all, and
so your whole morning of bee-stalking
has been wasted.

We now come to the animal world.
Or rather, first we come to One
Hundred and Twenty-fifth street, but
you don't get off there. The animal

world is next, and off you get. And what a sight meets
your eyes! My, my! It just seems as if the whole world
were topsy-turvy.

The next time you are at your grocer's buying gin,
take a look at his eggs. They really are some hen's eggs,
but they belong to the grocer now, as he has bought them
and is entitled to sell them. So they really *are* his eggs,
funny as it may sound to anyone who doesn't know.
If you will look at these eggs, you will see that each one
is *almost* round, but not *quite*. They are more of an
"egg-shape." This may strike you as odd at first, until
you learn that this is Nature's way of distinguishing
eggs from large golf balls. You see, Mother Nature
takes no chances. She used to, but she learned her
lesson. And that is a lesson that all of you must learn
as well. It is called Old Mother Nature's Lesson, and
begins on page 145.

Now, these eggs have not always been like this. That
stands to reason. They once had something to do with
a hen or they wouldn't be called hen's
eggs. If they are called duck's eggs,
that means that they had something
to do with a duck. Who can tell me
what it means if they are called
"ostrich's eggs?" . . . That's right.

But the egg is not the only thing
that had something to do with a hen.
Who knows what else there was? . . .
That's right.

Now the rooster is an entirely
different sort of bird from the hen. It
is very proud and has a red crest on
the top of his head. This red crest is
put there by Nature so that the hen
can see the rooster coming in a crowd
and can hop into a taxi or make a
previous engagement if she wants to.

A woman with a past.

A favorite dodge of a lot of hens when they see the red crest of the rooster making in their direction across the barnyard is to work up a sick headache. One of the happiest and most contented roosters I ever saw was one who had had his red crest chewed off in a fight with a dog. He also wore sneakers.

. But before we take up this phase of the question (for it is a question), let us go back to the fish kingdom. Fish are probably the worst example that you can find; in the first place, because they work under water, and in the second, because they don't know anything. You won't find one fish in a million that has enough sense to come in when it rains. They are just stupid, that's all, and nowhere is their stupidity more evident than in their sex life.

Take, for example, the carp. The carp is one of the least promising of all the fish. He has practically no forehead and brings nothing at all to a conversation. Now the mother carp is swimming around some fine spring day when suddenly she decides that it would be nice to have some children. So she makes out a deposit slip and deposits a couple of million eggs on a rock (all this goes on *under* water, mind you, of all places). This done, she adjusts her hat, powders her nose, and swims away, a woman with a past.

He also wore sneakers.

It is not until all this is over and done with that papa enters the picture, and then only in an official capacity. Papa's job is very casual. He swims over the couple of million eggs and takes a chance that by sheer force of personality he can induce half a dozen of them to hatch out. The remainder either go to waste or are blacked up to represent caviar.

So you will see that the sex life of a fish is nothing much to brag about. It never would present a problem in a fish community as it does in ours. No committees ever have to be formed to regulate it, and about the only way in which a fish can go wrong is through drink or stealing. This makes a fish's life highly unattractive, you will agree, for, after a time, one would get very tired of drinking and stealing.

We have now covered the various agencies of Nature for populating the earth with the lesser forms of life. We have purposely omitted any reference to the reproduction of those unicellular organisms which reproduce by dividing themselves up into two, four, eight, etc., parts without any outside assistance at all. This method is too silly even to discuss.

We now come to colors. You all know that if you mix yellow with blue you get green. You also get green if you mix cherries . milk. (Just kidding. Don't pay

any attention.) The derivation of one color from the mixture of two other colors is not generally considered a sexual phenomenon, but that is because the psychoanalysts haven't got around to it yet. By next season it won't be safe to admit that you like to paint, or you will be giving yourself away as an inhibited old uncle-lover and debauchee. The only thing that the sex-psychologists can't read a sexual significance into is trap-shooting, and they are working on that now.

All of which brings us to the point of wondering if it *all* isn't a gigantic hoax. If the specialists fall down on trap-shooting, they are going to begin to doubt the whole structure which they have erected, and before long there is going to be a reaction which will take the form of an absolute negation of sex. An Austrian scientist has already come out with the announcement that there is no such thing as a hundred per cent male or a hundred per cent female. This confirms the lay opinion, formed by observing women with brakemen's haircuts and men wearing tidies around their straw hats. It may result in the disappearance of the expression "One hundred per cent he-man," which in itself will be enough of a boon for July and the first part of August. This Austrian's announcement is really a big step forward. It is going to throw a lot of people out of work, but think of the money that will be saved!

And so, young men, my message to you is this: Think the thing over very carefully and examine the evidence with fair-minded detachment. And if you decide that, within the next ten years, sex is going out of style, make your plans accordingly. Why not be pioneers in the new movement?

ANOTHER BENCHLEY GEM

STORM Warnings for New York" is the title of one of the most amusing stories that Robert C. Benchley ever has written for the D. A. C. NEWS. It is scheduled for our August number and we do not hesitate to predict that our readers will get a genuine kick out of it.

The theme is that New York is getting so naughty that law-abiding and decorous citizens are already preparing their alibis against the Day of Judgment, so that they will not be blamed for the Sodom and Gomorrah goings-on of the night-club set. Mr. Benchley himself says that he is viewing the situation with such alarm that when he leaves his suburban home for the city he makes sure that a statement signed by his pastor absolving him from all blame for Gotham's wickedness is in his pocket.

There will be a parade showing how parsnips are cooked in all the different countries of the world.

STORM WARNINGS FOR NEW YORK

By
ROBERT C. BENCHLEY

Drawings by
REA IRVIN

ANYONE wishing to see New York summer shows, or any other New York shows for that matter, had better run like everything. Any day now the walls of the city are going to topple in, and, with a blare of trumpets, the Forces of the Lord are going to smite New York, even as Sodom and Gomorrah were smitten. New York is riding for its Big Fall, and it wouldn't be surprising if it came around the end of this week.

Probably never before in the history of disrobing (see Taine's "A Short History of Unhooking and Unbuttoning," Harpers', 1897, 1 vol., 345-pp. octavo) have so many young ladies appeared with so few clothes before so many people at once. It is recorded that in ancient Rome the *puellæ* wore fewer clothes at the annual outings, but their audiences were comparatively small and selected from a list of socially possible people. Today, in the Borough of Manhattan, the young folks appear before a Winter Garden full of practical strangers— that is, they are strangers at the beginning of the show. By the end of the first act, it is as if they had known them all their lives. Just as no man is a stranger (or a hero) to his Swedish rubber, so, by the price of a ticket to "The Great Temptations" you can have at least twenty people in New York whom you know awfully, awfully well. And yet they say that New York is cold and aloof!

All this levity on my part is just whistling past the graveyard. I, personally, am pretty worried. You can push the Forces of Vengeance just so far and then— buckety-buckety—down comes the ceiling. Ask the Sodom Chamber of Commerce. And the worst of it is, that just as the rain sheds its benefits on the just and the unjust alike, the fact that you have been home and in bed every night at ten o'clock isn't going to help you a bit when your whole city begins to smell as if something was burning and then suddenly goes up in a puff of brimstone. You can't go out and argue with a Pillar of Fire and explain that you, personally, have been spending your evenings building bookcases. If your town goes, you go too, and no back-talk.

Now, in my case, the prospects are even more depressing, because the job from which I eke out barely enough money to buy gin for my children makes it necessary that I attend the opening performances of all these wrath-provoking shows. I don't like them. I would never go to see them if it were not for the fact that it is my life-work. Often I sit through them with my eyes shut. But I *am* unquestionably on record in the office of the Snooping Angel as sitting in D-113 at the Winter Garden. And when they are making out their lists for culprits to be hit on the head by falling walls or swirled up into the skies on a fiery horse with nine heads, my name probably is right there among the "B's" as a constant and incorrigible attendant at these festivals of sin. The angel probably doesn't do more than take a look over the audience. You can't expect him to go to the box-office and see who paid to get in or find out why they are there.

If I get through this summer all right, I am going to hire an assistant. Then, whenever a Shubert show is announced or something called "A Nuit in Paree," I will slip him the seats and say: "Here, Joe, go and enjoy yourself." In this way I may be able to escape the extra-heavy punishment in store for participants and get out of the general cataclysm with perhaps just a broken ankle or singed eyelashes. It is going to be bad enough for the simple bystanders without getting mixed up in the private showing. The only break that I have ever had in this line was that I was in France at the time of Earl Carro'l's champagne-bath party in New York. When I got back I found my invitation on my desk. If I *had* been there, covering the affair for my paper, they would have taken flashlight photographs.

And, after all, what fun is there in going to these displays? "The Great Temptations," for example, probably contains fewer real temptations than a Christian Endeavor convention. The thing is too unreal ever to constitute an actual menace. You hear somebody announcing that, if the audience will remain seated, there will now be a parade showing the way parsnips are cooked in all the different countries of the world. Then eight girls walk across the stage, one representing Nell Gynne cooking parsnips, one Cleopatra, one Thais, and so forth. It is very dull indeed, and the fact that the girls are clad as if they were just getting ready to turn on

Why, you will probably get a mill'on years extra in the biscuit oven just for saying such a thing.

the hot water doesn't help, or hurt, anything. The whole thing is highly academic, and unless you are interested in the cooking of parsnips, you are going to find yourself looking at your program to see how long it will take to empty the theatre with every seat filled. If the Forces of Judgment only knew it, the display of what the advertisements call "feminine pulchritude" is one of the most innocuous of all forms of theatrical entertainment. It is like looking in at a delicatessen window. It is too much.

However, try to tell that to the Watch and Ward Society. Try to convince that great, big, old Nine-Headed Horse, when he comes snorting down out of a cloud of fire with a flaming subpena made out in your name, that these exhibitions bore you. Just say to him, if you can make your voice heard above the thunder and lightning and bellowing rocks, that a show where a nine-tenths naked lady walks across the stage means no more to you than watching the Stamford local go through New Rochelle, and listen to him laugh. Why, you will probably get a million years extra in the biscuit oven just for saying such a thing.

You see, he has heard that line a good many times and he is getting a little tired of it, just as you would, yourself, after the first few million years. He knows that nobody ever will admit that he goes where he shouldn't because he likes it. Every single time it is a case of being on duty, as you might say; making an investigation for some reform agency, or getting material for a book, or showing an out-of-town customer a good time. Even

the out-of-town customer has the alibi that he is just trying to find out whether things are really as bad in New York as the papers have been saying they are. He would much rather have spent the evening writing a report to the firm about conditions in the textile industry but he didn't think that he could afford to miss an opportunity to get some first-hand information about the decadence of the present age.

So the only thing that there is left to do, if we are going to save ourselves and the biggest city in the country from a horrible fate, is to stop the Messrs. Shubert from putting on shows like that. And the way to stop them from putting on shows like that is to go to them and say: "Messrs. Shubert, put down that mending for just a minute, I want to talk to you. I am a married man with a family and I have a lot of work that I have to do before I die. I have insurance to pay up and I have a house which has to be painted before it can be sold. Now, you and your shows are leading this whole city into inevitable destruction at the hands of the Forces of Vengeance. No city can go on as New York is going on, giving pageants about the twelve different ways of cooking parsnips, without incurring Divine Wrath to a fatal extent. Won't you, for the sake of the wife and kiddies, put, let us say, a girdle of large hydrangeas on your choruses and perhaps an old-fashioned shawl? Won't you arrange it so that it won't be quite so incriminating for a man who wants to go straight to be numbered among the patrons of your entertainments?"

And if the Messrs. Shubert just laugh and go on with their mending or whatever it is that they happen to be doing at the time, the only thing left for me to do, at any rate, is to do my duty without flinching—accept my complimentary tickets, and go to these shows wearing a tin helmet and carrying a letter from my pastor in my pocket against the Day of Judgment.

Often I sit through them with my eyes shut.

THE NEW VILLAINY

By
ROBERT C. BENCHLEY

Drawings by
REA IRVIN

There was a time when the entrance of the preachers
on the stage was the signal for a sigh of relief.

ALTHOUGH the new fall season in the drama is only just under way, it is not too early to view with alarm. Some Viewers-with-Alarm begin as early as September to view, but that doesn't give you much time to collect data. Perhaps all that you can get is a *datum*, but a good, healthy datum is enough to base a sizable alarm-view on, and, as you go along, you can make up a datum or two, so that you can refer to the whole as data.

This month we are chiefly worried about the status (or stata) of what used to be known as "the old-time religion." That is, its status in the world of drama. If the new season keeps on as the past two seasons have gone, being under suspicion of harboring religious thoughts will place one in the psychopathic class. For two years now, eight out of ten villains have been preachers and any layman with excessive religious tendencies has turned out to be just a repressed old sex-addict.

There was a time when the entrance of the preachers on the stage was the signal for a sigh of relief to go up, for you knew that so long as he stuck around, things were pretty sure to go as they should. The lowest he ever reached in the dramatic scale was when he was occasionally used for comedy purposes. Once in a while there was a comic bishop, but that was only natural. And any member of the cast who showed signs of quoting the Scriptures, or going to church, was pretty certain to be one of those whom you could trust to help foil the adventuress in the last act.

Then along about the time that "Rain" settled down for a run, we began to find preachers sneaking into plays whose minds were not on their work in the vineyard. Under the guise of evangelism they started in to cut up. At first we thought: "Oh, well, this is just an exception. Our Dr. Murnie at home wouldn't do anything like this." But gradually, after we had seen dozens and dozens of preachers come on in the first act, make a few sanctimonious remarks, and then sprout little horns and a goat's tail, we began to look askance at even Dr. Murnie of the Second Congregational Church.

Then the lay members of the congregation came in for analysis. The hand of Freud reached out and touched the brethren and sistren and we learned that whenever anyone is excessively religious, it is a sign that they are suffering from an inhibition which is likely some day to break loose and leave Broadway strewn with bits of broken bottles and confetti. The more

Then the lay members
of the congregation came
in for analysis.

religious they are, the more they crave a good, rip-snorting week-end at Atlantic City, registering under the wrong name. It is all very confusing.

In the old days, the minute a man came on with a mustache like Adolphe Menjou's and wearing a pair of riding boots with a crop to slap them with, you could be pretty sure that he was up to no good. If you were highly strung you whispered out loud to the heroine not to go to the city with him as he had no more intention of marrying her than—well, than anything at all, and you know how little that is.

Today, whenever a character in clerical cloth makes his entrance, the orchestra starts picking at the violin strings in the old *pizzicato* villain-entrance music, the young-lady members of the cast pick their exits and the audience settles back in preparation for the dirty work.

Pretty soon, we may have a scene like this:

Scene: Living room of the DeViblis home. Father, mother, and daughter are seated around the table, splicing rope.

DAUGHTER: Pa, there's somethin' I been a-wantin' to ask you fer a long time.

MOTHER: For heaven's sake, daughter, talk straight. This isn't a New England farm play we're in. You know how to talk better than that.

DAUGHTER: Well, anyway, I want to marry Arthur Arthritis.

FATHER: What does he do for a living?

DAUGHTER: Well, he's changing his job in a few months.

FATHER: What does he do now?

DAUGHTER: Why—er—well, I'll tell you; just now he's a preacher, but he's going to change——

MOTHER: A preacher! Oh, my!

FATHER: A minister of the gospel? Where did you meet him? I thought I told you not to run around with them religious folks. They are every one of them inhibited.

DAUGHTER: Oh, that's just because you don't know them, dad. They're just as decent as you or I when you get to know them. And Arthur isn't *really* a preacher. He's just filling-in.

FATHER: Just filling-in, eh? I suppose you know what that leads to? Next he'll be having a little parish of his own, then he'll get a call to a big city, or perhaps he'll even sink so low as to be a missionary. Them preachers are all missionaries at heart, and you know what missionaries are. No, sir, no daughter of mine gets mixed up in that crowd.

DAUGHTER: Well, he's coming here in a few minutes to hear your answer. There he is now!

(*Enter the Rev. Heemerson*).

The stage folk have found a comeback and are using it.

FATHER: Well, what do you want here?

THE REV. H.: Why, Brother——

FATHER: Don't you "brother" me.

THE REV. H.: I love your daughter and I want to marry her.

FATHER: You want to *marry* her, eh? When you get to New York, I suppose?

THE REV. H.: Why, I thought——

FATHER (*stepping to the telephone*): Oh, you thought, did you? (*To central*): Give me police headquarters . . . . hello, police headquarters? Well, there's a preacher in my house. Send an officer up right away!

THE REV. H. (*leaving*): I'm sorry, sir, that you feel this way, so I think I'll be saying "good-bye."

FATHER: Good-bye, and go back to your religious crowd and their loose ways and never darken my door again.

(*Curtain with daughter crying, and father and mother getting down the family volume of Freud to read by the lamplight.*)

* * *

All this is perhaps the result of years and years of bullyragging the stage and stage folk by preachers and religious zealots. The stage folk have found a comeback and are using it. It will be nip and tuck for awhile, with the stage folk slightly in the lead until it is discovered that all stage folk are not really saints and all religious zealots not really satyrs and nymphs. Then things will settle down again. In the meantime, let's have some more of that chicken potpie, please.

ON SAFE GROUND

WILLIE was fishing.

"Willie!"

It was his mother's voice, but he was sheltered from the house by trees, and she could not possibly see him. So Willie went on fishing.

"Willie!"

Still Willie went on fishing.

"Willie!"

Willie began rebaiting his hook as his friend Bert approached.

"Don't you hear your mother callin' you?" said Bert. "That's three times she's shouted. Aren't you going in?"

"No," responded Willie, imperturbably.

"Won't she punish you?" asked his friend.

"No," repeated Willie, disdainfully. "She ain't going to punish nobody. She's got company, so when I go in she'll just say: 'The poor little fellow's been so deaf since he was ill!' "—*Manchester Guardian.*

As I understand it, one hundred and fifty-one years ago next
year, we declared our independence from Great Britain.

PLANS FOR THE SESQUI-AND-ONE

By
ROBERT C. BENCHLEY

Drawings by
REA IRVIN

NOW that they have finally got the buildings finished at the Sesqui-centennial in Philadelphia it will be time to begin tearing them down pretty soon. That is, unless my plan is accepted by the committee. My plan . . . . oh, well, *listen* to it anyway! It can't cost you anything to *listen*, can it? . . . . my plan is to keep all the buildings standing and use them next year in a Sesqui-and-One-centennial, in celebration of the one hundred and fifty-first year of our independence.

There is something rather fine about having been free for one hundred and fifty-*one* years. Only first we shall have to decide what it is that we have been free *from*.

As I understand it, one hundred and fifty-one years ago next year, we declared our independence from Great Britain. I may be wrong. That is what I have been given to understand, however. And ever since that time we have been a free people, with no unjust taxes, no unreasonable prohibitory laws, and a complete representation for each and every one of us in the law-making body, with the most conscientious and most able men in the country looking after our interests.

(Fifteen minutes of laughter.)

So it would be my idea to arrange exhibits in the buildings at the Sesqui-and-One-centennial which would typify this independence which we, as a nation, have maintained for so long.

First, there would be the Tax Building, furnished to commemorate our liberation from the famous tax on tea. In this Tax Building there would be a process showing how we spend our money today. Beginning with the Filling-out Station, where Citizen is shown filling out his income-tax blanks with a smile on his lips and a song in his heart, we follow the money on its way from Citizen's pocket to its ultimate destination,

the great, big, beautiful United States Treasury. Then, by paying an extra admission price of fifteen cents, the visitor may go into a little room and see what happens to the money after it gets to the United States Treasury. Children will not be admitted to this exhibit.

In this little room we see a series of drain-openings, into which money is pouring from the Treasury. These drains are labeled: "Project for widening the Little Beebash River to permit of navigation as far north as Tillybury, La."; "Project for erection of million-dollar post office in Wheatcake, Idaho"; "Project for sending committee of congressmen on tour of investigation of trout streams in northern Ontario"; "Project for providing three hundred thousand silk mufflers to wrap around radium engines in case radium engines are ever invented"; and one enormous drain, with fifteen openings, labeled: "Miscellaneous government expenses—nobody's business."

This will conclude the exhibit in the Tax Building, except that at the exit gate there will be a large piece of statuary showing Uncle Sam striking off the shackles of war-taxation from Citizen, with the inscription: "The War Is Paid for Now." The date on this is left blank. For ten cents you may guess when this will happen.

Just south of the Tax Building, we will come to the Building of Prohibitory Laws. This will cover one hundred and fifty acres of floor space and will be the most impressive exhibit on the fair-grounds.

Here we will see a group of wax-works showing how strictly King George of England held his colonies in check, and then, in comparison, how comparatively free we are today. Citizen will be shown having dinner in his own home with a carafe of wine on the table, or sitting in an open-air garden drinking a stein of beer. There will be a scene in a night club with people dancing at 3:00 A. M. Another group will show a man standing on a soap box reading a copy of the preamble to the Constitution and excerpts from the Declaration of Independence. There will be a very amusing tableau depicting a negro citizen, in his World-War uniform, casting a ballot in Georgia. Both sides of this building will be lined with similar exhibits, and you can spend a whole afternoon walking up and down and thanking your lucky stars that you are not being ground under the despotic heel of the King of England.

At the exit gate to the Prohibitory Laws Building there will be a shady garden where you may sit at tables and drink a cooling and stimulating punch or perhaps a glass of Tokay.

The main comedy relief of the exhibition will come in the building containing evidences of Representative Government. Here we will see Average Citizen casting his ballot. This, in itself, is a pretty funny scene. Then there will be shown the different things that may happen to his ballot. It may get wet and be thrown out, it may be dropped into the wrong box and end up in the reading room of the public library, it may stick to another ballot and not get counted, or he may use a voting machine and slip one over on the officials.

Then, after the votes have been counted and the lucky candidate elected, we see his progress through congress, always in touch with Average Voter, always working in his interests, careful of Voter's money, jealous of his rights, in fact as well as in theory, Mr. Citizen's personal representative in the government. The big complaint in the days of King George was "Taxation without Representation." Thank God this exists no longer.

Citizen will be shown in an open-air garden drinking a stein of beer.

The rest of the fair-grounds will be given over to fun-making. The American Indian will have his own building, in which will be shown all the dandy things that have been done for him by the people who took his land. Adjoining the American Indian Building will be the negro exhibit, where every afternoon at three and every evening at seven-thirty there will be a lynching or a burning. There will be a program of old negro melodies in connection with this, sung by choruses of negro college-graduates who have taken advantage of the freedom accorded them and have found the way clear for their making good.

At the farther end of the grounds will be a reservation for World-War veterans where they may play whatever games they like and make whatever money they can. Over this reservation will be large signs reading: "Our Brave Boys"; "All Glory to Our Troops—Let Them Try and Get It"; "Remember Château-Thierry—Where Was That?" and the chorus of that old song: "When you come back, and you *will* come back, there's a whole world waiting for you."

All this has been put into shape and submitted to the committee as a proposal for next year's Sesqui-and-One-centennial. It is before the committee now: If you want it, and believe that it would be an inspiring exhibition, write to your congressman and ask him to push it. And then go back to bed and get a good sleep.

Every afternoon at three and every evening at seven-thirty there will be a lynching or a burning.

The best defense is a good offense in this case.

THROWING BACK THE EUROPEAN OFFENSIVE

By ROBERT C. BENCHLEY
Drawings by REA IRVIN

THIS is probably the hardest time of year for those of us who didn't go to Europe last summer. It was bad enough when the others were packing and outlining their trips for you. It was pretty bad when the postcards from Lausanne and Venice began coming in. But now, in the fall, when the travelers are returning with their Marco Polo travelogs, now is when we must be brave and give a cheer for the early frost.

There are several ways to combat this menace of returning travelers. The one that I have found most effective is based on the old football theory that a strong offense is the best defense. I rush them right off their feet, before they can get started.

In carrying out this system, it is well to remember that very few travelers know anything more about the places they have visited than the names of one hotel, two points of interest, and perhaps one street. You can bluff them into insensibility by making up a name and asking them if they saw that when they were in Florence. My whole strategy is based on my ability to make up names. You can do it, too, with practice.

Thus, let us say that I am confronted by Mrs. Reetaly who has just returned from a frantic tour of Spain, southern France, and the Ritz Hotel, Paris. You are inextricably cornered with her at a tea, or beer night, or something. Following is a transcript of the conversation. (Note the gathering power of my offense.)

MRS. R.: Well, we have just returned from Europe, and everything seems so strange here. I simply can't get used to our money.

MR. B.: I never see enough of it to get used to it myself. (*Just a pleasantry.*)

MRS. R.: When we were in Madrid, I just gave up trying to figure out the Spanish money. You see, they have *pesetas* and——

MR. B.: A very easy way to remember Spansh money is to count ten *segradas* to one *mesa*, ten *mesas* to one *rintilla* and twenty *rintillas* to one *peseta*.

MRS. R.: Oh, you have been to Spain? Did you go to Toledo?

MR. B.: Well, of course, Toledo is just the beginning. You pushed on to Mastilejo, of course?

MRS. R.: Why—er—no. We were in quite a hurry to get to Granada and——

MR. B.: You didn't see Mastilejo! That's too bad. Mastilejo is Toledo multiplied by a hundred. Such mountains! Such coloring! Leaving Mastilejo, one ascends by easy stages to the ridge behind the town from which is obtained an incomparable view of the entire Bobadilla Valley. It was here that, in 1476, the Moors——

MRS. R.: The Moorish relics in Granada——

MR. B.: The Moorish relics in Granada are like something you buy from Sears Roebuck compared to the remains in Tuna. You saw Tuna, of course?

MRS. R.: Well, no (*lying her head off*), we were going there, but Harry thought that it would just be repeating what——

MR. B.: The biggest mistake of your life, Mrs. Reetaly, the biggest mistake of your life! Unless you have seen Tuna, you haven't seen Spain.

MRS. R.: But Carcassonne——

MR. B.: Ah, Carcassonne! Now you're talking! Did you ever see anything to beat that old diamond mill in the *Vielle Ville?* Would they let you go through it when you were there?

MRS. R.: Why, I don't think that we saw any old diamond mill. We saw an old——

MR. B.: I know what you're going to say! You saw the old wheat sifter. Isn't that fascinating? Did you talk with the old courier there?

26

Mrs. R.: Why, I don't remember——

Mr. B.: And the hole in the wall where Louis the Neurotic escaped from the Saracens?

Mrs. R.: Yes, wasn't that—? (*Very weak.*)

Mr. B.: And the stream where they found the sword and buckler of the Man with the Iron Abdomen?

Mrs. R. (*edging away*): Yes, indeed.

Mr. B.: And old Vastelles? You visited Vastelles, surely? . . . . Mrs. Reetaly, come back here, please! I just love talking over these dear places with someone who has just been there. . . . . May I call on you some day soon and we'll just have a feast of reminiscence? . . . . Thank you. How about tomorrow?

And from that day to this, I am never bothered by Mrs. Reetaly's European trip, and you needn't be, either, if you will only study the above plan carefully.

The other method is based on just the opposite theory—that of no offense, or defense, at all. It is known as "dumb submission," and should be tried only by very phlegmatic people who can deaden their sensibilities so that they don't even hear the first ten minutes of the traveler's harangue. The idea is to let them proceed at will for a time and then give unmistakable evidence of not having heard a word they have said. Let us say that Mr. Thwomly has accosted me on the train.

Mt. T.: It certainly seems funny to be riding in trains like this again. We have been all summer in France, you know, and those French trains are all divided up into compartments. You get into a compartment—*compartimon*, they call them—and there you are with three or five other people, all cooped up together. On the way from Paris to Marseilles we had a funny experience. I was sitting next to a Frenchman

You are inextricably cornered.

"Did you get to France at all when you were away?"

who was getting off at Lyons—Lyons is about half way between Paris and Marseilles—and he was dozing when we got in. So I——

Mr. B.: Did you get to France at all when you were away?

Mr. T.: This was in *France* that I'm telling you about. On the way from Paris to Marseilles. We got into a railway carriage——

Mr. B.: The railway carriages there aren't like ours here, are they? I've seen pictures of them, and they seem to be more like compartments of some sort.

Mr. T. (*a little discouraged*): That was a French railway carriage I was just describing to you. I sat next to a man——

Mr. B.: A Frenchman?

Mr. T.: Sure, a Frenchman. That's the *point*.

Mr. B.: Oh, I see.

Mr. T.: Well, this Frenchman was asleep, and when we got in I stumbled over his feet. So he woke up and said something in French, which I couldn't understand, and I excused myself in English, which *he* couldn't understand, but I saw by his ticket that he was going only as far as Lyons——

Mr. B.: You were across the border into France, then?

Mr. T. (*giving the whole thing up as a bad job*): And what did *you* do this summer?

Whichever way you pick to defend yourself against the assaults of people who want to tell you about Europe, don't forget that it was I who told you how. I'm going to Europe myself next year, and if you try to pull either of these systems on *me* when I get back, I will recognize them at once, and it will just go all the harder with you. But, of course, *I* will have something to tell that will be worth hearing.

DECEMBER   **1 9 2 6**

UNCLE EDITH'S GHOST STORY

By ROBERT C. BENCHLEY
Drawings by **REA IRVIN**

"TELL us a ghost story, Uncle Edith," cried all the children late Christmas afternoon when everyone was cross and sweaty.

"Very well, then," said Uncle Edith, "it isn't much of a ghost story, but you will take it—and like it," he added, cheerfully. "And if I hear any whispering while it is going on, I will seize the luckless offender and baste him one.

"Well, to begin, my father was a poor wood-chopper, and we lived in a charcoal-burner's hut in the middle of a large, dark forest."

"That is the beginning of a fairy story, you big sap," cried little Dolly, a fat, disagreeable child who never should have been born, "and what we wanted was a *ghost* story."

"To be sure," cried Uncle Edith, "what a stupid old woopid I was. The ghost story begins as follows:

"It was late in November when my friend Warrington came up to me in the club one night and said: 'Craige, old man, I want you to come down to my place in Whoopshire for the week-end. There is greffle shooting to be done and grouse no end. What do you say?'

"I had been working hard that week, and the prospect pleased. And so it was that the 3:40 out of Charing Cross found Warrington and me on our way into Whoopshire, loaded down with guns, plenty of flints, and two of the most beautiful snootsfuls ever accumulated in Merrie England.

"It was getting dark when we reached Breeming Downs, where Warrington's place was, and as we drove up the shadowy path to the door, I felt Warrington's hand on my arm.

"'Cut that out!' I ordered, peremptorily. 'What is this I'm getting into?'

"Greffle shooting and grouse no end."

"'Sh-h-h!' he replied, and his grip tightened. With one sock I knocked him clean across the seat. There are some things which I simply will not stand for.

"He gathered himself together and spoke. 'I'm sorry,' he said. 'I was a bit unnerved. You see, there is a shadow against the pane in the guest room window.'

"'Well, what of it?' I asked. It was my turn to look astonished.

"Warrington lowered his voice. 'Whenever there is a shadow against the windowpane as I drive up with a guest, that guest is found dead in bed the next morning—dead from fright,' he added, significantly.

"I looked up at the window toward which he was pointing. There, silhouetted against the glass, was the shadow of a gigantic man. I say, 'a man,' but it was more the figure of a large weasel except for a fringe of dark-red clappers that it wore suspended from its beak."

"How do you know they were dark red," asked little Tom-Tit, "if it was the shadow you saw?"

"You shut your face," replied Uncle Edith. "I could hardly control my astonishment at the sight of this thing, it was so astonishing. 'That is in my room?' I asked Warrington.

"'Yes,' he replied, 'I am afraid that it is.'

"I said nothing, but got out of the automobile and collected my bags. 'Come on,' I announced, cheerfully, 'I'm going up and beard Mr. Ghost in his den.'

"So up the dark, winding stairway we went into the resounding corridors of the old seventeenth-century house, pausing only when we came to the door which Warrington indicated as being the door to my room. I knocked.

"There was a piercing scream from within as we pushed the

door open. But when we entered, we found the room empty. We searched high and low, but could find no sign of the man with the shadow. Neither could we discover the source of the terrible scream, although the echo of it was still ringing in our ears.

" 'I guess it was nothing,' said Warrington, cheerfully. 'Perhaps the wind in the trees,' he added.

" 'But the shadow on the pane?' I asked.

"He pointed to a fancily carved piece of guest soap on the washstand. 'The light was behind that,' he said, 'and from outside it looked like a man.'

" 'To be sure,' I said, but I could see that Warrington was as white as a sheet.

" 'Is there anything that you need?' he asked. 'Breakfast is at nine—if you're lucky,' he added, jokingly.

" 'I think that I have everything,' I said. 'I will do a little reading before going to sleep, and perhaps count my laundry. . . . . But stay,' I called him back, 'you might leave that revolver which I see sticking out of your hip pocket. I may need it more than you will.'

"He slapped me on the back and handed me the revolver as I had asked. 'Don't blow into the barrel,' he giggled, nervously.

" 'How many people have died of fright in this room?' I asked, turning over the leaves of a copy of *Town and Country*.

" 'Seven,' he replied. 'Four men and three women.'

" 'When was the last one here?'

" 'Last night,' he said.

" 'I wonder if I might have a glass of hot water with my breakfast,' I said. 'It warms your stomach.'

" 'Doesn't it though?' he agreed, and was gone.

"Very carefully I unpacked my bag and got into bed. I placed the revolver on the table by my pillow. Then I began reading.

"Suddenly the door to the closet at the farther end of the room opened slowly. It was in the shadows and so I could not make out whether there was a figure there or not. But nothing appeared. The door shut again, however, and I could hear footfalls coming across the soft carpet toward my bed. A chair which

"—into the resounding corridors of the old seventeenth-century house."

lay between me and the closet was upset as if by an unseen shin, and, simultaneously, the window was slammed shut and the shade pulled down. I looked, and there, against the shade, as if thrown from the *outside*, was the same shadow that we had seen as we came up the drive that afternoon."

"I have to go to the bathroom," said little Roger, aged six, at this point.

"Well, go ahead," said Uncle Edith. "You know where it is."

"I don't want to go alone," whined Roger.

"Go with Roger, Arthur," commanded Uncle Edith, "and bring me a glass of water when you come back."

"And whatever was this horrible thing that was in your room, Uncle Edith?" asked the rest of the children in unison when Roger and Arthur had left the room. "Go on with the story and don't keep us sitting here yawning all night. And don't hand us that old one about this being the ghost of a former butler who was murdered by the 'maarster' because he ran out of whisky."

"I can't tell you that," replied Uncle Edith, "for I packed my bag and got the 9:40 back to town."

"You mean that you walked right out on that mystery—left it flat?" queried the little ones, in disgust.

"Yes, I did exactly that," retorted Uncle Edith.

"That is the lousiest ghost story I have ever heard," said Peterkin.

And they all agreed with him.

"There against the shade was the same shadow."

THE BOYS' CAMP BUSINESS

By
ROBERT C. BENCHLEY

Drawings by
REA IRVIN

THERE seems to be an idea prevalent among parents that a good way to solve the summer problem for the boy is to send him to a boys' camp. At any rate, the idea seems to be prevalent in the advertising pages of the magazines.

If all the summer camps for boys and girls turn out the sterling citizens-in-embryo that they claim to do, the future of this country is as safe as if it were in the hands of a governing board consisting of the Twelve Apostles. From the folders and advertisements, we learn that "Camp Womagansett—in the foothills of the White Mountains" sends yearly into the world a bevy of "strong, manly boys, ready for the duties of citizenship and equipped to face life with a clear eye and a keen mind." It doesn't say anything about their digestions, but I suppose they are in tiptop shape, too.

The outlook for the next generation of mothers is no less dazzling. "Camp Wawilla for Girls," we learn, pays particular attention to the spiritual development of Tomorrow's Women and compared to the civic activities of the majority of alumnæ of Wawilla, those of Florence Nightingale or Frances Willard would have to be listed under the head of "Junior Girls' Work."

Now this is all very splendid, and it is comforting to think that when every boy and girl goes to Womagansett or Wawilla there will be no more Younger Generation problem and probably no crime waves worth mentioning. But there are several other features that go hand in hand with sending the boy to camp which I would like to take up from the parents' point of view, if I may. I will limit myself to twenty minutes.

In the first place, when your boy comes home from camp he is what is known in the circular as "manly and independent." This means that when you go swimming with him he pushes you off the raft and jumps on your shoulders, holding you under water until you are as good as drowned—better, in fact. Before he went to camp, you used to take a kindly interest in his swimming and tell him to "take your time, take it easy," with a feeling of superiority which, while it may have had no foundation in your own natatorial prowess, nevertheless was one of the few points of pride left to you in your obese middle-age. After watching one of

Soggy and waterlogged.

those brown heroes in one-piece suits and rubber helmets dive off a tower and swim under water to the raft and back, there was a sort of balm in being able to turn to your son and show him how to do the crawl stroke, even though you yourself weren't one of the seven foremost crawl experts in the country. You could do it better than your son could, and that was something.

It was also very comforting to be able to stand on the springboard and say: "Now watch Daddy. See? Hands like this, bend your knees. See?" The fact that such exhibitions usually culminated in your landing heavily on the area bounded by the knees and the chest was embarrassing, perhaps, but at that you weren't quite so bad as the boy when he tried the same thing.

But after a summer at camp, the "manly, independent" boy comes back and makes you look like Horace Greeley in his later years. "Do this one, Dad!" he says, turning a double flip off the springboard and cutting into the water like a knife blade. If you try it, you sprain your back. If you don't try it, your self-respect and prestige are shattered. The best thing to do is not to hear him. You can do this by disappearing under the surface every time it looks as if he were going to pull a new one. After a while, however, this ruse gets you pretty soggy and waterlogged and you might better just go in and get dressed as rapidly as possible.

The worst phase of this new-found "independence" is the romping instinct that seems to be developed to a high state of obnoxiousness at all boys' camps. I went to camp when I was a boy, but I don't remember being as unpleasant about my fun as boys today seem to be. I have done many mean things in my time. I have tortured flies and kicked crutches out from under cripples' arms. But I have never, so help me, Confucius, pushed anybody off a raft or come up behind anyone in the water and jumped up on his shoulders. And I don't think that Lincoln ever did, either.

There is evidently a course in raft pushing and back jumping in boys' camps today. Those photographs that you see in the camp advertisements, if you examine them closely, will disclose, in nine cases out of ten, a lot of boys pushing each other off rafts. You can't see the ones who are jumping on others' shoulders, as they are under water. But I want to serve notice right now that the next boy who pushes me off a raft when I am not looking, or tries to play leapfrog over me in ten feet of water, is going to be made practically useless as Tomorrow's Citizen, and I am going to do it myself, too. If it happens to be my own son, it will just make the affair the sadder.

Another thing that these manly boys learn at camp is a savage habit of getting up at sunrise. The normal, healthy boy should be a very late sleeper. Who does not remember in his own normal, healthy boyhood having to be called three, four, or even five times in the morning before it seemed sensible to get up? One of the happiest memories of childhood is that of the maternal voice calling up from downstairs, fading away into silence, and the realization that it would be possibly fifteen minutes before it called again.

All this is denied to the boy who goes to a summer camp. When he comes home, he is so steeped in the pernicious practice of early rising that he can't shake it off. Along about six o'clock in the morning he begins dropping shoes and fixing up a new stand for the radio in his room. Then he goes out into the back yard and practices tennis shots up against the house. Then he

The next boy who pushes me off a raft is going to be made practically useless as Tomorrow's Citizen.

He goes out into the back yard and practices tennis shots up against the house.

runs over a few whistling arrangements of popular songs and rides his bicycle up and down the gravel path. You would be surprised at the sound two bicycle wheels can make on a gravel path at six-thirty in the morning. A forest fire might make the same crackling sound, but you probably wouldn't be having a forest fire out in your yard at six-thirty in the morning. Not if you had any sense, you wouldn't.

Just what the boys do at camp when they get up at six is a mystery. They seem to have some sort of setting-up exercises and a swim—more pushing each other off the raft—but they could do that by getting up at eight and still have a good long day ahead of them. I never knew anyone yet who got up at six who did anything more useful between that time and breakfast than banging a tennis ball up against the side of the house, waiting for the civilized members of the party to get up. We have to do enough waiting in this life without getting up early to wait for breakfast.

Next summer I have a good mind to run a boys' camp of my own. It will be on Lake Chabonagogchabonagogchabonagungamog—yes, there is, too, in Webster, Massachusetts—and I will call it Camp Chabonagogchabonagogchabonagungamog for Manly Boys. And by the word "manly," I will mean "like men." In other words, everyone shall sleep just as long as he wants, and when he does get up there will be no depleting "setting-up" exercises. The day will be spent just as the individual camper gosh-darned pleases. No organized "hikes"—I'd like a word on the "hike" problem some day, too—no camp spirit, no talk about Tomorrow's Manhood, and *no pushing people off rafts.*

THE NEW SOCIAL BLIGHT

By
ROBERT C. BENCHLEY

Drawings by
R. F. HEINRICH

After a good warm, heavy dessert and a hot mug of coffee you are
supposed to settle down in the library and tell who wrote the poem
beginning: "If Niobe were here tonight—"

ONE of the big questions which is agitating society today is why I don't go out more to parties. You hear it on all sides. "What has become of Benchley?" they say; "we never see him around at people's houses any more."

There is one camp which claims that I am embarrassed in the presence of strangers because of some malformation, another that I shun my friends because of conspicuous pores, and still another that since I flunked my Alexander Hamilton finals I have taken to seclusion and will see no one. I have instructed my attorneys to deny all of these insinuations categorically.

The real reason is that society today has turned intellectual on me. You can't go out any more to parties without being asked questions on matters of general information. Immediately the supper dishes are cleared away someone comes out with a list of questions concerning famous characters in history or literature, and there's your evening—just sunk.

When I was younger, a party was a party, not a college-board examination. We used to sit around and kiss each other, or drop handkerchiefs, or get to fighting, and everything was just dandy. Sometimes even the rugs would be pushed back and the more nimble ones would wrestle about on the floor to music. Among the older boys and girls a deck of cards would be broken out, and everyone would enjoy an evening of re-nigging (not spelled right and I know it) and snarling at each other. This sometimes ran into money, which was not a bad idea provided it ran in the right direction. And whatever we did, almost anybody could do it. All that was necessary was a fairly good constitution and enough sobriety to keep from falling on your forehead.

But now everything is different. Someone, a few years ago, began a revival of an old high school game called Twenty Questions. This was considered pretty

effete when I was a boy and was indulged in by only those who didn't have the virility to play Post Office and other sex games. There would be one room (the warmest) devoted to Twenty Questions, and the rest, those who had any pride in their heritage, went into the next room and flung themselves about in various health-giving activities.

But suddenly Twenty Questions became *de rigueur*. You must be able to guess what someone was thinking of (as if anyone cared), or you must think of names of cities which began with "W" (even less tantalizing), or you must take a paper and pencil and jot down answers to such questions as "What famous Phœnician general, well known for his alto singing, was responsible for the Second Punic War?"

From this last game has developed the present pernicious custom of just plain General Information. After a good warm, heavy dessert and a hot mug of coffee you are supposed to settle down in the library and tell who wrote the poem beginning "If Niobe were here tonight, the moon in all her glory would—etc." Young people, with red blood coursing through their systems, must sit around in a circle and tell each other who invented amalgam fillings and what president of the United States studied palmistry until he was eleven years old. The future of the race is being placed in the hands of young men and women who spend their evenings together trying to remember who wrote the music to *Il Rogobo* and how many dreens there are in a gross gambut. If you were to ask me what we are coming to, as a nation, I should reply: "I don't know, *I'm* sure."

And now, to make things worse, they have gotten out a book full of questionnaires; so that hostesses who can't think up things to ask their guests can just turn to this book and have enough material to tire out several parties. There are questionnaires on literature, mining, engineering, bird calls, and comparative plumbing, and then ones on general information which include every-thing. In one of these General Information question-naires, Question No. 1 may be "What have the following in common: Alcibiades, Pepin the Great, Walter von der Vogelweide, and William A. Douglas?" and Ques-tion No. 2 may be "What is the coefficient of linear expansion in a steam pipe at 1367 South Water street?"

The worst feature of this questionnaire book is that it also contains the answers. This enables a lot of unscru-pulous people to cheat by peeking in the back of the book before they go to parties in which they know that the modern inquisition will be part of the program. Of course, the faster these cheaters rattle off the answers, the worse it makes me look. I wouldn't mind being shown up by college professors and people of that ilk, because I could make the perfectly legitimate claim that they were professionals and I would, therefore, be risking my amateur standing if I entered into any competition with them, lacking special permission from the A. A. U. It is, however, terribly humiliating to be outdone by those that I know are morons, who appear intelligent only because their minds, having nothing else on them, can retain a lot of "crammed" facts for a few minutes.

Now, in college, I took what was known as the "classical course," which meant that I had no courses after Friday and none before eleven in the morning. In the "classical course" it was also understood that there was to be no monkeying with mathematics or any of those fly-by-night sciences. A gentleman's education

Hostesses can just turn to this book and have material enough to tire out several parties.

A rather slick bit of trickery by means of which one can run out in Canfield.

was what I was to have—and what I got. And when-ever, in after life, I want to know anything, I go right to the encyclopedia and look it up. There was nothing said in the specifications about being able to answer on the dot any questions that a hostess might see fit to ask me after dinner.

When a man has reached my age, he can't afford to go around to parties being humiliated. I have, through certain studied facial expressions and a characteristic carriage, established a reputation for dignity and civic stability for myself. People have come to think of me as a pillar of some sort or other, a definite bulwark in the literary and social life of the community. This standing has been achieved through years of scowling and keep-ing quiet while others were talking, and by walking very slowly with my hands behind my back. I tried for a while wearing glasses to add to the effect, but I couldn't see with them on and kept tripping over things, which, in a way, detracted.

And now I am asked nightly to jeopardize this hard-earned reputation by sitting around and making a sap of myself in front of a lot of people. There isn't one of those questions that I couldn't find the answer to in five minutes if I really wanted to know it. But I have other things to take up my mind, and, until the present craze for general information dies down, I shall devote myself to my studies in the privacy of my own room. At present I am working on a rather slick bit of trickery by means of which I can run out in Canfield.

"I crab *your* scene! My Gawd, what makes you think this is *your* scene?"

THE MENACE OF THE TALKING MOVIE

By ROBERT C. BENCHLEY

Drawings by REA IRVIN

NOW that the talking movie is a *fait accompli*, we must look into the matter and see what can be done to spoil it. Or perhaps all that we shall have to do is sit still and let it spoil itself.

One of the encouraging features in favor of any plan to make the talking movies obnoxious is that the actors and actresses themselves will be doing the talking. If some way can be found to let them just talk naturally while the picture is being taken, everything will be good and terrible.

For example, if we could hear what Norman Cortezas really says to Vida LaPlante as they sit talking to each other in the old rose-covered bower on the estate of COLONEL WARREN, the old rose-covered Virginia planter, the talking movies would have justified their invention right there. Let us run off a few hundred feet of the big love scene, where JACK WESTBROOK (Norman Cortezas) is telling HELEN WARREN (Vida LaPlante) that he is going up North to make some money and then come back and put her family on its feet. If the talking movies are really on the job, we shall hear the following:

JACK *leans over the sundial and looks into* HELEN'S *eyes:*

"What are you trying to do—crab my scene? *Look* at me, fer cripes sake, *look* at me! How can I get any effect with you lookin' off at the scenery?"

HELEN *draws close to* JACK *and shyly puts her hand on the sundial so that it touches his:*

"*I* crab *your* scene! My Gawd, what makes you think this is *your* scene? The script calls for you to play up to *me*."

JACK *takes* HELEN'S *hand gently in his and then, as if his passion were beyond his control, raises it quickly to his lips, covering it with kisses:*

"That's right! Pull away! Pull away from me! I don't get any more fun out of this than you do, but I've got a *little* consideration for the picture. I'm an artist, at any rate!"

HELEN, *flinging her arms around his neck:*

"An *artist!* A tight-rope artist, that's what you are! I've got a contract, you know, that calls for better treatment than this, and, believe me, I'll take it up with Lasky himself, too."

JACK *tears himself away from her and dashes to the gate, where he stops and turns, hat in hand, to blow her a kiss:*

"I'd keep away from the office if I was you. You and your contract ain't so popular there right now, from all I hear. They'll jump you on the scales and check up on your weight. That's in your contract, too, baby, and don't forget that!"

Fade-out of JACK *walking slowly down the lane, with* HELEN *sobbing over the sundial.*

Of course, as soon as the actors realize that what they are saying is being recorded for the audience to hear, they will stop all these little intimate passages between themselves and talk for publication. So we shall probably have a line like this as soon as the thing is perfected:

PIERRE RAMSEY *is seen sitting in his chair at the club. He is the son of a rich banker and something of a lovable wastrel. His father has told him that he must go to work or lose his share of his inheritance. He is discussing his future with* TED ROSSITER, *his buddy:*

"In playing this rôle of the young wastrel, I am trying to *live* the part, although, I must admit, it is the farthest possible from my own personal private life off the screen. After graduation from college, my parents wanted me to study law, but it seemed to me that in the motion pictures there lay a great chance for someone who was a real artist. And so I came to Hollywood. I am up every morning at six for a canter over the hills and in bed every night at ten, after a hard day in the studio. But I never go to bed without first reading a chapter of Emerson. Emerson, it seems to me, is the greatest philosopher of them all."

PIERRE *rises, knocks the ashes off his cigarette, and . . . . cut to father's entrance.*

The one big problem which will arise out of the ultimate perfection of the talking movies is what to do with the subtitle writers.

There will always, of course, be the descriptive titles, such as "Came the Dawn." Who will speak these? Perhaps there will spring up an entirely new character in the movies, a little old man with dark glasses and a tall, gray beaver hat who, at appropriate intervals in the picture, will appear in the lower right-hand corner of the frame and, taking off his hat, will say:

"After three weeks of lonely heartache, Mona decided that the easiest way was perhaps the best, and down through the corridors of time echoed the sneering laughter of the gods. I thank you!"

Or perhaps *two* little men in beaver hats who will say in unison:

"And with the coming of a new spring, Roland and Betty found that their love had ripened into parent-hood . . . . . Tum-diddy-um-tum—tum-tum!" (*Into a dance and off.*)

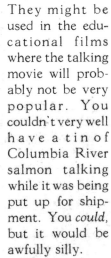

"And with the coming of a new spring, Roland and Betty found that their love had ripened into parenthood."

The question of what to do with the present writers of subtitles still remains unsolved. They might be used in the educational films where the talking movie will probably not be very popular. You couldn't very well have a tin of Columbia River salmon talking while it was being put up for shipment. You *could,* but it would be awfully silly.

If the educational films do claim the subtitle writers, educa-

"But I never go to bed without first reading a chapter of Emerson."

tional films are going to be a lot sexier than they are now. Let us imagine a picture showing the process of cutting and binding pampas grass, for example:

"Week after week the reapers toiled at their incessant ritual, until finally Love came."

"Later that night."

"In the morning, Luke realized that a great charge had been given into his keeping and that by the fifteenth all 10,000 of the bales must be shipped."

"Here work 400 girls, each binding a bale of grass, each thinking the long, long thoughts of youth."

"After three months of struggling against the forces of Nature, Phil, the foreman, at last made out his bill-of-lading."

"Came the government inspector."

"Next week: *Broken Oyster Shells, or The Romance of Road Building in Bermuda.*"

But the real trouble will come in the news reels. It will be all very well to have people talking on the screen when they have been told beforehand what to say, but what are you going to do when you have a reel showing marines ashore painting Ceylon red? No sub-title, reading "Uncle Sam's Boys on a Lark in Sunny Ceylon," will gloss over what you hear Uncle Sam's boys saying about the lark. In a picture showing dock-hands unloading the largest elephant ever brought into America, how are you going to explain to the kiddies that what the man in the dungarees is saying to the man in the undershirt is just elephant-talk? The news reels will probably become the worst moral influence in the movies and will have to be cut out.

But at any rate, we may get a chance to hear what that one word is that celebrities mutter just before they turn away from a close-up shot. President Coolidge blinks stupidly, looks to the left, salutes the camera, and then, just as the operator is about to cut, his lips move in one word. If we knew what that word is, we would know more about whom to vote for in 1928.

JUNE   1927

When I want a
vacation, I get
in a rowboat.

THE GREAT AMERICAN FOLLY

By Robert C. Benchley

Drawings by Burt Thomas

IT IS funny that going over Niagara Falls in a barrel never achieved more popularity in this country as a method of taking a trip. You would think that it would appeal to Americans to such an extent as to make it necessary to run excursion barrels over the Falls during July and August. For, as a nation, we seem to be more gluttonous for punishment in respect to uncomfortable traveling than any nation on earth. Witness the number of people who take train trips in the summer—for *pleasure*.

Here is a great nation confronted each summer with the problem of vacationing. Almost every locality has some spot within walking distance where a very passable vacation could be spent. But no! We must pack trunks and bags and go somewhere too far away even to motor, just so that we can go choo-choo during the hottest months of the year—or of any year, for that matter.

A foreigner visiting this country during a torrid spell and seeing the great terminals crowded with moist, bedraggled travelers, snapping at each other and pinching their children's arms to keep them in line, would surely think that nothing short of a great catastrophe or enemy invasion could set so many people on the march in such weather. And then next day he reads in the papers that "Record Crowd of Holiday-Makers Throng Terminals." Holiday-makers! A Roman holiday, such as Nero might have planned.

With the advent of the hot weather, your American citizen begins to get restless and to look up time tables. He finds that he can leave Cleveland at six and get into

Dallas at four-fifty or that he can leave Boston at noon and get into Los Angeles at nine-twenty. Of course, the railroads can't predict for him just what the hottest day of the month will be, but he has a fine instinct for picking it in advance. If he could pick horses or stocks with the same sagacity that he picks hot days for traveling, there would be less poverty in this country and fewer overdrafts.

If, by any chance, he hasn't got his ticket in advance, he waits until some evening the sun sets very round and red and all the natives say, "A hot day tomorrow, brother!" and then he rushes home and throws a few things into a bag, gets all his children (if he hasn't children, he borrows some from a neighbor) and sets his alarm for six in order to be up with the blistering sun and off on the 8:45 for a two-day cinder bath.

Probably one of the most depressing sights in the world is a family entering a train drawing room on a good steamy morning, all ready for a trip across the continent or as far as their money will take them. Their train has been frying in the yards all the day before and all night and as they all push their way into the little box they are to call "home" for two days, Mother and one of the frailer daughters faint immediately.

"Well, well," says Daddy, cheerily, "it's going to be a scorcher all right," and to hear him you might think that it was all his doing. The bags are put in the racks and piled up behind the door, Mother and the frailer daughter are brought to temporarily, Daddy takes off his coat and sits in that good American hot-weather institution, the woolen waistcoat, and everything is set.

Someone thinks of turning on the fan. This is a Pullman contrivance whereby heated air from the engine is brought through asbestos pipes and set in motion in the drawing rooms. Its effect is that of a soft sponge of chloroform held close against the nose. At the first whirl of the fan, out goes Mother again.

As the train starts, everyone crowds to the window to get whatever air there may be, and that is a good joke, too, for there isn't any air. There is something on which the soot travels, but it isn't air. Something for physicists to discover some day is what that element is that comes in at train windows in summer. It might be turned to some good use if it could only be isolated and harnessed, such as frying wheatcakes or popping corn, for instance.

Now all this would be very terrible if this family had *had* to make the trip at this particular time. It would be wrong for us to laugh at other people's sufferings. But this is the result of months' of careful planning and eager anticipation. Everybody knows what trains are in late June, July, and August, and that is evidently why everybody takes trains in late June, July, and August rather than at any other time.

If any one factor more than another is making for the gradual disintegration of the American family and the increase of divorce it is this custom of family traveling in summer. I saw a family of four leaving Chicago last summer on the way to the Coast. They had two drawing rooms and seemed to be the best of friends when the train pulled out of the Santa Fe station. (May I explain that I was taking the trip on *business?* When I want a vacation I get in a rowboat.) The next morning it was 98 in Kansas City and the sun wasn't up yet. By Emporia it was 105. The family in question were my next-door neighbors and gradually I began to hear voices being raised in querulous bickering. There seemed to be some argument as to whether they should have lunch brought in to them or go into the diner.

"It can't be any worse in the diner than it is in here," someone said.

"Oh, it can't, can't it? Have you ever *been* in a diner?"

"Yes, I've been in a diner and I know what I'm talking about."

"If you didn't have all those things hanging up on the hooks it would be a little cooler in here."

"*My* things! Two-thirds of them are yours."

Then there was a sound of things being yanked off hooks and packed into a suitcase.

"*Now*—I suppose you

are cooler! Now I guess you'll need an overcoat."

"Well, at any rate, the air gets a chance to circulate."

"*Air!* What air?"

This went on, sometimes louder, sometimes softer, according to the stamina of the speaker. Finally two of them went into the diner and two of them had lunch served in the drawing room. None of them ate anything; just sat around and gasped.

This went on all across Kansas, and during the night there were sounds of restless banging and murmured threats. At Albuquerque the next afternoon, one member of the family got off and took the next train back, another got off and bought a house in Albuquerque and I guess is living there yet. The other two continued on to the Coast but in separate drawing rooms and didn't speak to each other again. One of them was carried off on a stretcher at Pasadena.

This sort of thing is going on every summer in almost every train going in almost any direction. Is it any wonder that our people are becoming loosely knit?

Of course, the phenomenon of railroad excursions in summer is even more startling. In every railroad station in the country you will see great posters advertising cut-rate excursions for the Fourth of July. The one day in the year when anyone with any brains would plan to get into the bath tub with a good book and pull down the shades is the one day in the year when the citizenry put on stiff collars and take a round trip to Savannah, Georgia, Washington, D. C., or Old Point Comfort. And a round trip at that! None of this staying and getting a bath anywhere. Just jam on the train and sit in the heat until you get some place—and then jam on the train and sit in the heat until you get back. I don't know what to make of it.

Perhaps the explanation is that some of the people are crazy some of the time; some of the people are crazy all of the time, and in late June, July, and August all of the people are crazy all of the time.

"Well, well," says Daddy, "it's going to be a scorcher."

At this juncture I
decide to lie down.

"IN THIS CORNER—"

By ROBERT C. BENCHLEY
Drawings by
REA IRVIN

FRANKLY, I am not much of a fight fan. I always get sorry for the one who is getting socked. On the other hand, if *no* one is getting socked, I am bored and start screaming for blood. There is no such thing as pleasing me at a fight.

Of course, as I keep saying to myself when I get to worrying over the loser's suffering, he probably expects this sort of thing. When a man decides to be a fighter he must know that sooner or later he is going to get his nose mashed in. He takes that chance. So there is really no need for me to feel so bad about it. God knows, I have troubles enough of my own without sitting and wincing every time some Lithuanian bunker-boy gets punched in the side of the head.

But somehow I can't help feeling that the one who is getting mashed is pretty fairly surprised that things have taken this turn—and not a little mortified. I am afraid that he didn't want to fight in the first place, but was forced into it by his backers. Perhaps, if I read more of the fighters' statements before the fight, I would feel a little less sorry for them when I hear their faces give way. Once I read what a welterweight said on the day before the contest, and, for the first time, I actually enjoyed seeing his lip swell up.

Probably my tender feelings in the matter are due to an instinctive habit I have of putting myself in the place of anyone I am watching. I haven't been at a fight for more than three minutes before I begin indulging in one of my favorite nightmares. This consists of imagining that I myself am up in the ring facing the better of the two men.

Just how I am supposed to have got up in the ring is never quite clear. I don't believe that I ever would sign up deliberately for a prize fight, much as I need the money. I can think of at least fourteen thousand things that I would try first. But the idea seems to be that while drugged or under the influence of alcohol I have agreed to meet some prominent pugilist in the Yankee Stadium and, quite naturally, the affair has filled the mammoth bowl with a record crowd, all of

whom are cynically antagonistic to me.

Whatever my mental processes may have been which led me to don silken tights and crawl through the ropes, my reverie begins when I awake to find myself standing under the terrific glare of the lights going through the formality of shaking gloves with a very large man.

"Here, here, Benchley," I say to myself. "What's all this? This is a very foolhardy thing to be doing."

But there is no way of backing out now and the only thing that I can do is to throw a big bluff that I know something about boxing.

Now, as a matter of fact, my fighting technique is limited to a few elementary passes learned in a gymnasium class when I was in school, and consists of a rather trusting stance with the arms raised as if posing for a photograph, followed by a quick lunge forward with my left and an almost simultaneous jump backward. The fact that this is all done to a count, "one, two, three, and four," leaves something to be desired as strategy. I also have a nasty right hook—done to

Fortunately, I have
the reach.

"five, six, seven, and eight"—which, I think, would deceive no one. I have tried both of these on the younger of my two boys, and he found little difficulty in solving them the very first time. Fortunately, I had the reach, however.

Equipped with these two primary attacks, each of which resolves itself into the quick jump backward, I am supposed to pit myself against a trained fighter. The whole thing is pretty terrifying to start with and rapidly grows worse.

The trouble with my position No. 1 seems to be that my opponent doesn't wait for me. No sooner have I taken my stance and raised my fists than I am the recipient of a terrific clout on the ear, without even the formality of counting "one, two, three, and four." Without seeing very much of anything at the time, I try my left hook, which ends very badly somewhere in midair, and again take a rapid succession of neck-bending socks on either side of the jaw. At this juncture, I decide to lie down.

This strategy on my part is greeted with derisive hoots from the crowd, but there seems to be nothing else to be done about it. There is practically nothing that my opponent can't do to me and nobody knows it better than I do. Furthermore, I am not one of those people who develop a gameness under physical pain. I am not a glutton for punishment. If I had my way about it I would practically *never* let myself be hurt. In the waiting room of a dentist's office I have been known to develop a yellow streak which is clearly visible through my clothing. Gameness is a grand quality and it is all right as a last resort, but my motto is "Try everything else first."

Consequently, in the position in which I now find myself, my first thought is how to get out of the ring and into bed with the covers pulled over my head. I try crawling out through the ropes, but in this particular dream-fight of mine, there is a rule against throwing in the towel. Both fighters must go the entire fifteen rounds, dead or alive. So you can see my predicament.

I very seldom get much farther than this point in my reverie. I suppose that I would just lie there on the floor and make my opponent come to me if he wanted to hit me. I am very certain that I would not be fool enough to get up on my feet again. I might try kicking him in the shins from my recumbent position, but I doubt that I would bring myself to even that show of belligerence. I would simply have to trust in his seeing the humor of the thing and good-naturedly getting down on the floor beside me and wrestling the rest of the fight out. He would win that, too, but I wouldn't get those socks on the side of the head at any rate.

As I snap out of this dream state and find myself sitting in my safe ringside seat (from which I can see nothing, owing to the holders of ringside seats in front

If no one is getting socked, I am bored and start screaming for blood.

of me indulging in the good American custom of standing up whenever things get interesting) my first sensation is one of great relief at my good fortune in not being in the ring. But then I see some other poor son-of-a-gun getting what I might have had, and I can't help but wish that the whole thing would stop. Maybe he, too, found himself up there quite by accident.

Of course, there is one thing about prize fights that one sees nowadays. In a large majority of them no one gets hurt enough even to *want* to stop before it is over. Sometimes it is hard to tell who is the winner, and the most serious injury sustained by either fighter is a little skin rubbed off the inside of his arms from waltzing. At least, I have the distinction of having taken part in the most brutal fight of modern times.

D. A. C. JUNIORS HONORED

TWO Junior members of the D. A. C., Andrew J. Weatherwax, Jr., and Oliver W. Burke, Jr., have been selected to make a trip to Copenhagen, Denmark, this summer as members of the "My Friend Abroad" delegation of 100 American boys. This delegation is made up of lads from all sections of the United States, and the two D. A. C. representatives are the only ones selected from Detroit. Both attend the Shaw Country Day School. Prof. Sven Knudsen, of Copenhagen, personally picked the members of the party.

D'AC NEWS

COPYRIGHT, 1927, CHARLES A. HUGHES

AUGUST, 1927

This bombshell from Mr. Chapin precipitated a riot of controversy.

FROM A SANDWICH TO A NATIONAL INSTITUTION

By ROBERT C. BENCHLEY

Drawings by BURT THOMAS

IT WAS in the fall of 1912 that a little group of trappers met together in an old log hut situated where the Hotel Pontchartrain was then. They were a sturdy crew, these pioneers of old Detroit, and, although their manners were rough and their beards shaggy, they were God's green footstools, each and every one. And in their hearts was the dream of a great project—with a swimming pool in it.

Heating facilities were not so convenient in those days, and the little band of minute-men were huddled about a peat fire which had been carried in a brazier to the meeting to dispel the chill of the raw Michigan autumn. Old Charlie Hughes, the otter trapper (or "Otter Boy," as he was called), was the first to speak:

"Wall, men," he said, removing his coon-skin hat and substituting for it a golf cap (golfing togs being prescribed as parliamentary regalia in Detroit), "we are gathered here today on serious business." At this, several of those present began to cry.

"Come, come," said the sturdy trapper, "this will never do. We are men and we must do men's work." At this, several of those present began to laugh.

Things went on like this for quite a while, and it finally transpired that what Old Charlie had in mind was the formation of an organization of some sort to give entertainments. The long winter nights in Detroit had begun to get on the nerves of the out-of-door natives and the time seemed ripe for the establishment of some organized form of fun-making. "We should have a good restaurant in connection, too," said the kindly old woodsman; "the best in the country," he added, with a twinkle.

"What should we call it?" asked Hugh Chalmers (for it was indeed he).

"I would like to suggest," spoke up Roy Chapin (for it was indeed he, too), "that this organization be called 'The Detroit Athletic Club.'"

This bombshell from Mr. Chapin precipitated a riot of controversy. One faction among those present wanted it called "The Syracuse Athletic Club"; others felt that the word "athletic" was a little too effete and wanted it to be known as "The Detroit Meat-Tearers' Club." Others objected to the name "club."

It was finally decided to appoint a committee of seven to go into the matter and see what could be done by way of a compromise. Those present at the informal meeting were, besides those already cited, G. D. Pope, F. H. Holt, C. S. Vaughn, William R. Orr, Elmer J. Smith, Frederick S. Stearns, William E. Metzger, Robert B. Tannahill, William B. Wreford, E. H. Doyle, Harry J. Porter, Carl M. Green, and Frederick C. Ford. Otto H. Kahn sent a telegram saying that he could not be present, despite the fact that he had not been asked.

Of these, a committee of seven was elected, consisting of Messrs. Chalmers (captain), Hughes (yeoman), Chapin, Tannahill, Orr, Kelsey, Pope, and Hawkins. Otto H. Kahn sent a telegram saying that he regretted being unable to serve on the committee.

It was soon found out that a committee of seven could not function, as the only game that seven could play was hockey (hockey was played with seven men in those days). So three more were added (Messrs. Joy and Clark, and Judge Codd), which made just one too many to play baseball, but just enough for two regulation basketball teams.

So efficient was this group that within six weeks Detroit had grown from a small trading outpost to a city of quite a few thousand, 107 of whom were enrolled as charter members of the D. A. C., it having been

If the D. A. R. ever got any of the D. A. C.'s mail, they kept it.

decided to compromise on calling the organization the "D. A. C." instead of the "Detroit Athletic Club." There was some confusion at first, owing to the club's receiving mail meant for the D. A. R., but, as soon as the mail was opened, it was easy to tell that a mistake had been made and most of it was forwarded right on to the D. A. R. headquarters in Washington. If the D. A. R. ever got any of the D. A. C.'s mail, they kept it, but, as Secretary Hughes so gallantly said, "The old girls are welcome to it. They get little enough fun out of life as it is."

It was at first thought that an original investment of $800,000 would be enough, but, when pencils and paper had been brought to play, it was found that this sum wouldn't keep the pool supplied with fresh water. So the total was raised to $1,350,000, that seeming like a good round sum. The next question was, where to get it.

The first meeting of the club, as a club, was on December 7, 1912, just one hundred years (and a little over three weeks) after Napoleon's retreat from Moscow. Mr. Henry B. Joy made no mention of Napoleon in his speech from the floor (not that he was on the floor, you understand—this was a business meeting) but he did start the subscriptions for second-mortgage bonds and, before you could say "Detroit Athletic Club," $200,000 worth were pledged. On that very date the writer of this article was interviewing his boss (the advertising director of the Curtis Publishing Company) with a view to negotiating an increase in salary from $27.50 a week to $30—without success. All of which shows the difference between Philadelphia and Detroit.

The next big question was, where to build the clubhouse. Those with prophetic vision, foreseeing certain constitutional amendments (United States Constitution, not D. A. C.), advocated building on the Canadian side, but this was turned down. Had this been done, the D. A. C. would today have had a membership as large as the Boy Scouts of America. But soberer counsels prevailed, and it was decided to purchase the entire block bounded by Madison avenue, John R., and Cross streets, and the State of Ohio.

Now all that remained to be done was to build the house, get in a lot of new magazines, fry some eggs for the first meal, and elect a president. Taking them in their reverse order, Hugh Chalmers was elected the first president, with Henry B. Joy and George P. Codd, vice-presidents, N. A. Hawkins, treasurer, and Old Charlie Hughes, the original trapper and otter king, secretary. The limit of resident members was fixed at 1,500 and nonresident at 500, but with the building up of the Great Middle West and the coming of the White Man, it was found necessary to enlarge these quotas to let in all worthy petitioners who presented themselves.

The disposal of the bonds for the building of the clubhouse figures as one of the major financial *coups* of the United States. In his *History and Theory of Bond Selling in Christian Lands*, Prof. H. M. Dunhan says:

"Next to this (he has been discussing the financing of the Panama Canal) the most remarkable financial transaction of the early Twentieth Century took place in Detroit on December 16, 1913. Here, Mr. Abner E. Larned in the auditorium of the Board of Commerce not only floated an entire issue of $600,000 worth of bonds in two hours, but also floated the Cruiser 'Zippo' which had been grounded in the Detroit River for two weeks and had been given up as hopeless. It was found, after the meeting, that there was enough over-subscription to buy egg sandwiches all around and even then have enough to put by in case anything happened during the night."

And so it came about that the dream of those sixteen ragged pioneers in that little log cabin on the frontier blossomed into reality. The Detroit Athletic Club was built and turned out to be the biggest in the world (this is disputed by the Nordeutchersportgesellschaftundturnvereinbruderschaft of Ulm, Germany, but the Nordeutchersportgesellschaftundturnvereinbruderschaft is not really an athletic club, as many of its members are very fat). Visitors come from all over the world to taste its corned-beef hash and to splash in its pool, or, if cramps are feared, to splash in its pool first and *then* taste its corned-beef hash. It has a club magazine which rivals the best of the publishing world, enlisting as it does the services of such eminent writers as Robert C. Benchley. It has a grand staircase and, in the photograph of its gymnasium, no fewer than eleven medicine balls are clearly visible. On this, the fifteenth anniversary of its inception, we salute its brave founders.

The most remarkable financial transaction of the early Twentieth Century.

Meeting the Boats

By ROBERT C. BENCHLEY

Drawings by
GLUYAS WILLIAMS

A wild search reveals no familiar face.

ONE of the worst phases of staying in America all summer is what is known as "meeting the boats." By this is meant going down to the docks to welcome incoming travelers. It is an incredibly cruel rite and should be abolished.

In the first place, the boat-meeter has presumably been stewing in New York for at least three days before the boat is due—sometimes all summer. He is in no mood to meet anything—much less a boatful of buoyant vacationists. Even if it were possible for him just to go downstairs in his hotel and have the boat dock right in the lobby, he wouldn't be any too game. But docking in a hotel lobby is something they haven't worked up yet, modern science or no modern science. At present, it is the invariable rule of steamers to find out where you (the meeters) are and then to dock at a point as inaccessible as the topography of New York will permit. And the topography of New York permits almost anything.

It is always well to call up the office of the steamship company the day before the boat is due and ask at what hour she will dock. You will talk with some very small child who seems to be dazed by your question and who gives you an answer which is palpably wrong, provided it will parse at all. This will put you on your guard. You will then see that you are up against no ordinary emergency and will begin to worry. All this helps the general effect and makes the day more unpleasant.

There are two possibilities for the next day. One is that you will arrive at the dock (a) too early and (b) too late. The records show no instance of anyone's arriving just as the gangplank was put down. This would be contrary to maritime law.

Arriving too early is much the worse method of procedure, which is probably what makes so many people arrive late. When you arrive early there is grave danger of going insane while waiting. A rumor that the boat is due at 9 A.M. brings you sweating to the pier at 9:10.

You dash up the dock and see a boat already being unloaded and most of its passengers gone. This is terrifying. A wild search among the remaining battlers with the customs officers reveals no familiar face. Inquiries of stewards, if it is a non-English-speaking crew (and it always is), get you nothing but pleasant nods and queer noises. Just as you are about to leave the dock in a panic, you see the name of the ship on her bow. It is *not* the ship you are meeting. Your ship is due on the other side of the pier.

And then begins the long vigil. An official says that she is in Quarantine and will dock in half an hour. Another says she will be in in ten minutes. Another says she hasn't left Cherbourg yet. So you decide not to leave and go back to bed as you would like to do but to stick it out. Half an hour isn't bad. It isn't good, either.

Now half an hour—an hour—two hours—on a North River pier with nothing to do is what makes radicals of people. No matter what the weather may be out in the street, on the pier it is damp and cold. There is a preparation in the construction of piers which is calculated to eat through shoe soles in twenty minutes and freeze feet in forty-five. This gets in its work the minute you put foot on the dock.

The question of entertainment while you are waiting is a knotty one. You may run very fast up and down the pier until you are exhausted and fall unconscious. If unconsciousness is your aim, however, there are less nervous ways of acquiring it, although the use of stimulants to this end is to be deplored, as it is likely to result in nasty complications with dock officials and your being put off entirely. A slow, carefully nursed bun might work out well, but it is very hard to gauge those things. You think you are nursing it along carefully and the next thing you know you are over on your face with an ugly gash in your forehead.

There are games that the waiter can play among the boxes and crates on a pier provided he likes

No matter what the weather may be out in the street, on the pier it is damp and cold. There is a preparation in the construction of piers which is calculated to eat through shoe soles in twenty minutes and freeze feet in forty-five.

games, but, if you happen to be all alone, it is rather difficult not to look silly playing them. One of the least suspicious-looking games for the lone waiter to play is counting all the crates and seeing if he can give each one the name of a prominent character in history.

It is unwise to keep asking officials when the boat is going to dock, as they know no more about it than you do and it just irritates them. On the other hand, it is well to keep in friendly contact with some one of the pier authorities, otherwise they will think that you are a red, snooping about to blow up the dock. Either way, you are going to make yourself unpopular. Either way, you are going to catch cold.

Now, let us suppose for the sake of argument that the ship finally docks. You are standing in the crowd at the foot of the gangplank, trying to spot your mother or your wife or whatever it is you are meeting. After a few abortive waves at the wrong people, you decide that a sense of dignity alone requires you to keep your gestures under control; so you stand impassive until practically all the passengers are off. Then you begin to wonder. Has there been a burial at sea? Has your loved one fallen into the machinery? Whoever the people are that get off boats first, they are never by any chance *your* people. They must be *somebody's* people, because somebody is there to meet them. But *your* people are always the last to get off a train, a boat, or out of a theatre or football stadium. That's the way life is.

Whoever the people are that get off boats first, they are never by any chance your people.

Let us again suppose, for the sake of argument (if anybody cares to argue) that they finally appear, all very flustered and in somewhat of a daze. You rather expect to have them impressed at the sacrifice of time and money that you have made to be down at the pier to greet them, but no. This is taken for granted. Of course, your mother or your wife you *have* to be down at the pier to meet, but you *certainly* don't have to go out of your way to meet anybody else, and the next time they can just meet themselves and see how they like it.

Your presence is not only taken for granted but also your contribution toward the customs duties. "Oh, *have* you got fifty dollars with you, Bob?" they say, "we haven't had our money changed yet and this man says that I have to pay excess on my coat." So out comes the fifty dollars (if you are sap enough to have it on you) and away it goes into the coffers of the United States Customs House —zip! You can also take care of the bags and get them into a cab and you can see that the porters are taken care

of and that the steward (who has been so awfully nice) gets a little something extra for coming 'way out to the stairs with you.

I went to meet Donald Ogden Stewart (I mention no names) and bride on their return from their honeymoon. They landed in Hoboken, necessitating my leaving New York before daylight. Well, it seems that they had plans to go to Princeton to the Yale-Princeton game that afternoon, and, as it would be so much easier for them to drive right from the pier in Hoboken to Princeton, it was only logical that old Bob should take the bags (nineteen pieces) and little Lucy (the worst dog ever smuggled into America) over to New York for them and get them a room at a hotel—a hotel where one could keep dogs.

I didn't want to do this—and did it with very bad grace —but nevertheless I found myself in a cab with nineteen pieces of baggage (including Lucy's dog-house) *and* Lucy, bound for Manhattan. That was a Saturday noon.

Late Sunday afternoon we were found on the beach at Yaphank, Long Island. There were only five pieces of baggage left, and I had eaten part of Lucy while Lucy had eaten part of me. I remember nothing after visiting the eighth hotel and being told that one could not bring dogs in. The Stewarts tell me that they had a swell time at Princeton and that I ought to have gone.

This was the last boat that I met until I had to meet my wife this spring. I determined not to get there too early and consequently tore up just as the last passengers were leaving the pier. I had forgotten to get a dock permit and was forced to scream over the top of a picket fence at my wife and two little boys who were standing huddled under the "B" sign, crying softly and on the verge of being taken up by the Travelers' Aid Society.

"I got held up!" I yelled.

"That's nothing, we've been held up continually all summer!" somebody yelled back at me.

My wife beckoned for me to come over.

"I can't!" I replied. "I have trachoma."

At this my entire family burst into tears and got back on the boat to return to France. I couldn't get in touch with them until I had been to the American consul's and got a photograph of myself with two sides to it, one for the government and one for the class-book. Even then they were pretty cross at me.

So I have given up meeting boats. You can't win. The best way is to go abroad yourself and get met.

*By this time the crowd was
in an ugly humor.*

The Low State of Whippet Racing

By ROBERT C. BENCHLEY

Drawings by GLUYAS WILLIAMS

IT DOES not seem too soon now to begin formulating plans for next year's whippet racings. While there are still a few more races on the 1927 schedule, most of the important ones have been run off and the leading whippets have practically all broken training.

Whippet racing in recent years has deteriorated into a sordid spectacle, productive of only gigantic gate receipts for the promoters. At one whippet race on Long Island last summer, it is estimated that forty people lined the course, and, as each of these forty paid something in the neighborhood of a quarter for parking their cars in a nearby field, it will be seen that the thing has already got out of hand and is now in the class of mad sport carnivals. Tex Rickard is getting covetous.

This has naturally had its reaction on the whippets themselves. They have become mercenary and callous. All they think of is money, money, money. The idea of sport for sport's sake is a dream of the past as far as whippets are concerned. In order to make the game what it used to be, we shall have to bring up a whole new breed of whippets and send the present success-crazed organization out on the road in circuses where they may indulge their lust for gain without hindrance of any considerations of sportsmanship.

Perhaps a few examples may serve to illustrate my point. I witnessed a whippet race in California recently at which the gate happened to be very small. There had been no publicity worthy of the name and the word had simply got around among the racetrack gang that some whippets were going to race at three o'clock. This brought out a crowd of perhaps six people, exclusive of the owners and trainers. Four of the six were chance passers-by and the other two were state policemen.

Now evidently the small size of the crowd enraged the whippets or, at any rate, threw them into such a state of mind that they gave up all idea of racing and took to kidding. In the first race they were not half way down the lanes when two of them stopped and walked back, while the other two began wrestling good-naturedly. The owners at the finish line called frantically, but to no avail, and the race had to be called off.

In the second race they would not even start. When the gun was fired, they turned as if by prearranged mutiny and began jumping up and kissing their trainers. This race also had to be called off.

By this time the crowd was in an ugly humor and one or two started to boo. The state police, scenting trouble, went home. This left four spectators and further upset the whippets. A conference of the owners and trainers resulted in what you might call practically nothing. It got along toward supper time and even I went home. I looked in the papers the next morning but could find no news of the races, so I gathered that the rest of the heats had been called off too.

This pretty well indicates the state in which whippet racing now finds itself in this country. The remedy is up to those of us old whippet fanciers who have the time and the means to reform the thing from the ground up.

First, I would recommend a revision of the system of whippet-calling. As you no doubt know, a whippet race is at least one-third dependent on calling. The trainer leads the whippet from the finish line up the lane to the starting point (a silly procedure to begin with) and then holds him in leash until the gun. The owner, or some close personal friend, stands at the finish line and calls to the whippet, which is supposed to drive him crazy and make him run like mad back down the lane again in a desire to reach his owner. As we have seen, the whippet can take it or leave it and is by no means certain to show any desire at all to get back to the caller. Now this must be due to the calling. If the thing were made attractive at all for the whippet to reach the finish line, we would see no more of this hopping up and kissing trainers at the start. They would be in a better frame of mind.

As near as I could distinguish, most of the owners called out, "Come on, Luke!" or "Here, Bennie, here!" Now obviously there was nothing very exciting about these calls. You or I wouldn't run like mad down a lane to get to someone who was calling, "Come on, Charlie!" or "Here, Bob, here!" (unless, of course, it was Greta Garbo who was doing the calling. In that case, a short, sharp whistle would be O. K.)

There must be some more attractive sounds made to entice the whippets down the lanes. Not knowing exactly what it is that whippets like best, it is a little difficult for me to make suggestions. I suppose something that corresponds in whippet life to the sound of a cocktail shaker would be efficacious. Or perhaps the whippet equivalents of a Ziegfeld chorus. I don't know and I don't pretend to know. All I am sure of is that the whippets aren't particularly attracted by what is being held out to them now.

Now in the matter of blankets. On the way up the lanes to the starting point, the whippets are forced to wear blankets like race horses. This saps not only their vitality but their self-respect. It is all right for a race horse to wear a blanket if he wants to, because he is big and can carry it off well. But when you get a whippet who, even with everything showing, can hardly be seen unless you have him in your lap, and then cover him up in a blanket,

It just makes a nance out of him.

it just makes a nance out of him, that's all. They look like so many trotting blankets, and they must know it. A whippet has feelings as well as the rest of us. You can't make a dog ashamed to appear in public and then expect him to run a race. If they have to be kept warm, give each one a man's-size shot of rye before he starts up the course. You'd get better racing that way, too. With a good hooker of rye inside him, a whippet might not really be running fast but he would think that he was, and that's something. As it stands, they are so ashamed of their blankets that they have to do something on the way down the lanes to appear virile. So they stop right in the middle of the race and wrestle.

This wrestling business calls for attention, too. It is all right for dogs to kid, but they don't have to do it in the middle of a race. It is as if Charlie Paddock, while running the hundred, should stop after about fifty yards and push one of his opponents playfully on the shoulder and say, "Last tag!" and then as if his opponent should stop and chase Charlie around in the track trying to tag him back. What kind of time would they make in a race like that?

I don't think that the thing has ever been put up to the whippets quite frankly in this manner. If someone could take a few whippets to a track meet and (the whole gag having been worked up before, of course, among the runners) the thing should deteriorate into a rough-and-tumble clowning match of pushing and hauling one another, the whippets might see what it looks like. You could say to them: "Now you see, that's how *you* look when you stop in the middle of a race and wrestle all over the track." They would be pretty ashamed, I should think.

The less said about their jumping up and kissing their trainers at the start, the better. This is something that a good psychoanalyst ought to handle. But so long as it is allowed to go on, whippet racing will be in the doldrums. And so long as whippet racing is in the doldrums —well, it is in the doldrums, that's all.

Better in the doldrums, say I, than for the whippets to so far forget the principles of good, clean amateur sport as to pursue a mechanical rabbit.

The owner or some close personal friend stands at the finish line and calls to the whippet.

It was decided that the place in which we should have to simulate wetness the most was under bedroom windows.

Beating Nature at Her Own Game

At Last a Substitute for Snow

By ROBERT C. BENCHLEY

Drawings by REA IRVIN

WHILE rummaging through my desk drawer the other night I came upon a lot of old snow. I do not know how long it had been there. Possibly it was a memento of some college prank, long forgotten. But it suddenly struck me what a funny thing snow is, in a way, and how little need there really is for it in the world.

And then I said to myself, "I wonder if it would not be possible to work up some sort of mock snow, a substitute which would satisfy the snow people and yet cause just as much trouble as real snow." And that, my dears, is how I came to invent "Sno."

As you know, real snow is a compound of hydrogen, oxygen, soot, and some bleaching agent. There is a good bleaching agent who has an office in Room 476, Mechanics' Bank Building. He was formerly general passenger agent for the Boston and Maine, but decided that bleaching was more fun. As a matter of fact, his name is A. E. Roff, or some such thing.

Again, as you know, real snow is formed by the passage of clouds through pockets of air which are lighter than the air itself, if such a phenomenon were possible. That is to say, these clouds (A) passing through these air-pockets (C) create a certain atmospheric condition known as a "French vacuum." This, in turn, creates a certain amount of ill feeling, and the result is what we call "snow," or, more often, what we call "this lousy snow."

Now in figuring out what I would have to do to concoct a mock snow, it was necessary to run over in my mind the qualities of snow as we know it. What are the characteristic functions of snow?

Well, first, to block traffic. Any adequate substitute for snow must be of such a nature that it can be so applied to the streets of a city as to tie up all vehicular movement for at least two days. This, I thought, requires distribution. Our new snow must be easily and quickly distributed to all parts of town. This will necessitate trucks, and trucks will necessitate the employment of drivers. *Now,* if the weather is cold—and what good is snow unless the weather is cold enough to make it uncomfortable?—these drivers (B) will have to have mittens. So mittens are the first thing that we must get in the way of equipment. And I took a piece of paper and wrote down "Mittens." This I crossed out and in its place I wrote down "Mittens" again. So far, so good.

Next, one of the chief functions of real snow is to get up in under the cuffs of your sleeves and down inside the collar of your overcoat. Here was a tough one! How to work up something which could be placed up the sleeves and inside the overcoat collars of pedestrians without causing them the inconvenience of stopping and helping the process. For no substitute for snow could ever be popular which called for any effort on the part of the public. The public wants all the advantages of a thing. Oh, yes! But it doesn't want to go to any trouble to get them. Oh, no! No trouble! If it is going to have snow up its sleeves and in its collars, it wants it put there while it is walking along the street, and no stopping to unbutton or roll back.

So it was evident that, if this function of snow was to be imitated, it would be necessary to hire boys to run along beside people and tuck the substitute in their sleeves and collars as they walked. One boy could perhaps tuck two hundred handfuls in an afternoon, and when you figure out the number of people abroad on a good snowy afternoon, you will realize the enormous number of boys it would take to do the job. Girls would be even worse, because they would stop to talk with people.

The problem of distribution thus unsuccessfully met with, the next thing was to decide what other attribute our "Sno" should have that would give it a place in the hearts of millions of snow-lovers throughout the country. Someone suggested "wetness," and in half a second the cry had been taken up in all corners of the conference room—for we were in conference by now—"Wetness! Wetness! Our 'Sno' must be wet!"

It was decided that the place in which we should have to simulate wetness the most was under bedroom windows. Who does not remember getting up to shut the bedroom windows and stepping into a generous assortment of snowflakes in their prettiest form of disintegration — water? Or even into a drift 'way, 'way out in the middle of the room right where Daddy could slip in it on his way to and from the office? This is perhaps the most difficult feature of snow to imitate—this bedroom drifting, and if, in addition to getting our composition snow into bedroom windows, we could manage some appliance whereby it could be shot into the folds of whatever underclothing might be lying on the chair nearest the window, then indeed might we cry "Eureka!" or even "Huzzah!"

The way in which we decided on the name "Sno" for

Little girls would stop to talk.

our product would make a story all in itself. The copyright laws forbid one from naming anything "Snow," or "Gold," or "Rolls-Royce," or any such noun. This law was passed by some fanatics who took advantage of our boys' being away at war to plunge the country into an orgy of blue laws. However, we have no other course than to abide by this unjust code as it stands.

We therefore decided that, by dropping the *w*, we could make a word which would sound almost like the real word and yet evade the technical provisions of the law. Some of the backers held out for a name like "Flakies" or "Lumpps," but our advertising man, who specializes on consumer light refractions, told us that the effect of a word like "Sno" on the eye of the reader would telegraph a more favorable message to his brain than that of a longer word ending in "ies" or "umpps." Look at the word "Ford," for instance. The success of the Ford product is almost entirely due to favorable light refractions of the name on the consumer's retina.

This decided us on the tradename "Sno" and left nothing more for us to do but work out the actual physical make-up of the product and the sort of package to put it out in. The package is also an important feature of any merchandising scheme, and it was decided that a miniature snowshoe would be appropriate and rather smart for our particular article. If we could work out some way in which "Sno" could be wrapped up in a six-inch snowshoe it would not only give the dealer something snappy to display but would make a nice-looking package for the consumer to take home—nicer-looking than a snootful of Scotch, for example. You would be surprised, however, to find how difficult it is to wrap up a unit of imitation snow in a snowshoe, unless you put them both in a box together, which runs into too much money.

And now all that remains to divulge is the physical make-up of "Sno." That is what we are working on now.

The problem of distribution thus unsuccessfully met with, the next thing was to decide what other attribute our "Sno" should have. Someone suggested "wetness," and in half a second the cry had been taken up in all corners of the conference room: "Wetness! Wetness! Our 'Sno' must be wet!"

Getting In on the Ground Floor

By Robert C. Benchley

Drawings by Burt Thomas

*Mr. Walter M. Teevish discovers
the Atlantic Ocean.*

EDITOR'S NOTE—*The following inimitable burlesque on the methods of some "high-power" bond salesmen was delivered by Robert C. Benchley at the club's recent bond-fire dinner. It was so well received by those present that it is printed here in order that all readers of the D. A. C. NEWS may enjoy the same treat that was necessarily limited to a small percentage of them upon the occasion of its original presentation.*

As I UNDERSTAND this dinner, it is given in celebration of one of the few instances in financial history where the sucker gets his money back. This constitutes a very auspicious occasion, but I hope it does not get back to some bond salesmen in New York that I know about. There is one guy in particular who has been chasing me around for three months now, trying to sell me something in an athletic club which, I gathered from him, is to be erected on the site where the present New York Public Library stands, with an outdoor swimming pool where Bryant Park is now. Inside, there are to be grass tennis courts, a two-mile straightaway course for crew racing, hot and cold Scotch in the lockers, and a complete file of *La Vie Parisienne* way back to Ninety-eight. That is the way he outlines it now. I gather it is a very fair proposition. Anybody that comes in on it can count on giving up work after 1929. But if he ever hears about this D. A. C. business, I will have to shoot him.

Since you D. A. C. men have been so fortunate in this instance, I wonder if I could interest you in a little proposition that *our* house is sponsoring. Just a little something that we are getting out for a few of our old customers. Really, gentlemen, I have no personal interest in whether you buy the bonds or not. As a matter of fact, the fewer bonds I sell, the more I have left for myself, and I am no fool. But really, I figure this out to be one of the nicest little propositions I have ever seen, and I have not seen many propositions, either. I almost saw Niagara Falls coming up here, but it was on the other side of the car.

The firm that we are getting these out for is the American Transcontinental Manufacturing & Holding Company, or, as it is jokingly known on Wall Street, the A. T. M. & H., sometimes the W. and Y. This is a new company, but a reorganization of the old A. T. M. N. & B., which in turn was a reorganization of the old A. T. M. N. & B.- sharp, some of the directors of which are to this very day where they were put after the company's first reorganization.

Now this new bond issue simply means that while the company already has plenty of money to go ahead with —well, within fifteen dollars of enough—we want to get as many different people in as many different sections of the country interested, so that we won't grow provincial or narrow in our policies; and also so that a bondholder, when he is traveling through the country, no matter what city he is in, can call up another bondholder and say hello, or spend the night. We are selling these to both sexes. It is to be just a great sort of fraternal organization, everybody bound together by the ties of a common worry.

Now perhaps you would be interested in a slight financial prospectus of this company. If you are not interested, you are going to hear it anyway, unless you have got some way of getting out of this room.

In 1904, this commodity was exported at the value of $34,000,000. In 1905, or ten years later, the exports had risen to $155,000, or an increase of 111 per cent over the preceding February. Now, this does not include turnover. As a matter of fact, the company had very little trouble with its turnover during that period. I once knew of a company in Minneapolis that hadn't had a turnover for fifteen years. Nobody seemed to know or mind, it was just one of those things. You either have it, or you don't.

Now, continuing, in 1912, the year of the war, there were 160,000 of those sold in Michigan alone. Now, I want to bring this down to the present time and place, with time and one-half for overtime, so you will see what I mean. Of these, 60,000 were white, 4,500 were practically white, and 6,000 were the same as those in Group A, or white. This makes twelve and four, which is fourteen; no, fifteen.

Now, let us take bank clearings. The penalty for taking them is fifteen years, I believe. In 1907, National Bicarb went off forty points. In 1908 it went off again, this time to Atlantic City. There was quite a scandal about it at the time, I think. Late in the evening of August 10 of that same year, credit became inflated. This inflation was first noticed by a passerby, who in turn notified the police, which caused a panic, as well it might.

This much is history. What is not generally known is that the Federal Reserve Board, then known as the State Boxing Commission, in an attempt to stabilize the situation and bring chaos out of order, threw on the market 30,000 shares of United States Whistle, with the result, of course, that there was an influx of gold, and another panic. Now, at this point, the directors of the A. S. M. & B. solved the problem by substituting the word "assets" for the word "liabilities." This made the monthly statement read as follows:

Assets unearned, as of July, 1921, 3,000,000. Liabilities, also unearned, subject to change, 1,250,000. That is dollars. That makes sixty per cent to be divided among eleven people, or a per capita distribution of approximately —oh, never mind.

Now, according to the tabulations of *The Commercial and Financial Chronicle*, in its Saint Valentine's Day number, the bank clearings were—, oh, I guess we have taken up bank clearings already.

Well, anyway, the point I want to bring out is that all of this is the result of the commercial foresight and sagacity of one man; one man who, as early as 1848, saw that within fifty years the Atlantic Ocean would one day become the great trade route between our country and Europe. This man dreamed a great dream. He saw that if someone could take the Atlantic Ocean and utilize it and bring it up to date, he would have in his control one of the great means of communication between America and Europe. And to this end, this man devoted his energy. I need hardly say that I refer to Mr. Walter M. Teevish, our assistant sales manager.

Oh, I remember in the early days of the business, when we had the shop at the corner of Worth and Cheever streets, now the corner of Cheever and Worth, my father used to tell this story, before he had that trouble with his hip— that was a funny thing about my father's hip. People used to laugh and say that he would not live the day out. But he went to Florida in 1892, and when he came back he could use that hip just as well as he could the other. Of course, he never used either hip very much at his age.

But, my father used to tell of this day he went into the shop and Mr. Teevish was sitting by the window, and my father said, "Well, for heaven's sake, Walter, what are you doing?" I make no attempt to reproduce the dialect. Mr. Teevish turned, and with the twinkle in his eye for which he afterwards became famous, said, "Harry, you can fool some of the people all of the time; you can fool all of the people some of the time; but you can't fool all of the people all of the time."

Well, the whole town was laughing for days over this. And my father used to tell the story, to anyone who would listen, although in a way, he was the goat, sort of.

It is to be just a great sort of fraternal organization, everybody bound together by the ties of a common worry.

Well, that will give you some idea of the obstacles this little man had to encounter in bringing his dream to fulfillment. People used to laugh and call it Teevish's folly, this plan to utilize the Atlantic. But I ask you gentlemen tonight, where would American commerce be today if it were not for the Atlantic Ocean? Where, indeed?

So much for the manufacturing end of it.

I think you have got some idea from these figures as to what we are trying to do in this bond issue. And while, as I say, I have no personal interest in selling them, because I probably could not collect my commission anyway, I sort of like your looks, and I want to do a little good, I want to render a little service, for after all, doing good and rendering service are the things that count. I remember once hearing Harry Sinclair say that, and I have never forgotten it.

So, in conclusion, I will say that just so long as the flood of alien labor is allowed to come into this country, just so long as our national divorce laws flaunt themselves in the face of public decency, just so long as the forces of unrest are allowed to agitate against our Constitution—I thank you.

Oh, yes, I understand I neglected to mention to you what it is we manufacture. This will be announced next Friday, December 2 (the date of the first public showing of the new Ford car).

✓ ✓ ✓ ✓

Employees Are Grateful

Employees of the D. A. C. have asked the D. A. C. NEWS once again to convey to the members their thanks for the generous contributions to the Christmas Fund. At this writing, the contributions are still pouring in and it is impossible to judge just how much will be totaled for the employees, but probably about $20,000.

However, there is no backing out now and Grandpa steps to the machine. He has his little piece all fixed up, but it suddenly doesn't seem so good.

On the Air

By ROBERT C. BENCHLEY

Drawings by
GLUYAS WILLIAMS

WHAT with General Motors, Palm-Olive Soap, and all the other commercial products going into the radio-broadcasting business and giving out high-class musical and literary numbers, it may soon be so that Mr. Gabrilowitsch will have to don a yellow slicker and carry a fish for Cod Liver Oil if he wants to get a hearing. This commercialization is killing us artists.

It almost killed Grandpa, the author of this essay, the other night, when, for General Motors, he prostituted his art and stepped in front of a microphone to talk precious words and literary nuggets out into the air for millions of unappreciative citizens to hear—and to shut off on. Grandpa isn't used to having such a big audience and it made him a little jittery.

The worst part about a radio audience is that it is so cold. You stand up in front of that pole and pull some of your best stuff right into it—and what do you get? Not even Magnolia. You get a stony silence that hasn't been equaled since they asked for a rising vote of thanks to Tad Jones at a Harvard Club dinner.

The old boy who tried to neck one of the lions in front of the New York Public Library was up against a hot-blooded proposition compared to Grandpa Benchley when he tried to make a radio audience laugh. It is one of the most discouraging experiences I have ever had, not forgetting the time when I winked at the Queen Mother in London once. I am practically crushed and bleeding, and I may go in for writing the Incoming Ships Department in *The Wall Street Journal* as a result.

In the first place, you have to *rehearse* these broadcasting acts. You have to go around at about five o'clock in the afternoon of the day when you are "going on the air" and run over your number just as if somebody were going to hear it. The "studio" is full of people even at that time of the day, musicians, timekeepers, trainers, and managers (there are sixteen managers to every program, each one under the impression that he is boss), and you have to say your piece out loud and try not to look silly. It was all I could do to say my piece out loud. I gave up trying not to look silly right at the start.

Come with me into the broadcasting studio in the afternoon, just as the shadows are beginning to deepen, and let us wander, hand in hand, through Radio Land. A big room, with perhaps seventy-five people in it roaming aimlessly about, just like a *real* business office. What you are supposed to do is to run over your number to see how long it takes. Everyone has a stop-watch, including the girl who checks your coat. And while the orchestra is trying to find "*a*," and the boy who works the dynamo is trying to find his helper, and the assistant manager is trying to find the second assistant manager, and the sunshine is trying to find the roses, *you* mutter in a low tone whatever it is you think you are going to say that night while a lady holds a stop-watch on you without even listening. She's no fool. Her job is just to find out how long it takes. She isn't paid for *listening* to a lot of junk. She isn't even paid for *looking* at you.

All right. You say your piece and your rehearsal is over. You find that you did it in 9-2/5 minutes flat, on a wet track, too. That's great, they tell you. The week before, Irvin Cobb did only 10 flat. You then rush into the showers and have a rubdown, followed by a test to see if your voice can be heard in the next room. If they can't hear your voice in the next room, there isn't much chance of its being heard in Flagstaff, Arizona.

So you go into a little box and say the first paragraph over again, this time into what they jokingly call the "mike." Sometimes you say it into the "mike" and sometimes into the "pat," but it's always the same old story about the two Irishmen. Well, it turns out that your voice

The leader is looking out the window and dreaming of the days when he thought he was going to be a drum-major.

saying that no one could smoke, but you couldn't help it. You were lucky if you didn't burst into flames.

Nine-thirty! The program begins! Mr. Carlin, the announcer, steps to the "mike" and says: "Good evening, everybody! We are going to listen tonight to Mr. Robert Benchley who—" and you can just hear radio machines from Maine to California being shut off. There were probably more people tuning in on weather reports that night than at any other time in radio history.

However, there is no backing out now and Grandpa steps to the machine. He has his little piece all fixed up, but it suddenly doesn't seem so good. The first wise-crack is pulled into silence. When you are working on a stage, at least you can hear yourself getting the razzberry. On the radio you feel as if you were saying it into Grant's Tomb after he had been taken out. The second wise-crack, and an even worse silence. Grandpa looks around to see if maybe the orchestra isn't laughing. The banjo player is puttering with a hangnail. The drummer and the flute player are working on a problem on tick-tack-toe. The leader is looking out the window and dreaming of the days when he thought he was going to be a drum-major. And here are you, broken hearted, and wondering what it's all about.

The funny thing about wise-cracks is that, if you don't get any reaction, they cease being wise-cracks, even to you. The funniest line in the world (which I would like to think up some day but never seem to), if spoken into a vacuum, would sound like the biggest flop in the world. But that is a psychological feature which needs elaboration and this is no place for elaboration. The only thing that can be said here is that if nobody laughs, it isn't funny, that's all.

This goes on for fifteen minutes. All there is in the room is the sound of your own voice, which suddenly becomes the most revolting sound you have ever heard. In the middle of my little act, it was necessary for the male quartet to step up and break the silence with a song. This gave me my chance. I grabbed my hat and said to Mr. Carlin: "Well, I'll be off! See you later." Mr. Carlin said that I was still expected to do more after the quartet stopped. I asked him to do it. "Tell them anything," I said; "tell

isn't much good. You must raise it a little—not louder, mind you, just higher. Or else you must lower it. Not softer, but deeper. Mr. Werrenrath, the celebrated Danny Deever hummer, was one of those in charge at my tryout and he made the big mistake of telling me that I ought to make my voice sound more like a nance. "'Way up here," he said, indicating where he puts "The Road to Mandalay" when he isn't using it, "'way up here in the roof of the mouth." So I socked him and left in a huff. Mr. Werrenrath ought to know better than that.

I was told to come back at nine, as the concert was to begin at nine-thirty. Just what I was supposed to do between nine and nine-thirty I never could figure out, because if there ever was a dull period in the world's activities it is while people are waiting to begin a radio program. You can't even peek out through the curtain and see who is coming in—because there is nobody coming in.

We all got in a little room, the orchestra, the male quartet, six representatives of the advertising agency who were running the show, a delegation of rooters from General Motors, and a dozen substitutes who were on hand in case that anything went wrong. The windows were then closed and the steam turned on. There was a sign up

(Continued on page 144)

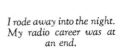

I rode away into the night. My radio career was at an end.

On the Air
(Continued from page 29)

them that I got a telephone call that my little boy has been arrested. Tell them I have fainted. I'm going!" But the quartet had stopped and I was "on the air" again. Five more minutes of silent prayer and the act was over. Jumping on my horse, which I had left saddled and bridled at the door, I rode away into the night. My radio career was at an end.

Ever since then I have been getting letters from Montgomery, Alabama, and Wichita, Kansas, giving answers to some riddles I had asked. I happened to say in the course of my talk that I had lost my hat at the Harvard-Yale game and that if any of my radio audience knew where it was I would appreciate their letting me know. To date, I have received six old hats, C. O. D., seventeen telegrams saying that my hat was in New Rochelle, St. Louis, and Buffalo, and four proposals of marriage. My mother, who heard the thing from Worcester, Mass., called up that night and asked if I had a cold and was I taking good care of myself. My wife and children, who had gathered around the family radio to hear Daddy make a fool of himself, couldn't get the radio to work and heard only an SOS from a ship at sea. As a matter of fact, that SOS was from Daddy himself. From now on I do my act on a stage in front of people where I can see the vegetables coming in time to dodge.

Fast Contests in Ladies' Volleyball

Two ladies' volleyball leagues are playing regular schedules in the club gymnasium this winter and, according to all accounts, the competition is the liveliest in the history of this excellent sport. On Monday and Thursday mornings, the more experienced players perform, teams being captained respectively by Mrs. Charles W. Burton and Mrs. W. H. Graham, with the latter now leading.

The teams are made up as follows:

Burton's Belles—Mesdames Charles W. Burton, C. P. Craine, W. H. Roberts, F. D. Eaman, Andrew Lorimer, H. E. Hund, J. T. Sinclair, E. N. Hayes, R. C. Handloser, Misses Alice and Gertrude Weeks.

Graham Gems—Mesdames W. H. Graham, Edward L. Warner, Theodore Gorenflo, Jr., George D. Lorimer, F. L. Radford, R. M. Connor, C. L. Severy, H. A. Coffin, G. C. Clark, H. C. Capman, C. W. Jinnette, J. A. Moynihan.

In the Tuesday-Friday group, Mrs. W. B. Maurice's team was leading Miss Carrie McMillan's team with five games won and two lost.

The personnel of the contending factions is as follows:

Maurice's Marvels—Mesdames W. B. Maurice, G. Hubert Noble, C. W. Neumann, H. H. Flint, Robert McFate, T. D. Stewart, C. H. Stever, A. F. Malow.

McMillan's Miracles—Miss Carrie McMillan, Mesdames Charles S. Ritter, Gordon B. Raymond, F. H. Phelps, C. G. Franklin, A. B. Hoffman, F. C. Thompson, H. R. Crusoe.

Recent additions to the ladies' classes are Mesdames H. W. Plaggemeyer, R. B. Alling, Michael McNamara, Edward L. Wetstein, J. F. McGough, H. A. Hamlin, and P. E. Marion.

DAC NEWS

RFH

January, 1920

Click Here to Search

D'AC NEWS

COPYRIGHT, 1928, CHARLES A. HUGHES

March   1928

Hockey was played mostly by small boys with a view to hogging the ice when others, including little girls and myself, wanted to skate.

Shinny with Starched-Shirted Spectators and Salaried Sluggers

By Robert C. Benchley

Drawings by Gluyas Williams

THE growth of hockey in the brief period which spans my own life is a matter of great interest to me. Sometimes I sit and think about it for hours at a time. "How hockey has grown!" I muse, "How hockey has grown!" And then it is dinnertime and I have done no work.

But, frankly, hockey is a great big sport now, and I can remember when its only function was to humiliate me personally. I never was very good at it, owing to weak ankles which bent at right angles whenever I started out to skate fast after the puck. I was all right standing still or gliding slowly along, but let me make a spurt and—bendo —out they would go! This made me more or less the butt of the game and I finally gave the whole thing up and took to drinking.

But, at that time, hockey was an informal game, played mostly by small boys with a view to hogging the ice when others, including little girls and myself, wanted to skate. It is true, there was a sort of professional hockey played on an indoor rink at Mechanics' Hall, but that was done on roller skates and was called "polo."

"Polo," as played by the professional teams from Fall River and Providence, was the forerunner of the more intimate maneuvers of the Great War. The players were all state charges out on probation, large men who had given their lives over to some form of violence or other, and the idea was to catch the opposing player with the polo stick as near to the temple as possible and so end the game sooner. A good, livid welt across the cheek was considered a compromise, but counted the striker three points, nevertheless, just to encourage marksmanship. It was estimated that the life of an average indoor polo-player was anywhere from six to eight hours.

Then, gradually, the game of ice-hockey came into ascendancy in the colleges. It was made a major sport in many of them, the players winning their letter for playing in the big games and falling behind in their studies, just as in football and baseball. I was on the student council in my own university when the decision was made to give the members of the hockey team a straight letter without the humiliation of crossed hockey sticks as a bar-sinister as heretofore, and the strain of the debate and momentousness of the question was so great

21

that, after it had all been decided and the letters had been awarded, we all had to go and lie down and rest. Some of us didn't get up again for four or five days. I sometimes wonder if I *ever* got up.

And then came professional hockey as we know it now, with the construction of mammoth rinks and the introduction of frankfurters in the lobbies. Every large city bought itself a hockey team to foster civic spirit, each team composed almost exclusively of Canadians, thereby making the thing a local matter—local to the North American continent, that is.

As at present played, hockey is a fast game, expert and clean, which gives the players plenty of chance to skate very fast from one end of a rink to the other and the spectators a chance to catch that cold in the head they have been looking for. Thousands of people flock to the arenas to witness the progress of the teams in the league and to cheer their fellow townsmen from Canada in their fierce rivalry with players, also from Canada, who wear the colors of Boston, New York, Detroit, and other presumptuous cities. As the number of cities which support hockey teams increases, the difficulty is going to come in impressing on the French-Canadian players the names of the cities they are playing for, so that they won't get mixed up in the middle of the game and start working for the wrong side. A Frenchman playing for Chillicothe or Amagansett will have to watch himself pretty carefully.

However, this is all beside the point—or beside the cover-point, if you want to be comical, even though there aren't any more cover-points. What this article set out

You can slip out and have a session with a frankfurter.

GW

to do was to explain how hockey may be watched with a minimum of discomfort and an inside knowledge of the finer points of the game.

As it is necessary to have ice in order to play ice-hockey, I have invented a system, now in use in most rinks, whereby an artificial ice may be made by the passage of ammonia through pipes and one thing and another. The result is much the same as regular ice except that you can't use it in high-balls. It hurts just as much to fall down on and is just as easily fallen on as the real thing. In fact, it *is* ice, except that—well, as a matter of fact, although I invented the thing I can't explain it, and, what is more, I don't *want* to explain it. If you don't already know what artificial ice is, I don't care if you never know.

If you arrive at the hockey game just a little bit late, you will be able to annoy people around you by asking what has taken place since the game began. There is a place where the score is indicated, it is true, but it is difficult to find, especially if you come in late. In the Madison Square Garden in New York, where every night some different kind of sport is indulged in (one night, hockey; the next night, prize-fighting; the next night, bicycle-racing; and so on and so forth) the same scoreboard is used except that the numbers are lighted up differently. I went to a hockey game late the other night and, looking up at the scoreboard, figured it out that Spandino and Milani had three more laps to go before they were three laps ahead of anyone else. This confused me a little, but not enough. I knew, in a way, that I was not at a bicycle race but I didn't feel in a position to argue with any scoreboard. So I went home rather than cause trouble.

Spectators at a hockey game, however, are generally pretty well up in the tactics of the game, always, as usual, excepting the women spectators. I would like to bet that a woman could have played hockey herself for five years and yet, if put among the spectators, wouldn't know what that man was doing with the little round disc. However, poking fun at women for not knowing games is old stuff, and we must always remember that we men ourselves don't know everything about baking pop-overs. Not any more than women do. (Heh-heh!)

The man who thought of installing frankfurter stands in the lobby of hockey arenas had a great idea. If it looks as if there might not be any scoring done for a long time (and, what with goal-tenders as efficient as they are, it most always does look that way) you can slip out and have a session with a frankfurter or even a bar of nougatine and get back in time to see the end of the period. The trouble with professional hockey as played today is that the goal-tenders are too good. A player may carry the puck down the ice as far as the goal and then, owing to the goal-tender's being just an old fool and not caring at all about the spectators, never get it in at all. This makes it difficult to get up any enthusiasm when you see things quickening up, because you know that nothing much will come of it anyway. My plan would be to eliminate the goal-tenders entirely and speed up the game. The officials could help some by sending them to the penalty box now and then.

As a matter of fact, I have never even seen a hockey game in my whole life.

Orchids, Street Cleaning, and Mr. Benchley

By Donald Ogden Stewart

Drawing by Burt Thomas

NEW YORK, May 20.—My little warning in last month's issue to the effect that I was getting fed up on these official New York "welcomes" to distinguished visitors doesn't seem to have done much good and I must therefore repeat that if they don't stop the whole business immediately I shall go some place else and live. I don't think that they realize here that I don't have to live in New York if I don't want to. Who do they think they are, anyway? Well, I'll show them. Some one of these days New York will wake up and find that I have moved to Bridgeport—and then where will they be? I can hear them now, saying, "Please, Don, come back. Please—we were just fooling. Honest, we won't welcome any more flyers." Well, it will be too late. New York will have lost me—and it will have been New York's own fault. So there. How do they like that for an ultimatum?

Not that the flyers didn't deserve their welcome —and in case twenty-five or thirty more flyers have flown across the Atlantic before this article comes out, I mean the German-Irish team of Koehl, Von Huenefeld, and Fitzmaurice—and it was really fairly exciting at first. Tugs whistling, bands playing, silk hats waving in the breeze, "Die Wacht am Mother Machree"—you'd think

that there never had been a war with Ireland—or was it Germany? Anyway, the whole war had evidently been a great big mistake and we were only too glad to show Germany that we forgave her for all those mean things we had said about her, so for a week the whole city was a mass of German flags—with the exception of one large hotel which made the rather tactless mistake of hanging out the French and British banners in quite a conspicuous place. And the flyers seemed to be having a very good time, too. I didn't get down to the city hall for the official speeches, but I heard them over the radio and, best of all, I heard Mrs. Koehl, who had just arrived from Germany that day. The radio announcer said, "And now Mrs. Koehl will say 'Hello,'" so Mrs. Koehl stepped up to the microphone and guess what she said! She said "Hello"— which showed that Mrs. Koehl was picking up our language very quickly.

And I won't say, either, that the flyers stayed too long, or wore out their welcome— because they didn't. But it got to be sort of tough on the boys who happened to be trying

(Continued on Page 44)

Mr. Benchley returns from Europe with no more baggage than he took.

(Continued from Page 42)

to entertain the public at the various theatres, etc., which the distinguished guests happened to visit. I was at Madison Square Garden the night of the Sharkey-Delaney fight and they arrived right in the middle of a swell preliminary and I wish that you could have seen the look on the winning boxer's face when he realized that all that cheering wasn't for him—that, in fact, nobody in the Garden was even looking at him. And the next night they arrived at *Here's Howe* just as "Fuzzy" Knight was trying to put over some humor on a tough first-night audience—and you can imagine how it helped "Fuzzy" to hear "There's the flyers" run through the house, at which everyone stood up and cheered. That's what's called, in the theatrical profession, "a swell break"—especially as it was "Fuzzy's" first chance with a big musical show. I might add, however, that he made good with what Mr. Benchley calls a "bang"—and if you want to see some grand crazy humor be sure and go to the Broadhurst.

Mr. Benchley Is Back—Fairly Sound

And speaking of Mr. Benchley, he returned safe and sound (well, pretty sound) from his Continental exploration trip and reports that Europe is recovering rapidly from the war, with the exception of two bad oysters in Munich. His reception was not quite as boisterous as that which greeted the flyers—partly owing to Mr. Benchley's wishes, and partly because he doesn't own a silk hat—but several whistles blew as he came up the harbor and Mr. Benchley made a brief speech of reply in which he said he was very glad to get back to America, although he liked Europe, too. Mr. Benchley thinks that there is a great future for America if we can only eliminate communism and hay fever, and that jazz music is dying out and will be replaced by dirigibles and the eight-hour day.

Mr. Benchley, if you remember, left very suddenly for Europe late one evening. His baggage had not been conspicuously augmented on the trip, either; and the customs people just couldn't understand him.

That brings us to the subject of the Pulitzer prizes, which are prizes awarded each year by a man named Pulitzer. He doesn't actually award them himself, as he is dead, but a committee does, and the idea seems to be to combine art with uplift, virtue, and clean underwear. At least, that seems to have been Mr. Pulitzer's original intention. The drama prize, for example, is supposed to go to that play which best "represents the educational value and power of the stage in raising the standard of good morals, good taste, and good manners." Well, the prize winner this year was Eugene O'Neill's *Strange Interlude,* and if that play raises the standards of good morals, good taste, and good manners, "Texas" Guinan is Martha Washington. The prize novel, similarly, is supposed to present "the wholesome atmosphere of American life and the highest standard of American manners and manhood"—and the award this year went to *The Bridge of San Luis Rey* by Thornton Wilder, which, as you know, is a tale of Peru in about seventeen hundred and something. So how do you know where you are? Other prizes were:

Excellence in Greek and Water Polo—Marc Connelly.

High Diving and Domestic Science—Dorothy Parker.
Fattest—Charles Puffy.
Longest Under Water—Hergesheimer.

Speaking of prizes, the prize something-or-other was handed to Jack Delaney the night he fought Sharkey in the Garden, and I never saw a man hit the floor as quickly or as hard. It was a little embarrassing for me, too, because I had just finished assuring the gentleman on my left that Sharkey was a loud-mouthed bum from Boston who didn't have a chance, when I looked up and there was Delaney flat on his face. Well, we all make mistakes.

Howling Mob at Orchid Show

Following the Sharkey-Delaney fight at the Garden came, naturally enough, the annual orchid show, with all the excitement and hubbub which attend such an event, and for three days the Garden was a mass of seething, milling orchid lovers. I shall never forget the scene on the last night of the judging—the hush in the air—the tense faces of the spectators—and then the sudden announcement that *pithicanthicus diplodidorum* of Boston had won. Why, I tell you, hell broke loose. Hats were tossed in air—frenzied women embraced equally frenzied gentlemen—the hall shook with cheers. Nothing since the Armistice has equalled it. The owner of *pithicanthicus diplodidorum* was carried around the Garden on the shoulders of her friends and was finally induced to make a brief speech, in which she said that she was glad an American flower had won, and called for three cheers for *sombottica pysistratus,* the former champion.

Then, forgetting orchids for the moment, there was the big new scandal in the street cleaning department in which it seems that something like $200,000,000 has been grafted from us taxpayers in the course of ten years. If there must be graft, I don't know anybody I would rather see get it than a street cleaner—but $200,000,000 is an awful lot of money, especially with horses becoming scarcer and scarcer every day. What with the sewer scandal on one hand, and the street cleaning on the other, it looks as if Thornton Wilder ought to have plenty of material for another work presenting "the wholesome atmosphere of American life and the highest standard of American manners and manhood." And what a sap I was, to go to college instead of starting right to work with a broom and shovel.

Jimmy Defends the "Peepul"

And so, between denouncing graft and entertaining aviators, Mayor Walker has been kept pretty busy—not to mention the fight which he has on his hands over the proposed increase of subway fares from five to seven cents. It seems that he was elected on a promise to the "sardines" that they would never have to pay more than a nickel for the privilege of hanging onto a subway strap, and now the Interborough has announced that they are going to charge two cents more. Personally, I haven't gone down into a subway since the day I tried to get from Times Square to the Grand Central and ended up over in Brooklyn, so that I really can't take sides in the matter—but it does seem an awful lot of fuss to make over two cents. Why, I often give that amount to a cloakroom girl.

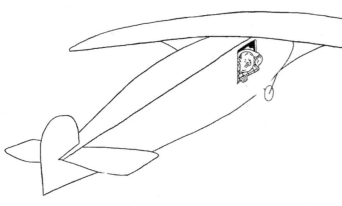

Leg Number One

(Starting the Log of the Transcontinental Benchley Endurance Flight of 1928)

By ROBERT C. BENCHLEY

Drawings by GLUYAS WILLIAMS

IT SEEMS very funny that, with all this talk and to-do over transoceanic fliers, nothing has ever got around about the big Benchley Endurance Flight from London to Budapest (and return) in March of this current year. I guess you have to have a drag with the newspapers, or with the group that eats lunch at the Hotel Algonquin, to get any publicity these days. However, I had just as soon the whole daring exploit went unheralded and unsung, except that there are a few points which I *would* like to have straight on the records. In the first place, I did *not* promise that waitress in Vienna that I would send her to Vassar if she would come to America, and in the second— well, we might as well take the log of the flight, day by day, and clear the whole thing up.

As far as distance went, we flew over 3,000 miles, far enough to have crossed the Atlantic if we had wanted to spend our mileage over that route. The reason we chose the route that we did was because it had landing fields like Paris, Berlin, Vienna, and Munich, on which we could alight, whereas the Atlantic had nothing but a lot of dull water. If the Atlantic wants to get people like us to fly over it, it has got to make itself more attractive. People can't be coming down in the middle of it with nothing to do with their evenings.

In a sense, however, we were really pioneers in the air, for our 3,000-mile flight was the first flight to be made *not* in the interests of aviation. In fact, so far as I am concerned, aviation can stop tomorrow.

I can't really say that the idea of flying to Budapest from London was mine. I had had some notion of going by train. In fact, I had the trains all looked up and marked in red on the timetable. But not one of them was ever used, except once when I missed the plane. During our preliminary stay in London, however, I lived in the fool's paradise of thinking that we were going to Budapest like other people.

The two young men who were fortunate enough to be my traveling companions at the moment (and whom I will call Luther and Erman just in kidding)* had, it seems, other plans. They didn't say anything about them to me at the time, partly because they wanted the whole thing to come as a surprise and partly because I am older than they are and have soberer judgment in such matters as flying to Budapest. (As a matter of fact, granting me a wee bit of precocity in adolescence and a certain laxity in state marriage-laws, I am old enough to be their father, but really more a pal than a father).

So, on the morning of March 6, when we left our hotel in London for Paris, I was under the impression that we were headed for that most charming of all trains—the Golden Arrow. I was very gay at the thought of the Channel crossing, for I am a good sailor and had reason to believe that Luther was not.

"Never mind, Luther," I said, "grandpa will tell you all about the big ships we pass if you can't see them yourself."

It was not until we had been driving for half an hour that I sensed trouble.

"I didn't realize that the station was so far from the hotel," I said.

"It isn't," said Erman. "You're just tired, that's all. Why don't you take a little nap, grandpa?"

This was followed by considerable giggling on the part of the boys. Just then we turned sharply to the right by a big sign which said: "CROYDON."

"What are we going to do, *fly* to Paris?" I said, joining in the laughter. "I didn't bring my helmet." I can joke as well as the next man.

"We've got a helmet for you, grandpa," said Luther.

*TRANSLATOR'S NOTE: "Luther" and "Erman" have been pretty well identified from police-records as John H. Whitney and James D. Altemus.

I looked at the young man suspiciously between narrowed eyelids.

"And a dandy little parachute, too, in case you want to get out and pick some daisies on the route."

I looked at the young man suspiciously between narrowed eyelids, but, as I had been out late the night before, they couldn't tell the difference between that look and the one I had had all morning. And, even as I withered them with my glance, we turned in at the big airdrome at Croydon and piled out like a crowd of happy schoolboys.

"Well, lads," I said, "grandpa will be going back to London now. And the best of luck to you!"

But I said it rather weakly, for I knew that I was caught like a rat. I had never flown before and had often boasted that I never *would* fly, not so long as my ankles held out, but I really couldn't see any way out of this box unless I were to fall down and play dead. And even then the boys would probably have taken me in the plane to Paris for burial; so that was out. My only course was to spoil their little joke by making believe I didn't care.

"You young scoundrels!" I said, laughing. "How did you know I wanted to fly to Paris? Aha-ha-ha-ha! I haven't flown since the war."

"What war was that, grandpa," said Erman, "the War of the Roses?"

"There was a rose in it," I said, reminiscently. "A yellow rose, and it belonged to a little girl, a vintner's daughter, who lived on the road to Senlis—"

But the boys were already out of sight and in the big waiting room where travelers on the Imperial Airways sit and wait for the big white birds which are to make them so sick.

I was a little reassured by the everyday commercial aspect of the place. Bulletin boards announced the locations of the planes which had started out earlier, and a pretty map with little lights on it told what the weather was at various points along the route. Porters apologized by with truck-loads of baggage and there was a general air of nothing-much-to-get-excited-about which made me feel that perhaps everything was going to be all right after all. And certainly enough people were doing it every day. Furthermore, the pilots on these big passenger planes must be very expert fliers, or a great big company like the Imperial Airways wouldn't let them take their precious cargo of human freight up and across the Channel daily. I began to get rather enthusiastic about the prospect.

I was not so enthusiastic, however, but what I could experience quite a thrill of relief when I heard an official say that there would be no more passenger planes leaving Croydon that day because of fog over the Channel and general bad weather over the route. We were going to take the Golden Arrow after all! Oh, well, I had *tried* to fly, hadn't I? A man can't do any more than ride 'way out to Croydon, can he?

Luther and Erman were looking at the map and talking with a pilot in flying togs when I rushed up to join them.

"Toughest kind of luck, boys!" I said. "No more passenger planes out today. Fog over the Channel." I felt a little like Lindbergh as I said it.

"O. K. here!" said Luther. "That means we'll have less traffic to get through."

"If you want to, we might as well get started now as anytime," said the pilot. "I've just got word that things are temporarily a little better along the coast and we ought to take advantage of it."

I looked at the boys, who had started giggling again.

"Never mind, grandpa," Erman said, taking me by the arm. "You don't have to go in a nasty crowded old common passenger plane. We have chartered one all our own, just so that you can stretch your legs out."

"I'll stretch my legs out between here and London, if you don't mind," I said, starting for the exit, this time in earnest.

"Your bags are all aboard the plane now," said Luther, "and your umbrella, too. You can't go back to London without your umbrella."

"Toughest kind of luck, boys!" I said. "No more passenger planes out today. Fog over the Channel."

This was a poser.

"You boys aren't going to fly this private plane yourselves, are you?" I asked.

"Just a little, now and then," said Erman. "I've got a pilot's license, you know."

"So had Mark Twain," I said, "but a Mississippi River steamer has different controls from an airplane."

"I can get the hang of it all right, grandpa, don't worry, once we get up in the air. And Luther here can drive an automobile. They all work on the same principle, don't they, Luther?"

"Sure," said Luther. "All you have to do is not look down. And if you are a good boy, grandpa, maybe you can fly her a little, too. Won't that be fun?"

And the boys took me, each by an arm, and we hopped-skipped-and-jumped out of the waiting room and onto the big field, singing "Fly-away, birdie, fly-away home."

There, on the concrete plaza, stood the "City of Melbourne," with her twin motors roaring, as pretty a Handley-Page as you would care to see someone else going up in. I started to run over in my mind all the sins of my past life, but had got only as far as my sixteenth year when someone said, "Up you go, gramp!" And, sure enough, up I went.

Editor's Note: The log of the great Benchley Endurance Flight in the "City of Melbourne" will be continued in the September number, telling of the daredevil journey from Croydon to Le Bourget and of the monster reception to the fliers in Paris.

The main idea is to tell members of the club where they live, but it would be simpler to ask a taxi-driver if he knows.

How to Use Your Club Year Book

By ROBERT C. BENCHLEY

Drawings by BURT THOMAS

THIS issue of the D. A. C. NEWS which you hold in your hand (or are getting your little boy to hold for you) is the August Number or "Year Book," so-called (a) because it comes out in August (b) because it is the only issue of its kind during the year, thank God.

Its main idea, as you will see by looking through it hurriedly, is to tell the members of the club where they live, although on such occasions as they are likely to forget where they live they would not be likely to have a copy of the Year Book along. It would be simpler to ask a taxi-driver if he knows. However, you never can tell when you are going to need an address of some sort, and it is to fill this growing demand that the Year Book is issued every August.

This particular edition for 1928 is especially valuable and different from last year's in that a finer screen is used in the Ben Day borders on the photographs of directors. This was decided upon after an all-night editorial conference between Mr. Hughes and Mr. Batchelor, during which considerable hard feeling was aroused by Mr. Batchelor's suggesting hand-drawn borders showing cupids

with cornucopiae and dolphins. Mr. Hughes said that what was good enough for Ben Day was good enough for him and that he didn't think that the directors would like the idea of cornucopiae and dolphins, especially held by cupids. The argument raged back and forth all night and into the next day (Thursday) until finally a compromise was effected, in deciding on a Ben Day border *but* with a finer screen. A telegram of congratulation was sent to Ben Day, but the Western Union returned it "not known at this address."

Not many of the club members, as they sit up in bed pouring over their Year Book these summer nights, know anything of the story of the book from its first printing to the present edition. It is a story known chiefly to bibliophiles throughout the country, but to them it presents a yarn of considerable fascination. Ask the librarian of the Widener Memorial Collection to tell you some day and watch his color change.

The original folio of the D. A. C. NEWS Year Book is now in the possession of C. M. Rathbone, a Philadelphian —a fact which should be a living reproach to all Detroiters. Mr. Rathbone is said to have paid $16,000 for it at an auction in London in 1920. Just how it happened to be in London nobody knows, but it is thought that somebody left it there in the Savoy bar believing it to be an illegitimate baby (it was wrapped up in a blanket when found and was soaking wet).

This folio is interesting in comparison with the modern editions in that it contained a glossary in the back giving the French equivalent of all the names in the directory, Detroit having originally been founded by the French and the word *detroit* itself meaning (business of thumbing through dictionary: *detrop-detromper-detruir-detroisser* — there's a funny word, *detroisser*, meaning to churn butter with a left-handed churn—here we are—*detroit*) "straits." The first edition also contains a club by-law reading, "members shall not hitch their dog-sleds to the club porch without written permission from the house committee and not even then."

But enough of this rummaging around among old books. Detroiters may look at this original folio themselves when in Philadelphia by visiting the Rathbone Collection and getting Mr. Rathbone stewed enough to show it to them. It is under glass (*sous cloche*) and is delicious with a strip of Virginia ham underneath.

It is the present edition to which we wish to call attention today, however, and, if you will glance through its pages you will see why the editors are so proud of it. But you must know how to use your directory, otherwise you may get one man's name and another man's address, a complication that has caused most of the wars in history.

Suppose you want to look up the address of the writer of this article, for instance. You first look under "B" in the "Resident Members" which is a fool thing to do as I do not live in Detroit. (And incidentally, this issue is much duller for me than it is for you because I don't know where any of the streets in Detroit are—and don't much care, for when I am in Detroit, Mr. Hughes tells me anything I want to know. If there is anything duller to read than a list of addresses in a strange city, it is looking at the signs on the trolley-cars in a strange city. I gather that Wildemere avenue is a long avenue because here is a No. 17606, but it conveys no picture to my mind. True, I used to do my courting on a Wild*wood* avenue but that was in Worcester, Massachusetts. I used to take my mandolin along to Wildwood avenue and, if I could get my "A" to stay in tune, used to play "Call Me Up Some Rainy Afternoon," but this reminiscence is getting me a long way from 17606 Wildemere avenue, Detroit. And I can't tie *anything* up to Pallister avenue. So you see, I personally don't get much fun out of the August issue).

But you are looking up my name. It's not in the Resident List; so you try, in succession "Nonresident Members," "Associate Members" (all ladies) "Athletic" (I used to be athletic until I threw my knee out being best man at

(*Continued on Page 162*)

The original folio of the "D. A. C. News" Year Book is now in the possession of C. M. Rathbone, a Philadelphian—a fact which should be a living reproach to all Detroiters.

How to Use Your Club Year Book

(Continued from Page 22)

Donald Ogden Stewart's wedding in 1926. Now it is much as I can do to bend it prettily in walking. So I am not under "Athletic" and there is no use looking). You will probably pass over without trying the list headed "Army and Navy" and "Clergy," especially as there are no "B's" at all in the "Army and Navy" list. As there are only four Honorary Members and two of them are Lindberghs and the other two are Rickenbacker and Yost, it is easy to see that the club has been currying favor with the Middle-West vote, which lets me out. All that is left are the "Junior" and "College" lists, and anybody who has seen the weight that I have been putting on in the last twenty years would know better than to look for me there.

So the first use to which you have put your Club Directory has proved fruitless and you have spent the whole morning at it. Think up another name—your own—for instance—and try that. If you can't find it, call up Mr. Hughes or Mr. Batchelor and ask him how to spell it.

If, however, it is found that your name is not in the list under any spelling, don't let that worry you. There are some people whose names *never* are printed in any lists no matter whether they belong there or not. Mine is one. I have sailed on maybe eight or ten ocean liners and my name has never appeared on any passenger-list. (Once I found an "R. C. Bonney" but it never was proved that it was meant for me.) I belong to several clubs in my home town and each year, when the club-book is issued, they

evidently get a man to go through the list especially to delete any reference to me by name. "Here's Benchley's name again" they say in going over the proof sheets, "we'll have to fire that proof reader." The man who sends out the bills is the only one who seems to have my name spelled correctly. He never misses.

But this ability to keep out of sailing and club lists is not an unfortunate one. It keeps hundreds of insurance agents and summer-camp circularizers away and you can live, for the most part, as unmolested by charity organizations as if you were captain of a coal barge. If you are on shipboard you have nobody looking you up on the third day out and asking you if you are any relation to a friend of theirs in Utica, and if you are in a club you have no one calling up to ask if you will write a letter to the Membership Committee in behalf of a perfectly dandy chap, who doesn't happen to be known to three members as yet. And if your good luck happens to follow you into your relations with the telephone company and you are not even in the list of subscribers, there is no reason why you shouldn't live a peaceful and fairly private life.

So take this issue of the D. A. C. News and look at the ads, glance over the by-laws again just to refresh your memory, make a few personal remarks about the photographs of the Club Officers, and let it go at that. As far as your own name goes, take my advice and don't trifle with your luck.

GLUYAS
WILLIAMS

*It was found snugly hidden in
a nest of cartons of American
cigarettes.*

Leg Number Two

of the Benchley Endurance Flight

By ROBERT C. BENCHLEY

Drawings by GLUYAS WILLIAMS

YOU will remember—if you can remember anything at all—that I had promised to tell you all about the big Benchley Endurance Flight from London to Budapest (and return) in March of whatever year this is now. We had just taken off in the twin-motor Handley-Page plane from Croydon and were headed for Paris. (As a matter of fact, we were headed at first for Liverpool, but we soon got that straightened out all right.) You will also remember that I personally was not crazy about flying.

It is now my plan to tell some of the more technical details of the flight, and, although this expedition was unique in that it was *not* made in the interests of aviation, perhaps some of the facts recorded here may be of value to fliers who plan to go over the same route in the future.

In the first place, keep your eyes shut. This does away with what is known as "flier's disease, or throw-up," and,

if you happen to be a little sleepy when you get into the plane, it may result in a refreshing doze. I myself shut my eyes as we left the ground at Croydon and, before I knew it, was lulled by the drone of the motors into a fitful, but life-giving, sleep. When I awoke, we were swooping down onto the field at Le Bourget.

Emerging from the cabin, after a perfect landing (kindness of Captain Olley of the Imperial Airways), I approached the first official in sight and said modestly: "I am Charles Lindbergh." As it was a French official, however, that did not get me a thing. All he wanted to know was if I had a passport. By a lucky chance, I did *not* have one with me, the one I had been using being locked up in my bag in the baggage compartment of the plane. This broke the ice, in a way, and there followed a good-natured hunt through bags and beards until it was found, snugly hidden in a nest of cartons of American cigarettes, which I was smuggling into France. So the French customs officials and I got to laughing and, as a gesture of good grace, I gave them the cigarettes for having helped me hunt for my passport.

There was a tremendous crowd on hand to see us land, the word having got around Paris that we were on our way, but most of them were busy wheeling our baggage into the waiting room and the other two didn't seem to care. So, after nibbling at the sandwich they keep in the Le Bourget restaurant for just such emergencies (Lindbergh is said to have taken the first bite out of it, although the ham has been changed since), we soon found ourselves in Paris, ready for a good night's sleep (a hundred francs extra with wine).

For aviators who have just finished the London-to-Paris flight I would recommend (stop me if I get too technical) a place called Sheherazade, or Florence's, on the Rue

Blanche. Here you can get rid of the deafness which comes from sitting next to the motors, and also of about three thousand francs on a clear night.

We had planned to hop off for Berlin the following morning, but there *was* no following morning that day (it being a church holiday and everything running right into afternoon without stop); so ten days later we felt able to get our shoes on again and in no time at all were on our way out to Le Bourget, which, as everyone knows, is the landing field outside of Paris that Lindbergh made famous by dropping in one evening without an introduction.

A pleasant feature of the automobile trip from Paris to Le Bourget for those who are about to get into a plane is the large number of funeral processions one passes en route. A French funeral procession (there is a dandy cemetery just handy to the flying field) is none of your closed-in affairs like those in America. A French funeral procession *is* a procession and everything but the head of the deceased is on view. The mourners walk behind in snake-dance formation and there are lots of plumes and palms and transparencies, all indicative of the transitory nature of our little life in this vale of tears. After riding through five of these cortèges, the inclination on the part of the prospective flier is to shoot himself right there and save all that gasoline and oil.

However, nobody seemed to have a gun handy and even if there had been one, no one would have had the strength to pull the trigger. So we postponed it all until we should be up about three thousand feet.

The things that fliers should remember about the hop from Paris to Berlin is that, immediately you land at the Templehoffer Flugfeld in Berlin, you should go right to the Adlon Hotel and take a good bath in *kirschwasser*. This wine of the country started out by being straight alcohol, but felt that it didn't have quite enough zip; so, rather than be a nance's drink, it doubled itself up and became alcohol squared (Al^2). That will take care of you for a day and a half and will get all that wind out of your eyes.

Other good landing fields in Berlin besides the Templehoffer are, the Moulin Rouge (a French name, but they are all blondes), Barberina (Hardenbergstrasse 18 . . . . Telefon-Steinplatz 11821), Casanova, and a little place called Bajadere. These fields are all well lighted for night flying, and the hangar service is excellent.

Flying from Berlin to Vienna is a bit different, because you have to come down at either Prague or Dresden, and the flying fields there are 'way outside the city, with no attractions of any sort whatsoever. We chose Prague because we had no Czechoslovak visés and that caused quite a little excitement until we proved that we had $10 (35,000 *zippers*) apiece. Once this had been ascertained, the Czech officials—or maybe they were Slovak, they didn't turn around—were very friendly and allowed us to get out of the plane to buy them a drink. We took one of them with us as a mascot when we

flew off again, but, as he got sulky later, we threw him overboard. We said that he mistook the door of the plane for the door of the washroom and he never knew the difference.

Aviation conditions in Vienna are not what they were before the war. There are plenty of places to land, but the old spirit doesn't seem to be there. They sing too much in Vienna. You can't turn your back but what the Viennese are putting on a Schubert Centenary or a Strauss Field-Day, and a people who sing as much as that get too tired to be much fun in the evening. As far as the progress of aviation was concerned, Vienna was a bust. Mushrooms, yes. At the Restaurant Schöner you can get as nice a mess of mushrooms (fried, like clams) as any flier could ask for, but you can't sit eating mushrooms all night.

From Vienna to Budapest I personally went by train, having got into a windmill by mistake, thinking it was the plane. The others waited for me awhile, but figured out that I was flying ahead of them on my own power and so went on. The train ride from Vienna to Budapest, not being strictly aviation material, I shall omit mention of.

We are now in Budapest and it was here that we decided to turn our plane homeward, first, because one wing was gone and, second, because the inside of the cabin was so full of funny papers we couldn't move about. But I would like to warn fliers about one feature of Budapest as an aviation center—"slivovitz" is *not* a dentifrice, no matter how much like one it may smell. The farther away you keep it from your mouth the better.

And so, happy but tired, we flew home to London, stopping only at Vienna, Munich, and Paris again to collect our laundry and say good-bye to our countless friends who had been so kind to us pioneers of the air.

One more technical detail before closing—our motors were 750-horsepower Napiers and I cannot say too much in praise of them.

A pleasant feature of the ride to Le Bourget is the large number of funeral processions one passes.

Heard in the Lobby

ROM J. U. Higinbotham, our Saratoga, Cal., correspondent, comes the following anecdote regarding an infant prodigy of the Golden State:

"Saratoga rejoices in a hotel (make it 'an hotel' for your British readers) which it has the daring originality to call an inn. We christen the boarders 'inn-mates' and have some wonderful friends among them. The summer run sometimes reaches as high as fifty or more guests. At this time there is parked at the inn a lovely young matron and her three-year-old daughter, the latter a raving favorite with all of the innmates. She is a serious-minded infant and not in the least degree spoiled by the undisguised admiration of which she is the center. Her diction is perfect and her fluty, child-like voice would penetrate through other sounds, only there are never any other sounds when she opens her mouth.

"The other evening, after dinner, the guests were assembled in the living room and The Littlest Girl approached one of the male boarders, a self-conscious bachelor in the dubious forties.

"'Mr. Wilson,' she said, 'will you do something for me?'

"'Of course I will, my dear,' said the flattered gentleman.

"'Please go up in our room and look in the upper drawer of the dresser on the right-hand side under mama's panties and there's a box of chocolates, and please bring me down one.'"

H G. SALSINGER, the eminent sportologist of *The Detroit News*, contributes and guarantees this bit of history:

"When Mr. Robert Benchley, the Deauville crime reporter, took his mysterious trip to Europe last spring, the usual party was held on the eve of his departure. Mr. Benchley was to sail on the 'Ile de France' and all French liners depart at midnight, so the boys generally start at noon celebrating the occasion.

"Plenty of boys enlisted in the cause of Mr. Benchley, and it was 11:45 P. M. when Mr. Benchely and his chorus men arrived at the dock. The ship's huskies were preparing to lift the gangplank and the boys yelled to Mr. France, the owner, that Mr. Benchley was on the passenger list and would be along in a minute. A purser, or some other rude moron, came down to help Mr. Benchley aboard, and just as he got Mr. Benchley's face set toward the 'Ile de France' there was a new commotion. Mr. Benchley stopped, the purser stopped, the boys stopped. Through the hilarious mob came a woman, screaming a path for herself. She rushed up to Mr. Benchley and thrust something into his clammy hands.

"'Here, Bob,' she said, 'I heard they didn't have any

in Europe, so you take these along with my best love.'

"Mr. Benchley looked down upon what he held in his hands and discovered a platter heaped high with wheatcakes. They had been covered with butter and spread with sirup, and the sirup and the molten butter were drooling down over Mr. Benchley's hands and what was left of his immaculate clothes, and some drooled over on the purser.

"Thus was Mr. Benchley started for Europe, and need I mention that his last well-wisher, the donor of the steaming wheatcakes, was none other than the roaring lioness of the drawing rooms—Dorothy Parker?

"Which reminds me of what that droll person, Mr. Franklin P. Adams, once included in his column:

"'Here is how I should answer if someone asked me, "Who was that lady I seen you with last night?"—"That wasn't no lady; that was Dorothy Parker."'"

WHEN "Ted" Paramore and Gene Buck were in town last month in connection with the launching of their new show, *Ringside*, they regaled a group of friends with stories of that inimitable wag, Wilson Mizner, who is said to be the real author of almost every *bon mot* that gets a footing on Broadway. One of these stories has to do with Mizner's ventures in Florida real estate at the height of the boom. It seems that the New Yorker persuaded a man to buy a considerable piece of property that did not turn out to be just what the purchaser had believed he was getting. A suit was started and Mizner was one of the witnesses. In the course of his testimony the plaintiff asserted that Mizner had told him that he could grow nuts on the property. So when Wilson took the stand, the plaintiff's lawyer asked him:

"Did you not tell Mr. Blank that he could grow nuts on that property?"

"No, sir," replied Mizner. "What I said was that he would *go* nuts on that property."

THE movie-talker evolution in the cinema production industry has given rise to one pseudo-story concerning a movie supervisor who, like the majority of the Big Boss's relatives on the payroll, was linguistically handicapped. The supervisor is supposed to have taken in a pre-view of a new talking film and ordered a "retake" on it.

"Why?" queried the director. "It sounds all right to me. It has action, speed, dramatic suspense, and everything."

"Yeh," replied the super, "but I don't like the pronunciation of that guy—I can't even hear the final *k* in 'swimming.'"

"I Am in the Book"

By Robert C. Benchley

Drawings by Gluyas Williams

I need a valet to follow me about, everywhere I go.

THERE are several natural phenomena which I shall have to have explained to me before I can consent to keep on going as a resident member of the human race. One is the metamorphosis which hats and suits undergo exactly one week after their purchase, whereby they are changed from smart, intensely becoming articles of apparel into something children use when they want to "dress up like daddy." Another is the almost identical change undergone by people whom you have known under one set of conditions when they are transferred to another locale.

Perhaps the first phenomenon, in my case, may be explained by the fact that I need a valet. Not a valet to come in two or three times a week and sneak my clothes away, but a valet to follow me about, everywhere I go, with a whiskbroom in one hand and an electric iron in the other, brushing off a bit of lint here, giving an occasional *coup de fer* there, and whispering in my ear every once in a while, for God's sake not to turn my hat brim down that way. Then perhaps my hats and suits would remain the hats and suits they were when I bought them.

But the second mysterious transformation—that of people of one sort into people of another sort, simply by moving them from one place to another in different clothes—here is a problem for the scientists; that is, if they are at all interested.

Perhaps I do not make myself clear. (I have had quite a bit of trouble that way lately.) I will give an example if you can get ten other people to give, too. Let us say that you went to Europe this summer. You were that rosy-faced man in a straw hat who went to Europe this summer. Or you went to the seashore. My God, man, you must have gone *somewhere!*

Wherever you were, you made new acquaintances, unless you had whooping cough all the time. On the voyage home, let us say, you sat next to some awfully nice

people from Grand Rapids, or were ill at practically the same time as a very congenial man from Philadelphia. These chance acquaintances ripened into friendships, and perhaps into something even more beautiful (although I often think that *nothing* is really more beautiful than friendship), and before long you were talking over all kinds of things and perhaps exchanging bits of fruit from your steamer baskets. By the day before you landed you were practically brother and sister—or, what is worse, brother and brother.

"Now we must get together in the fall," you say. "I am in the book. The first time you come to town give me a ring and we'll go places and see things." And you promise to do the same thing whenever you happen to be in Grand Rapids or Philadelphia. You even think that you might make a trip to Grand Rapids or Philadelphia especially to stage a get-together.

The first inkling you have that maybe you won't quite take a trip to Grand Rapids or Philadelphia is on the day when you land in New York. That morning everyone appears on deck dressed in traveling clothes which they haven't worn since they got on board. They may be very nice clothes and you may all look very smart, but something is different. A strange tenseness has sprung up and everyone walks around the deck trying to act natural, without any more success than seeming singularly unattractive. Some of your bosom friends, with whom you have practically been on the floor of the bar all the way over, you don't even recognize in their civilian clothes.

"Why, look who's here!" you say. "It's Eddie! I didn't know you, Eddie,

Before long you were exchanging bits of fruit from your baskets.

with that great, big, beautiful collar on." And Eddie asks you where you got that hat, accompanying the question with a playful jab in the ribs which doesn't quite come off. A rift has already appeared in the lute and you haven't even been examined yet by the doctors for trachoma.

By the time you get on the dock and are standing around among the trunks and dogs, you may catch sight of those darling people, the Dibbles, standing in the next section under "C," and you wave weakly and call out, "Don't forget, I'm in the book!" but you know in your heart that you could be in a book of French drawings and the Dibbles wouldn't look you up—which is O. K. with you.

Sometimes, however, they do look you up. Perhaps you have parted at the beach on a bright morning in September before you went up to get dressed for the trip to the city. The Durkinses (dear old Durkinses!) were lying around in their bathing suits and you were just out from your last swim preparatory to getting into the blue suit.

"Well, you old sons-of-guns," you say, smiling through your tears, "the minute you hit town give us a ring and we'll begin right where we left off. I know a good place. We can't swim there, but, boy, we can get wet!"

At which Mr. and Mrs. Durkins scream with laughter and report to Mr. and Mrs. Weffer, who are sitting next, that you have said that you know a place in town where you can't swim but, boy, you can get wet. This pleases the Weffers, too, and they are included in the invitation.

"We'll have a regular Throg's Point reunion," Mrs. Weffer says. Mrs. Weffer isn't so hot at making wise-cracks, but she has a good heart. Sure, bring her along!

Along about October you come into the office and find that a Mr. Durkins has called and wants you to call him at his hotel. "Durkins? Durkins? Oh, *Durkins!* Sure thing! Get me Mr. Durkins, please." And a big party is arranged for that night.

At six o'clock you call for the Durkinses at their hotel. (The Weffers have lost interest long before this and dropped out. The Durkinses don't even know where they are—in Montclair, New Jersey, they think.) The Durkinses are dressed in their traveling clothes and you are in your business suit, such as it is (such as *business* is). You are not quite sure that it *is* Mrs. Durkins at first without that yellow sweater she used to wear all the time at the beach. And Mr. Durkins looks like a house-detective in that collar and tie. They both look ten years older and not very well. You have a feeling that you look pretty seedy, too.

"Well, well, here we are again! How are you all?"

"Fine and dandy. How are you—and the missus?"

"Couldn't be better. She's awfully sorry she couldn't get in town tonight. (You haven't even told her that the Durkinses were here.) What's the news at dear old Throg's Point?"

"Oh, nothing much. Very dead after you left."

"Well, well— (A pause.) How have you *been* anyway, you old son of a gun?"

"Oh, fine; fine and dandy! You all been well?"

"Couldn't be better. What was going on at the old dump when you left? Any news? Any scandal?

"Not a thing."

"Well, well— Not a thing, eh?— Well, that's the way

it goes, you know; that's the way it goes."

"Yes, sir, I guess you're right— You look fine."

"Feel fine— I could use a little swim right now, though."

"Oh, boy, couldn't I though!" (The weather being very cold for October, this is recognized by both sides as an entirely false enthusiasm, as neither of you ever really cared for swimming even in summer.)

"How would you like to take a walk up to Sammy's for a lobster sandwich, eh?"

"Say, what I couldn't do to one right now! *Boy!* Or one of those hot dogs!"

"One of Sammy's hot dogs *wouldn't* go bad right now, you're right."

"Well, well— You've lost all your tan, haven't you?"

"Lost it when I took my first hot-water bath."

This gets a big laugh, the first, and last, of the evening. You are talking to a couple of strangers and the conversation has to be given adrenaline every three minutes to keep it alive. The general atmosphere is that of a meeting in a doctor's office.

The general atmosphere is that of a meeting in a doctor's office.

It all ends up by your remembering that, after dinner, you have to go to a committee meeting which may be over at nine o'clock or may last until midnight and they had better not wait for you. You will meet them after the theatre if you can. And you know that you can't, and *they* know that you can't, and, what is more, they don't care.

So there you are! The example that I gave has been rather long; so there isn't much room left for a real discussion of the problem. But the fact remains that people are one thing in one place and another thing in another place, just as a hat that you buy in the store for a natty gray sport model turns out to be a Confederate general's fatigue-cap when you get it home. And if you know of any explanation, I don't care to hear about it. I'm sick of the subject by now anyway.

*A couple of young men come in
and, seeing you, go right out again.*

Back for the Big Game

By ROBERT C. BENCHLEY

Drawings by GLUYAS WILLIAMS

THIS is about the time of year—it would be a good joke on me if this article were held over until spring —when the old boys begin thinking of going back to college to the Big Game. All during the year they have never given a thought to whether they were alumni of Yale or the New York Pharmaceutical College, but as soon as the sporting pages begin telling about O'Brienstein of Harvard and what a wonderful back he is, all Harvard men with cigar ashes on their waistcoats suddenly remember that they went to Harvard and send in their applications for the Yale game. There is nothing like a college education to broaden a man.

Going back to the old college town is something of an ordeal, in case you want to know. You think it's going to be all right and you have a little dream-picture of how glad the boys will be to see you. "Weekins, 1914," you will say, and there will be a big demonstration, with fireworks and retchings. The word will go around that Weekins, 1914, is back and professors in everything but Greek will say to

their classes: "Dismissed for the day, gentlemen, Weekins, 1914, is back!" And a happy crowd of boys will rush pellmell out of the recitation-hall and down to the inn to take the horses from your carriage (or put horses into it) and drag you all around the campus. (My using the word "campus" is just a concession to the rabble. Where I come from, a "campus" is a place where stage-collegians in skullcaps romp around and sing "When Love Is Young in Spring-time" in four-part harmony. The reservation in question is properly known as "the yard," and I will thank you to call it that in the future, if you please.)

Anyone who has ever gone back to the old college town after, let us say, ten years, will realize that this country is going to the dogs, especially as regards its youth in the colleges. You get your tickets for the Big Game and you spend a lot of money on railroad fare. (That's all right; you have made a lot of money since getting out. You can afford it.) When you get to the old railroad station you can at least expect that Eddie, the hack-driver, will remember you. Eddie, however, is now pretty fat and has five men working for him. You can't even get one of his cabs, much less a nod out of him. "O. K. Eddie! The hell with you!"

You go to the fraternity house (another concession on my part to my Middle West readers) and announce yourself as "Weekins, 1914." (My class was 1912, as a matter of fact. I am giving myself a slight break and trying to be mysterious about the whole thing.) A lone Junior who is hanging around in the front room says, "How do you do? Come on in," and excuses himself immediately. The old place looks about the same, except that an odd-looking banner on the wall says "1930," there being no such year. A couple of young men come in and, seeing you, go right out again. Welcome back to the old house, Weekins!

A steward of some sort enters the room and arranges the magazines on the table.

"Rather quiet for the day of the Big Game," you say to him. "Where is everybody?"

This frightens him and he says, "Thank you, sir!" and also disappears.

Well, after all, you *do* have a certain claim on this place. You helped raise the money for the mission furniture and somewhere up on the wall is a stein with your name on it. There is no reason why you should feel like an intruder. This gives you courage to meet the three young men who enter with books under their arms and pass right by into the hall.

"My name is Weekins, 1914," you say. "Where is everybody?"

"Classes are just over," one of them explains. "Make yourself at home. My name is Hammerbiddle, 1931."

Somehow the mention of such a year as "1931" enrages you. "1931 what? Electrons?" But the three young men have gone down the hall; so you will never know.

A familiar face! In between the bead portières comes a man, bald and fat, yet with something about him that strikes an old G chord.

"Billigs!" you cry.

"Stanpfer is the name," he says. "Think of seeing you here!"

You try to make believe that you knew that it was Stanpfer all the time and were just saying Billigs to be funny.

"It must be fifteen years," you say.

"Well, not quite," says Stanpfer, "I saw you two years ago in New York."

"Oh, yes, I know, *that*! (Where the hell did you see him two years ago? The man is crazy.) But I mean it must be fifteen years since we were here together."

"Fourteen," he corrects.

"I guess you're right. Fourteen. Well, how the hell are you?"

There is no sign of recognition on either side.

"Great! How are you?"

"Great! How are you?"

"Great! Couldn't be better. Everything going all right?"

"Great! All right with you?"

"Great! All right with you?"

"You bet."

"That's fine! Kind of quiet around here."

"That's right! Not much like the old days."

"That's right."

"Yes, sir! That's right!"

Perhaps it would be better if the 1931 boys came back. At least, you wouldn't have to recall old days with them. You could start at scratch. Here comes somebody! Somebody older than you, if such a thing is possible.

"Hello," he says, and falls on his face against the edge of the table, cutting his forehead rather badly.

"Up you get!" you say, suiting the action to the word.

"A very nasty turn there," he says, crossly. "They should have that banked."

"That's right," you agree. You remember him as a Senior who was particularly snooty to you when you were a Sophomore.

"My name is Feemer, 1911," he says, dabbing his forehead with his handkerchief.

"Weekins, 1914," you say.

"Stanpfer, 1914," says Billigs.

"I remember you," says Feemer, "you certainly were an awful ass."

You give a short laugh.

Feemer begins to sing loudly and hits his head again against the table, this time on purpose. Several of the undergraduates enter and look disapprovingly at all three of you.

By this time Feemer, through constant hitting of his head and lurching about, is slightly ill. The general impression is that you and Stanpfer (or Billigs) are drunk, too. These old grads!

The undergraduates (of whom there are now eight or ten) move unpleasantly about the room, rearranging furniture that Feemer has upset and showing in every way at their disposal that they wish you had never come.

"What time is the game?" you ask. You know very well what time the game is.

Nobody answers.

"How are the chances?" Just why you should be making *all* the advances you don't know. After all, you are fourteen years out and these boys could almost be your sons.

"I want everybody here to come to Chicago with me after the game," says Feemer, tying his tie. "I live in Chicago and I want everybody here to come to Chicago with me after the game. I live in Chicago and I want everybody here to come to Chicago with me after the game. I live in Chicago ——"

Having issued this blanket invitation, Feemer goes to sleep standing up.

The undergraduates' disapproval is manifest and includes you and Billigs (or Stanpfer) to such an

(Continued on Page 134)

Back for the Big Game

(Continued from Page 29)

extent that you might better be at the bottom of the lake.

"How are the chances?" you ask again. "Is Derkwillig going to play?"

"Derkwillig has left college," says one of the undergraduates, scornfully. "He hasn't played since the Penn State game."

"Too bad," you say. "He was good, wasn't he?"

"Not so good."

"I'm sorry. I thought he was, from what I read in the papers."

"The papers are crazy," says a very young man, and immediately leaves the room.

There is a long silence, during which Feemer comes to and looks anxiously into each face as if trying to get his bearings, which is exactly what he is trying to do.

"We might as well clear the room out," says one of the undergraduates. "The girls will be coming pretty soon and we don't want to have it looking messy."

Evidently "looking messy" means the presence of you, Feemer, and Stanpfer. This is plain to be seen. So you and Stanpfer each take an arm of Feemer and leave the house. Just as you are going down the steps—a process which includes lurching with Feemer from side to side—you meet Dr. Raddiwell and his wife. There is no sign of recognition on either side.

There is a train leaving town at 1:55. You get it and read about the game in the evening papers.

No "Staff Photographer" Is Retained by This Magazine

THIS magazine has been informed that a Detroit photographer has been soliciting sittings from D. A. C. members on the basis that he has been commissioned to secure pictures for publication in the D. A. C. NEWS. Absolutely no such relation between the D. A. C. NEWS and any photographer exists or ever has existed. Any promises of the sort implied are without foundation. This magazine never has had an "official photographer" or a "staff photographer," nor has it ever authorized the solicitation of sittings on its behalf. Whenever this magazine desires a photograph it will communicate directly with the person to be photographed and will make arrangements to have the sitting made without expense to the subject or any obligation to order prints for the subject's own use.

The D. A. C. NEWS is always glad to receive pictures of members and their families and accepts these if suitable for publication, regardless of where they have been made. From time to time it uses the work of all of Detroit's first-class studios. It cannot, however, guarantee that pictures submitted unsolicited will be published, as this is a matter depending on many changing conditions that only the editor is in a position to weigh.

Photographs submitted for publication should be sent to the editorial office of the D. A. C. NEWS, 5940 Cass avenue. They will be returned if desired.

D'AC NEWS

Copyright, 1928, Charles A. Hughes

December ⸱ 1928

Gradually, during the Reconstruction Period following the Civil War, carpetbaggers from the North came in and organized these singing groups into glee-clubs.

"Go Down, Sweet Jordan"

By ROBERT C. BENCHLEY

Drawings by R. F. HEINRICH

THERE used to be a time when four Negroes could get together and tear off a little ripe harmony and nobody thought anything of it except that it sounded great. Now, since spirituals have been taken up socially, you have got to know counterpoint and the "History of the Key of Four Flats" in order really to appreciate them.

What used to be just plain "Swing Low, Sweet Chariot" in the old brown book of college songs, along with "Seeing Nellie Home" and "Clementine," is now a manifestation of the growth of the Chariot Motif from the ancient African tap-dance through the muted eighth-note into assonance and dissonance. And over your ears.

Having heard and read so much about the history of the Negro spiritual, I have been moved to look into the matter myself and have unearthed a large block of data which I am going to work into a book, to be called *The Legal Aspects of the Negro Spiritual*. It will take up the little-known origins of the spiritual in Africa and bring it right down to the present day, or rather to December 5, when the book will come out (and go in again after seeing its own shadow).

Commentators and experts on the spiritual do not seem to realize that this particular form of harmony comes from the old African "vegetable-humming," dating back to the early seventeenth century and perhaps later. "Vegetable-humming" or *blakawa* was a chant taken part in by certain members of the tribe who wished they were vegetables and who thought that by humming loudly enough (with the tenor carrying the air) the God of the Harvest would turn them into vegetables and they could get their wish. There is no case on record of any one of them ever having been turned into a vegetable, but they kept on humming just the same, and it is in this strange form of religious ecstasy that the spiritual as we know it had its origin.

Let us take, for example, the spiritual, "Roll Down Jordan, Roll Up de Lord." This is one of the best songs for our purpose, as it contains the particular harmonic combinations which are also found in the "vegetable-humming," that is, C, G-sharp, A, and E, sliding up very wickedly into D-flat, G-natural, B-flat, and E-sharp. In case the G-sharp slips a little too much and gets into H, the singer must open his mouth very wide but stop making sounds altogether.

The first verse to "Roll Down Jordan, Roll Up de Lord" goes:

> "Roll down Jordan; roll up de Lord;
> Roll down Jordan; roll up de Lord;
> Roll down Jordan; roll up de Lord;
> Roll down Jordan; roll up de Lord!"

We then find the whole spirit of the thing changing and the evangelical note so common among Africans creeping into the second verse:

> "Roll down de Lord; roll up Jordan;
> Roll down de Lord; roll up Jordan;

Roll down de Lord; roll up Jordan;
Roll down de Lord; roll up Jordan;
Hey-hey!"

Thus, you will see, does the modern chant derive from the old wheat-cake dance, which in its turn, derived from Chicago to Elkhart in four hours (baby talk). In this dance we seem to see the native women filing into the market-place in the early morning to offer up their prayer to the God of the Harvest for better and more edible crops ("O God of the Harvest! Give us some corn that we can eat. That last was terrible! Amen"). The dance itself was taken part in by the local virgins and such young men of the tribe as were willing to be seen out with them. They marched once around the market-place beating drums until someone told them to shut up. Then they seated themselves in a semicircle, facing inward, and rocked back and forth, back and forth. This made some of them sick and they had to be led out. The rest sat there rocking and crooning until they were eighteen years old, at which time they all got up and went home, pretty sore at themselves for having wasted so much time.

We have now seen how the old tribes handled the problem of what to sing and how to prevent people from singing it. The slave trade, bringing these Negroes and their descendants over to America, foisted the problem on the United States. For a long time, owing to the colored people not knowing that they were developing a national folk song, nothing was done about it. The Negroes just sat around on pieces of corn-pone and tried out various kinds of swipes which they aggravated by the use of the banjo. One of the favorite songs of this era ran thus:

(*Basses*) M-m-m-m-m-m-m-m-m.
(*Tenors*) M-m-m-m-m-m-m-m-m.

(*First tenor solo*) M-m-m-m-m-m-m-m-m-m.
(*Second tenor solo*) M-m-m-m-m-m-m-m-m-m.
(*Unison*) Comin' fer to carry me home.

Under this ran the banjo accompaniment something like this:

Plunky-plunky-plunky-plunky,
Plunky-plunky-plunky-plunky,
Plunky-plunky-plunky-plunky,
Plunky-plunky-plunky-plunky,
Plunk!

Here we find for the first time some evidence of the spirit of the whole race stirring in its captivity. We seem to see the women filing into the market-place in the early morning to raise their prayer to the God of the Harvest— I guess that goes with the other song.

Gradually, during the Reconstruction Period following the Civil War, carpetbaggers from the North came in and organized these singing groups into glee-clubs, each with a leader and white gloves. They taught the basses to sing "Zum-zum-zum-zum" instead of "M-m-m-m-m-m-m" and wrote extra verses to many of the numbers to be sung as encores. The colored people didn't know what to make of all this and many of them stopped singing entirely and went in for tap-dancing. But the popularization of the Negro spiritual was on its way and special writers were assigned to the job of making up words which would sound rather native and yet would tell a story. It was found that only four words were needed for each song, as they were always repeated. Thus we have the growth of such songs as "Carryin' de Clouds on Jehovah's Back," "Ain't Gwine ter Pray fer de Old Black Roan," and "Ramona." The growth of the narrative in such songs can be traced

(*Continued on Page 128*)

The rest sat there rocking and crooning until they were eighteen years old, at which time they all got up and went home, pretty sore at themselves for having wasted so much time.

RFH

(Continued from Page 126)

among Mrs. Moore's works, deserves immortality. Mark Twain, in an ancient day, was enchanted with it. Everyone who has ever learned to know and love Mrs. Moore has done it honor. Thus it runs:

> Many a man joined the club
> That never drank a drachm,
> These noble men were kind and brave,
> They did not care ——

How do you suppose Mrs. Moore ends that line? You have probably concluded already. But you conclude without Mrs. Moore. Incredible as it may appear, those two inevitable words—which so earnestly recommend themselves to you—never entered the sweet head of Michigan's sweet singer. No. Grandly she completes her strophe: "They did not care for slang."

This epitomizes Mrs. Moore. And, in a way, it epitomizes also the unbelievable epoch in which she lived, for there must have been some persons who read her and admired her. Old newspapers reveal criticisms that are little more than screams—of laughter, or of anguish. But on she wrote and somebody published her. Let that be sufficient token that the world does move.

Poor soul, she was hurt by the critics. No better conclusion could be given this article than the words with which she herself concluded a notable lyric entitled "The Author's Early Life." Thus, plaintively, she addresses her public:

> And now, kind friends, what I have wrote,
> I hope you will pass o'er,
> And not criticize as some have done,
> Hitherto herebefore.

"Go Down, Sweet Jordan"

(Continued from Page 22)

in the following, entitled "All God's Chillun Roll Their Own":

> "Oh, I went fer ter see de lightnin',
> Oh, I went fer ter see de lightnin',
> Oh, I went fer ter see de lightnin',
> But de lightnin' warn't ter home.
> "Oh, I went fer ter see de thunder,
> Oh, I went fer ter see de thunder,
> Oh, I went fer ter see de thunder,
> But de thunder warn't ter home.
> "Oh, I went fer ter see de rain (pronounced 'ray-un'),
> Oh, I went fer ter see de rain,
> Oh, I went fer ter see de rain,
> But de rain warn't ter home."

And so on the song goes, with the singer going to see, in rapid succession, the fog, the light mist, the snow, the oysters, the river, Lake Placid, the man about coming to carry away the ashes, and finally the Lord, none of them being at home except the Lord and he was busy.

This marks the final development of the spiritual as a regenerative force and also marks the point at which I give up. I would, however, like to hear four good colored singers again without having to put my glasses on to follow the libretto.

The lisp of the letter "s" has ruined more than one promising "talkie" career.

How I Became a Screen Hero

By ROBERT C. BENCHLEY

Drawings by BURT THOMAS

A GREAT many of my movie public must wonder how I became a star at my age and with my build. Perhaps some of them even wonder how it is that I keep from falling over on my face when I try to walk. My fan mail each day tells me of the curiosity which my meteoric rise in the movies has aroused throughout the country. One fan wrote me last week, saying, in part: "Now I know where you are, you dirty bum, you! You thought you could walk out on that dentist bill of $48, didn't you? Just because you don't live in Worcester any more, you thought you had given me the slip. Well, I saw your pan in the Strand the other night. . . . etc., etc." And so it goes, letter after letter, some requesting my signature to a check for five or ten dollars. or whatever the bill happens to be, some telling me that the writer has changed from Lerny, Hatch, Rabfuggest, and Sloan to Breeck & Company and will be glad to call on me sometime and talk over adequate protection for my old age. I sometimes sit and cry over my fan mail like a little child. It is all so wonderful, so wonderful, that people should be so kind to me.

And now I am going to tell you, my great movie public, just how a sound picture is made. By "sound picture" I mean those moving pictures in which the sound is distinctly heard coming from under the speaker's left arm while his lips move half a beat ahead of the words. It is the Western Electric Company's gift to Mankind (leased out to the movie companies at a nominal sum) and has resulted in such a marvelous reproduction of the human voice that I predict that, within ten years, there

will be nothing but silent pictures on view in movie houses throughout the country.

First, let us take up the mechanical principle which is behind this reproduction of the human voice and accompanying noises. As you know, all sound is a series of waves set in motion through the ether by—all sound is a series of waves set in motion through the ether. Now these sound waves are very much like the ripples on the surface of a pond, except that they do not have little bits of straw and crumbs floating on them. If you have ever fallen into a pond you have seen the ripples go off in all directions toward the shores of the pond, like the lot of yellow cowards that they are. This is exactly the way in which sound waves go through the ether, and with just about as much sense to it, too.

Now, in making a sound picture, the camera not only records the impression of the light waves (I forgot to tell you about the light waves, but if you have ever seen the ripples on the surface of a pond you will understand the principle of light waves, too) but, thanks to a wonderful machine called the "sound machine" (they worked a long time on that one, a lot of people wanting to call it the "sewing machine," but "sewing machine" had already been used), the camera also records the sound waves as well. (Those of you who have ever seen the ripples on the surface of a pond will understand the sound waves.)

Having thus explained the principle of the talking movie, I will now let you in on how they are made.

First, you must go to California. . . . . All right, then, you can't make talking movies.

✓ ✓ ✓ ✓

(*Five minutes later:*) Are you ready to listen to reason now? What's so bad about going to California? (*On saying this, I break out laughing in spite of myself and have to give in.*)

Very well, then. Make them in the East. You won't get any of that delicious California sunshine, though. (*Here I lose complete control of myself and laugh maybe for five minutes.*) Come on, now, let's quit fooling and get down to business.

In making a talking movie you have to remember one thing: Anything that you say while making it will be used against you. You can't mutter little oaths under your breath or hiccough slightly behind your hand. It all comes out in the blueprint, a little louder than the rest of your talk, if anything. An actor of my acquaintance (one meets all kinds of people in that sort of work), who was accustomed to working in a regular theatre, had a scene with a young lady who was playing the part of a nun. The actor, according to the time-honored stage custom, was trying to queer the young lady's big speech by walking up-stage while she was talking, thus making it necessary for her to turn her face away from the audience. The young lady saw what was going on and, as she finished a line which was written: "My vows make it impossible for me to go with you, but I shall always love you," she added, under her breath: "Come back down-stage, you dirty snake, you! I'm on to you and don't try any of that stuff with me." All of which came out on the film and caused no end of hard feeling, especially as the actor was John Barrymore and the actress was Vilma Banky.

As a matter of fact, the above incident never happened at all and I just made it up out of whole cloth, putting in John Barrymore's and Vilma Banky's names to make it even more interesting, if such a thing were possible. That just shows how easy it is to get stories like that started unless one is very careful.

All this, however, is just chitchat and is getting us nowhere in our search for the secret of artificial rubber—or is it Edison who is trying to make artificial rubber? I guess it's Edison. What we are after is a clear and explicit demonstration of the principle of sound-photography

All is grist that comes to the sound machine's mill.

as applied to the talking picture. That's more like it.

Now there are two methods of making talking movies, both pretty lousy. One method, however, is a little better than the other, because it has the sound photographed right on the film with the picture instead of its being made on a phonograph record and synchronized. In the first system there is some illusion of the sound coming from the mouth of the speaker and his lips seem to move approximately in unison with the sound, so that he does not give the appearance of saying "oh" with his upper teeth pressed against his under lip. In the second method there is nothing to keep him from finishing his little talk as far as his face goes but still giving forth the last eight words from somewhere up in a nearby tree.

There is also a big problem which male actors have to face in talking for the films, and that is the lisping "s." Apparently the "s" in talkie reproduction fills up with ink or something, for when it comes out the speaker has as nice a little lisp as a Shubert-chorus man. This, together with the naturally rich and luscious quality which the voice takes on in reproduction, is likely to cause all kinds of unfair speculation in those districts where the speaker is not known personally. After the appearance of one of my big, super-one-reel features I got a duck of a note from a boy living in Cleveland, asking if I wanted to paint lampshades in my spare time. It's things like that which make me wonder if perhaps it wouldn't be better to stick to writing and let my other talents lie dormant until such time as I cannot be misunderstood.

The lisping "s," then, is one of the big things which we who have the good of the talking movies at heart have got to face and overcome. One way would be not to use any words which have an "s" in them, or to substitute another letter for "s" whenever it occurred. This would be rather trying, however, and would probably get you into just as much difficulty as lisping would—maybe more. People would stand for just so much of that sort of thing and then they just wouldn't listen any more.

Of course, the scientific departments in the picture studios are working on these things all the time, and perhaps it would be just as well to leave it to them. If I can just devote myself to my public and live just the kind of life that my thousands and thousands of fans would like to have me lead, I will be doing my share toward making the talking movies a great influence for good in the world. And, if someone else can fix up that "s" so that I won't give the wrong impression to those of my public who don't know me personally, then everything will be all right and I can devote myself to my books, of which I have a great many, and which I love to curl up and read—or maybe just curl up.

Please write and tell me whether you want my mustache to be blonde or brunette in my next picture. I can make it either. Or perhaps you would prefer me without any mustache at all, though in that event you doubtless will be just wasting your vote, because it has been endorsed heartily by the great majority of my admirers.

Somebody evidently called the bluff when Messrs. Stewart and Gilbert shouted, "My kingdom for a horse!"

Hollywood High Life

By ROBERT C. BENCHLEY

Drawings by BURT THOMAS

ONE of the reasons why I didn't want to come out here to Hollywood, California, was because I was afraid that I would have to lead a fast life. I am by nature something of a recluse, owing to one of my ancestors having been a Franciscan monk (good at legerdemain), and the pleasures of this world are gall and wormword (equal parts) to me. Having heard of the fleshpots of Hollywood and the gay life led by the movie colony, I was a little apprehensive that I might be caught up in its whirlpool through sheer naïveté and inexperience and that I might find myself, before I knew it, drinking cocktails and engaging in a brawl with John Gilbert over Greta Garbo. At least, that is what I hoped.

The very first night I spent in Hollywood I took part in an orgy at John Gilbert's house. I had known Mr. Gilbert slightly in New York, having found him in my bed one morning with Donald Ogden Stewart and a small Shetland pony named Black Beauty. Mr. Gilbert and Mr. Stewart had set out on Black Beauty for the country that night and had been overtaken by a blizzard just outside my shack; so what was more natural than that they should crawl into my bed and wait to surprise me when I came in? As good luck would have it, the same blizzard had caught me just as I was rounding the turn from Fifty-third street into Sixth avenue and I had pluckily made up my mind to

spend the night at the trading post. So it was not until eight in the morning that I beat my way through the drifts to find my bed occupied by the cozy trio outlined in the first chapter of this story, and it was but the work of a minute for me to set the bed on fire by a carelessly dropped cigarette stub as I dozed off beside them. Soon we were all fast friends (except Black Beauty, who got to coughing) and it was thus that, on my first night in Hollywood, Mr. Gilbert returned the compliment and asked me up to his house to a typical movie debauch.

Mr. Gilbert's house is situated on top of a mountain and is best reached by tying yourself with a rope to the air-mail plane and dropping off when you are directly over the Gilbert estate. You should let go just a little before you get over the house, as the rotation of the earth will carry you in a slight arc forward and land you just about right. Living like this on a practically inaccessible plateau limits Mr. Gilbert's guests to those who can yodle or have goat-blood in them. The house is of that Spanish mission type of architecture so popular with Californians and so unpopular with me—but there, each man to his own *gout*.

This bacchanalia at John Gilbert's began about nine in the evening and must have lasted easily until a quarter to ten. After a delicious dinner which made up, in a way, for the absence of wine, Mr. Gilbert and I sat around in his vast living room and discussed the question of whether representatives chosen by popular vote should always reflect the opinions of their constituencies or should use their own judgment in questions of public good (*res publicae*, Mr. Gilbert called it). This got pretty dull after a while, as we both agreed on the subject, and, along about half past nine, Mr. Gilbert yawned slightly and looked at his watch. This set me to yawning and looking at my watch, and we both went to the window and looked down at the lights of Hollywood, the wickedest city in the world. They were street lights, as it turned out, all the lights in the houses being extinguished. "Well, Bob, old man," said Jack, reeling to the door, "I think I'll turn in. I have to be at work at eight-thirty tomorrow in Arizona. You can sit around if you like. There are some bound volumes of law-reports for 1927 over there and if you want a drink, just ring the bell. I don't think Nomba has gone to bed yet. He doesn't usually turn in before ten. When you want breakfast, just ring for him. I shall probably be gone. Good night, old timer!" And the Great Lover of the Silver Screen staggered to bed, leaving me to survey the wreckage of my first Hollywood party and cool off my befuddled brain as best I might.

And so it goes up and down the length and breadth of Hollywood, one party after another. If you happen to be dining with one of the big stars and stay after ten in the evening, your host, or hostess, will disappear quietly, leaving you to fight it out alone with the books and magazines. They have to be "on the lot" at nine in the morning, looking very handsome or beautiful, as the case may be, and having probably tried once, in the early days of their careers, looking handsome with a size eleven head and eyes like the hanging gardens of Babylon, have decided that the best thing to do is go to bed early before they get into trouble. It is probably a very sensible policy, but it certainly cuts in on the debauchery of those who are looking to the movie star to debauch them.

Let me describe to you a typical night among the flesh-pots of Hollywood. Don't send the children away—they can listen. They may be bored, but they won't be shocked.

We enter the old Moorish home of our host and slip down an old Moorish hallway on our old Moorish seats until we reach the living room, which is long and high and made of stucco with rugs hanging on the walls. Here we are greeted by the screen hero or heroine in person and the bacchanalia begins. If it is to be a particularly rowdy party one cocktail is served, made of the extract of those citrus fruits for which California is famous and a dash of bitters. This gets the party into a wild frame of mind and then the fun starts. People walk about from group to group saying, "Hello, how are you?" and, before long, are shaking hands and answering, "Fine!" There being no second round of orange juice and bitters, the crowd lurches into dinner.

During dinner the talk drifts gradually to the movie business and the various executives are taken up, one by one, and discussed in low tones. There is also general conversation on the subject of contracts, salaries, options (an option is evidently something that has one more month to run and there is always the

question of whether or not it is to be "taken up." It never is.) This sort of thing goes on in riotous fashion all through dinner, with a climax of a large pie being brought on and fifteen raisins jumping out and taking their places on the guests' plates. By this time coffee is ready, and such a time as there is, stirring it and drinking it and asking for more! It is hell cut loose! Only those who are not actors or actresses take sugar, but you may be sure that the rest more than make up for the abstemious ones and soon there is sugar all over the place. It is like the days when Rome tottered on the brink of self-destruction.

After dinner, the guests are escorted into a private projection room, and, not having seen or heard of the movies for perhaps six minutes, are shown several reels of old comedies, with now and then a scene of two people kissing each other over a rose gate just for sex interest. During the running off of these reels most of the important people take advantage of the dark and the soft hum of the machine to doze off into a quiet nap.

And then comes the mystic hour of ten when the lights are turned on and everyone begins to yawn. Those who have to be up early in the morning (comprising seven-eighths of the company present) go home, and the remaining eighth go home, too. Thus comes to an end one more Hollywood *soirée* and one more step is taken toward the ultimate degeneration of this modern Babylon.

After about a week of this sort of thing, the new member of the movie colony begins to show the strain. His eyes become heavy with too much sleep and his brain becomes deadened with the fumes of ripe figs and avocados. A strange flush begins to creep into his cheeks and unless he watches out, he begins to look healthy. A man can't go to bed at ten-thirty every night and not show it. So one evening Mr. George Jessell, Mr. Marc Connelly, and I decided to take matters into our own hands and see if we couldn't start some of this debauchery we had heard about. Seated in Mr. Jessell's hotel we got out the telephone book. Mr. Jessell claimed to know some numbers.

So Mr. Jessell knew some numbers. He called them, one by one, hoping to find someone who would perhaps give us a clue as to where all this night-life (Continued on Page 168)

Hollywood debauchées, worn out by an evening of conversation washed down with orange juice, go reeling to bed.

Many Seek This Title

THE annual Club handball doubles championships are well under way as these lines go to press. An even dozen combinations are engaged in trying to wrest from Stanley Dickinson and Charlie Dohany the title that they won a year ago.

Two teams are ranked as low handicap pairs, both being given a minus five ranking. These are Lea Henry and Jules Ayers, and Oscar Erickson and Pete Revelt. Incidentally, this is Erickson's first appearance in a doubles event for a long period of time.

Al Schaufelberger, winner of the city championships, last month failed to realize his ambition to annex the state title along with the city honors. Everyone expected Al to go through this tournament, held at the Cadillac A. C., with ease, but apparently he was the victim of a mixture of overconfidence and a right arm that seemed to worry him in his match with Chet York, of the K. of C.

, , , ,

Hollywood High Life
(Continued from Page 29)

was going on. And one by one the same answer came back: "Awfully sorry, Georgie, but I have to be 'on the lot' and made-up at nine tomorrow. Why don't you and your boy friends come around tomorrow afternoon and play some tennis? I won't be here, but you can use the courts." One young lady in particular was press-agented by Mr. Jessell as being very beautiful. "The most beautiful girl you ever saw," was the way he phrased it as he gave central her number. "You wait till you see her," he said, holding the mouthpiece against his chest, "the most beautiful girl in the world." He repeated this several times, still listening to central ringing, and finally looked up to say: "She's so beautiful she ain't at home!" But even that consolation was denied us, for central at last took a hand in the thing and told Mr. Jessell that there was no use in ringing the number any longer as the receiver had been taken off the hook on the other end, indicating distaste. So the three of us took a walk along Hollywood boulevard until we reached the point where the street lights stop (five blocks away) and then walked back to Henry's (the only place in Hollywood which stays open after midnight) and had a glass of milk and a cheese sandwich apiece. This brought to a close our gayest night in Hollywood and us to bed at 12:15.

As I write this I am seated in my own hotel room at 8:30 P. M. Outside some frogs are croaking and pretty soon the night air-mail will hum over, marking the last sound to be heard until morning. Slowly Old Captain Sand-Man is creeping up on me and it won't be long now before I begin hitting the "g" on my typewriter when I mean "f" and leaving out the middle "e" in "every." And then I will totter over to my little white bed and leave a call for seven, for I have to be "on the lot" and made-up at nine. Hollywood has got me in its siren grasp and one more good rounder-in-the-making will have gone rustic. It must have been this way in Sodom and Gomorrah.

The quaint effect of Spring upon some of our workmen

Introducing Spring and Mr. Benchley's Dog-Eared Pansy

By Donald Ogden Stewart

Drawings by Constantin Aladjálov

New York, March 20.—Well, here it is *Spring* again and little birds are singing and crocuses are budding and steel riveters are dancing and leaping around the tops of unfinished fifty-eight story buildings and "something" is in the air. And I, for one, am very glad that the winter is over. It's been a hard winter——

For instance, our radiator pipes. Never has there been such a bad year for radiator pipes. Never before except for the winter of 1908 have they started pounding at 6:30 in the morning.

And cracked derbies. This has been an awfully hard winter on derbies. I cracked three getting in and out of taxicabs, I think, and two some place else, and then one on New Year's Eve.

And moths—I've never seen so many moths. I've tried everything. Flit, Twink, Listerine. I've posted large signs in every closet—"No Moths—this Means YOU." I've sat up all night trying to find out how they get in—and still they come. I've tried being nice to them and reasoning with them, and I've even tried force.

And rust—What a winter this has been for rust! Phew! I don't know where it all comes from. About the only thing that hasn't got rust on it is our cocktail shaker, but mummy says dats 'cause we used it so g-- d--- much.

And chewing gum on the heel of my shoe—Really, you can't imagine what we New Yorkers have been through this winter.

But now Spring is here—and everything is lovely. At least, I hope it is going to be lovely. There seems to be a little doubt yet as to just how this Jones law is going to affect the speakeasy business and for the past few weeks the boys have been running very quietly until they see just what is in the cards. Five years in jail doesn't really appeal very much even to anyone who wants to catch up on his reading, and if the local judges decide to get a little nasty, it may frighten some of the better (Continued on Page 44)

(Continued from Page 42)

class places out of business. However, a number of prominent young attorneys have got up an organization for the purpose of "educating jurors" as to the injustice of sending anyone to jail for selling really good liquor and that ought to do some good—especially to the jurors who are being "educated." Meanwhile a great many places have actually closed up and St. Patrick himself (bless his owld soul) couldn't get in, let alone any one like myself whose interest in snakes is comparatively occasional.

Speaking of speakeasies, the annual St. Patrick's Day parade was a big success and no one enjoyed it more than your correspondent and his friend, Robert Benchley, whom you all probably remember for his splendid work on the screen in "Intolerance." At least, I think it was "Intolerance"—either that or "The Big Parade," although I'm pretty sure it was John Gilbert in "The Big Parade." At any rate, Mr. Benchley, the actor, (to distinguish him from Benchley the man) and I were crossing Fifth Avenue, or, rather, we were just about to cross Fifth Avenue when what should come along but the St. Patrick's Day parade. Now both Benchley and I, by a curious coincidence, come from an old Irish family, although my family is quite a bit better than his on my mother's side and, in fact, my grandfather wasn't allowed to play with Benchley's grandmother until he was twenty-one, although that is another story and can be found in Elwell on Torts, State of Ohio vs. Benchley et al; pp. 124 ff. On Benchley's father's side, however, were several first string men and in spite of an acknowledged weakness behind the bat, he managed to finish well up in the first division so that when the parade came along, as I have mentioned, we were both not only ready but willing to "join in." And "join in" we did.

Well, it being Spring as it was, one thing led to another and after we had passed the reviewing stand several times without receiving more than a brief nod and a curt "good morning" from Mayor Walker, we decided to go over to the Flower Show at Madison Square Garden—an interesting decision in view of the fact that Mr. Benchley had entered several flowers this year without dreaming that he would receive the "premier prix" (second prize) for unclassified violets. As a matter of fact, Benchley hadn't entered a violet at all but had brought in from his summer place in Scarsdale a rara avis, which is known to scientists as a dog-eared or Benchley pansy and thereby (as is so often the case) hangs a tale. One morning Mr. Benchley was walking in his

semienclosed hanging-standing-sitting-garden and he happened to trip over a flower and fall flat on his face. Surprised and not a little vexed, he eventually picked himself up and began to look for the offending rodent which he happened finally to discover to be a pansy of a species which he had long ago believed extinct.

Interested, Mr. Benchley immediately tried breeding the flower with various flora and fauna in his neighborhood but with no apparent success until July 14, 1928, when his little boy, Nathaniel, came running into the house with tales of a strange new plant in the south portion of the garden. Mr. and Mrs. Benchley rushed out of the house without stopping to put on their respective hats and coats and to their intense delight discovered that Nathaniel had indeed "told the whole truth" and that they were the proud possessors of a dog-eared pansy. To make a long story short, both of them caught bad colds, but, as soon as the little stranger was old enough to be (Continued on Page 92)

St. Patrick investigating the speakeasy question

Introducing Spring and Mr. Benchley's Dog-Eared Pansy

(Continued from Page 44)

separated from its parents, they took several photographs and awaited developments. Nor did they have to wait long. On the following Monday a representative of the National Horticultural Society waited on Mr. Benchley and after Mr. Benchley had finished his salad, he led the conversation adroitly around to the subject of pansies and got Mr. Benchley to show him the photographs in question. Mr. Benchley also showed him pictures of his two boys and himself in bathing at Siasconset, but the other was not to be put off and on August 3, the world received the news that an American had indeed discovered the bête noire of every flower lover's heart—a dog-eared pansy.

Telegrams of congratulation poured in from every quarter of the globe, but Mr. Benchley wisely and patriotically decided to exhibit the little gem first in America, and thus it was that on the afternoon of March 16, he and I found ourselves in Madison Square Garden, the center of an admiring throng and the cynosure of every feminine heart. And need I add that he went to bed that night very happy.

Detroit Shorn of Handball Titles

FOR the first time in a number of years Detroit is without an A. A. U. national title. During the week of March 18, at the New York Athletic Club, Joe Griffin, of Detroit, lost his national single honors and Al Schaufelberger, and Willis Kamman, national doubles champs representing the D. A. C. also dropped their title. In both instances, the honors went to the Pacific Coast which hasn't had a titleholder since Maynard Laswell's unsuccessful defense of his championship at Detroit three years ago.

Alfredo Banuet of the Olympic Club of San Francisco, won the singles, beating Griffin 21-17—21-17. Then, with Lane McMillan, Banuet beat "Schauf" and Kamman in two comparatively easy games.

Banuet was the sensation of the tournament.

54-40 or Fight

TWO members of the club met in the lobby the other day and Smith asked Jones where he was living.

"I've moved to the Belcrest Apartments, 5440 Cass avenue," replied Jones.

"Why, that's strange. I thought that you told me the last time I saw you that you were looking at an apartment on East Jefferson and had just about decided to take it."

"Yes, I had decided to move to the East Side, but my wife insisted on 5440 Cass and, rather than run the risk of a serious row, I agreed. Anything for peace in the family."

"Ah, I see," concluded Smith. "It was a case of 'Fifty-Four, Forty or Fight'; and you backed down."

Bringing Back the Morris Dance

By Robert C. Benchley

Drawings by
Gluyas Williams

I DON'T know why I never thought to speak of it before, but we don't do nearly enough Morris-dancing in this country. These fine early summer days (I take it for granted that, by the time this appears, there will have been some fine days, although I have no grounds on which to base this assumption.) it seems a shame to be devoting ourselves to golf and tennis and drinking when we might be out of doors prancing around a pole and falling down every few feet.

In Merrie Englandie they used to have quite a good time doing this, and there is no reason why we shouldn't today, except that good poles are hard to get. Poles with ribands on them are practically unknown. The thing to do is get a pole and put the ribands on yourself, and then you are sure that they are fresh.

Of course, it is not necessary to have a pole for your Morris dance, but it is better because then you have something to lean against when you get tired. (I am tired before I start, just thinking about it.) The chief thing for Morris dancing is a smock and lots of ribands. I am sorry to keep harping on this riband business, but you are just nobody in Morris-dancing circles unless you have a lot of ribands hanging off you. These serve to float in the wind and to trip you up. I am going right ahead in this thesis on the assumption that "ribands" are the same as our "ribbons," although I haven't looked it up. If they are something entirely different, then I am getting myself into a terrible mix-up and might better stop right here.

Bells are also worn strapped to the dancers' legs to give warning to the other dancers and show where each individual is at any given time. These dances used to run on 'way into the night sometimes and, without the bells, there would be nasty collisions and perhaps serious

Then you have something to lean against when you get tired

injury. It is essential that the bells be strapped tightly to the legs, otherwise the dancer will have to keep stooping and hitching them up every few steps, thereby spoiling the symmetry of the dance figure. If the bells *are* loose and there is no way of tightening them, the next best thing is to have a very small child run along beside the dancer and hold them up. It would have to be a *very* small child, though, so small as to be almost repulsive.

I had always thought (when I thought of it at all) that the name "Morris dance" came from William Morris who designed the old Morris chairs. By the way, did you ever see a Morris chair that wasn't old? They must have been new *some* time, when they were bought, but by the time anyone ever got to looking at them the seats were all sunken in and the arms covered with cigarette burns. Perhaps that was the way William Morris designed them. I frankly don't know, as I never happened to see any of his blue prints on that particular job. As I look back on them now, it also seems that they were always awfully low, so low as to be almost a part of the floor. It was always very difficult to get up out of one once you got in, and I wouldn't be surprised if a great many people are still sitting in them, which would account for where a great many people that have been missing still are. Expeditions might be started to go and get missing people out of Morris chairs—or maybe you don't care.

Well, anyway, it *wasn't* that William Morris who worked up the Morris dance, because he came a great deal later and was too busy with chairs, anyway. I understand that the Moors in Spain did the first Morris dances, and called it the "Morisco," probably a trade name like "Nabisco" and "Delco." It is barely possible that one of the Marx Brothers' ancestors, named Mawruss, invented it and began

21

that pleasing trick of nomenclature which has resulted in "Groucho," "Harpo," "Chico," and "Zeppo" among his descendants. At any rate, the dance that the Moors used to do was the "Morisco" and "Morris" was as near as the English could get the name. You would think that a great big nation like England could get the little name "Morisco" right. But no.

We are told that, in Merrie Englandie, one of the dancers was always decked out as Robin Hood "with a magpye's plume to hys capp and a russat bearde compos'd of horses hair," which is as lousy spelling as you will see grouped together in any one sentence anywhere. At first, the only music was that of the bells, but that got pretty tiresome after a while and they brought out a flute or "tabor," which probably added nothing. I can, offhand, think of nothing more dismal than that must have been.

Of course, I hope that you don't think that I am under the impression that the Morris dance was the *first* outdoor dancing done by people. I am not quite *that* much of a ninny. The first records that we have of such things are those of the Egyptians about 5000 B. C. (And what a long time ago *that* was!) Nobody knows what they had to dance about in 5000 B. C., but they were hard at it, for we find pictures of them dancing on their sarcophagi. That is, they didn't *dance* on their sarcophagi but they drew pictures on their sarcophagi of dancing, which must have been almost as painful. In this dance, eight maidens from the local maidenry danced around and around with no particular idea in mind, finally falling down when they got tired, which was in anywhere from ten to fifteen minutes. This left them with the rest of the afternoon free, but they probably weren't good for much.

Sex is about the last thing that would enter your head

Most all folk dancing that followed this has been based on the same idea—round, and round, and round, and then stop. In the Chinese court dances they did a great deal of banging as they danced, striking swords on shields and scowling, but there is no record of anyone ever getting hurt. They got awfully tired, though. That seems to be the story of all group dancing down through the ages, people getting awfully tired. It is a wonder that no one ever thought of just not dancing at all.

Sometimes, of course, the dances did mean something, usually an appeal to the Rain God to do something about the crops. The Egyptians had a dance like this, but one year they did it *too* well and got nothing *but* rain; so they had to work in a figure, which was an appeal to the Sun God, to come and drive away the Rain God. This resulted in a lot of hard feeling between the Sun God and the Rain God and the entire dance had to be discontinued, with the result that, for about fifty years, no crops at all came up.

But we are getting away from our Morris dance, which is perhaps just as well. By the Sixteenth Century you would have thought that people would be working up something new in the line of dancing, but the only difference between the Morris dance and that one of the Egyptians was the bells on the legs. The Egyptians also danced sideways a lot which made it difficult for them to get anywhere much. The English rustics did know enough to dance forward and back, but that isn't much of a development for over six thousand years, is it?

A lot of people try to read a sex meaning into dancing, but that seems to me to be pretty far-fetched. By the time you have been panting and blowing around in a circle for five or ten (Continued on Page 96)

It was always very difficult to get out of one once you got in

Bringing Back the Morris Dance

(Continued from Page 22)

minutes, keeping your mind steadily on maintaining your balance and not tripping, sex is about the *last* thing that would enter your head. Havelock Ellis even goes so far as to say that all life is essentially a dance, that we live in a rhythm which is nothing but a more cosmic form of dancing. This may be true of some people, but there are others, among whom I am proud to count myself, to whom life is static, even lethargic, and who are disciples of the Morris who designed the Morris chair rather than the Morris of the dance.

Havelock Ellis can dance through life if he wants to, but I think I'll sit this one out, if you don't mind.

, , , ,

If Thugs Were as Cultured as Their Autobiographies

UPON my word, if it isn't my good friend, Red the Slasher!"

"Well, for goodness sake, Shotgun Nick! Fancy seeing you here!"

"And how, may I ask, has the world been treating you?"

"Splendidly, Nick, splendidly. I've been somewhat er—preoccupied disposing of the Green street gang."

"And the disposal has taken place satisfactorily, I trust."

"Extremely so. Their defeat was as thorough as that of the Angles and the Saxons at the Battle of Hastings."

"Indeed? Including Mike Poliski, he of the Reubenesque physique."

"Yes, even he was, as the racing fraternity would phrase it, destroyed."

"He was a vulgar fellow, half humanitarian and half humanist."

"Your distinction between the two is both witty and penetrating. It describes him as accurately as Voltaire so famously described the Holy Roman Empire. And how are you occupying yourself?"

"Well, I am at this time immersed in plans to throw a snag in the madly whirling wheels of capitalism."

"You mean—"

"Exactly. I have decided, with the help of a few trusty marksmen, to remove a few million dollars from the reserve of the Harrimeyer National Bank."

"And will, if I understand you rightly, not hesitate to dispatch any dissenting guards to limbo if the necessity arises."

"Most decidedly not. After all, modern civilization tends to attach too much importance to the individual human life.

"Exactly. We forget that *man* is, after all, a biological organism relatively unimportant. But I shall be late to the opera. Farewell."

"And I must hie me home to a quiet evening with Spinoza. *Au revoir.*"

—*Parke Cummings.*

DAC NEWS

DRAWING BY R. F. HEINRICH

July - 1921

Some day you may hear of my dare-devil escapades on the Riviera

Mr. Benchley Goes to the Races

By ROBERT C. BENCHLEY

Drawings by GLUYAS WILLIAMS

THERE are several spectacular ways in which I could dissipate a fortune, if I were to have one left to me, but one of them is not horse-racing.

Some day you may read of my daredevil escapades with a team of arch-duchesses on the Riviera in which "Mad Bob" (that will be I) rides up and down the Promenade des Anglais on a high-powered running-board throwing out burning mille-franc notes at the people (all of whom love me for my wild, likeable eccentricities). You may read of someone who has discovered me, a gray-haired, distinguished-looking old derelict, pacing the water-front of Port Said, living on the pittance furnished me by friends whom I had wined and dined in the old days when I was known as "The Playboy of Two Continents," before a group of international bankers conspired against me to wipe out my entire fortune at one *coup.* (I hate those bankers already, just thinking about it.) But you will never hear about my taking my life at a racecourse—unless it is from sheer boredom. That is one thing you don't have to worry about, in case you worry about me at all.

In the first place, I never can *see* a horse-race. Of course, when you go to a race in England, like the Grand National, you don't expect to see. All you do is listen very carefully and peer into the mist and, when you hear the crowd murmur "They're off!" go around back to a refreshment tent and munch on a cold meat-pie until you think it is time for the race to be finished. Then go to the door of the tent and someone (who didn't see the finish either) will tell you who won. That is the Sport of Kings as England knows it.

In this country, you usually can see the course, but I personally have a great deal of trouble in finding out where the horses are. Part of this is due to my inability to manipulate long-range glasses. I can swing them jauntily by my side before the race starts, and I can hold them up to my eyes (until my arms get tired—then to hell with them) but I can't seem to see anything except an indistinct blur of grass and an object which later turns out to be the back of the head of one of the officials. Even if I find the horses when they are grouped at the barrier, I lose them the minute they start out and spend my time sweeping the horizon for them while my friends are muttering "Look at that! Look at him come up! There goes Captain's Garter! Here comes Onion Soup!"

I have therefore given up the use of glasses entirely and carry them just for looks. (I am even thinking of giving that up, too, as I have been told that they don't *look* right on me.) With the naked eye at least I can see the grass clearly and, at Belmont Park, there are some very pretty fountains to watch in case the race itself has eluded you. Even with my eyes free to roam as they will, I lose the horses before they have gone a hundred yards. Everyone else seems to know where they are, even people with much worse eyesight than mine (and I may say that my eyesight is very good as a general thing), but the whole affair becomes a mystery to me until suddenly I find that they are at the last turn and into the homestretch. Then comes the problem of finding out which horse is which.

It is, I will admit, a very pretty sight to see a lot of horses coming in at the finish, but it would be much more exciting for me if I could distinguish the various colors. Insofar as I have any favorites at all, they are always the horses who carry a bright red, because that is the only color that means anything to me at the finish. These yellow and pink mixtures get all confused with the baby-blues and blood-oranges when they get bunched together,

I spend my time sweeping the horizon

and I am constantly upset by the spectacle of what seems to me to be two jockeys on one horse. I don't like to admit after the finish that I haven't been able to detect the winner, and so a great many times I am completely in the dark unless I overhear a chance remark or see an early edition of the papers. This makes going to the races something of a mockery.

Then, too, there is another source of confusion for me in the varying lengths of the races they see fit to run. I think that I am correct in saying that one has a right to expect that any race shall finish down in front of the grand stands. I don't mean to be arbitrary about this, but that is the way it seems to me. All right, then. The last race I saw at Belmont Park (New York) began where they all begin—that is, just beyond my range of vision, over at the right. The horses, as near as I could tell, ran straight away along the other side of the course, meaning nothing as far as I was concerned. Then, just as they reached the far turn, they seemed to give the whole thing up as a bad job and began running in different directions. I thought that maybe it was a game like hare-and-hounds, that one bunch of horses went North and another went South and still others East and West, with the ones who got back onto the course first, winning. But no. It seems that the race was over, 'way out there, and they were simply dispersing for the afternoon. In other words, nobody in the stands (unless they happened to know black art and were able to work long-range glasses) had any idea as to which horse won. I was particularly fortunate in not caring.

But, aside from the strain of trying to keep the horses within your range of vision and telling which is which, there is another feature of horse-racing which seems to me a little irksome. That is the intervals between races. If left to myself I would be inclined to read a good book between times, or even during the races themselves. But this, evidently, is not allowed. You must get up as soon as a race is over and go out behind the stands and walk around in the paddock. Just what good this is supposed to do I never could figure out. You look at the horses and you look at the jockeys and you say "how are you" to a lot of people who are walking around looking at the horses and the jockeys. But as for changing anything at that late hour, even your mind on a bet, the whole thing seems a little futile. Most of the people who walk around in the paddock just before a race don't know whether a horse looks good or not. They just look. They make marks with a pencil and try to appear "in the know" (*slang phrase*), but even *I* know that they aren't getting anywhere by doing it. Unless a horse in the paddock is obviously walking on three legs, or a jockey is obviously cockeyed, this walking around is just walking around and I can just walk around at home (*Continued on Page 129*)

Then I get a little panicky. I begin rushing

GW

Mr. Benchley Goes to the Races
(Continued from Page 23)

or in Times Square. I don't have to go out to a race-course to do it.

Of course, you do get your picture taken. Perhaps that is why people go out into the paddock. But there must be a lot of people who *don't* get their pictures taken, and there must be a lot of people to whom, like me, the whole thing is an empty formality. Certainly there are a lot of people who bet without knowing the first thing about horses. They are the ones whom I would put up for life membership in the International Whatsis Club. I may do a lot of incomprehensible things in my life (and the records show that I do) but I don't do that.

Personally, I always get lost when I walk around in the paddock. I start out with, let us say, three friends, whose company is sufficiently pleasing to me to make me leave my comfortable subway or speakeasy and go out to the track in the first place. We amble around under the trees for a few minutes, look at a couple of horses who would much rather not be looked at, and then, all of a sudden, I am alone. My friends have disappeared into comparatively thin air. I turn to the right and run into a horse. I turn to the left and run into several people who might as well be horses as far as anything in common we have together. Then I get a little panicky. I begin rushing. I try to find the clubhouse. It, too, has disappeared. There are a lot of people about, but I don't seem to know any of them. Once in a while I recognize

a man who works in the box office of a theatre I know, but he always looks so worried that I dare not speak to him. I feel that maybe I am out of place. Later I find that I am. The hot sun beats down on me and I get to crying. The whole thing takes on the aspect of a bad dream. Even if I do get back to the stands, I merely am getting back to further confusion. There really is nothing left for me to do but go home.

Perhaps I was a little sanguine when I said, earlier in this article, that you will never find me dead at a race-course. Perhaps that is just exactly where I shall die. I have one plan to avoid this horrible contingency—never to go again.

English by a Frenchman

HERE's a circumlocution written by a Frenchman who is still struggling to get the upper hand of our peculiar language. The incident is cited by Frank Roche, of New York, the publisher of Automobile Topics.

The Frenchman recently invented an automobile device which he was eager to advertise in Mr. Roche's paper. However, in the rush of things he was unable to get the copy ready at the required time. So he wrote to Mr. Roche: "Dear Sir, I'll have to escape your July issue."

Mr. Roche wonders just what was implied by that.

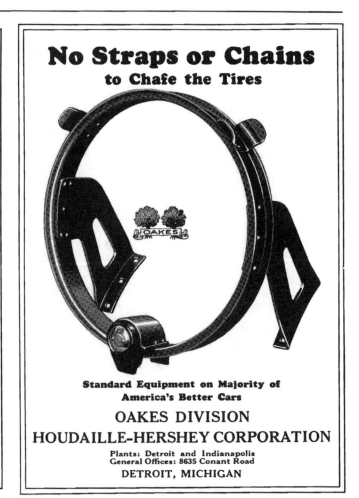

August   1929

Exercise For Those At Sea

By ROBERT C. BENCHLEY

Drawings by GLUYAS WILLIAMS

ONE of the most pernicious effects of ocean-travel, as far as I am concerned, is the exercise one feels obliged to take. I sit at home for 10 months of the year, right on one chair, getting no more exercise than is involved in thumbing a cigarette-lighter and turning the pages of a newspaper. (Sometimes, after turning all the pages of one of those big Sunday editions, I have to go and lie down for a little while). And my health during those 10 months is simply elegant. Rosy cheeks, a good digestion, and sleep as soon as I hit the pillow (or whatever I happen to be sleeping on) are the rewards of my lethargic and sedentary life. If I were any healthier I would smell of pine-needles, and I wouldn't take a walk around the Reservoir if Greta Garbo were to offer to go along with me. I wouldn't take a walk around the Reservoir even if I could be assured of being alone.

But once on shipboard I feel that I must exercise. I listen to people who say: "Of course, if you don't get exercise on board ship you will get logy." Logy? Boy, you don't know what logy is! If I were to get any logier than I am during the winter months they could prop me up in Wanamaker's window and hang dress-goods on me. But somehow this never occurs to me at sea. I believe everyone who tells me that I must keep my blood circulating—my blood, which hasn't known what it was to circulate since I used

One of the most pernicious effects of ocean-travel, as far as I am concerned, is the exercise one feels obliged to take

to ride a Columbia bicycle (without a coaster brake, because it was $5 extra). And, as a result, I go crazy mad for exercise and get myself good and sick.

I will say this for myself—I don't walk decks for exercise. I am not one of those who go barging past deck chairs, counting the rounds, and making everybody who is trying to get a little rest feel guilty and irritated. Once in a while, when most of the passengers have gone to bed, I may sneak out and take a few turns around alone, but that is just to get some air into my lungs before turning in. Those smoking rooms on our more expensive ships get awfully stuffy, especially if you have been eating olives.

No, sir! When I take exercise on shipboard, I take *exercise*. I go the whole hog—and the whole camel and horse and elephant and every one of those inventions of a German devil with which ships' gymnasiums are equipped. From a sedentary, sluggish, and almost entirely motionless human being, I turn into a bouncing, whirling, and perspiring dervish, bent on shaking a leg or an arm completely off and giving my liver and kidneys the surprise of their middle-aged lives. I often wonder what my liver and kidneys think when, along about May or June of each year, they are suddenly prodded out of a sound sleep and twisted and hammered about at five o'clock each afternoon for a week and then put back to sleep again until the return trip in August. Not being an A. A. Milne, I can't get them to talk to me and *tell* me what they think, but I *do* know how they behave in return—and that it isn't very nicely.

At five o'clock sharp each afternoon on board ship, I don a strange costume which I feel, in a way, is rather dashing and athletic-looking, but which really is made up of such unimpressive articles as an undershirt, a pair of trousers, and bed slippers. Then it is up to the gymnasium, two steps at a time, and onto the first piece of apparatus which is vacant. This usually is an electric horse, which has a gait something between a trot and a canter, with just a suspicion of lope thrown in. I haven't been on a real horse since I discovered that horse hair gave me hay fever (and what a relief *that* was, to know that I had a good excuse for not riding!) but that does not deter me from letting myself be jounced up and down, with occasional attempts at posting, until my lower grinders are firmly imbedded in my upper ones and my head a throbbing mass of temples. You have no idea what a sensation *that* is.

You would think that, as I survey my mates at work on the other pieces of apparatus, I would see how foolish I myself must look. Here they are, a lot of middle-aged men (with occasionally a real good *old* boy) dressed like people who rush out of a hotel in a fire, steaming around on bits of machinery, trying one until they get tired (which is almost immediately) then switching to another until they give every indication of bursting, all of them pudgy beyond repair and all of them thinking that in one week's time they are going to whip themselves back into some sort of shape. I will say this for most of them—they don't keep it up for more than three days. The last part of the trip I have the gymnasium almost to myself. That is because I am not so smart as they are. I bide my time.

After the horse has had its pleasure with me, I submit myself to what is humorously known as the "camel." Here the twisting is done, first to the right, so that my left hip is dislocated, then to the left, throwing out my right hip. This goes on for some time, as the attendant forgets me and lets me sit there longer than I should. I make no move to get off, for I am afraid of getting a leg caught in the machinery, and so there I sit, writhing and twisting from the hips up, until the man has finished showing an old gentleman how to race himself on a stationary bicycle and then comes and mercifully lifts me off.

The rowing-machine and weights are more easily regulated, for I can stop doing those myself when I am exhausted. What is more, I *do* stop. I don't care what the attendant thinks—when I begin to see great red flames rising through the sweat which is pouring down over my eyes, I stop. I know when I've had enough. Sometimes I am not able to get up out of the machine right away, but I stop at any rate. Someone will come along and lift me out before long. Red flames I don't like. Not for long at a time, anyway.

Then come the massage machines, which, after all

this wrenching and rowing, seem like mechanical godsends. There is one in particular which comes as a grateful relief, and that is the pair of leather-bound rings which wriggle up and down your back. Prop me up against a pair of those and I am set for the afternoon. After a strenuous hour of punishment, I have been known to lean against those grinding rings and drop off into a fitful doze. Even if I do not go so far as to shut my eyes, I fall under the spell of the massage to such an extent that my eyes become fixed on the fencing foils hanging on the wall, my jaw drops, and my whole body twists loosely in rhythm to the crawling knobs. It is the height of ecstacy (or *one* of the heights) and on such occasions my mind wanders far from the ship and the sea and I dream that I am back in my little old chair at home, far from the apparatus and deck-tennis (as a matter of fact, I am bothered very little by deck-tennis, for no matter how much I feel that I ought to be playing, there is always somebody using the courts, thank God).

Thus do I undo all the good that a winter of lethargy has done me. After three days of exercising I find myself unable to sleep, my digestion suffers a complete disruption, and I feel strange pains creeping over me in parts of my body which I never knew that I had. My skin gets sallow and my eyes sunken, and, the day before I land, I come down with some sort of joint disintegration or other and have to be carried off the boat.

I come down with some sort of joint disintegration or other and have to be carried off the boat

A Message to D.A.C. Members

By ROBERT C. BENCHLEY

Drawings by
GLUYAS WILLIAMS

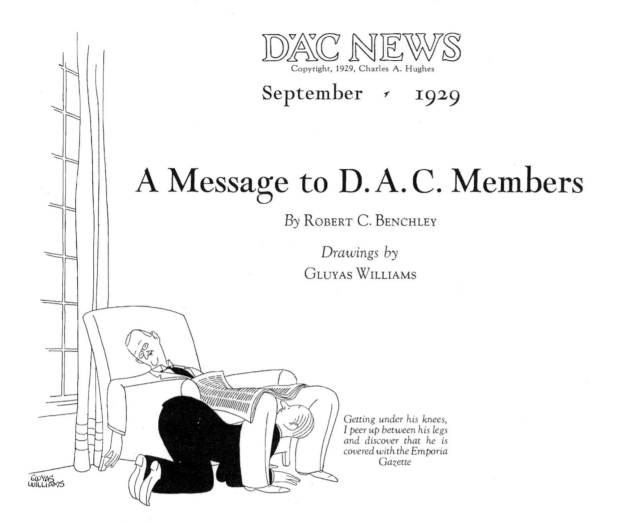

Getting under his knees, I peer up between his legs and discover that he is covered with the Emporia Gazette

M ANY of you men who sit here today without reading this article are club members. You are the elite of America. You have either founded a club, or have been elected to a club, or have been on the waiting-list of a club and forgotten about it. This country is a land of clubs and you are its chosen people. What are you going to do about it?

There really isn't much that you can do about it. Your responsibility is such that, no matter what you do, you are not doing the right thing. But, as members of the Detroit Athletic Club (everybody up, please!) you have a special responsibility to the nation. I was in Washington only 11 years ago and President Hoover (who was then head of the Masticating League) said to me—or rather said to another man who said to me— "What are the members of the Detroit Athletic Club doing about it?" And I—or the man who told me—was unable to answer, owing to having left the room.

There are three things a club member can do to justify his special privileges as a citizen. He can go to his club and help make it just the very best club in the country. (2) (The other was 1). He can never go to his club at all, or (3) he can go to it and hide copies of the magazines that other members want.

It is with the third class of club members that I would like to deal in the beginning. I have been a guest in the Detroit Athletic Club (and when I say guest I *mean* guest). It has never cost me a nickel. (On the contrary). And there is only one suggestion that I would have to make

to its management: Find the man who hides the copies of the N. Y. *Times* in the reading room. I would like to talk to him. Not that I care especially about the N. Y. *Times,* but it is a part of my job to read it when I am in other cities. I have to keep tabs on the number of Finns who advertise for jobs in the *Times* as I am working on a thesis dealing with the unemployment situation among Finns and Letts. (I don't keep track of the Letts really, but I am supposed to). So when I am in Detroit, naturally the first thing I look for is the N. Y. *Times,* in order to make my report, which I do every so often.

Well, I goes to the reading room of the D. A. C. and what do I find? The Toledo *Blade,* the St. Louis *Post-Dispatch,* the Minneapolis *Svenska-Dag-blat,* and *Farm and Fireside.* But no N. Y.

But, thanks to the club luncheons at the D. A. C., there are at least three hours of the day when you are no good as business men

Times. I go over to the corner of the room where a gentleman who has been playing a luncheon game of handball is asleep with a paper over his chest. Getting under his knees, I peer up between his legs and discover that he is covered with the Emporia *Gazette* (I know William Allen White very well, and like him personally, but I do not happen to want to see the Emporia *Gazette* at that particular moment). On the other side of the room are two men who are talking about Mr. Raskob. One of them is waving a paper which, by sidling up alongside and making believe I am fainting, I discover to be the Denver *Post.* There are copies of the N. Y. *Times* on the rack for all those dates on which I was in New York myself, but the copy for that particular day for which I am looking has evidently been taken and used to wrap up lunch with. I do not mean to be captious, or ungrateful, but I do think that you men, as members of the Detroit Athletic Club, might see to it that this particular *Times* fancier is told that the Los Angeles *Examiner* would do just as well for his purpose.

So much for the civic duty of club members. The next point is Charlie Hughes. I am a very busy man, what with building all those New York subways and that new bridge across the North river, and gave up writing a long time ago. But Charlie Hughes comes to New York and calls me up. "This is Charlie Hughes," he says, "why don't you drop around to my room this afternoon about five o'clock? I have some snapshots of the Byrd expedition I would like to show you." So I drop around to Charlie's room about five o'clock and the shapshots are so good that it is eight o'clock before I am out again and by that time, in spite of my having renounced writing as a profession three years ago, I have asked him what he would think of a piece about clam digging for the October issue. He has probably said that it sounds all right, if he can read my spelling, and there I am, writing a piece on clam digging, with the North river bridge hanging in mid-air and no subways built. If I ever become a writer it will be because Charlie Hughes kept calling up and asking me to look at snapshots of the Byrd expedition, and God

knows I have no desire to become a writer. The members of the Detroit Athletic Club can do a great service to American letters by keeping him in Detroit.

But all this must be very uninteresting to you, who are captains of industry and busy with banquets and things; so we will drop the personal element and get down to the main point of this speech (I really am speaking this out loud to myself and making stenographic notes of it), which is: What can the club members of America do today to elevate the cultural tone of the country?

Being members of an athletic club you are naturally interested in the restaurant side of the problem. I think that the club luncheon is one of the greatest factors in the development of cultural America. (If you don't think so, then you don't think so, that's all). But it is generally agreed that the menace of America today is a preoccupation with business and money making. Money, money, money, that is all you Americans think of. Detroit is practically the seat of this money making. I have seen enough money in Detroit to pay all of my bill at Brooks Brothers and make quite a dent in my dentist's account. It's a wonder that some of you Detroiters wouldn't see that what I need is leisure and peace of mind and freedom from creditors and start an endowment on which I could just investigate fish eggs and sip juleps. However, that is none of my business, I suppose.

Well, here you are, anyway, in grave danger of becoming obsessed with money making, and a very nasty habit it is, too. But, thanks to the club luncheons at the D. A. C., there are at least three hours of the day when you are no good as business men. I am no business man myself, but I have had a corned-beef hash at the D. A. C. for lunch which would have reduced the entire firm of J. P. Morgan to a group of dreamy poets until four o'clock in the afternoon—and by then it is too late to do anything anyway. If you men will just stick to those luncheons, especially during the (Continued on Page 28)

Some of the worst cases of drowning on record have been where the victim was dozing off after a bread pudding

36. Women holding cards, or properly registered at the door, or accompanied by a member may be admitted on evenings of special entertainment to such departments as may be designated by the house committee.

37. Women to whom cards of admission have been issued may introduce other women for the day only, and name of guest so introduced must be entered in the guest register at the Randolph street entrance.

38. Women who are not associate members shall be required to sign the name of the member responsible for them and affix his account number to a ticket for everything ordered by them in the clubhouse. Their own initials should also be written after the member's name.

39. Associate members and women holding admission cards may use the gymnasium and swimming pool on Mondays, Wednesdays, and Thursdays from 9 to 11:30 o'clock A.M. Tuesdays and Fridays the pool is available to the daughters of members—no adults or women over seventeen (17) years of age. The hours are from 2:30 to 4:30. At no other time will women be permitted to go above the second floor of the clubhouse excepting to the women's locker room, unless on special occasions designated by the house committee. The swimming pool or other athletic departments shall not be available to women on holidays, unless by permission of the house committee.

40. The women's department, to which women have access regularly, is restricted to the women's reception room on the first floor (entrance from Randolph street), ladies' dining rooms and palm room on the second floor, and women's locker rooms. Except on special occasions, to be designated by the house committee, women are not permitted the use of the main stairway, main elevators, or main hallway on the second floor.

41. Women holding admission cards have not the privilege of taking residents of Detroit to the swimming pool or other athletic departments. Those wishing to take nonresident guests to the pool should make written application to the house committee forty-eight (48) hours in advance. The number of guests will be limited according to the season of the year.

42. No checks will be cashed for women on account of the inaccessibility of the club office from the women's department.

43. Guest cards are not issued to women.

MISCELLANEOUS

44. The bringing of liquor into the dining rooms or locker rooms is prohibited.

45. Junior members are privileged to use the athletic department Monday, Tuesday, Wednesday, Thursday, and Friday (except that the swimming pool is not available to them on Tuesday and Friday afternoons), from 2:30 to 4:30 P.M., and Saturdays from 9 to 11:30 A.M.

46. Complaints, requests, and suggestions must be made in writing, signed by the member, and sent to the committee in charge of the department to which they refer.

47. Any or all of these rules may be changed or rescinded by the house committee at any time, if the committee deems that the best interests of the club demand it.

48. The manager is required to notify members of any violation of the rules of the club and to report the same to the house committee.

49. Guest cards will be issued only upon written order of a member.

50. Children must not be brought into any of the social rooms of the club and must not be allowed to go unattended on the dining room floor. Dining service for parties containing children under five (5) years of age can be had only in private dining rooms, except on Sundays before 6 P.M. Children under fifteen (15) years of age are not allowed at club entertainments, unless the notice of such entertainment otherwise provides.

51. The club shall not be responsible for the loss of property from bedrooms occupied by members or guests, or for any other loss sustained in the clubhouse by members or guests. Valuables may be placed in the office safe.

Checks will be given at the coat room for articles left there, but the club will not be responsible for any loss in connection therewith.

A Message to D. A. C. Members

(Continued from Page 22)

warm weather, and will get other business men throughout the country to follow your example, you will have America on an equal footing with Persia as a land of aesthetes and will kill forever the rumor that America has no soul.

There is one thing about D. A. C. luncheons, however, that I would like to issue a word of warning about. That is this business of having food served on the edge of the swimming pool. Once, when I was in your beautiful city, I attended a weekly swimming affair in the Club pool, at which members of various boards of directors, after knocking each other off a pole into the water for half an hour, sat around the edge of the tank and, in their *robes de bain*, partook of a dainty snack of wiener schnitzel, lyonnaise potatoes, several of the heavier vegetables, and a good bread pudding. "After swimming, you know," was the excuse, "a man needs good hearty food."

Now that may be all very true, and I would be the first to deny that a man who has been swashing about in the water for an hour deserves to be bolstered up by at least a wiener schnitzel, but I would recommend having it

DAC NEWS

Vol. 14   September, 1929   No. 9

CHARLES A. HUGHES . *Editor and Publisher*
GEORGE W. STARK . . . *Managing Editor*
MISS HELEN WHITELEY . . *Society Editor*
J. C. FAUST . . . . *Art Director*

Published monthly by the Detroit Athletic Club. Subscription to members, $1.00 a year; to nonmembers, $2.50. Single copy, twenty-five cents. Entered as second-class matter July 29, 1916, at the post office at Detroit, Michigan, under the act of March 3, 1879.
Advertising rates on application.
Trade-mark registered, U. S. Patent Office.

served downstairs or somewhere in the building where there is not so much danger of falling back into the water again after eating. After a meal like that the natural tendency is to lean over backward and snatch 40 or 45 winks, especially when there are speakers such as I was on that occasion, and any doctor will tell you that going in swimming after a heavy meal is likely to result in cramps. Drowning after eating is even worse, and there is no reason to suppose that a member of the Club who is dozing off after a bread pudding will have enough originality to strike out after hitting the water, even to keep his head above the surface. Some of the worst cases of drowning on record have been where the victims were dozing after a bread pudding.

Now I don't want you members of the D. A. C. to feel that I am finding fault with you or with your Club. It is all for your own good that I am saying these things, and to perpetuate your membership into a robust old age, for your continuance means a lot to me. If you don't believe it, just look back over the files of this paper and try to figure out where else I could have sold the things I write.

DAC NEWS

DRAWING BY R. F. HEINRICH

August - 1920

Click Here to Search

Football Rules or Whatever They Are

By ROBERT C. BENCHLEY

Drawings by GLUYAS WILLIAMS

How many of my little readers remember the day when a perfectly ordinary citizen could watch a football game and know what was going on? Rather than wait for an answer to this question, which would have to be obtained by a post-card ballot and might take months, I will make a stab at the answer and venture to say that it is only the older boys who remember. For during the last 10 years the Football Rules Committee has seen to it that no one who understood the game the year before should understand it this year. The motto of the Rules Committee seems to have been: "New rules and new rooters each year."

In the old days, when they changed the rules maybe once every 10 years, watching football was something of a pastime. You took your seat in the stands and, provided you knew anything at all about the game, you followed the plays as they were executed and knew at least which side had the ball and what their general line of attack was. Oftentimes you knew enough about the game to yell suggestions to the quarterback or to tell the man next to you where the boys would have done well to try rushing on the third down. (If you did do this, however, you are not alive today—not if the man next you was I.)

Once they changed the number of points gained by a goal from the field, but that wasn't very hard for me to remember, as I worked out a system which made it practically impossible for me to go wrong. My freshman year in college, Harvard beat Yale by one goal from the field, which then counted four points. The next year the scoring was changed to three points. Well, all I had to do to remember how much a goal from the field counted under the new ruling was to think back on that 4-0 score of my

They sit up nights trying to think of new rules to confuse the graduate

freshman year, subtract one and there I was with the answer! By that time the goal from the field had either been kicked or missed and perhaps another score made, but I had the general principle down pretty cold anyway, and it seemed to me that I had accomplished something.

It wasn't so bad even when they began tampering with the number of downs to go 10 yards in. It was confusing at first, but they let you alone and didn't try to rattle you by changing it again the next year, and before long you got to liking the four downs to 10 yards better than the old way. I sometimes wonder how we ever got along with the old way, but I suppose it was all right for that period, what with gas lights and everything. But I certainly should resent any move to go back to the old number of downs, although, for all I know now, they *have* gone back to them. The spectator would never know.

For after the war the Rules Committee began to get jittery. They acted as if they thought somebody was following them. First they would put on a beard, then they would take it off and walk on their hands, then they would duck around a corner and then appear walking very tall. They changed rules every season as if they were trying to work up a new game out of football and make it into something they didn't quite know about. They made illegal all the old plays that used to be the essence of the game and sat up nights trying to think up new things to put in their places. It has got so now that the Rules Committee itself is about the only body of men who know enough about the game to play it, and they haven't anybody to play it with.

The freshman teams, or better the prep-school teams, who learn the game for the first time each year, have the drop on veterans, for they don't have to forget anything that they learned the year before. A senior, who has been taught all his life to pick up a fumble and run with it, suddenly finds that he can't do this, but must, when an opponent drops the ball, place his right hand to his mouth and call out "Co-e-e-e!" until a substitute quarter runs out from the side lines and shoots the ball with a revolver. This naturally confuses the senior. What it does to the spectators in the stands can be judged by the way they instinctively jump up and yell "Fumble!" only to sink back a second later and go back to reading the program.

All that the spectator gets out of a game now is the fresh air, the comical articles in his program, the sight of 22 young men rushing about in mysterious formations, and whatever he brought along in his flask. The murmur which you hear running through the stands after each play is caused by people asking other people what the idea of that was and other people trying to explain.

The thing to do is to change the rules for good and all this winter and then let us take a couple of years to learn them. It is this dribbling along, a couple of changes this year and a couple more next, which is driving us old boys crazy. I would suggest the following outline of rule revisions for the year 1930 along the lines of the changes to

date, this revision to stand for 10 years or until the game has been discontinued entirely.

Early Season Rules

(SEPTEMBER 22 TO OCTOBER 6)

1. Only the quarterback shall be allowed to carry the ball and he shall run only when there is nobody after him. At other times he shall walk, dribbling the ball as in basket ball. He must keep whistling at all times.

2. A touchdown shall be considered made when the quarterback has placed the ball on the 55-yard line, with each team lined up on its own goal line. As soon as the quarterback shall have made a touchdown thus, he shall call out "Come out, come out, wherever you are, or else I'll catch you standing still!" At this signal both teams shall run very fast and try to get to the opposite goal line without being tagged. A penalty of 10 points shall be accorded to the team making the touchdown.

3. A fumble shall count four points for the side making it, except in the following instances: (1) when made by a right guard (2) when made by a

He must place his right hand to his mouth and call out "Co-e-e-e!"

man in a white head guard (3) when made by a player who shall have first signalled to the referee indicating that he is about to fumble (4) when made by a professor who has got onto the field by mistake and can't find his way out.

Mid-Season Rules

(OCTOBER 13 TO NOVEMBER 3)

1. Only a left tackle shall be allowed to carry the ball, and he shall not weigh more than 190 pounds (with the ball). He need not whistle.

2. A touchdown shall be considered made when the left tackle shall have tossed the ball into a basket held on the 30-yard side line by an assistant manager, who shall run to the coach with it and say: "Look! A ball in the basket!" A touchdown thus made shall count seven points, providing nine rahs are given. (*Continued on Page 138*)

Football Rules or Whatever They Are

(Continued from Page 23)

3. When the ball is fumbled, nobody shall pay any attention to it at all, but another ball shall be brought out and put into play on the 10-yard line. If the old ball rolls into a pocket (there shall be four pockets dug into the field 20-yards apart on the side-lines) it counts 10 if it be in a 20-pocket, 20 if in a 10-pocket and 100 if in either of the booby-pockets.

Late-Season Rules

(NOVEMBER 10 TO NOVEMBER 30)

1. Nobody at all shall be allowed to touch the ball with his hands, but it shall be kicked along with the right side of the ankle of the right foot. Any player may kick it but he must first run to the referee and hold up two fingers, saying "Kick, sir?" The referee shall answer: "Please do."

2. There shall be no touchdowns, as such, and no scoring, as such. The side winning the game shall be the one which can prove that it has had the most exercise. After all, the game should be played for the game's sake, not to score points.

3. All spectators shall be blindfolded and made to sit with their backs to the field so that none shall peek. This will do away with overemphasis on football in college life and prevent the game from becoming a gigantic spectacle. It will also do away with graduate-domination. It may even do away with the graduates. The money hitherto furnished by the graduates can be made up by the sale of banners and arm bands to residents of the town in which the game is played.

With these new rules definitely in force, so that the spectators will know what to expect each year, they can make their own plans for Saturday afternoons during October and November.

And probably, at that, the stands will be crowded.

, , , ,

"What the Servants Despise—"

ANTON HAUPTMANN, who has collected 4000 signatures of the world's most important people and has been thrown out of so many places that he remembers only the best, tells his experience with the ex-Crown Prince of Germany, who, according to this story, seemed to be quite an expert in psychology—since the war, anyway.

As Hauptmann was being put off the grounds of the Crown Prince's retreat in Naples for the sixth time, the Prince came out and asked him what he wanted. Interested, he looked through the book of signatures, saw many of his own family, signed, then called his staff.

"Listen and don't forget this," he warned them. "Know in the future that always what the servants despise the master would like to see. That is life."

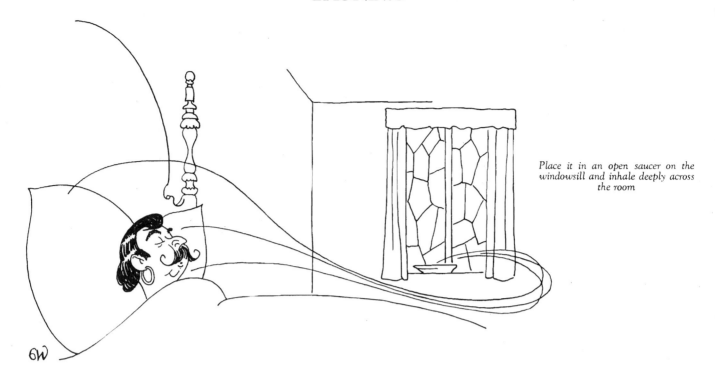

Place it in an open saucer on the windowsill and inhale deeply across the room

Carnival Week In Sunny Las Los

By ROBERT C. BENCHLEY

Drawings by GLUYAS WILLIAMS

You have all doubtless wanted to know, at one time or another, a few of the quaint customs which residents of the continent of Europe seem to feel called upon to perpetuate from one century to another. You may know about a few of them already, such as child-bearing (which has been taken up on this continent to such an alarming extent) and others of the more common variety of folk mannerisms, but I am very proud and happy to be able to tell you today of some of the less generally known customs of the inhabitants of that medieval Spanish province Las Los (or Los Las, as it was formerly called, either way meaning "The The" *pl.*) where I have had the extremely bad fortune to be spending the summer.

Las Los, nestling, as it does, in the intercostal nooks of the Pyrenees, makes up into one of the nicest little plague-spots on the continent of Europe. Europe has often claimed that Las Los was *not* a part of it, and in 1356 Spain began a long and costly war with France, the loser to take Los Las and two outfielders. France won and Spain built an extension onto the Pyrenees in which to hide Los Las. They succeeded in hiding it from view, but there was one thing about Los Las that they forgot; so you always know that it is there.

It was in this little out-of-the-way corner of the world, then, that I set up my easel and began painting my fingers and wrists. I soon made friends with the natives (all of whom were named Pedro) and it was not long before they were bringing me their best Sunday knives and sticking them in my back for me to try and tell which was which. And such laughter would go up when I guessed the wrong one! All Latins, after all, are just children at heart.

But I am not here to tell you of the many merry days I myself spent in Las Los, but of some of the native customs which I was privileged to see, and, once in a while, take part in. They rather resent an outsider taking part in most of them, however, for there is an old saying in Las Los that "when an outsider takes part, rain will surely dart" (meaning "dart" from the clouds, you see) and above all things rain is abhorred in that section of the country, as rain has a tendency to cleanse whatever it touches, and, as another old proverb has it, "clean things, dead things"—which isn't exactly accurate, but appeals to these simple, childish people, to whom cleanliness is next to a broken hip.

First of all, then, let us tiptoe up on the natives of Las Los during their carnival time. The carnival week comes during the last week in July, just when it is hottest. This makes it really ideal for the Los Lasians, for extreme heat, added to everything else, renders their charming little town practically unbearable. This week was chosen many hundreds of years ago and is supposed to mark the anniversary of the marriage of old Don Pedro's daughter to a thunderbolt, a union which was so unsatisfactory to the young lady that she left her husband in two days and married a boy named Carlos, who sold tortillas. This so enraged the thunderbolt that he swore never to come to Los Las again, and, from that day to this (so the saying goes, I know not whether it be true or not) that region has never had any locusts. (This would almost make it seem that the repulsed bridegroom had been a locust, but the natives, on being questioned, explain that the *patois* for "thunderbolt" (*enjuejoz*) is very much like the *patois* for "locust" (*enjuejoz*) and that the thunder

Occasionally someone hits a tambourine

GLUYAS WILLIAMS

papers, and if they were to pass up one year without riding in decorated ox carts, it wouldn't seem like carnival week to the readers of the London illustrated papers. You can hardly blame a man with a *wheero* hang-over, however, for not wanting to bump around over cobblestones in an old two-wheeled cart, even if it has got paper flowers strung all over it. One of the saddest sights in the world is to see a native, all dressed up in red and yellow, with a garland of orange roses around his neck, jolting and jouncing along over hard stone bumps with a girl on his knee, and trying to simulate that famous Spanish smile and gay abandon, all the time feeling that one more bump and away goes that meal he ate several days ago, along with his legs and arms and portions of his lower jaw. No wonder Spaniards look worried.

However, there is a great deal of shouting and cawing among those who can open their mouths, and occasionally someone hits a tambourine. This is usually frowned upon by the person standing next to the tam-bourine-hitter and a remark, in Spanish, is made which could roughly be translated as: "For the love of God, shut up that incessant banging!"

The carnival, which is known as *Romeria*, is supposed to be a festival of the picnic type combined with a reli-gious pilgrimage to some sort of shrine. (Continued on Page 82)

god, in giving his order for the future of Los Las, put the accent on the wrong syllable and cut them off from lo-custs instead of thunder storms). This may, or may not, be the truth, but, as I said to the old man who told me "Who the hell cares?"

The first day of the Carnival of the Absence of Locusts (just why they should be so cocky about having no locusts is not clear. Locusts would be a god-send com-pared to some of the things they *have* got) is spent in bed, storing up strength for the festival. On this day all the shops, except those selling wine, are closed. This means that a little shop down by the river which sells sieves is closed. People lie in bed and send out to the wine-shops for the native drink, which is known as *wheero*. All that is necessary to do with this drink is to place it in an open saucer on the window sill and inhale deeply from across the room. In about eight seconds the top of the inhaler's head rises slowly and in a dignified manner until it reaches the ceiling where it floats, bumping gently up and down. The teeth then drop out and arrange themselves on the floor to spell "Portage High School, 1929," the eyes roll upward and backward, and a strange odor of burning rubber fills the room. This is followed by an unaccount-able feeling of intense lassitude.

Thus we may expect nothing from the natives for the first two days of the carnival, for the second day is spent in looking for bits of head and teeth, and in general moaning. (A sorry carnival, you will say—and *I* will say, too). But later on, things will brighten up.

On the third day the inhabitants emerge, walking very carefully in order not to jar off their ears, and get into a lot of decorated ox carts. They are not very crazy about getting into these ox carts, but it is more or less expected of them at carnival time. Pictures are taken of them riding about and are sent to the London illustrated

The two of us sat all alone in the public square.... drinking a lemon-squash together

GW

Carnival Week In Sunny Las Los

(*Continued from Page 30*)

This shrine, however, is never reached, as along about noon of the third day some desperate guy, with a hangover no longer to be borne, evolves a cure on the "hair of the dog that bit you" theory, and the *wheero* is brought out again. The village watering trough is filled with it and a sort of native dance is held around the trough, everyone inhaling deeply. Those who are still unable to inhale are carried to the edge of the trough and a little *wheero* is rubbed on their upperlips, just under the nose. Then it is "goodnight all, and a merry, merry trip to Blanket Bay" for the festive villagers, and the carnival is shot to hell. A week later business is quietly resumed.

On the fifth day of the carnival there is supposed to be a bull chase through the streets. The principle of the thing is that a bull is let loose and everyone chases it, or vice versa. As, however, there was nobody fit to chase a butterfly, much less a bull, on the fifth day of this carnival, I had to take care of the bull myself. The two of us sat all alone in the public square among the cadavers drinking a sort of lemon squash together.

"A dash of *wheero?*" I asked the bull.

Well, you should have heard him laugh! After that, I got up on his back and rode all around the town, visiting the points of interest and climbing several of the better looking mountains. Pretty soon we were in Turkey, where we saw many interesting sights and then, swinging around through the Balkans, got back just in time for me to scramble into bed. I must have hit my head on the footboard while pulling up the sheet, for the next morning (or whenever it was) when I awoke, I had quite a bad headache. Thank Heaven I knew enough to lay off that *wheero*, however. I'm no fool.

A-Hunting We Won't Go

(*Continued from Page 33*)

After a discreet interval, Mr. Milfret followed, feeling unaccountably light of heart and clear of conscience.

So complacent was his mood that he had difficulty in displaying a proper degree of regret when Doc Snedecker called on him a day or two later. "Doggoned if I can understand how we happened to miss connections," said Doc. "I was looking all around for you at the station Saturday morning."

"I was looking for you, too," said Mr. Milfret truthfully.

There was an awkward silence. "I don't suppose we'll have a chance to go hunting now until next fall," said Doc at length, "but I sure enjoy thinking about it. I tell you, there's nothing like the thrill of watching a swarm of mallock ducks come flying toward you, closer and closer— while you snuggle your good old gun against your shoulder and draw a bead on 'em, and then—bingo!"

"Bingo—bingo!" agreed Mr. Milfred.

Whereupon Uncle Beauregard's stuffed owl on the bookcase winked its solitary glass eye, and summed up the matter by remarking, "Hooey!"

Another Uncle Edith Christmas Yarn

By ROBERT C. BENCHLEY

Drawings by GLUYAS WILLIAMS

UNCLE EDITH said: "I think it is about time that I told you a good old-fashioned Christmas story about the raging sea."

"Aw, nuts!" said little Philip.

"As you will," said Uncle Edith, "but I shall tell it just the same. I am not to be intimidated by a three-year-old child. Where was I?"

"You were over backwards, with your feet in the air, if I know anything about you," said Marian, who had golden hair and wore it in an unbecoming orange ribbon.

"I guess that you probably are right," said Uncle Edith, "although who am I to say? Anyway, I *do* know that we sailed from Nahant on the fourteenth March."

"What are you—French?" asked little Philip, "the fourteenth March."

"The fourteenth *of* March, then," said Uncle Edith, "and if you don't shut up I will keep right on with the story. You can't intimidate me."

"Done and done," said little Philip, who bled quite a lot from a wound in his head inflicted a few seconds before by Uncle Edith.

"We set sail from Nahant on the fourteenth *of* March (nya-a-a-a-a) on the good ship *Mary W. Rosenthal,* with a cargo of old thread and bound for dear old Algeciras."

The Captain

"End of story!" announced Marian in a throaty baritone.

"It is *not* the end of the story, and I will sue anyone who says that it is," petulated Uncle Edith. "You will know well enough when I come to the end of the story, because I shall fall over on my face. Now be quiet or Uncle Edith will give you a great big abrasion on the forehead."

"I can hardly wait," said little Philip, or whichever the hell one of those children it was, I can't keep them all straight, they are all so much alike.

"Aboard," continued Uncle Edith, "aboard were myself, as skipper——"

"Skippered herring," (*a whisper*).

"—Lars Jannssenn, first mate; Max Schnirr, second mate; Enoch Olds, third base; and a crew of seven whose names you wouldn't recognize. However, there we were.

"The first 709 days were uneventful. The sailmaker (a man by the name of Sailmaker, oddly enough) made eleven sails, but, as we had no more ships to put them on, and as our sails were O. K., we had to throw them overboard. This made the men discontented, and there were rumors of mutiny. I sent a reporter up to see the men, however, and the rumors were unconfirmed; so I killed the story. NO MUTINY was the head I put on it in the ship's paper that night, and everybody was satisfied."

"You great big wonderful animal," said Marian, running

her tiny hand through Uncle Edith's hair.

"It was nothing," said Uncle Edith, and everybody agreed that it was.

"However," continued the old salt pork, "everyone on board felt that something was wrong. We were at that time at Lat. seventy-eight, Long. seventy-eight, which cancelled each other, making us right back where we started from—"

"Don't tell me that we are back at Nahant again," said little Philip, throwing up.

"Not exactly Nahant," said Uncle Edith, "but within hailing distance of a Nahanted ship."

"You just used Nahant in the first place so that you could pull that gag," said Primrose, who, up to this time, had taken no part in the conversation, not having been born.

"So help me God," said Uncle Edith, "it came to me like *that!*" And he snapped a finger, breaking it. "The

Max Schnirr,
second mate

ha'nted ship lay just off our starboard bow, and seemed to be manned by mosquitoes. As we drew alongside, however, we found that there was not a soul on board. Not a soul on board."

"That is the second time you have said that," said little whatever-his-name-is—Philip.

Uncle Edith made no reply other than to throw nasty little Philip into irons.

"'Prepare to board!' was the order given. And everybody, ignoring the chance for a pun, prepared to board the derelict. In a few seconds we were swarming over the side of the empty ship and searching every nook and cranny of her. The search, however, was fruitless. The ship's log was found in the wheelhouse, but, as the last entry read, 'Fair and warm. Billy said he didn't love me as much as he does Anna' we discarded that as evidence. In the galley we found a fried egg, done on only one side, and an old bo'sun who was no good to anybody. Other than these two things, the mystery was complete."

"Not that I give a damn," said Marian, "but what was the explanation to this almost complete mystery?"

"If you will shut your trap," said Uncle Edith, "I will tell you. As I may not have told you, the mystery ship was full of sleeping Hessian troops, such as were used against the colonists in the Revolutionary War. They were very gay in their red coats and powdered wigs, and, had they been awake, might have offered some solution of the problem which now presented itself to us.

" 'What shall I do, cap'n?' asked Lars Jannssenn, who has been promoted to purser.

" 'What would you *like* to do, Lars?' I asked him.

" 'Me, I would like to have three wishes,' was the typically Scandinavian reply. (Lars had belonged to the Scandi-navy before he joined up with us.)

" 'They are yours,' I said, more on the spur of the moment than anything else. 'You take your three wishes and put them in your hat and pull it down over your ears. Anybody else?'

"Suddenly there was a scream from below decks. I have heard screams in my day, but never anything like this one. It was dark by now, and there were a lot of couples necking in the lifeboats. But this scream was different. It was like nothing human. It came from the bowels of the ship, and you know that's bad.

" 'All hands below!' I cried, and just as everybody was rushing down the hatchways there came a great explosion, seemingly from the jib.

" 'All hands to the jib!' I cried in my excitement.

A member of the crew singing at his work

Old Sail-maker, the sailmaker

" 'What is all this — a game?' asked the crew, as one man.

" 'I am captain here,' I said, boxing the compass roundly, 'and what I say goes! In the future please try to remember that fact.'

"Well, this sort of thing went on for hours. Up and down the ship we went, throwing overboard Hessians in our rush, until finally the cook came to me and said: 'Cap'n, I frankly am sick of this. Are there, or are there

not, any reasons why we should be behaving like a pack of schoolboys?'

"This was a poser. I called the crew together and we decided to go back to the *Mary W. Rosenthal*. But, on looking over the side, we found a very suspicious circumstance. *The Mary W. Rosenthal was gone!*"

"I don't believe it!" said little Philip, from the brig.

Uncle Edith turned sharply. "I thought you were in irons," he said.

"You think a lot," replied little Philip, and the entire casino burst into a gale of laughter, although it was a pretty lousy come-back, even for a three-year-old.

Just then somebody noticed that there was a small triangular cut in little Philip's right eyelid.

"A mere trifle," said Philip. "I got it in the charge up San Juan Hill. I was

Lars Jannssenn

riding right alongside Colonel Roosevelt. Shot and shell were falling all about us, but nothing daunted, the Colonel and I urged our mounts up the hill and won the day. The Colonel was the first to observe that my right eye had been shot out. 'We've got to get *that* back,' he cried, and the entire regiment charged down the hill again looking for the missing eye, loyal fellows that they were!

"Well, sir, you can believe it or not, but we found all the pieces of the eye except this one little triangular slit. Surgeons came from far and wide and a marvelous job of patching resulted in the eye's being put back in its old accustomed place. And outside of slight headaches in the morning, I have felt just dandy ever since."

"Very well, then," said Uncle Edith. "I am sorry if you feel that way. For I was just going to end the story by saying that we sailed the mystery ship back to Nahant."

"And where does Christmas come in?" piped up Marian, who hadn't heard a word of Uncle Edith's story.

"Who the hell said anything about Christmas?" asked Uncle Edith in a rage.

And who the hell did?

Robert Benchley Spreads Some

Sauce For the Propaganda

Gluyas Williams' idea of Mr. Benchley enjoying his own radio

Reading all this stuff in the newspapers about propaganda is getting me a little jittery. Now I think *everyone* is trying to influence my mind. I can't read a story about an approaching cold snap without thinking that maybe it was inspired by the mitten people. Little items about robberies I suspect to be insurance propaganda. And who knows who slips all these

He will say that 209 cases have been caused by listening to pipe organ recitals

accounts of immorality into the papers? Old Nick himself, I'll be bound!

We are being influenced in this insidious manner to call for the building of more battleships, or fewer battleships, or painting green those battleships which we now have and trimming them with fur. Evidently, by a careful and expert campaign, you can get the public mind to thinking anything—provided you can get it to thinking at all.

I have a little plan here to abolish the radio, except for ships at sea and reporting ball games. I want to get Congress and the nation anti-radio-minded. I should rather like to keep my own radio, if it could be so worked, but I definitely want to put a stop to other people's radios. And the way to go about this is a campaign of insidious propaganda, based on those executed by large organizations and corporations as brought to light in the recent disclosures. We can't hope to get the thing across much before 1932, but I can wait. If by then Congress will have passed a bill making illegal all radio sets but mine, I shall feel that I have done a patriotic service. And, let it be understood, it is purely patriotism which is motivating me.

The initial step will probably be stories in the Sunday papers, printed in the magazine sections. They must have nothing to do with radio, as such. There will be one called: "Is America Going Mad? Noted Ear-Specialist Says Incessant Sound-Waves Degenerate Ear Drums." Another will be written by a noted orchestra leader who says that too much music, day in and day out, rots the brain cells and makes the listener incapable of appreciating good music when he hears it. Another will be a series of charts showing that guinea-pigs, when subjected to *Land of the Sky-Blue Waters* eighteen times a day for four weeks, became stupid and lethargic and beat their wives.

In these stories the word "radio" will never be mentioned, but the public will be prepared, in a general way, for what is to come. They will become "noise-conscious" and may even begin feeling of their own ear drums (or as near their ear drums as they can get) and wondering nervously if they are still there.

Next, we will import a German scientist from Bad-Neuheim who, in the course of a series of lectures on "Liver Control," will say that, out of 300 cases of liver-elevation, or Stratt's Disease, which have come to his attention, 209 have been caused by listening to pipe organ recitals. "Pipe organ recitals," to quote from his lecture, "are all right so long as the listener is *in the room* with the pipe organ, but if the sound is brought to him by means of an apparatus, such as the telephone, telegraph, radio (the word "radio" will be tucked in among the others, as if incidental) or by the American Express, there will be an electro-magnetic contact established which will act on the human liver both as a dissolvent and hoister, resulting in a wasting away of the organ, and, at the same time, a lifting of it to a position slightly below the thorax." This ought to frighten them.

In order to get the newspapers lined up with us we will send to the editors about 20,000 letters cancelling subscriptions on the ground that, so long as baseball and football scores, racing results, and general news items are being broadcast every day, there is no longer any need for buying a newspaper. The form of the letters will be something like this:

Dear Sir: My attention has been called to the fact that I can get everything out of the radio that I get out of your paper, and I am therefore stopping my subscription. Not only will this save me the eye-strain of reading, but also I shall not have to go to the door every morning in my pajamas to pick the newspaper up. This is no small item, I can assure you, as stooping over to pick up a paper in the morning (especially after drinking the night before) is always productive of a giddiness which sometimes makes it necessary to remain stooped over, even on my hands and knees, until my breakfast is brought to me. I also find it difficult to keep the bottoms of my pajamas from dropping down when stooping over, even though I am able to come back to an erect position myself. I dare you to print this letter. Yours, etc.

This will make the editors furious and they will be only too glad to write editorials against the radio when the time comes. They can tie radio-abolition up to such editorial topics as the repaving of Center street and littering up Prospect Park, and will send reporters out to get statistics on the number of residents of the city who have gone mad listening to radios in the next apartments. Once we get the newspapers with us, we are good as set.

For the monthly magazines we have stuff already lined up. Nice, gentlemanly essays on "The Quiet Home," "Is the Art of Conversation Dying Out?", "Dare You Be Alone with your Wife?" and "Fireside Chats without the Aid of the Birnheimer Fur Trappers' Quartet." Perhaps a series showing that the decay of family life in America is due to the family's never having a chance to talk to one another, and several pieces decrying the use of the ukelele as a substitute for religion.

Of course, in the field of religion we can get a great deal of good work across. Personal conversation with the pastors, slipped in by paid propagandists who go around joining churches and making friends with vestrymen, to the effect that every man, woman, and child who listens to sermons over the radio is a man, woman, and child who is not dropping a quarter into the contribution box and is also a man, woman, and child who can shut the thing off the minute the sermon gets dull; all this will soon result in sermons against the radio as a menace to our national integrity. "If the Lord had meant us to hear a lot of things over the air we would have been equipped with antennæ in the first place," will be a good angle. (*Continued on Page 70*)

They will shout horrible things before they can be shut off

(Continued from Page 68)

down in Belgium and France. Nobody has a greater horror of war than I have, or would work more enthusiastically for universal peace, but I seriously doubt if all these books, evidently written to show the folly and brutality of nations under arms, will avail much when, under the sting of some national affront, the flag goes by in front of the fife and drum corps. And Mr. Tomlinson's title indicates why they won't. When Macbeth said that all our yesterdays have lighted fools the way to dusty death, he knew whereof he spoke, and the young man in the flip novel mentioned at the top of this article knew the same thing when he remarked that the world won't alter much, simply because there is no such thing as inherited memory. ·Mr. Tomlinson is a splendid writer, however, and if we must relive those tragic four years between book-covers, they might as well bear his name.

, , , ,

Sauce for the Propaganda

(Continued from Page 27)

And now it will be time for us to come out into the open. We will have employees who insinuate themselves into the radio programs themselves and, under cover of delivering an address on "Stewing Apricots for Fun" or "Ten Little Fingers and Nine Little Toes," will make ghastly noises and shout horrible things before they can be shut off. This will, of course, tip the radio companies off as to what is on foot, but by that time it will be too late

for them to do anything about it. They can apologize to their audiences all they want to, but if we can get enough performers to be insulting all at once, the impression will have been made. I can hardly wait for *that* night.

By this time, Congress will have been drawn into it. Not only will the congressmen have received letters galore from their constituents demanding the abolition of the radio, but our lobbyists in Washington will have been at work showing them that campaign speeches over the radio mean nothing to them, as they give them no chance to exert the old personal appeal which comes flashing out from those black eyes of theirs. Furthermore, their eloquent gestures go for naught over the radio and, most important of all, they can no longer get away with a speech which says nothing. The wonder is that they have stood for radio campaigning as long as they have. Show me the senator or member of the House of Representatives who can withstand that argument!

So it looks as if I were about to get my wish. All I need is a good big fund and a clever campaign manager, perhaps Mr. Shearer, now that he is free. Just how I am going to be able to abolish other people's radios and still keep mine is a problem I haven't worked out yet. I don't suppose that many broadcasting stations would want to send out programs just for me alone. It would seem kind of silly to go to all that expense to entertain only one person.

Well, all right! Supposing I *can't* keep my own radio. Take it away from me and see if I care.

I would always feel that sooner or later he would turn into a fairy prince and whisk me off to the moon

A Dark Horse In British Sports

« « Who but Benchley could get this much out of a travel folder? « «

I had just about decided that I was getting too old for athletic sports, what with my left knee bending backward just as easily as it does forward and my face getting purple when I so much as lift an arm, but now everything is different. I am going in training again. And it is the Travel Association of Great Britain and Ireland which has done this for me.

The T. A. of G. B. and I. has sent me a pamphlet called "Calendar of Historic and Important Events in 1930," and it is full of the peachiest things. A lot of them are aimed at the indoor trade, such as the Carnation Show on November twenty-sixth in the Royal Horticultural Hall (I'm afraid I can't make the Carnation Show and I am simply sick about it) or the Scottish Home Life Exhibition (whee-e-e!) at Edinburgh in April. These things which are held in halls are too sedentary. I must be up and about.

For me, there seem to be countless forms of healthful exercise available in the British Isles during 1930. In September there will be "tossing the caber" at the Braemar Highland Gathering; on April twenty-second there will be "street football" at Workington, Cumberland, "played through the streets of the town with hundreds of players on each side"; in June there will be the Uphellya at Lerwick, Shetland, and on Shrove Tuesday, Westminster School will indulge in its rite of "tossing the pancake."

As Shrove Tuesday is nearest at hand, let us get down to training for "tossing the pancake" first. I am taking it for granted that "tossing the pancake" corresponds to our American "snapping the cookies," and, if it does, I am in pretty good training right now. A little more control in the matter of direction, and I am set for the contest at Westminster. I may not be quite so young as the boys who go to school there, but I have given my system some pretty tough treatment in the past ten years and there ought to be no difficulty in keeping up with the sickliest of them. I held the transatlantic cookie-putting (or snapping) cup for 1928 and lost it in 1929 only to a man who had a complication of other troubles, which more or less rendered him a professional. For an amateur, otherwise in good health (which ought to be a specification in any cookie-snapping, or pancake-tossing competition). I have every confidence that I can hold my own against the field. The only part about this Westminster meeting that I don't like is its coming on Shrove Tuesday. I usually have other things to do on Shrove Tuesday.

I would know more how to train for the Lerwick "Uphellya" if I knew what they did there. It sounds a little unpleasant. I rather imagine that some fighting goes on and maybe a little preliminary drinking. I might enter my name for the preliminary drinking and then see how I liked the rest of it. After the preliminary drinking, however, I probably would like—and enter—anything. That might be bad, as there are a lot of things which I really shouldn't enter. I don't know much about the residents of Lerwick, or what they are likely to do at an "Uphellya," but so long as it doesn't involve running more than ten yards or vaulting, I guess that I can keep up. I never could vault, even in my heyday (1846-1847), owing to a third leg which always seemed to appear just as I was about to clear the bar and drag about three inches too low. I never could find that leg after the vaulting was over, and it is something I would rather not talk about, if you don't mind.

Of course, taking place on the island of Shetland, the whole thing may be done on ponies, which wouldn't be so good. I know that it sounds silly, but I have always been just a little afraid of Shetland ponies. No horse would be so small as that unless he had something up his sleeve to make up for it. It isn't natural for a horse to be so small. I wouldn't get on one for $1,000,000 (well anyway, for $5) because I would always feel that, sooner or later, he would grow big on me or turn into a fairy prince and whisk me off to the moon. Perhaps I haven't communicated to you my feeling about Shetland ponies, but it is a pretty subtle one, and if you haven't already got it for yourself, I could talk all night without making you understand. When I have said that, for grown-up horses, they are *too small*, I have said everything. And if the Shetland "Uphellya" is held on Shetland ponies, they can scratch me.

The "street football" in Workington, Cumberland, with hundreds of players on each side rushing through the streets of the town, sounds pretty uninteresting. I don't think that I shall even enter that. It is the sort of thing which sounds like a lot of fun when you are planning it, but which works out to be a terrible flop. In the first place, the streets of Workington can't be very wide, as none of the streets is wide in an English town. This means that only about five or six men can possibly be in line from one wall to another. In other words, there are going to be about 192 players on each side who have nothing to do but giggle and push each other about. This is going to be not only dull but bad for the morale. Before the game has been on for fifteen minutes those who are unwilling non-participants are going to get tired of pushing each other about and are going to slide into the nearest pub and wait for the thing to be over. Pretty soon those in the front line are going to realize what fools they are making of themselves by kicking a football around when they might be with their teammates in a nice warm pub, and they are going to stop, too. This will leave just the football rolling by itself in the streets and all the women and visitors sitting up in windows, wondering where the two teams are. My suggestion would be that they save time by getting

Gluyas Williams drew the pictures

I have asked several sporting goods dealers if they have a caber

Slip your money very quietly on "Daisy Bob"

the two teams in the pub right at the start, and letting the women and visitors kick the ball about. My interest in it is purely academic, however, as I shall not be there.

The last event for which I have to train is the one held at the Braemar Highland Gathering in September, "tossing the caber." I have asked several sporting goods dealers if they have a caber and they have told me that they are all out. There seems to be a big run on cabers this season. As I remember it, a caber is either a pole about the size of a flagstaff or a small animal like an anteater. In either case, I would not be particularly crazy about tossing it. I seem to have seen pictures of men in kilts hoisting a great pole into the air, but never any pictures of its landing; so I don't know whether you actually throw it or just stand there and hold it up until somebody comes along and tells you to drop it. Hoisting the pole might be all right, but I would rather not wear the kilts, if it is all the same to the committee. I once wore kilts to a fancy dress party and I am still blushing over what happened.

I rather think that my best event will be tossing the pancake at Westminster School on Shrove Tuesday. I am not making book on it, and I don't want to lead any of my friends into betting, but I will say this much: if you have a little cash that you want to invest and will take a fifteen to one bet (I am a dark horse in Westminster and the favorite, I understand, is a boy with a very weak stomach who won last year) you could do worse than send your money to "Duggie," the London bookmaker who advertises on the back pages of the London weeklies, with instructions

for him to do what he thinks best, but, if possible, to slip it in very quietly on "Daisy Bob" (my stable name).

At any rate, I shall be back in athletic circles again and getting exercise. I never can thank the Travel Association of Great Britain and Ireland enough.

Falling Stars
» » »

Away down South in the Training Camps
The embryonic base ball champs
Are catching flies and pounding pills
And giving sporting writers thrills.
Writes Old Bill Bosh in *The Tanktown Times*,
"The Yellow Sox have a second Grimes."
Writes Sammy Splish in *The Daily Chatter*,
"The Purple Shirts have a great new batter."

When Mamselle Spring to summer yields
And rooters crowd the base ball fields,
When frantic fans their foreheads mop
And gurgle quarts of soda pop
The featured "finds" we marvelled at
Hardly ever come to bat!
But don't condemn the sport page sages—
It's hard to fill up winter pages!

» » Arthur Lippmann

Mr. McNamee Opens A New Theatre

There follows a page from the log of a radio addict, who tried, with almost fatal results, to make a transcription of the breathless remarks of Mr. Graham McNamee, de luxe radio announcer, on the occasion of the dedication of the Punch and Judy Theatre in Grosse Pointe:

Well, folks, this is a great evening out here in Grosse Pointe. . . . . When the folks out here decide to do things, they don't fool, and I want to tell you as I stand here at this microphone in the lobby of the beautiful Punch and Judy Theatre in Grosse Pointe, Michigan, surrounded by the flower of the wealth and beauty of this beautiful little suburb, I am having the thrill of my life. . . . . Of course, I already had the thrill of my life at the opening game of the World Series last fall and again at the Yale-Harvard game and again at practically every heavyweight prize fight I have ever broadcast, but this is the real thing this time . . . . I am having the thrill of my life, and what is life without feeling once in a while the thrill of it? . . . . People are pouring into the stadium—no, I mean they are pouring into the theatre now, the wealth and beauty of this famous suburb by the sun-kissed shores of Lake Erie. . . . . "Bugs" Baer is expected any minute, and I don't need to tell you who *he* is. . . . . So is Elsie Ferguson, the darling of Broadway, and I don't need to tell you who *she* is. . . . . You never saw such clothes and such beauty, the

wealth and flower of this famous suburb. . . . . Here comes Mr. and Mrs. W. E. Scripps, and I don't need to tell you who *they* are. . . . . And here comes Philip Newburg, and I don't need to tell you who *he* is—I beg your pardon, I meant Phelps Newberry, who now has the ball on the Dartmouth twenty-five yard line. . . . . He's getting ready to kick, probably to the management. . . . . M. J. Kavanagh is the manager and I don't need to tell you who *he* is . . . . One of the Fisher brothers just entered . . . . I think it's Lawrence . . . . No, it's Fred . . . . On the other hand it's William . . . . Anyway, it's one of the Fisher brothers, and I don't need to tell you who *they* are. . . . . Here comes Tessa Kosta, the darling of Broadway, and I don't need to tell you who *she* is. . . . . "Bugs" Baer is expected any minute now, and I don't need to tell you who *he* is. . . . . And just now there entered the most gorgeous creature I have ever seen . . . . In a minute I'll tell you who she is . . . . Nobody seems to know . . . . She's the women nobody knows . . . . Anyway, I don't *need* to tell you who she is . . . . And folks, here in person is Henry Ford . . . . And Mrs. Ford. . . . . Mr. Ford, you know, is the inventor of the Ford motor and the richest man in the world. . . . . Well, that's the way it's been out here in this famous suburb all evening long. . . . . Edsel Ford just came in and I don't need to tell you who *he* is.

A Trip with

To the Tomb of Benchley

I wonder who the fellow is who is doing dramatic comment and other odd humor jobs around New York, Detroit, and elsewhere, under the name of Benchley. Whoever he is, he is grossly minimizing the reports of the death of the real Benchley, whose tomb I visited at Cap d'Antibes on the French Riviera last summer. And whoever he is, he is, incidentally, doing a darned good job of filling the Benchley shoes, and my Benchley ear is one of the best in America. He is doing such a good job that I sometimes wonder if I ought to run the risk of silencing this finished imposter.

But, after all, it is no secret. The Benchley tomb is a veritable mecca for all humor lovers who visit France, so who am I to think I am spilling secrets? Harpo Marx knows; I know he knows; what's he so quiet about? It was he who, clad in a copy of *Variety* and a coat of tan on the beach at Cap d'Antibes, directed me to the Benchley crypt back of the lumber yard. Not that I, as a rule, go in for tombs or shrines or such, but my hay fever was so bad that day that I was ready to try anything—chiropractors, osteopaths, or even *faith*. Yes, even Benchley worship.

Anyway, it couldn't hurt me to go see Benchley in his box. Like a fool I had made it worse by sticking my nose in a bin of orris root in a perfume factory in Grasse, not far away, that morning, and my chauffeur for the day had suggested Benchley. "I take 'em there for everything from rickets up," he said. "The alley out in front of the house is piled high with crutches. They take one look at the motto over the tomb and throw their crutches in the alley. The lumber yard saws 'em up into fagots every few days. You'll see them piled up all around that end of the village."

"Mots the whato?" I asked my guide eagerly, having just come over from England.

"How's that?"

"What's the motto?"

"*There's nothing as funny as a crutch.* It hangs right over Benchley, clear as day."

"Do you think there is any possible collusion between the ex-Benchley and the fagot yard?" I asked meaningly.

The body is down back of the lumber yard

Harpo Marx can talk when he wants to

To one who has spent much time in California and can either take his sunshine or leave it, it seems utterly silly that a man should make a beast of himself and kill himself with sunshine as Benchley did—they say he was a mere crisp when they shoveled him up that evening—and Benchley, although he brought cheer to many aching hearts in America (I always say that a man who can make people laugh is one of God's greatest gifts to the world), well, he was not what you would call one of our sunshine boys. Benchley dying of sunshine! Imagine that! Ha! ha! ha! Him weathering the Kleig lights of Hollywood and then going to France and dying of sunburn, with all the other things there are to die of in France!

If the place hadn't been so hard to find, we wouldn't have found it. *Ferme des Orangers,* or Orange Farm, they call it, though *Ferme de Gin* might have been a better name for it, for all the oranges I saw. After we had visited the hotel and the club and beach and had been up a lot of alleys, I was ready to quit, but my guide was only growing more and more determined, and it was really due to his French bullfrog-headedness that we finally got there. Only to find that the tomb was closed on the last Saturday of every week! And this was on a Saturday.

I offered the attendant five francs to look at the body, but she wanted ten. So I pretended to leave, and slipped around and looked in the tomb room window and there

was Benchley looking as much like Benchley as Grant looks like Grant in *his* tomb. If Benchley wasn't dead, he was so far gone that this boy in New York who is saying he is Benchley is a whole lot more apt to be Lon Chaney, if you ask me. I don't want to be nosey, but I'd like for everybody who comes in contact with this new Benchley to watch him closely when he isn't looking, and look under his toupee when they get the chance, and find out who it really is. We owe it to American letters to get to the bottom of this. God, it might be James M. Barrie!

But let's not stop him. It's magnificent. It's one of the most beautiful and most successful hoaxes that have been perpetrated on readers of English literature since the beginning of time. Let's see how far the fellow will go. And maybe one of these days he will take off his false whiskers and show himself.

Lord, I'd like to be present at the unveiling!

If you catch this Benchley imposter napping I wish you'd lift his toupee and see who it really is

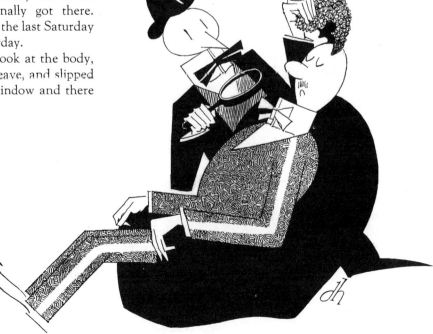

D'AC NEWS

Copyright, 1930, Charles A. Hughes

» The Making of a Play «

by Robert Benchley

An interview with the author of "The Green Pastures"

It is not generally known that Mr. Marc Connelly, author of *The Shanghai Pasture* (or *The Green Gestures*, which is its sub-title) is the same Marc Connelly who was the center of a debating scandal in Detroit a year or so ago when he crossed words with the author of this article on the subject of "Who Won the National Election?," it having been thought at the time that Hoover had. (I need hardly say that *The Shanghai Pasture* is the all-Indian play now running at the rate of $60 a minute in New York City.)

Mr. Connelly was so badly beaten in that debate and in the fist-fight which followed in an alley immediately afterward, that he resolved to go to New York and "make good." As my resentment against him had vanished almost as soon as it had come (all the Benchleys have been hot-headed, which accounts for so much hair falling out) I felt that the least that I could do would be to give him a few suggestions to help him in his climb toward regaining the respect of his fellow-men. So, following the flash-in-the-pan success of his play, I decided to interview him and send the original manuscript of the interview to Detroit. Here it is, or whatever is left of it after the editors of the D. A. C. News get through monkeying with it.

Climbing the four flights of rickety stairs which lead to Mr. Connelly's suffocating attic on Fifty-seventh street, I found that the *soi-disant* playwright was in Europe (32 Rue Blondel, Paris, to be exact).

"Tell me, Mr. Connelly," I said, taking out my electric pad and pencil, "how did you come to write a play calling for an all-Indian cast? You know what Indians do, don't you?"

The Great Emancipator looked slowly around the room and went back to sleep again.

"That is an exploded theory," he said, mumbling through his toothless gums, "the Indians are just the same as any of the rest of us, only feathery."

Gluyas Williams drew the pictures

Mr. Benchley, the well-known
interviewer

"When I wrote *The Shanghai Pasture*," he said, picking up an old banjo to strum, "I wanted to show the public that the North American Indian had a soul, that he was not the sex-crazed beast that Longfellow made of him in *Hiawatha*, that——"

"You mean Gandhi?" I asked.

"I do *not* mean Gandhi," said Connelly, laughing in spite of himself. "Gandhi makes salt."

"Not any more, he doesn't," I twitted. "The British government has seen to that. All the salt he makes now you could put into your right eye."

"Ouch!" winced Connelly, "just thinking of it makes my right eye smart. . . . . But tell me, Mr. Benchley, did you think, when you wrote *The Green Gestures*, that it would be the success that it is?"

"I thought nothing," I said sulkily," except that the world needed a little kindness, a little tolerance,——"

"—a little kiss each morning, a little kiss each night," we both joined in together, Mr. Connelly singing a lousy tenor.

"Let's try that from the beginning," he suggested, arousing himself for the first time during the interview. That Mr. Connelly loves part-singing is a fact known to only about nine-tenths of the population of New York.

And then the dream changed, and we all seemed to be in some place like Wisconsin.

"Do you really believe all those things which you put in your play?" I asked, not caring.

"You will have to be a little more specific," said Pinero. This stumped me, as I had not yet seen the play.

"Why—er—" I hesitated, "for example, that part where —you know—Lief and Edna are out in the green pastures and meet—what's his name?" (Continued on Page 54)

"That's just it," I countered, with that same relentless logic with which I had crushed him on that memorable evening in Detroit, "would you want your sister to marry one?"

"She did," said Mr. Connelly, and added, "if I had a sister."

"You don't mean Mahatma Gandhi, do you?" I asked.

"*You* don't mean Mahatma Gandhi, do *you*?" he replied. "Gandhi is an Indian of a different feather. My play deals with North American Indians."

"The same thing," I said. "The same thing, except that you add the words 'North American' in front of it."

"When I wrote this play," (it was Connelly speaking) "I had no idea that it would bring you around here to ask me questions about it. What are you trying to do, drive me mad-mad-*mad?*"

I laughed an irritating laugh.

Mr. Connelly, the well-known
playwright

The Making of a Play

(Continued from Page 22)

"You mean Gandhi?" Mr. C. was trying to help me out.

"Gandhi, that's it! Where Lief and Edna meet Gandhi. Did you mean that, really and truly mean it, I mean?"

"It is funny that you should have hit on just that one scene," said Marc, "because that is taken right out of my own experience. There was really a Lief, and there was really an Edna, only her name was Edna Gough."

"Did you really believe that Noah built an ark when the flood came?" he asked. I had him confused.

"I should answer questions about *your* play," I smiled. "However, I *will* say that I have great respect for Noah."

"Noah was a sincere man, there can be no doubt about that," said the creator of the character. "I was always convinced, while I was writing about him, that he really believed that there was going to be a flood."

"Oh, I think that everyone who saw the play got that. In fact, I'm sure they did. But, if you were to do the thing over again, don't you think that you could bring out the motivation a little clearer?"

"Noah left Elsie because Elsie didn't fit in with his new life as he saw it."

I saw that I was on a rather tender subject.

"I'm sorry, Marc," I said. "I didn't know."

"Das aw rite, Massa Bawb," said the old darkie.

"Listen, Connolly," I said angrily, "you don't have to talk that way to me. I knew you when you were Irish."

"Then please spell my name with an 'e'," he said testily. "It is 'C-o-n-n-e-l-l-y'."

"There is a man in *Uncle Vanya* who spells it 'C-o-n-n-o-l-l-y'," I argued.

"Are you sure?" he asked nervously.

"I ought to be sure," I said, "I saw the show last week."

"I'm glad you told me," he said. "Maybe *I'm* wrong. It looked like an "e" to me when I read my birth certificate."

"You can't go by those," I reassured him. "They are all politics. In my certificate my name was spelled 'Baltch'."

"But why are you asking me all this?" asked Mr. Connolly's secretary. "I told you when you came in that Mr. Connolly was in Europe."

"I heard you the first time," I said. "When do you think he will be back? I would like to interview him."

"I doubt if he ever comes back," said the secretary sadly. "He is trying to figure out how he can do his play in Germany, and there aren't any Indians in Germany, at least none who do not speak with a Bavarian accent."

"You mean Gandhi?" I asked for, I hope, the last time.

"That isn't funny any more," said the secretary. "It wasn't ever *very* funny."

"As funny as you are," I snapped back.

But she was gone, and I was left alone with my dreams.

(Next month: An interview with Marc Connolly, author of The Three Sisters*)*

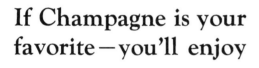

HEARD IN

In these troublous days, when it would appear that practically every Detroit policeman is in peril of losing his job, it is refreshing to note the calm that attends the affairs of the police department of our little cousin, Highland Park, the suburb which we entirely surround.

Highland Park had until recently for its chief of police a soft-spoken and a mild-mannered gentleman named William Cross. His placid demeanor is all the more marked in contrast to the fierce mien of his hard-boiled predecessor, Charles Seymour, once a Detroit dick.

At any rate, Walter Boynton was telling us that recently a couple of slick racketeers decided to open a very expensive gambling house in Highland Park. Preparations were carefully made. Nice furniture was installed. Roulette wheels were all ready for the first whirl. Tables for dicing and for cards were neatly placed. Certain people of influence were seen and attended to. In short, everything and everybody was fixed.

That is, everybody but the docile Mr. Cross. And on the morning of the day that the place was to open, with everything ready for the Big Shots of the gambling world, Mr. Cross called around.

"I want to see the proprietor," he calmly announced to the sleek-haired fellow who let him in.

"He ain't here," was the inelegant reply.

"I want to see the proprietor," reiterated Mr. Cross, with just a shade of irritation in his voice.

"Who th' hell are you?" countered the man.

"I'm the chief of police," said Mr. Cross sweetly.

"Oh," said the man, at once adopting the ingratiating manner. "Well, I'm the proprietor. You see, we have to be careful. And I was going to get around to see you.

We're goin' to have a real toney place here. You know, no cheap stuff, jus' ladies and gents will get in here. And we're goin' to open tonight. I've got everything all fixed. I've seen all the boys and I got everything fixed."

"I see," said Mr. Cross. "Well, you neglected to see the chief of police."

"I know, I know," said the proprietor eagerly. "I was gettin' around to that. And now how much is my place here goin' to cost me?"

"How much did you spend fitting it out?"

"Oh, about $75,000," said the gam.

"Well," said Mr. Cross very pleasantly, "that's just about what it'll cost you."

And with that he opened the door to admit three stalwart policemen with axes.

⸝ ⸝ ⸝ ⸝

The energetic salesmen of the Detroit Aircraft Corporation are pretty mad about an expense account that re-

cently came into the office of Edward S. Evans, the president. Mr. Evans assigned Carl Squier to take charge of a Lockheed plant in one of the towns in Southern California. A short time ago it became Mr. Squier's important duty to entertain two fairly well-known aviators, Art Goebel and Col. Lindbergh, no less.

Mr. Squier did a handsome job and when it was all over he sent in his expense voucher. On it was an item that read as follows: To one breakfast for Col. Lindbergh, Mr. Goebel, and self, ninety cents.

This was a very great shock to Mr. Evans, who is used to scanning expense accounts. And you can just imagine the chagrin of all the high-powered salesmen, who are used to making them out in a big way.

⸝ ⸝ ⸝ ⸝

Walter F. Zimmer confesses that it is a real hardship for him to adopt a diet, as he has recently done, especially when the medics tell him to lay off pie. For years and years, Mr. Zimmer says, it has been his policy to consider that day lost that does not see him consume at least one piece of pie, and make it blueberry please.

"It all goes back to the days when I was a struggling young advertising man on the staff of the Chicago Daily News. I used to eat in a small restaurant across from the old Tribune office and believe me, I wasn't exactly living off the fat of the land. I had a habit of flipping a dime and

catching it in the palm of my hand. If it came heads, my lunch was a hot dog and a cup of coffee; if it was tails, I treated myself to pie and coffee. Just a superstition.

"One day I flipped my dime in the air and missed the catch. The dime fell through a grating and was lost to sight. I didn't eat at all that day."

THE LOBBY

ONE of the reasons why Gene Tunney is a pain in the neck to the newspapermen and many others is his affected manner of putting on the Ritz. The former champeen pug was a guest at Jimmy Cox's buffet supper the night of the Sharkey-Scott fight at Miami. Naturally, all the guests were going to the fight and that was about the only topic of conversation during the informal meal

One of the company said to Tunney: "I suppose, Mr. Tunney, that you will be introduced to the crowd from the ring?" But Gene scorned the racket that made a celebrity of him in this fashion, which would have forced the swankiest English lord to take a long count: "Oh, no! It has all been quite arranged that I shall not be put to that inconvenience. Blah, Blah, and still more Blah."

⸜ ⸜ ⸜ ⸜

SPEAKING of hush-huts, Walter Winchell relates that during the intermission of a new Broadway show a water wagon paused in front of the theatre and the driver inspected the first-nighters. Dorothy Parker, of whom you've probably heard, asked the driver if she could sit up there with him.

He was an agreeable guy and he nodded assent. Parker climbed up, while the crowd on the pavement roared.

Then she persuaded Robert Benchley to join her and the best humorist in America struggled to the perch.

"Where to?" kidded the water wagon driver.

"James," cried Dorothy, "drive to so and so West Forty-ninth street," the same being the address of one of the speakeasies frequented by the New York literati.

And, by golly, the affable fellow drove them there. Dorothy and Bob were so happy they urged the man to join them for a bit of a nip.

"No, thanks," he said, "I'm on the wagon," and so saying drove away.

A thing like that could happen only in the biggest village in the world, you know.

⸜ ⸜ ⸜ ⸜

MIGHTY names were bandied about the ringside at Miami and many of their owners were there to listen. When Tommy Loughran was slapping Pierre Charles with his cream-puff punches, a fan who had never seen Loughran before and didn't know that he couldn't dent a plate of butter, yelled at him: "Hey, you been training at the Stotesburys?"

⸜ ⸜ ⸜ ⸜

GEORGE ADE was authority for this one: During the short time that Phil Scott remained perpendicular, he was busy warding off Sharkey's vicious blows but never attempting to lead and plant his fist on Jack's anatomy. That kind of tactics prompted a front pew-holder to shout: "Say, Scott, having tea with them Rodman Wanamakers don't get you anything!"

⸜ ⸜ ⸜ ⸜

GEORGE BERNARD SHAW was Lady Astor's chief lion recently at a tea she gave on her French estate in honor of Ambassador Dwight W. Morrow and Senator David A. Reed. After Shaw, who is very fond of sweets, had devoured the greater part of a chocolate cake meant for the American guests, he attacked all countries in general—except Ireland and Russia—and Lady Astor in particular.

"What would you and I have done in Russia?" asked Lady Astor of her great guest.

Stroking his beard thoughtfully, Shaw replied, "If you and I had been in Russia we would have been married and divorced a long time ago."

⸜ ⸜ ⸜ ⸜

SUZANNE LENGLEN, French tennis star, has exchanged her deadly racquet for a commercial needle. As director of the sports department for a Paris dressmaking firm, she is designing more of those short sleeveless dresses which she made so popular on all the tennis courts of Europe that no woman player would think of appearing in anything but this familiar uniform. She also introduced the famous bandeau which later Helen Wills rivaled with her no less famous eyeshade. Suzanne, in spite of her prima donna temperament, is a good business woman with an eye to her bank account, as her having turned pro indicated. In France she is more famous than beloved. And she is the only woman of her generation to be molded in wax and placed (among murderers and presidents) in the Musée Grévin, Paris' wax works of celebrities.

Merely by making little check-marks on a sheet and thumbing passport leaves, they can hold things up until noon

Browsing Through the Passport

by Robert Benchley

It won't be long now before they'll all be coming home —all those Americans who weren't going to Europe this summer because of the old Wall street plague of last November. They are hanging on their elbows over the counters in London and Paris steamship offices this very minute, trying to get reservations back to New York, and saying: "The price doesn't matter. Just something on A deck, if you can." How did they get abroad, after all that moaning about money? How are they going to get back? Or maybe you don't care.

Considering how easy it is to get out of this country, the getting-back-in is made very discouraging. Not only is there the question of passage-money for the return trip (a feat in itself of no mean proportions after you have discovered that those purple Bank of France notes that you had tucked away in the reserve wallet against a rainy day were for 500 francs apiece instead of 1000), but there is also the unpleasant reception you get when you reach the harbor of your native land. It is almost as if the Government didn't want you. Well, I don't want the Government—so we're even.

The thing that makes it confusing is that everyone on board an ocean-liner, bright and early on the morning when she is supposed to dock in New York, gets out on deck all dressed in street clothes, looking very stuffy and strange, just as if it were simply a question of finishing the second cup of breakfast coffee (if you can get the first one down, the second doesn't taste so frightful) and then stepping right off the side of the ship into a taxi. If the thing is supposed to dock at 11, everyone is all set to land at 8 A. M., with umbrellas rolled up and cameras slung over the shoulders, and with nothing to do but walk up and down the deck and fret.

This is all due to the fact that our beloved Government, by way of a welcome home, meets us with little reception committees of doctors and passport tasters, who have to come out to the ship in a little boat with what are known as the "delay papers." The idea is simply to delay things. Some of these officials have been in the business of delaying for as much as twenty-five years and have it down to a fine art. They can take a ship which is ready to dock at 9 A. M. and, merely by making little check-marks on a sheet and thumbing passport leaves, with an occasional look under the eyelids of a passenger, hold things up until noon. And not very nicely, either. You would think that they, instead of you, were the ones who had just come from abroad and from seeing the *Winged Victory* in the Louvre and the Rosetta Stone in the British Museum. You would think that the Old World air, which you have paid at least $3000 to acquire, gave you no rights at all.

This hanging around for hours and hours on shipboard between quarantine and the pier can spoil an entire summer of travel for a nervous man. If he has packed his bags and got everything out of his stateroom, donned his straw hat and wrapped his raincoat over his arm (with every indication of the hottest day of the year wafting down the

Gluyas Williams
drew the pictures

And what a bit of read-
ing matter that is!

bay from the city) he has nothing to do but pace about and think. He suddenly finds that his shipmates are very dull, at practically the same moment in which they found that he is very dull himself, and there is nothing to talk about. People who have been the life of the ship on the way over, when they get dressed in their landing-suits and come under the influence of the Long Interval, change into flat-footed Babbitts with nothing to say but: "Well, there's Little Old New York" or some crack about the Statue of Liberty and Prohibition. Everyone seems to have produced a dog from somewhere, and there is the constant threat of fighting to keep what little breath of life there is left alive. But there never is a dog-fight, much as it would be wel-comed. Even the dogs are let down.

It is at this time, when all one's books and magazines are packed, that one takes out the old passport and reads every word in it just out of sheer boredom. Standing in line waiting for Uncle Sam to look at your tongue or hanging around on deck waiting for the tide to turn, there is nothing like a little red passport to while away the time. And what a bit of reading-matter *that* is!

To start with, there is the unpleasant line on the front page: "In Case of Death or Accident Notify—" Well, unless something happens between quarantine and the pier, you have made a bum out of that. It is nothing to read on the trip across. It brings up too many mental pictures of avalanches or bad fish.

"This passport is a valuable document. Due care should be taken to see that it does not pass into the possession of an unauthorized person." A fine time to be reading that! Practically everybody on the continent of Europe, includ-ing bartenders and the young ladies at the Belles Poules,

have had a crack at this passport, if only to see how you spell your name. What would "due care" be? What would an "unauthorized person" be? So far as I am concerned, everybody in Europe is unauthorized. I recognize no authority but the Constitution of the United States (some parts of it) and the bouncer at Jack's and Charlie's. And yet my passport has been practically the picture-book of the Continent. More people have read it than have read the Book of Ruth.

Here is a man named "D. Lorinas" or "D. Toinaz" who messed up one whole page under the pretext of getting me into England. I must write him a postcard from America just to show that all Americans aren't rude. Then there is somebody connected with the French govern-ment whose name is just nothing but a long line of "m's" written in that dandy purple ink which has made France the backward nation that she is. According to the stamp under his name (I translate literally and without any attempt at style) "The present visa does not dispense the porter to conform to dispositions regulating in France the day of strangers." O. K. Monsieur, the porter gets you! No monkey business. (Continued on Page 70)

He suddenly finds his shipmates
are very dull

Browsing Through the Passport

(Continued from Page 27)

The German one I am not so sure about. It seems to be signed by a man named "Grosvenor" who should, I should think, have signed the British one instead of Mr. Lorinas. Perhaps there was an exchange professorship, with Mr. Grosvenor filling in for Mr. Lorinas at Köln and Mr. Lorinas doing the Dover trick. I'll bet they were both glad to get home and get some real cooking. Mr. Grosvenor, doubtless due to unfamiliarity with German, has filled in a line which, according to my knowledge of the language, would have me traveling backwards, which I certainly never did. I traveled sideways for a couple of days in Paris, but never backwards, especially in Germany. I must check Mr. Grosvenor up on this.

I sincerely hope Mr. Grosvenor will be able to straighten me out on this, because nobody wants to be barging backwards about the continent of Europe, especially when you are unconscious that you are facing in the wrong direction.

The next two pages frankly baffle me. One is headed "Érvényes Magyarországba" and is signed "S. N." I guess that I am supposed to be on very friendly terms with "S. N." and recognize his initials, but, unless it is Sam Northrup, I haven't the slightest idea who it is. And Sam Northrup certainly wouldn't be writing in my book about "Érvényes Magyarországba," not after all we went through together in the old days. Either the same man went right on into the next page of my passport, or it is another language entirely. I wouldn't know. But evidently on the sixteenth of Brez, 1928 (prijezd odjezo) I rated a paragraph from Str. (name undecipherable) saying that "Plati ve smyslu vynosu nitra ze dne. 31/VII 1925 cis 52858 vyjimeene k jedomu prujezdu pres uzemi csr."

Now I have done some unaccountable things in my travels abroad and have turned up with a lot of little knickknacks that I don't remember buying, but I would swear that, wherever I was on the sixteenth of Brez, 1928, I had nothing to do with "vyjimeene k jedomu." I'll bet that the official, Sam Northrup or whoever it was, just was trying to be funny and confuse me. And, if we hadn't been held up so long in the harbor, I never should have seen it. That's the way with those jokes like that. You go to all the trouble of writing them in books, and then the person who is supposed to be the goat never even sees them. I am a little sorry that I looked now.

Perhaps it would be a good idea if the professional joke makers would make it a practice to notify their intended victims well in advance. This would avoid complete confusion as well as doing away with wasted effort. Goodness knows that the life of a jokesmith is full enough of bitter disappointments and disillusionments. We should all do our utmost to make life simpler and sweeter for them.

Of course, this reading over of a passport will not take up *all* the time between quarantine and the pier. You will still have opportunity to walk around the deck eight or ten times and go back to your stateroom to pick up the things you forgot to pack. But it will help to while away a little of the tedium, and also may make you more reconciled to staying home next summer.

The Menace of Buttered Toast

by R-b-t B-n-c-l-y

Confessional » »
In Which An Author Tells All

Maybe I am a fool, but I want to go in for bulb culture. Oh, I know there is no money in it! I know that I shall just get attached to the bulbs when I shall have to give them away to somebody who wants to grow crocuses or tulips or something, and there I shall be, alone in that great, big, lonely old house that my grandfather, the Duke, left me.

This will mean, naturally, that I shall have to give up writing for a living. This God-given talent which I have must be tossed aside like an old mistress (or is it "mattress"?) and my whole energy must be devoted to the creation and nurture of little bulbs which someday will grow into great, big, ugly crocuses, defacing beautiful green lawns all over the country. But I feel the call, and what else is there to do?

Now, since I am resolved to abandon the belles-lettres, the only decent thing is to pass on the secret of word magic to someone else. Having held the reading public spellbound for ten years with my witchery, I must disclose its secret in order that some poor sucker may take it up and carry on the torch, bringing cheer to the sick and infirm and evasive notes to Brooks Brothers and the Westchester Light and Power Company. I have therefore decided to set down here the magic formula, by means of which I have, for ten years, kept the wolf from getting upstairs into the bedrooms. Here is a sample of a typical Benchley piece:

Gluyas Williams pictures Mr. Benchley as a young man before he had a mustache

Personally, if you ask me (and, so far as I have heard, nobody has asked me yet, but I shall go right ahead just the same) I feel that we, as a nation (and when I say "as a nation" I mean "as a nation") eat too much buttered toast.

Buttered toast is all right, provided neither of my little boys butters it (my two little boys seem to have an idea that butter grows on trees, when everybody knows that it is cut in great sheets by a butter-cutter [butter-cutter, butter-cutter, where have you been?] whence it is shipped to the stamping-room where it is stamped by large blonde ladies with their favorite initials and done up in bundles of twenty-five to be sent to the Tissue Paper Department for wrapping), but I *do* think, and I am sure that *you* would think so, too, if you gave the thing a minute's thought, that there is such a thing as overdoing buttered toast.

In the first place, you order breakfast. (By ordering breakfast, I mean that you get up out of bed, go into the kitchen in your bathrobe, cut three slices of whatever happens to be in the bread box [usually cake], toast it, and butter it yourself.) The words "buttered toast" come naturally in any breakfast order. "Orange juice, two four-minute eggs, *buttered toast,* and coffee." Buttered toast and coffee must be spoken together, otherwise you will hear from the State Department. (And how I hate the State Department! *Boy,* I could kill it!)

Here is where we make our big mistake. If, for once (or even twice), we could say "coffee" without adding "buttered toast," it wouldn't be so bad, but, as my old friend, President James Buchanan, used to say (he was President more as a favor to Mrs. Buchanan than anything else), "You can't eat your cake and eat it too."

It being Christmas Eve (or isn't it? I am all mixed up), we ought not to be very hard on buttered toast, because it was on a Christmas Eve that buttered toast was invented. There were six of us (five counting the Captain) all seated around an old stove (the stove was only eleven years old, but that seemed old in those days, and I guess that it *is* old for a stove), when up spoke Baby Puggy, the daughter of the termagant.

"What's all this?" said Baby Puggy. (All *what* never seemed to occur to her to explain, and if she was satisfied, what the hell are you kicking about?)

"I am in no state to bandy legs about," replied her uncle, who, up to this time, had entirely monopolized the conversation.

"I am getting awfully sick of this sort of thing," said Old Doctor Dalyrimple (they called Dr. Dalyrimple "old" because he was 107, and a very good reason, too, for calling him old), "and I have a good mind to go home and go to bed."

"You are in bed, but you're not at home," piped up little Primrose, a frightful child. "They gave your bed at home away to the Salvation Army."

"It serves them right—I mean the Salvation Army," said Old Doctor Meesky (who had changed his name from Dalyrimple to Meesky since we last saw him). And there, so far as anybody can tell, ends the story of Little Red Mother Hubbard, and, I can almost hear you say, "Who cares?"

But about buttered toast. (Not that I care about buttered toast, and not that I think you care.) If we are to have buttered toast brought to us on our breakfast trays (or is it "drays"?) I would suggest the following ways to get around the unbearable boredom of the thing:

1. Have the Football Rules Committee decree that no buttered toast shall be dunked in coffee which does not fill at least one-half (¾) the cup. This will do away with fumbling.

2. Nobody connected with the theatre, either in a managerial capacity (this includes calling "half-hour" and holding up the left leg of the tenor's trousers while he is stepping into the right leg) or as an actor (God knows what this includes) shall sell tickets to any performance for more than $11.50 over and above the box office price—or, at any rate, shall not boast about it.

3. My two small boys shall not throw paper aeroplanes so that they hit Daddy any nearer his eye than his temple.

4. I forget what this rule is.

5. I remember this, but wish I hadn't.

6. Nobody named "Cheeky" shall be allowed to compete.

This, I think, will fix matters up. And if you find that your buttered toast has become soggy after having lain under a small china Taj Mahal with a hole in the top (maybe the *real* Taj Mahal has a hole in the top, for all I know. It ought to have, to let all those people in and out) then just send for the Captain (you remember the Captain!) and tell your troubles to him (song cue: "Tell Your Troubles to the Captain. He Will Weather or Not").

But I *do* think that something has got to be done about buttered toast. I am not one to cavil (cavil me back to Old Virginny) but I do think, if you ask me (and I don't remember anyone's asking me [oh, I guess I said that in the beginning of this article. Sorry!]) I do think, personally, that—where was I?

᾿ ᾿ ᾿ ᾿

I guess that that successfully bugs any more writing I may want to do for the D. A. C. News. Unless, by some wild chance, I should get some new stuff. Well, anyway, I had a good time while it lasted.

Mr. Benchley inspecting one of the country's largest buttered toast factories to gather material for this article

Growing Old With Football

by Robert Benchley

I rise four feet straight into the air

drew the pictures

frightful brownish-colored tie which I had worn at the 42-0 game. This had to be unbent and rolled into some sort of knot. Unfortunately, I had lost one of the shoes I had worn at the 36-0 game, so I wore the one I had and an old white sneaker to match it, necessitating telling people that I had a lame foot. I had to take the pipe I had been smoking at the 15-0 game, and, what was worse, I had to smoke it, meaning that I would be deathly ill after the third puff, as the years had left their deposit in the bowl until you could have raised tomatoes in it. Thus equipped with *porte-bonheurs* and good-luck tokens, I would totter to the field and take my seat.

I never saw anything of the game, because when the whistle blew for the kick-off I would shut my eyes, relying on the location of the following cheers to tell me whether it had been run back or fumbled. The only times that I could bring myself to open my eyes and watch were when there was time out or between the halves. The rest of the time I sat trying to keep my pipe from flying out of my mouth and wishing I had gone to the country for the week-end, preferably the Swedish country.

This was the way I used to take my football. This was the reason why I was always underweight and had no thumbnails. It was a form of self-flagellation, and I loved it. Wasn't it all for the dear old Alma Mater?

I first noticed that the old flame was dying down when I picked up the Sunday paper one October morning and found that my Alma Mater had already played her first game of the season. Hitherto I had been able to recite the schedule by heart by the middle of September. Then I began seeing items in the paper that "Wheedon would be out of the line-up for the Michigan game," and that "the berth at right tackle would be in the capable hands of Thorley," and I had never heard of either Wheedon or

It is getting harder and harder to write about football as I grow older. (I take it for granted that I *am* growing older, although, except for a slight arteriosclerosis and an inability to hear, I would never know it.) This is either because the game is changed every year so that it is difficult to follow, or because I just don't care any more.

There was a time when, two weeks before the Big Game, I began biting my fingernails and having heartburn after eating. From then on until the final Saturday morning I did nothing but pace the floor and look out the window. In my more quiet moments, I made block letters on blotters and the backs of envelopes spelling out "HARVARD" and "YALE," shading each letter very carefully until I broke and had to start walking again. My friends shunned me, and I snapped at all relatives who tried to be nice.

On the morning of the Big Game I was of two minds: either to pull the bedclothes up over my head and hide in bed all day or to drop dead. It was obviously impossible for me to attend the game in the state I was in. However, I compromised by arraying myself in a set of old articles of clothing, each of which had been worn on some previous occasion when the home team had won. I had a

What was worse, I had to smoke it

Thorley. I would send in my applications for the Big Game as usual, but it wasn't until the preceding Friday that I began having trouble keeping my food down. Evidently things were cooling off in my system.

The final collapse of my youthful enthusiasm came during the Big Game when I realized that I was not only watching the kick-off but fair-catches as well. They were the first fair-catches I had ever seen made by the home team. That game I kept my eyes open during every minute of play, except for one or two seconds when a goal from the field was being tried. I was evidently getting very, very old. But I was enjoying football for the first time in my life.

The Rules Cross Him Up

Then the Rules Committee heard that I was having a good time, and set out to fix that up right away. They changed all the rules that I liked and substituted rules that I didn't understand. They not only did this once, but every year they did something different, so that, even if I tried to learn the new rules one year, it did me no good the next. I finally got so that I didn't know which side had the ball. So just as I reached the happy stage of cool-headedness where I could watch football, I found that I didn't understand football any more.

Now I find that I don't get the late editions of Saturday night's papers to find out the early season scores, but wait until I have had my coffee on Sunday morning and usually until I have read the news in the first section. (Sometimes I peek just a little into the sporting section, but it is really just a nervous reaction left over from the old days.) I get my tickets for the Big Game and make plans to go up to it, but along about the Friday night before, when I should be refusing my dinner and gnawing on my knuckles, I

begin to think of that long ride in the cold, that slow procession of fur coats from the parking place or station to the field, and the long ride back. I think of the drunks and the guys who stand up in front of you on every play. I think of the arrival at the seats, when it is discovered that there are two very small spaces left for the six members of your party, spaces which seem so tiny at first and so roomy when that icy wind begins to sweep up from underneath and destroy your shins. And, above all, I think of not knowing what the players are doing and not even knowing the players. And a great lassitude comes over me, and I spend Saturday in my warm room listening to Graham McNamee report the wrong plays over the radio.

Oh, Boy, That Forward Pass!

At least, this is what I would like to do at the time. What I really do is start out with the party on Saturday morning, grousing and unpleasant and saying that I see little percentage in taking such a long trip just to freeze to death. I snarl at my companions all during the motor ride, arguing that we would have been much better off if we had taken the train. I laugh with great sarcasm at the difficulty we experience in trying to find a place to park. I get cinders in my shoes during the walk to the stadium. I complain of the crowds and of the drunks and of the small spaces left for us to sit in. I watch the kick-off with complete indifference and even read the program and see where every player went to preparatory school. And, along about the middle of the first period, the home team gets the ball down on those rats' twenty-yard line and I watch the conference preceding the forward pass as I would watch a group of Electric Light and Power officials deciding whether or not to pass a dividend. But as the quarterback falls back with the ball in his hand and the end suddenly appears over at the left somewhere, a slight stirring of the sap begins in my old bones and I raise a languid eyelid to see what happens. And, as the boy (God bless his heart, the rascal!) goes over the line with the ball tucked nicely against his jersey, my eyes pop out, my hat flies off, I leave my seat and, to the astonishment of my neighbors, rise four feet straight into the air, while a hoarse shriek tears my thorax and I collapse in a faint.

But I still feel that football isn't what it used to be.

Sometimes I just peek a little into the sporting section

D'AC NEWS

Copyright, 1930, Charles A. Hughes

December » 1930

Trying to catch Mrs. Ransome Nevillsby by the shoulder-strap

"I Spy Backgammon"

by Robert Benchley

Having nothing to worry me right now (except a slight dropping away of bits of the base of my brain, which any good doctor can fix up in no time) I am beginning to fret about children's games. What are our children going to play if all their little games are to be appropriated by the grown-ups? With Mama and Papa playing parchesi, backgammon, and "run-sheep-run," there isn't much left for the kiddies to play except the old-time grown-up games. And we wouldn't want to see that, I am sure.

I can remember the time when backgammon was something you played only when you had tonsillitis, and didn't think it was so hot even then. Children in the old steel engravings always seem to have been playing backgammon, that is, when they weren't hanging on the necks of St. Bernard dogs or dressing up in "Dranma's" spectacles. (Children in steel engravings had no fun. I think one may put that down as a definite generalization.) In fact, backgammon was the spinach of indoor sports, and something that was reserved almost exclusively for little visiting cousins and children who "weren't very well."

On the back of my backgammon board there was a layout for a game called "Nine Men's Morris." I never knew how to play "Nine Men's Morris" and I never found anyone who did, but it always seemed to me to be just one short step duller than backgammon. I thought that some day, when I was really sick, I would have to learn to play "Nine Men's Morris," and that is one of the things

which kept me so well as a child. I expect any day now to hear that "Nine Men's Morris" has become all the rage in smart gaming circles; that there are Nine Men's Morris clubs and to read in *Vanity Fair's* "Nine Men's Morris Department" that the strategy of the game comes in so lining up your "davits" that your opponent can not release his "morrises" without opening up an "alley" for your "sub-davits" or "dangoons."

Another game which I as a child used to let myself in for only when I thought that I might possibly be allowed to sit up after eight o'clock by playing it, was parchesi. I now find out that backgammon is an outgrowth of parchesi and that some of our best young bloods have lost or gained as much as a thousand dollars a night on parchesi. I must have been a particularly dull child, for I never made a nickel out of parchesi and I was runner-up in the South End Parchesi Tournament, which lasted from Friday at ice-cream time until Saturday just before dancing-school. In fact, I was so good at parchesi that I even went in for bamboozle, which was a lot more complicated because it had more pictures on the board and you spun a little arrow to get your points. There was a time, when I was about ten years old, during which all the cuticle on my right forefinger was worn off from spinning the arrow on a bamboozle set. I got my letter for it.

Now it is all right if grown-ups want to play bamboozle and parchesi and backgammon, because they are games which can be played sitting down and in evening clothes. But if this invasion of childhood sports is going to continue, it can't be kept sedentary. Are we coming to "run-sheep-run" and "reliev-o"? Are our restricted streets going to echo with "Hill-Dill, come over the hill, or else I'll catch you

Drawings by Gluyas Williams

I very often just stood still and shook hands with my pursuer

Mr. Theodore M. Sturfish as he lunges himself at your flying form. This is *not* going to be fun.

Wholly aside from the physical risk and exertion of crashing around in the open, gambling is going to be introduced into "run-sheep-run" just as it has been introduced in backgammon and parchesi.

This will run into money. If everyone who catches his opponent wins ten bucks, with a bonus of two-fifty if you tear his or her clothing, I am going to stand for a pretty loss. Even in the old days I was never much of a hand at running games. I was the last one to be chosen on a side; and if there was any possible way of getting caught on the pickets of a fence in the general scramble, I found it and did my best with it. My wind was all right (and still is, unless I go crazy and start walking fast), but I somehow lacked the knack of lifting one leg above the other with any kind of deftness and when it came to dodging I very often just stood still and shook hands with my pursuer with a sportsmanlike gesture, saying "After all, it's only a game."

So I am worrying about the children's games, not so much for the children's sake (they didn't ask to be born; let them take care of themselves) but because I see a time coming when I am going to be entirely at a loss for something to do after dinner. I used to be able to play bridge a little, but that soon got beyond me. I don't want to play backgammon and parchesi, and I certainly do not intend to let myself in for "Hill-Dill, come over the hill" or "reliev-o," or even "duck-on-the-rock." I bruise too easily now. So what am I to do after I have finished coffee? I can't do much reading at that time, owing to the jumping type the printers seem to be using these days. Cigars make me sick. I can't play tennis, immaculately groomed as I always am, and I can't seem to find anyone who will roll a hoop with me. I guess the best thing for me to do is just to go and lie down.

standing still"? I hate to think that time will ever come.

When I go out to a party, I realize that I am in for almost anything in the way of games. I dress my prettiest (which, if I happen to be feeling in the mood, is gosh-darned pretty, if I do say so) and I make a point of holding my knife and fork so that they don't fly up and cut people sitting near me. And when, after dinner, I am told that everybody is to think up an adverb and act like it, or stumble through the dark and murder people and then guess who, or even go into the gaming-room and play backgammon or bridge, I make no protest. I make no protest aloud, that is. In my heart I say: "Oh, I am, am I?" and find some kindred soul who doesn't want to play games and we get off in a corner of some room upstairs and crash into glasses and small tables. I have learned to find my way about at parties, and can locate upstairs libraries and hideaways with rare cunning, so that I am practically never hooked in games of chance. There is always somebody else who feels "Let's get the hell out of this!" and, with a couple of good cigars and plenty of ice, we can pass the evening very pleasantly without having the hostess find us.

But if this appropriating children's games is going on to its logical conclusion, and the more rowdy forms of childhood sport are going to be taken up, it is not going to be possible to slip away upstairs and read English weeklies. For example, if our best families take up "run-sheep-run" as an after-dinner entertainment for guests, the thing is going to start right after dinner and *out-of-doors.* Everybody is going to be herded out into the side yard, with his coffee cup in his hand, and sides are going to be chosen-up before the quieter members of the party have had time to slip away. Before you know it, you are going to find yourself standing in a long line in front of the garage and having to dash feverishly back and forth trying to catch Mrs. Ransome Nevillsby by her shoulder-strap or dodge

I can locate upstairs libraries and hideaways with rare cunning

"Cheerio 1931!"

Says Robert Benchley

"Tell us, Grampy, of the morning four days after Christmas"

As illustrated by Gluyas Williams

Isn't it wonderful, wonderful, *wonderful*, to have Christmas over and done with? My! I think that we should all be just as happy and grateful at the thought as any little people *could* be! Just think! Christmas is *over!* Do you hear, Lazy-bones? Christmas is *over!*

This year, of all years, Christmas was top-hole. (That top hole over there under the sign reading "Ashes.") What could be more thrilling than the feeling, on awakening bright and early on the morning of December twenty-eighth, that this was *not* the week in which Christmas came, that it was all over *last* week, and that here you were, safe and sound (when I say "sound," I mean "still breathing"), with only a broken leg, $3845.50 in unpaid bills, and an overdraft of $45 to show for it! Ding-dong! Ding-dong!

Just imagine the joy, in future years, of telling your grandchildren about the morning of December twenty-eighth, 1930!

"Tell us, Grampy," they will shout (and I hope that if any of them ever call you "Grampy" you will strike them down like small dogs and cut them off without a sixty-day note to their names), "tell us of the morning four days after Christmas when *you* were a little boy!"

"Well, kiddikins," you will reply (and I hope that if you ever call them "kiddikins" they will set fire to you and tell the process-server where you are), "well, kiddikins, it was this-a-way: I wasn't exactly a little boy at the time, being old enough to have kidney-trouble and four store-teeth at the time. I also had a lot of fifteen-and-a-half

shirts which I couldn't wear any more on account of strangulation. But I *was* a little boy at heart—and, I am afraid, in mind—a sort of Peter Pan who just wouldn't grow up enough to hold his money in his mouth after he had made it. I was awfully cute, but not so cute that I didn't want to smack myself on the nose every time I looked at myself in the mirror. I wish that you kiddies could have seen me then. You would have had so much material to come back at Grandpa with when he scolds you now for being careless.

"Well, along about the first of December in 1930, there came rumors that Christmas was coming. 'What Christmas is that?' people said. 'The time of good cheer,' was the answer (over the radio, by agencies who were trying to buck the public up so that they would buy some of that stock the stores had on hand), 'the time when everybody gives presents to everyone else.'

" 'I've given my presents already,' I said, crossly. 'I've been giving presents since a year ago last November.' And I showed my broker's handwriting to prove it. '*Dear Mr. Benchley: Thank you for your present of December sixth. It was just what we wanted—only not enough. How about a rocking-horse before three p. m., December ninth? Yours for a Merry Christmas, Goldman, Sachs Co.*'

"But the authorities insisted that Christmas 1930 was different from Christmas November 1929-November 1930, inclusive, and, being a nation of weaklings, we submitted. We even went to the extent of buying holly-wreaths in place of the old laurel and waxed-ivy ones we had been using. That is what comes, my children, of belonging to a democracy. You have to take your holidays when they are forced on you, and not, as one would do in a properly regulated system, take them when you have $50 in your pocket and *feel* like a holiday.

"The morning of December twenty-eighth dawned cold and clear. I was sound asleep in my little trundle-bed in Bryant Park when I was awakened by my mother (who had come down from the old farm to live with us, owing to the fact that the old farm was occupied at the time by the First National Bank and Mortgage Co. of Bellows Falls, Vt.). 'Come, come, get up, Robert!' my mother said. 'This is the week in which Christmas doesn't come!'

"With a bound I was out of bed and on my feet and washing in the fountain. (We had to break the ice in the fountains to wash in those days, not so fortunate as you today who can go to the nice, warm, public baths to wash.)

"The air was alive with excitement. People were walking up and down the streets, greeting each other with 'Merry Week-after-Christmas, neighbor!' and 'Better luck next time, brother!' while clear on the frosty December morning air came the ringing words of the carol:

" '*It's all over now, ye merry gentlemen!*'

"And, boys and girls, it *was* all over! Nothing to worry about between then and December, 1931, nothing except the cream for the coffee, the studs for the shirt, and the laces for the shoes. I could hardly contain myself, but ran up and down the streets, stopping everybody I met and singing at the top of my lungs: 'How about a nickel for a cup of coffee?' adding, as a special inducement, 'No more Christmas, remember!' "

At the conclusion of this tale of Christmas Aftermath, 1930, Grandpa will probably have to be comforted with a rich, hot grog, which, by that time, will have become so legal that he won't be liable for more than sixty days in the cooler for smelling of it. (In those days, when you and I are telling our stories of 1930, the great "avalanche of wet votes" will have swept the country to such an extent that selling liquor will no longer be a misdemeanor. It will be witchcraft, punishable by a dipping in hot oil and the application of a quick match.)

It is all very well to talk like this about what we are going to tell our grandchildren in twenty years (or, for some of us, two or three years), but right now is the time to sit down and count our blessings, so that we may enter 1931 with a cheerful spirit and a wave of the sword. Maybe we won't have to sit down to count them, or even stop what we are doing, but let's count anyway.

In the first place, 1931 won't be 1930. You can't get around that. It will have a figure "1" in it, no matter what else it hasn't. It's those zeros that make all the trouble. Look at 1907, 1921, and the Great Dark Day of 1888.

Then, too, Sophie Tucker has made a great hit in London and will probably stay there for at least a year.

In addition to all this, Amos 'n' Andy are on the skids, Helen Kane's baby-talk won't be bothering us much longer, and Hollywood has definitely decided that the talkies are not suitable for musical comedies. In fact, Hollywood is wondering just a teenty-weenty bit about the talkies themselves. Next year at this time we may have something very cheering to report in this connection. In the meantime you'll just have to be patient, that's all.

As we begin the new year, there are also indications that the martini has withstood the onslaughts of the fruit-juice cocktail (the hotel room orange-juice and gin horror has almost entirely been discarded) and, *en règle* or not, the turndown collar is being more and more worn with a dinner coat by those who have caught the real spirit of the dinner coat. And there are fewer and fewer banquets. Consequently there are fewer and fewer after-dinner speeches. As a result, I, personally, have lost six pounds.

Another thing for which we should all feel grateful is that there is every indication that the prohibition law will be enforced. I mean, the Government will undoubtedly make what is known as another concerted drive. This will be Series VII, No. 8296, of our best concerted drives, guaranteed against inflation or shrinkage. The new drive will, of course, permanently dry up the United States again and what a load that will be off our minds!

Radio crooning is on the wane, and I don't care whether you are a Rudy Vallée fan or not. It *is* on the wane, and you've even got to admit that we've heard just about the last of the University of Maine *Stein Song*. There is no doubt in my mind but that radio crooning did a lot toward making a bum out of 1930. Radio crooning lulled our most dynamic citizens into a state of lethargic indifference.

All in all, things look brighter for 1931. I don't want to be a Pollyanna about it, and I don't want any of you to go ahead with any fly-by-night schemes just because I have held out this word of encouragement. It will pay you to exercise a little caution. But there is always one thing—if 1931 is any *worse* than 1930, there won't be any 1932.

I ran up and down the streets singing, "How about a nickel for a cup of coffee?"

June » 1931

The Five-Year Menace

by Robert Benchley

Drawings by Gluyas Williams

"Well, there goes another day!"

Engineers and other people with close-cropped mustaches who are returning from Latvia (Öst-Schlem) tell remarkable tales of conditions in that country and of the much-discussed "Five-Year-Plan" by which the Litvoks (or Latvooks) expect to rehabilitate their country's economic system in two years. Well, maybe three.

The Litvakian government calls it the "Five-Year-Plan" as a subterfuge, the idea being to confuse the capitalistic nations of the world and make them think that it is going to take five years, when, as a matter of fact, the whole thing will be completed in three. Well, maybe four. This will give the Latvarks at least a whole extra year to rest up in. If they don't feel like resting, they can dress up funny and march around the streets singing "*Niji-niji-nonjgero,*" the national rolling-song.

In order to facilitate this remarkable economic readjustment, Listvia has been subdivided into 300,000 *lerkjes* or subdivisions, each one presided over by a *rovzki* or sub-thyroid. It is the duty of each one of these *rovskis* to cross off a day on the calendar every three days and to say: "Well, there goes another day!" Then, assisted by six or seven selected henchmen, he dumps 3,000,000 bushels of wheat on the European market. You can see what that is going to amount to in the course of a year. Three million bushels of wheat, @ so much per bushel, bring down your four and carry your eight and, *boy,* will you have *some* wheat!

According to the returning engineers and business men, conditions in Lakvia are pretty bad, although, of course, some people might call them pretty good. It all depends on what you call bad and good, or what you call business men. Certain it is that the inhabitants of that unfortunate country are oppressed by the economic dictatorship and are not allowed to go out of their houses at night unless accompanied by some younger person.

On being interviewed, as he landed last week, Orsen S. Merple, construction engineer for the Alamo Steel Sheeting and Pillow-Casing Co., told the reporters:

"One would have to see conditions in Lotvio at first hand to appreciate them. Imagine a city of 500,000 souls, each one of whom has to get up at six every morning and do setting-up exercises to the command of a radio announcer when the radio announcer himself can not count above

Little wonder that the people are on the verge of a revolution

three. In other words, in an exercise calling for four counts—one-two-three-four—500,000 people are left on the count of three, standing on tiptoes with their arms stretched out sideways, eyes to the front, abdomen drawn in, and lungs well filled without any chance to exhale. From this position they are expected to go into the next exercise, in which there are also only three counts. Little wonder that the people are on the verge of a revolution. It's just such things, trivial as they may appear, that cause nations to sever diplomatic relations with one another.

"My wife, who has stayed behind in Bargak because she was still standing in line to get last month's allotment of black bread and Bass' ale, suffered perhaps worse than any of our little colony because of her susceptibility to hay fever. As you know, some people get hay fever from the tiny particles of hair which come from horses. My wife has tried everything for it, and, even in America, we had to get rid of our old horse Ralph just as he was getting to be good company of an evening, because he got her to sneezing so. Well, sir, in Bargak you can imagine her predicament when we found that the local authorities had decreed that every housewife should walk one of the state's horses around the block every morning for an airing and curry-comb him every night. This was because, in the present deplorable condition of things, the state's horses were getting no exercise and were becoming logy and irritable. As all the men were conscripted for the heavy manual labor and all the children were forced to play hop-scotch under the direction of the Overseer of Public Play, there was no one left but the women for this humiliating task. It was just sneeze-sneeze-sneeze for my wife all day long, and hell for the rest of us."

The Department of State has compiled a set of figures on the progress of the Letvio Five-Year-Plan, designed to show the menace to American standards and institutions of this system. We have room for only a section of these, but feel that they ought to be given publicity of some sort, if only to fill what little space we have. After looking over this handsome set of statistics you are privileged to draw your own conclusions.

Statistics Prove All

During the year 1930, Litvokia exported to the other countries of the world the following astounding items:

Navy beans (undressed)...............45,000,000
Owing to the obstructionist tactics of the Little Navy Bean group in Congress, only eleven of these were bought in America, and those were navy beans of the third class.
Wheat (in units of a thousand).......89,000,000
Other Things......................79,000,000
Old Litvok Noblemen..............   7,000
All of these came to America.
Handlebars, bells, and other bicycle accessories........................ 10,000

This will give some idea of what we in America are up against with this constant Litvok dumping. There are two things that we can do about it. One is to add more figures to the above list, making 57,000,000,000 in all. The other is to stop reading them.

It was just sneeze-sneeze-sneeze for my wife all day long

22

D'AC NEWS
Copyright, 1931, Charles A. Hughes

August ⟩ 1931

A Day Among the Nudists

I was met by my host, Dr. Fuszbein

by
Robert
Benchley

Drawings by
Gluyas
Williams

The cult of nudism, which seems to be sweeping Germany and, during the hot days of summer, the upstairs sections of our house, has certain political significances which must not be overlooked. As soon as it hits the Reichstag, Germany is through. Revolution, followed by long fits of laughing, will be the result, and it will be a matter of only a few months before the Powers will have to intervene. Then *they* might get to undressing, too.

It was to investigate this phase of the question that I decided to visit the nudist colony at Kartoffelburger Heide, having first made sure that anyone holding a two weeks' guest card at the club does not necessarily have to play games or use the pool. I have no moral scruples against undressing in public, but I just don't feel comfortable about it. Twenty years ago I might have listened to reason.

On alighting at the little station at Kartoffelsburg, I was met by my host, Dr. Fuszbein, who had taken the precaution, in coming to the station through the business center of the town, of donning a gray fedora turned down jauntily on one side. He also carried gloves and a stick in true Continental fashion.

"A little concession to public opinion," he said, smiling, as he pointed to the gloves and stick. "The townspeople are still sticklers for form in such matters. For evening wear, we have white buckskin gloves and use the regulation evening stick with a silver knob—and, naturally, the silk hat. We find that it makes the tradesmen more respectful in their attitude toward us."

"I should think that it would," I said, not being able to think of anything else at the moment.

Dr. Fuszbein then led me to two bicycles which were standing against the station platform and gave every indication of mounting one of them himself.

"But my luggage?" I asked, with some trepidation.

"You will not need any luggage at the camp," he said pleasantly, and then added—"on the contrary."

I did not like his tone. I had been assured by the tourist agency who sold me my tickets that I should not have to get undressed and, what was more, I did not intend to. But I dreaded having a scene with my host, for he seemed a genial sort of man although quite bowlegged. But, as there was not the slightest chance of my taking my clothes off for anybody, much less a doctor of social ethics, I thought that I ought to warn him.

"I don't—er—you know I am not going to—I'm going to keep on wearing my tweeds, you know," I said, ringing my bicycle-bell nervously.

"My dear man," said the doctor, laughing heartily, "you are going to Liberty Hall and may wear whatever you like. But let us leave all that until we get there. Come on—hop aboard!" And we were off down the road toward the Kartoffelburger Heide.

As we pedaled along, the doctor asked me questions about America, but seemed a little distrait owing to a large humming bird which kept pecking at him from above and around the waistline. What with managing his gloves and stick and bicycle, and at the same time giving the humming bird as good as he sent, Dr. Fuszbein's interest in America struck me as being a little casual and insincere. As we descended into a valley and a rather sizeable group

We started off across the field at a dogtrot

of moths and June bugs took up the chase, the questions ceased entirely and the rest of the trip was given over to furious pedaling and loud slaps.

On our arrival at the Kartoffelburger Heide, we were met by the Greens Committee and escorted to a sort of meadow where we sat down on an embankment. As the grass was more of a wheat stubble than real grass, I was the only one who remained seated long, the Greens Committee choosing to walk about aimlessly and to strike various unimpressive poses like brokers in a Turkish bath. Here, in the center of their cult, the formality of stick and gloves was dispensed with, although several of the older men wore bérets. I almost regretted having taken the long trip from America.

"We were discussing the reparation situation when you came in," said one, a portly burgher whose name I later found out to be Reigenvolker. "The moratorium meant a great deal to us here in Germany, you know."

"So I see, so I see," I commented.

"But in the end there will have to be a more complete readjustment of the whole financial arrangement," he continued, arms akimbo. The cigar which he held firmly in his mouth had gone completely out and he turned to his neighbor, who was busy beating a faint tattoo on his hips with the palms of his hands, evidently to some tune in three-four time (that's the German of it for you!).

"Have you a match, Herr Rasmussen?" he interrogated.

"Don't be silly, Doktor," replied Herr Rasmussen, still continuing his patting.

"Sorry, I forgot," said the Doktor, smiling. And then, turning to me, he explained: "We are apt to forget here that we do not wear clothes. It is all so exhilarating, *nicht wahr?* Do you happen to have a match about you?"

By great good luck I did not, so the Doktor tossed his cigar away into the stubble, where it was later stepped on by a newcomer to the cult who seemed a little upset by the *contretemps.*

As a rather heavy mist had begun drifting in from the North Sea, the Greens Committee showed signs of impatience, but there seemed to be no one who wanted to call it a day. Instead, a rather specious air of nonchalance descended on the group and an attempt was made to carry on the conversation where it had been left off. Finally a start was made.

It was later stepped on by a newcomer

"The work of post-war reconstruction has only just begun," said a large brewer, wrapping his arms about his shoulders to keep off the steadily-falling mist which was by now a light rain. Occasionally he gave himself a slight hug to keep warm, although this was evidently against the rules and was frowned on by several of the brothers.

"I am often reminded of the words of Heine," he continued, "in which he tells of Man's struggle against the various forces of Nature, such as Unhappinesskeit, Unbrotherlyloveforgivenesskeit, Imponderabilityness, and concludes with these words:

> 'Du bist wie eine Blume
> So hold, so schön und rein.' "

At this several of the group burst into tears, while others turned to part-singing to hide their emotions. It was a sight I never shall forget and I thought of the horror of the situation if the Metropolitan Opera Company in New York should ever go nudist and put on *Lohengrin.*

As the rain was now coming down in torrents, I asked my host if he would mind if I ducked back to the station as I was afraid of getting my suit wet. So we all started off across the field at a dogtrot. As we ran, I was conscious of an attempt on the part of one of my companions to speak to me under his breath. Leaning over toward him, I distinguished the following words as well as my knowledge of German would allow me:

"Buddie, you don't happen to have an extra pair of pants about you, do you?"

I told him that I had some in my luggage at the station, at which he muttered through the side of his mouth:

"Don't say anything now, but I'll be standing out at the corner of the baggage room when you come out. I'll pay top price for them. I'm getting goddam sick of this, I'll tell you."

Which gave me an idea. An excellent business could be done in bootlegging little articles of clothing to nudist camps, the bootlegger to hide behind bushes and trees and slip out a pair of drawers here or a sweater there to those members of the cult who were fed up with the routine. They could wear them around for a while in places where they wouldn't be seen by the cops, and then, when they were warm, return them for pressing and laundering. All I need is a little capital.

To have the whole township prancing through must be pretty discouraging

What We Missed

by

Robert Benchley

Here it is autumn again, and a great many of us didn't get to Europe—again. What with one thing and another (both really the same thing in banking circles) we decided that it would be more fun this year just to stick around home. One can always dash off on little week-end trips and get just as dusty and grimy and lose just as much luggage as on a whole European tour. And it really doesn't cost so very much more money to stay at home than it does to travel abroad.

However, it looks as if we really had missed something this year by spending the season in the United States. According to that little schedule which is sent out every year telling what is going on in the British Isles (we took up last year's in these columns a year ago—remember what fun we had?), we missed some perfectly corking sporting events in England. If I were quite sure how it is done, I would kick myself for having let the chance go by.

According to my schedule (this is as of 1931, mind you, so don't try to go by it for next year), on May eighth there was the "Furry Dance" at Helston in Cornwall; on May fourteenth the "Ceremony of Well-Dressing" at Tissington in Derbyshire; on May twenty-fifth the "Ceremony of Dunmow Flitch" at Little Dunmow, Essex; on August eighth "Rush-Bearing" was revived at Grasmere in the Lake District; and on September seventh the "Dance of the Deer Men" came off at Abbots in Staffordshire. All **Drawings by Gluyas Williams**

of these come under the head of "Old Customs," so I gather that the people concerned know what to do when the time comes.

I think that most of all I should have liked to see the "Ceremony of Dunmow Flitch" at Little Dunmow. I don't imagine that bad weather would interfere very much with flitching, for it sounds like something that you could do just as well indoors as out in the open. I suppose that, for weeks ahead of the celebration, the young men of Little Dunmow train and diet and practice in order to be in perfect condition for May twenty-fifth.

"It's no good asking Georgie to the party," they probably say. "He's saving himself for the Flitch next week."

And when the Big Day arrives, and the flitchers are all assembled in their gay costumes (I have a feeling that a flitching costume cannot be worn for anything else but flitching and is put away in the attic directly the ceremony is over) the excitement in Little Dunmow passes belief, and the chorus of "Gorms" and "Oooms!" which shake the walls of the old town probably make our cheering sections sound like classes of deaf mutes. (I know that they don't say "Gorm" and "Ooom" in Essex so much, but there is nothing to prevent them from importing a gorming and oooming section from Yorkshire in case they want to have things correct for the occasion.)

The "Furry Dance" in Cornwall has, as its main feature, a maneuver which might, and then again might not, be agreeable. In the "Furry Dance" all the inhabitants of Helston dance right through each house in town, in the front door and out the back, until they have been the rounds. Now this might be all very well for the dancers, provided each house *has* a back door, but I can imagine some unfortunate citizen who, having spent the evening before in the tap-room getting primed for the event, might possibly not be so crazy about having the entire township dancing through his bedroom in the morning. I should think that to wake up with a hangover, in a condition where every consideration and tenderness

Junket and carnations

should be shown, and just as you were wondering which head to put on, to have the front door flung open and a line of cheering, merry-making dancers come tripping through, around the chairs, over the sofas, huzza-huzzoo, and out the back door, would be just a little more than one sick man could stand. And I'll bet they don't stop at just dancing through the house, either. There are probably bucolic wisecracks and a great deal of "Get up, get up, you lazyhead!" as they skip around. One person alone coming in, all fresh and brisk, would be too many under the circumstances. To have the whole township prancing through must be pretty discouraging. The wonder is that there are any people left in Helston at all.

Although I am sorry to have missed the National Carnation Show in London on July fourteenth, I have already got my disappointment under control. The carnation, or "pink," has really very little to recommend it as a source of excitement. Carnations and a species of dessert called "junket" always seemed to me to be in the same class spiritually, and although the young bloods have taken to wearing them (carnations, not junket) in their lapels with evening clothes, they still remain pretty fairly limited in their appeal to the senses. I hope that the Carnation Show was not held in a large hall, for it must have been difficult to think up combinations of carnations which would impel the visitor to go on from exhibit to exhibit. Aside from a display of the conventional red, pink, and white (with possibly those which are dyed green for St. Patrick's Day) there doesn't seem to be much that can be done with carnations except to bank them together in floral pieces with "Dear Bill" or "Success" picked out in red letters. They also make up into a tasty "Gates Ajar." But a whole horticultural hall full of them might pall a little, unless the visitor had been drinking before

he came. On the whole, I am least sorry to have missed the National Carnation Show of all the treats offered by Great Britain during the summer.

August was a big month in British sports, with "Shakespeare Week for Overseas Bowlers" from the first to the fifth at Stratford-on-Avon and the rowing race "for Doggett's Coat and Badge" on the second. The English Folk Dance Society also had a meeting at Malvern during the first two weeks of the month. Whatever the English Folk Dance Society worked up during their festivities we shall probably get over here in America in some form or other during the coming year, so it doesn't make much difference having been absent from that. (And it won't make any difference if we are absent from the demonstrations when they are brought over here, either.)

The race for "Doggett's Coat and Badge" was probably just a boat race which, unless the speaker of the day got nervous and called the prize "Badgett's Cat and Dog" (which is unlikely), would offer no more startling features than a regular boat race—or, in other words, no startling features at all.

But in the "Shakespeare Week for Overseas Bowlers" there is a certain element of mystery. A "Shakespeare Week" would be understandable (though not to be recommended) and overseas bowlers are probably very nice people who bowl well, otherwise they wouldn't have taken the trouble to come across the ocean to do it. But where is the tie-up between Shakespeare and bowlers? I haven't gone through my Shakespeare much lately, and I certainly don't intend to for the purposes of this summary. But, as I run his plays and sonnets over in my mind, I can remember nothing which would have made him the patron saint of bowling, or would have endeared him to bowlers, especially overseas bowlers. The local bowling club at Stratford-on-Avon might well be called the Shakespeare Social and Nine-Pin Club, just as there might be a Henry Wadsworth Longfellow Skating Rink in Cambridge or a Betsy Ross Pimiento-and-Cream-Cheese Sandwich in Philadelphia. But, for overseas bowlers to make a pilgrimage to the shrine of the Bard of Avon can be explained only by the possibility of their having seen pictures of the beard and neck-ruffle and mistaking Sir Francis Drake for Shakespeare, a confusion that could so easily happen.

For weeks ahead of the celebration, the young men of Little Dunmow train

D'AC NEWS

December 1931

Copyright, 1931, Charles A. Hughes

The Lost Continent of Mee »» by Robert Benchley

Drawings by Gluyas Williams

For centuries Mankind has been fascinated (perhaps "fascinated" is too strong a word—"left cold" might be nearer it) by the theory that most of the Atlantic Ocean was once a continent, called, by a great stroke of luck, "Atlantis." This continent is supposed to have got fed up with the whole thing one day and just dropped out of sight—gentlemen, ladies, and all. (There is an idea here for Europe and America, in case things get too jammed up. Any day after Wednesday will be O. K. for me. My laundry comes back on Wednesdays.)

Now along comes a man named Colonel Churchward, who says that there used to be another continent, right where the Pacific is now, and just to be different (and a little silly, I am afraid) he calls that continent "Mu." It does seem as if, while he was working up a continent 5000 miles wide and 3000 miles long, he might have thought up a better name than "Mu" for it,

but I suppose he knew what he was about. It couldn't have sounded very impressive, when anyone asked a resident of North America where he spent his summer, to have him say: "Oh, the wife and I batted around Mu most of the time," but perhaps they didn't care so much how things sounded in those days. They certainly didn't care how things *looked*.

But these theories about Atlantis and Mu (I still blush a little when I say it) have given me courage to promulgate a theory which I have been working on ever since my other work stopped, namely, that there was also once a continent where the Indian Ocean now is (I am not quite sure *where* the Indian Ocean now is, but it is down there somewhere) and that its name was Mee. (Future lost continents are to be known as "Mi," "Mo," and "Mum.") I see no reason why I haven't just as much right as anyone to say that something used to be where there is nothing now. How can I be proved wrong? I can be proved irritating, or tiresome, but not wrong.

I have given quite a little research to this matter, including falling overboard into the Indian Ocean while trying to peer down to its bottom, and I am more and more convinced that I am right. And even if I am not right, has any harm been done? Have I hurt anyone's feelings? Have I embroiled this country in war? In these days of vicious theorizing, it seems to me that a good, innocuous, easy-going theory like that of the Lost Continent of Mee ought to come as a relief.

My researches have been chiefly with sources, such as native writings and anthropological specimens found in the countries adjacent to the region where Mee was supposed to exist. The island of Madagascar, the coastline of East Africa along by Zanzibar (*there's* a mighty pretty place I must tell you about some time—Zanzibar), the tip-tippity end of the island of Ceylon, and the west coasts of Sumatra and Australia. (I have a map right here before me and know what I am talking about, so don't try to get fresh and trip me up.) You may think that these countries are pretty far away for a little boy to be researching about in, but I had my books and my thoughts to keep me company—and besides, I slept most of the time. I guess that I'm just a vagabond at heart.

First it was necessary to master the language in which these relics of a bygone day were written, and that was the toughest part of all. The natives of this district 20,000 years ago (which is when I figure out Mee was at the top of its stride) evidently spoke a mixture of Ossip and parrot-talk, with the sound of the vowels made by striking two flints together. Now there is very little Ossip spoken at the present day, except on the island of Cocos, which was closed the day I was there. So I was forced more or less to make up the translations out of my own head, which, in a way, was fortunate, as I could make them say

GW

I guess that I'm just a vagabond at heart

just about what I wanted them to say. It was in this way that I worked out a translation of an inscription on an old bone (found in an old beef stew) to read: "Right around about here somewhere is a continent called 'Mee'." The day I found this I fairly screamed "Eureka!"

But my chief discoveries to substantiate my theory were those made working out from the west coast of Australia into the Indian Ocean. I waded out as far as I could go into the water and then began feeling around on the bottom, doing my best to keep my chin from getting wet. (I gave up trying to keep my chin dry almost immediately and got right down up to my mustache. If a thing is worth doing at all, it is worth doing well.) Several Australians got together in a group on the beach and asked me if I had lost anything, suggesting that I would find better clams and mussels up the coast aways, off Dickey's Point. One of them even tossed some pennies out for me to dive for, a taunt which infuriated me slightly, but which I was able to pass off without comment as my mouth was under water at the time. And very shortly I was rewarded for my humiliating labors. Just how, I will leave for the next paragraph.

Having brought up, in succession, the wheel to a child's express-cart, one white sneaker, a tin box for lozenges (glycerine, for the throat, it said on the cover, although I, personally, prefer a gargle), and a native policeman, who said that he must have dozed off on a rock just before the tide came in and who wanted to know, with some anxiety, what time it was, I at last came upon something which I really could use as evidence of the existence of a former continent on this site. It was a large galley (I had to pull and tug quite a bit to get it to shore) which had evidently been used as a ferry between Australia and Mee, plying back and forth across the stream which divided Australia from what was then the mainland. I take it for granted that it was a galley *and* a ferry, although several of the spectators (not one of whom would help me drag it to shore) said that it was a diving-raft which had been sunk

The day I found this I fairly screamed "Eureka!"

GLUYAS WILLIAMS

in the Big Blow of 1888. That's the sort of thing one has to contend with in scientific research.

It now being established that there *was* a continent connecting South Africa with Australia, even though separated by fjords and little rivers (the cute rascals!) on either side, we have a perfect explanation for the ethnological puzzle which has been driving experts crazy for hundreds of years, *viz:* the presence in Australia of the Negroid or Hamitic type of skull when Australia is really a dependency of Great Britain. It is obvious that with a perfect passageway between South Africa and Australia, through what was probably a civilization superior to ours (and what civilization wouldn't be?) it was quite easy for the Broad Nose, or Hyperplatyrrhine (there should be a "w" in that word, I think, but let it pass) émigré to make his way from one land to another, provided he wanted to. The question now remains: "Why would he want to?" This, I feel, is none of our business.

I hope that I have not disturbed any of my readers by this rather startling theory and above all would I be sorry to have contributed in any way to the present World Unrest! But it has been a lot of fun for me, and I am hoping to get right to work, as soon as I have had my maps made up for Mee, to show the former existence of a continent known as "Moo." The only trouble that presents itself is that I don't know just where to place it, unless possibly where Lake Erie is now. I must ask the folks around Lake Erie if they mind.

✓ ✓ ✓ ✓

(The real truth about Russia may be difficult to find out and even more difficult to take out of the land of the Communists, but leave it to Mr. Benchley. He has just sailed for Russia with Douglas Fairbanks, and what that pair will soon know about Russia!

Before the five-year plan is working, we hope to present to our readers Mr. Benchley's important findings in the domain of Brother Stalin. What Stalin and his boys find out about Benchley might make a better story, but until Stalin joins the staff of the D. A. C. NEWS we shall have to play the game the other way around. — The Editor.)

GW

I waded out as far as I could

Odd Accidents In the Theatre

by Robert Benchley

We were seated around the fire in the Green Room of the old Peanut Street Theatre in Philadelphia, talking of strange mistakes which have occurred on the stage. There was Sir Alfred Beeziz (one of the strangest mistakes, himself), old George Milgrick, as good a Third Citizen as ever trod the boards, Lawrence ("Ham") Lingleigh, and myself. We were talking about strange mistakes which have happened in the theatre—or did I say that before?

"I shall never forget," said Sir Alfred—and then forgot, so it was old George Milgrick's turn. Sir Alfred was wild, and left the room to try to recall what it was he had been going to say. George, in the meantime, was well launched into one of the most unbelievable, as well as one of the dullest, anecdotes ever recounted in the old Green Room. And if those old walls could talk they would probably say: "Old stuff, buddie, old stuff!"

"We were playing *The Merchant*," said old George, "in the old Rollic's Theatre in old San Francisco. In the casket scene, where Bassanio, or Malvolio, or one of those boys whose names end in 'io,' was trying to guess which box contained the orange and the free ride on the whirligig, the property man had made a mistake and had put a small puppy (one of his own and one which had always wanted to go on the stage) into the second casket. When Mercutio (who was being played by Ralph Persist, by the way, who later came to be quite unknown) opened the casket and put in his hand, he said: 'I am being bitten! God! Will it be what I think it is?'—and fainted. The puppy, in the meantime, had jumped from the casket and was in Portia's lap, clawing at her spangles (Portia was being played at the time by Lillie Barrison, one of the Seven Barrison sisters, not one of whom knew anything about acting except acting-up) and had completely taken over the scene. In another minute he would have been playing Shylock."

"Is that all there is to the story?" I asked. I was very unpleasant in those days.

"What more do you expect of a story?" asked old George, bridling.

"What about the love interest?" I asked. "You certainly should put in some love interest."

"Don't you ever think of anything but love?" asked George, double-bridling.

"Well, I have to *eat* three times a day," I replied, cagily,

"but I am not a heavy eater." (This last was added in an undertone, not intended for any ears, but which George and Lawrence heard distinctly.)

"I have a story to match that and, I think, to go it one better," announced Lawrence, without waiting to be asked. "Have I an audience?"

"That depends upon how much paper you want to give out," I laughed. (The term "paper," in those days, meant free passes. Today business is so good that the word has become almost obsolete.)

"We were putting on a play on a show boat," said Lawrence, handing out passes galore, "and it looked for a while as if there might not be anybody 'out front' at all. (The phrase 'out front,' in theatrical parlance, means those half-wits and bitter enemies who sit on the other side of the footlights and refuse to applaud.) The Old Man, as we called the company manager, had come to us and said: 'Boys and girls, we may have to give a private performance tonight—private to ourselves. The water is so rough that nobody on shore wants to take a chance on getting aboard the boat, even though she is tied up to the dock. What are we going to do?' "

" 'Give the show on the dock,' I suggested, hoping that the suggestion would not be taken up. But it was, and we gave the show on the dock."

"I see," I said, looking at my thumb nail in a vain effort to conceal my boredom, "and then——?"

"And then we gave the show on the dock," replied Lawrence, a little coolly, I thought.

"Didn't anything unusual happen?" I asked, trying to work up some dramatic interest. "Didn't the show boat drift off, or the hawsers trip you up?"

"I don't know what you want in a story," said Lawrence, testily. "Murder?"

"That would be O.K. with me," I said. "Giving a show

Drawings by Gluyas Williams

on a dock is no story. At least it doesn't interest me. Why, I have given plenty of shows on docks myself. There was the time I was carried off the *Europa*, for instance. 'Show' was no name for it."

"Perhaps you have something better to offer out of your own experience?" said George, who felt as I did about Lawrence's yarn but also didn't like me particularly. "You *have* something out of your own experience, haven't you?"

"If I hadn't, I wouldn't start talking," I said. "Do you remember the Old Howard, in Boston?"

"Perfectly," replied old George.

"Well, you keep on remembering the Old Howard," I said, "and I will tell you a story of a strange mistake which happened in the old Bijou in New York. We were rehearsing a play called *The Old Homestead*——"

"I remember that!" said Lawrence.

"Well, you remember that and George remembers the Old Howard," I said, "and I will continue with my story. There was a part in *The Old Homestead* which had to be played by an ox, and the ox belonged to Denman Thompson, who, in turn, owned the show. Now the ox was, at the time, up in Swanzy, New Hampshire, on the Denman Thompson estate, playing around with another ox. (They cut up so that the natives used to call them 'a team,' a team of oxen.) We had, therefore, to find some-one to read the ox's lines in rehearsal, as he wasn't coming into the show until opening night. The stage manager picked old Harry Efferts, who was a great card in his day and who looked something like an ox, except for the ring in his nose, and he ran through the part while the rest of us were learning our lines."

"I am not crazy about animal stories," interrupted George. "I have disliked them since childhood. Is that all that this is going to be?"

"In a way—yes," I responded, glowering.

"Well, then, in a way I am going to duck, if you don't mind," said George. "Anyway, I know what happened. On the opening night Harry Efferts forgot that the ox was on-stage and walked on himself, reading the ox's lines and completely bugging the show. Am I right?"

"You're right in a way," I said, somewhat disappointed, "but there is another ending that I could work up which would make an entirely different story out of it. I could say that——"

At this moment Sir Alfred returned to the room and announced that he had remembered what it was he was going to contribute to the symposium of strange mistakes in the theatre. We had not counted on this and I can tell you that it gave us all quite a start.

"Well, what was it?" I said. "I have three minutes in which to listen to you."

"We were rehearsing *The Old Homestead*," began the old bore, laying down his pipe, "and there was one character missing——"

"The ox," supplied George, putting on his hat and pre-paring to leave the theatre.

"Exactly," said Sir Alfred. "And how did you know that it was the ox?"

"And you were a man who was then known as 'Harry Efferts,' " continued George, continuing putting on his hat.

"No, I was the ox," said Sir Alfred.

And so our little party broke up, voting that the evening had been one of the pleasantest we had ever spent. But it really had not been.

Ralph Persist in one of his rôles

One of the Seven Barrison sisters as "Portia"

Mr. Benchley in "The Old Homestead"

The Murder Without Interest

by
Robert
Benchley

Drawings by
Gluyas Williams

**Every night
Pierre used to come to the
hedge and whistle**

People interested in murders (and who, aside possibly from the victims themselves, are not interested in murders?) have been reminded by the recent strange killings in the little French town of Messy-sur-Saône of a famous case twenty-five years ago in the same neighborhood, which, up until now, has remained unsolved. One of the reasons why it has remained unsolved is probably that nobody gave much of a hang. It was known as the Murder Case Without Interest.

In the early spring of 1907, the little French village of Ouilly-Oise, fifteen kilometers from Messy-sur-Saône, was asleep among its apple blossoms and Cinzano signs, little dreaming that it was soon to become the center of activity for one of the dullest murders on record. In fact, immediately after the murder had been committed, and all during the long months of the investigation and subsequent trial, Ouilly-Oise (and its neighbor, Oisey-Ouille, which lies directly across the little river) still continued to sleep. Even the oldest inhabitant of the town, when confronted today with a request for the details of the crime, does not remember that any crime ever took place. And this, please remember, in spite of the fact that he himself was one of the murders.

It was late in April (still 1907) that the murder occurred, although it was not discovered until the first two weeks in June, and even then only half-heartedly. Old Lucien Delabriex and his daughter, Anisette, lived together under the schoolhouse, in the place where all the old algebra books were stored, and this kept them more or less out of the social life of the town, as nobody liked algebra. (Algebra in English is silly enough. You can imagine what it is in French.) The young girl, however, did not care

whether or not she and her father were accepted socially, for she had a young and handsome lover in Pierre Vineuille, cadet at the local *épicerie*, and her father gave her little or no trouble as he was murdered most of the time. So life went on at its quiet pace in Ouilly-Oise, with the drums of the Great War still seven years in the future.

Every night Pierre used to come to the hedge in front of the schoolhouse and whistle: "*The French they are a funny race—parlay—voo!*" and every night Anisette would creep out from under the schoolhouse, go to the gate, and tell him (in French) for Heaven's sake to cut out that incessant whistling and go home. Then she would go back to bed, for she had to get up very early in the morning and drive the geese down the village street in rehearsal for *The Big Parade* and *What Price Glory?* and all the other war pictures which were scheduled to come. (It has been estimated that those French geese cleaned up over $250,000 from Metro-Goldwyn alone during the post-war period.)

This routine began finally to get on the nerves of the cadet Pierre, and one night he didn't whistle at all, which so irritated Anisette that she went off to the village movies with him. The next morning the geese ran through their act alone. Pierre and Anisette were never seen again. With this, the mystery, such as it is, begins. And from now on the story begins to lose interest.

On the morning of the eighth, the town barber, making his daily rounds to collect old mustaches (the French even then were a thrifty race and saved everything, just in case), knocked at the door of the schoolhouse, and receiving no answer thought nothing of it and went on to the next house. So the barber cannot possibly be under suspicion, although he later claimed to have committed the murder. It was not until the following week that it was discovered that old Lucien Delabriex was no more.

We use the phrase "was no more," not as a euphemism for "was dead," but as a literal translation of the French "*etait non plus.*" This seems to be about the only way to describe what the old gentleman was. For some algebra agents, on a search for contraband algebra books, on forcing an entrance to the cellar of the schoolhouse found that not only was the octogenarian not there, but that he seemed never to have been there. There was an octogenarian suit hanging in the closet and evidences of an octogenarian debauch (beaver hats, carpet slippers, and spilled oatmeal) scattered about the room, but on the mantelpiece was a note, written in a round schoolgirl hand (round schoolgirls write with difficulty, owing to being so round) which read:

> "*To Whom It Probably Will Not Concern: You are just making a monkey of yourself looking for Lucien Delabriex. What do you care?*"

This was a question which nobody seemed able to answer, but the law made a coroner's inquest obligatory, so a coroner's inquest there was. The coroner couldn't be there himself, but he sent flowers and saw to it that everybody had plenty of rice and old shoes. There was nobody to question, but, as there were no questions to be asked except "How are you?" and "Did you have a pleasant vacation?" the lack of testimony did not seem so glaring. One of the villagers who had crashed the gate, Emu Vandouze by name, offered to pose as a witness, and we have been able to salvage a transcript of his testimony. It follows:

Q. Did you know the deceased personally?

A. How did you ever come to ask me that question?

Q. Oh, I don't know. It just popped into my head. Why?

A. Well, it's very funny—almost spooky. I was just about to ask you the same question myself.

Q. Mental telepathy, I guess. It happens to me all the time.

A. You can kid all you like, but I think there is a great deal more to this mental telepathy than we think.

Q. *You* think there is more to it than we think? What are you talking about? Make up your mind who you are.

A. I'm Bon-Bon Buddie, the Chocolate Drop——

Q. (*Joining in*)—the Chocolate Drop, that's me-e-e!

A. What else do you know?

Q. Don't ask me—I might tell you.

A. Witness excused.

Q. Where do you get off to excuse the witness? You *are* the witness.

Counsel for the Defense: I move to have that last remark stricken from the record as irrelevant, irrelevant, and irrelevant.

The Court: Motion denied, but thought awfully well of.

Counsel for the Defense: That's cold comfort. Thank you for nothing.

Q. Court adjourned.

The Court: Sez you!

This sort of thing dragged on for days, until finally it got so that nobody went into the court room at all, not even the Court. Another family moved into the courthouse and changed all the furniture around so that the room where the trial was being held became the baby's room and before long was all cluttered up with broken toys and picture books. Every once in a while some one connected with the trial would drop in to see how things were going and they would be shushed up for fear they would wake the baby. This more or less made a mockery of the law, and, after a year or two, the citizens of the town took the matter into their own hands (known as the Lynch Law in America) and stopped the whole thing for good.

Thus ended one of the strangest murder mysteries in the annals of French jurisprudence, ending where it had begun —in a deadlock. And yet some people hold that Truth is stranger than Fiction!

She had to drive the geese down the village street in rehearsal for "The Big Parade"

The Devil's Diamond

by Robert Benchley

Is the famous Imky diamond a hoodoo? Is it a diamond? Is it Imky? These are three of the five questions that students of the occult are asking themselves. (The other two questions are: 1. What three famous generals never saw each other? 2. Where is Arithmetic?) That low buzz-buzz-buzz is the sound of students of the occult asking themselves questions. The following silence is their failure to reply

He immediately fell down and broke both hips

GLUYAS WILLIAMS

For the riddle of the Imky diamond has been a source of puzzlement to scientists for the past fifty years. . . . Oh, well, forty-five then. . . . Thirty. . . . Twenty. . . . Six, and not a year less. That's final. Since it was first brought from India by Lieutenant Colonel Irving Imky, shortly after the Ski Rebellion, it has been passed from generation to generation of this unhappy family, always bringing death, famine, and similar bits of hard luck in its wake until the present members of the family have begun to wonder if perhaps it would not be better to get rid of it altogether. In fact, they *would* get rid of it—if they could find it. For in addition to its almost spooky quality of bearing misfortune to its owner, it has added insult to injury and got itself lost.

"It is somewhere about the house, I am sure," said Mrs. The Honorable Imky to a reporter yesterday, "for it is still giving off hard luck. That is the unfortunate part of the affair—we haven't the satisfaction of taking it out and looking at it, but it is being just as naughty as it was in the old days. If we could find it, we would throw it out and maybe get some sleep."

The first indication that the diamond was not a good-luck piece was when the old Lieutenant Colonel bought it from the Indian rajah and immediately fell down and broke both hips. He did not at first attribute the accident to the diamond, as he had been drinking rather heavily (otherwise he never would have bought it) and had been falling down constantly for two years. But this was the first time that he had suffered any injury more serious than slight abrasions and nose-bendings. They put him on a boat bound for England, he still clutching the jewel in his hand, as he would not trust it to his *punkah*. Shortly after leaving Singapore, the ship ran into a large rock (which later turned out to be the mainland) and the unlucky Imky's stateroom, which was forward on the starboard side, was pushed aft and slightly to port so far that

he ended up in the galley, in no very good frame of mind I can assure you. In fact, there was some doubt as to whether his stateroom was on the ship at all and, for a day or two, he was listed as "not having sailed." This little *contretemps* did his hips no good, either, and by the time he had landed in London he was far from the dapper young officer who had sailed ten years before to serve Her Majesty the Queen. But he still held the diamond clutched in his chubby fist and showed it to people with great pride, saying "Look!"

During the rest of his life (about four days) he refused to relinquish his prize, and when he was buried in Westminster Abbey (he was a very large man and there was some talk of burying Westminster Abbey in *him*, but this was given up because of the engineering difficulties in the way) another stone, of the same size and shape, had to be substituted for the real diamond, otherwise they never could have got him to lie down.

The gem then passed into the possession of his eldest son, Lord Inverness Imky, who was asleep at the time and didn't realize what he had inherited until the next day when the roof fell in. "What is this?" he asked, petulantly, from under a large glass chandelier. "Somebody wise-cracking?" When he was told that it was probably the work of the Imky diamond, which was then reposing in his strong box along with 3000 pounds worth of bills which his father had bequeathed him, he merely nodded (as well as he could with the chandelier around his neck) and said: "We Imkys must play the game and carry on to see it through, and cheerie-ho!" Then he collapsed and was buried in Westminster Abbey, much to the surprise of Lord Alfred Tennyson.

The next of kin to catch hell was the younger brother of Lord Inverness, who, by now, was in so much trouble in his own right that he hardly noticed the effect of the diamond. When, one day shortly after he had come into

Drawings by Gluyas Williams

his heritage, his right arm dropped off, he laid it to some boyhood prank and thought nothing of it. "I shall be all right," he said, pluckily. "I've seen everything, anyway." But he was *not* all right, and the diamond, evidently piqued at not being credited with this odd piece of misfortune, set itself to showing the young man what was what.

Hearing that there was a great future for left-handed men in America, the scion of this ancient family migrated and settled in New York (in the State of New York). He did not take the diamond with him, as he left England rather hurriedly, owing to a little killing in which he had played quarterback, but he had not been in New York for more than a month before the precious stone

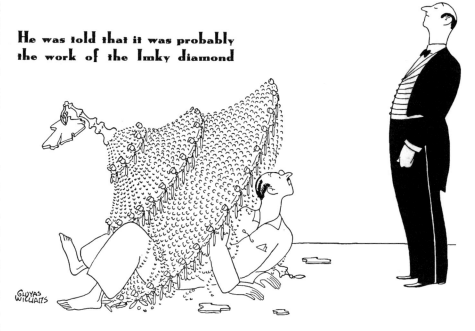

He was told that it was probably the work of the Imky diamond

followed him, working its way over on a cattleship under the name of Townsend. It showed up one day at his lodgings and that very evening New York was destroyed by the Great Chicago Fire. So much for superstition.

And so it has gone. The Imkys have prospered, in the material sense of the word (which is about as good a sense as you can get out of a word like "prospered"), having sold old Indians to New York for a string of beads and then flooded the market with new Indians. The Indians themselves enjoyed this little game of give and take and the Indian trade was brisk on Broadway for a good many years; so brisk indeed that additions had to be built to most of the speakeasies just to accommodate the Indian trade. Most of the drinking Indians

Said it must be somewhere about the house because she remembers having put it there herself

were two-bottle men and always after the second bottle they would insist upon giving portions of Manhattan to their white friends. And it was precisely in this manner that the island of Manhattan and subsequently all of America came finally into the hands of the White Fathers. So the Imkys have established a business here which, while it sagged a little during the Depression of 1929-78, has brought them in thousands of inquiries and promises to pay. They own a house on Fifth Avenue, which is now a Japanese back scratcher emporium with Turkish rugs in the window, and their children go to Public School No. 86. But they are not happy.

Thus we find that the great Imky diamond has proved more of a liability than an asset. During the past ten years hard luck has become so much of a staple in this rare old family that they hardly notice it, and it was not until one of the little Imky girls read about the Evil Eye, which is supposed to watch over her relatives (she gets the Sunday papers before her father and takes out the funnies and most of the interesting sections and makes birds' nests out of them), that the present generation of Imkys realized that they were harboring a viper in their midst. It was then that they began to look for it. The first thing to do in getting rid of a viper is to find it. "First catch your viper," as Mark Twain said when told of reports of his death having been greatly exaggerated.

And so we find ourselves confronted, not only by the problem of disposing of the famous Imky diamond but of unearthing its whereabouts. If the Imky family could locate their trouble (and Mrs. Imky, as we have seen, has said that it must be somewhere about the house because she remembers having put it there herself) they could give it to the Salvation Army, for the Salvation Army just eats up hard luck. But, so far, like the salt mill in the fairy story which ground out salt even from the bottom of the sea, the Imky diamond, wherever it is, is grinding out headaches for its owners, and nobody can stop it. Perhaps the best thing for the Imky family to do would be just to stop having children and die out.

Is the Sea Serpent "A Myth"?

by Robert Benchley

Drawings by Gluyas Williams

Now that people are again summering at the seashore, we shall doubtless begin getting those exciting reports on sea serpents, and maybe it won't seem good! All winter, spring, and early summer we got reports on budgets, taxes, and the increase in pellagra, and a good sea serpent report will come in the nature of a relief. At least, there is some ground for argument about a sea serpent.

So many things have turned out to be true, which everyone had scoffed at (who would have believed ten years ago that we should today be using matches instead of rubbing two pieces of wood together?), that it has to be a pretty wise man who will sneer at a sea serpent story. If we knew some of the things that are at the bottom of the sea, I guess a sea serpent would seem no more strange than an Airedale. I'll bet even that old sneaker that I dropped overboard while fishing in 1911 looks pretty startling by now.

There have been several sea serpent stories which have been fairly well authenticated, and if you were out in a rowboat in the territory supposed to be frequented by one of these monsters of the deep, you wouldn't be so cocksure. You might *think* that there were no such things, but you'd be a fool to say it. I understand that they have very sharp ears and don't take kidding very well.

There was, for instance, the famous serpent seen by the members of the crew of the schooner *Mrs. Ella B. Margolies*, off Gloucester, in 1896. This one, according to all reports, was a darb. I myself am not very crazy about talking about it, so I will set down the excerpt from the ship's log for what it is worth (closing price .003).

On Board "Mrs. Ella B. Margolies," August 6, 1896. Lat. 24°57′ S., long. 16 ft. E. . . . Brooklyn—8; St. Louis—4. . . . Am. T&T .20½.

In the four-to-six watch, at about five o'clock, we observed a most remarkable fish on our lee quarter, crossing the stern in a S. W. direction; the appearance of the head, which, with the back fin (or upper leg), was the only portion of the animal visible, was something similar to that of a rabbit, only without the ears. Perhaps we should not have said rabbit at all. The fin (or upper leg) seemed to be sometimes here and sometimes there, and might possibly have belonged

Right by the little door where clerks went in and out, something caught my eye

You might think that there were no such things, but you'd be a fool to say it

to some other animal. It (the animal) pursued a steady undeviating course, keeping its head horizontal with the surface of the water except when it turned to look backward, as if flirting with something. Once a small pennant was raised just above where the tail should be, a pennant which, according to the code of the sea, signified "Owner on Board."

No one on the ship has ever seen anything similar, and very few wanted to look a second time. There was a slight sea running and the wind was from the northeast quarter. We had lobscouse for supper.

This log was sworn to by the yeoman, who later deserted and went to work on a farm in Kansas.

This same animal was seen from points along the shore at Gloucester and Bass Rocks, and officials of the Odd Creatures Society took the trouble to investigate, armed with a set of questions which were designed to determine the exact nature of the alleged monster and to check on the habits of those who claimed to have seen it. The answers given by Roger Bivalve, a fisherman living in a lobster trap on Point Pixie, are representative as well as enlightening. Following are the questions asked by a representative of the society and the answers given, in an affidavit, by Mr. Bivalve:

Q. When did you first see the animal?

A. I should say shortly after falling down on the rocks in front of my place.

Q. At what distance?

A. Once it was in my lap. Other times about fifty yards out.

Q. What was its general appearance?

A. Something awful.

Q. Was it in motion or at rest?

A. There you have me.

Q. What parts of it were above the water and how high?

A. That depends on what you call "the water" and what you mean by "high."

Q. Did it appear jointed or serpentine?

A. Serpentine, by all means.

Q. If serpentine, were its sinuosities horizontal or vertical?

A. What was that again?

Q. What were its color, length, and thickness?

A. I am trying to think.

Q. Describe its eyes and mouth.

A. Well, its eyes were beautiful. I thought for a while that I was in love with it. Its mouth was more mocking than anything, which gave me the tip-off.

Q. Had it fins or legs, and where?

A. Do I have to answer that?

Q. Did it make any sound or noise?

A. I should say it was more of a cackle, or perhaps a laugh. I know I didn't like it.

Q. Did it appear to pursue, avoid, or notice anything?

A. It looked in my direction once or twice and winked. I take that back.

Q. Did you see more than one?

A. I didn't look.

Q. How many other persons saw it?

A. Oh, I see! You don't take my word for it.

Q. Do you drink?

A. Only medicinally, and then never after I fall over.

This affidavit, together with a dozen others of a similar nature, convinced the society that there undoubtedly *was* something in the water off Gloucester on August sixth, 1896. A report was drawn up on the subject, and it is from this record that we have taken the evidence submitted herewith.

It will be seen from all this cross-questioning that you can't walk into a newspaper office and say, "I have seen a sea serpent" and get away with it. There are a great many skeptics about, especially since liquor became more expensive, and a man who really wants to go down in history as a bona fide serpent-viewer has got to present his credentials and stick pretty closely to the same story. It would also be well if he took a mouthful of cloves before beginning to talk.

It is too bad that there should be this suspicion of excess drinking attached to reports of sea serpents, because it tends to lower the whole tone of that type of reporting and perhaps keeps people from telling all they might tell about the wonders of the deep. I know that I, myself, have a story which might help solve a great many

I saw a sight which made my blood run cold

problems in marine mystery, but which I do not feel like telling because it might alter my children's opinion of me.

Oh, well, I might as well get it off my chest! I am not a drinking man by nature, and although on this particular day I had rubbed a little alcohol into my hair to keep the flies away, I have every reason to believe that I was in full possession of my senses (I don't suppose that I can say *full* possession, for I have three more payments to make before they are really mine). I had been talking to an old friend whom I hadn't seen for years, and the next time we looked at the clock it was Friday; so I said: "Well, Harry, what do you say we call it a week and knock off?" Harry was agreeable (or as agreeable as he *ever* was, being a morose man at best) and we went and bought two hats to put on so that we wouldn't have to go home bareheaded. It was in the hat store that I caught my first glimpse of the sea serpent.

I know that this sounds fishy—and that is why I have waited all these years to tell about it. But, just as sure

as I am standing here at this minute, I looked down the length of the hat store (it was a very long hat store, made to seem even longer by the mirrors at the end), and there, right by the little door where the clerks went in and out, something caught my eye, no mean trick in itself, as my eye was not in a roving mood right then, as I was concentrating on a fedora which I fortunately did not buy. It was as if something with a long tail had just disappeared around the corner of the door and had run out into the back of the shop.

I thought nothing of it at first, thinking that it was probably a salesman who had a long tail and who was going about his business. But the more I thought it over, the stranger it seemed to me that I had not noticed a salesman with a long tail before, as we had been in the shop several hours by this time.

So I excused myself very politely to my friend and to the man who was waiting on us and tip-toed down to the door where I had seen the disappearing object. It was quite a long walk, as I got into another store by mistake and had to inquire my way back, but soon I reached the rear of the original hat store and looked out into the workroom. There, stretched across an ironing board, where they had been reblocking old derbies, I saw a sight which made my blood run cold.

Beginning at one end of the ironing board and stretching across it and off the other end into the window——

I guess that I was right in the first place. I never should have begun to tell about it. You wouldn't understand.

Now That We Think of It » » »

Only $1400 was lost in operations by the Club in June. Of course, lots of pastimes are pleasanter than losing money, but for a big institution like the D. A. C. to squeeze through a dull month with a loss of only $1400 amounts to almost a sensation. Naturally, the restaurant business in the Club at this time of year is pretty light, but the room business is holding up unusually well.

Two of the rubber industry's leading magnates were at the Club last month, Harvey S. Firestone and W. O. Rutherford, president of the Pennsylvania Rubber Company. They were in Detroit on one of their frequent visits to look over the situation. Mr. Firestone was accompanied by his son, Leonard. These famous men of the rubber industry all breathed a tone of optimism.

Directors of the D. A. C. were signally honored by Gar Wood last month. He invited them up to Algonac to see *Miss America* X. The directors made the trip to Algonac on the eleventh and up to that time no one but Mr. Wood and his coworkers had ever seen the boat with which he hopes to successfully defend the Harmsworth Trophy. In honor of the Club directors, the four titanic Packard motors were set off for the first time. The power plant in the new Wood boat is something to marvel at.

Kaye Don will need all of his 120-miles-an-hour speed if he is to finish ahead of the Detroit boat in the big races next month on Lake St. Clair. The 6800 horsepower that the engines in *Miss America* X are capable of developing is one-fourth of the horsepower in some of the big transatlantic liners, so when it is remembered that Mr. Wood's boat is only thirty-eight feet long it is not hard to realize that the turning on of all that power is going to move his boat through the water at a terrific speed. The coming Harmsworth race looks like the greatest battle of horsepower ever known on the water up to this time.

Les Dryden, chairman of the athletic committee, is a great booster for the sun bath on the roof of the clubhouse. The way to avail yourselves of the rays of the sun on the roof is to go into the locker room, undress, put on a bathrobe, go up to the roof, disrobe, and the sun bath is on. Plenty of cots are available. There is nothing fancy about the Club's solarium on the roof, but results are guaranteed. If the sun is shining, you will get your tan from a contented sun. Make no mistake about that. Sun bathing is quite the rage now. The University Club has just opened a new solarium on the roof of its clubhouse.

But what if we haven't got the five cents?

As I Understand It

by Robert Benchley

Here we are, face to face with the most momentous national election that this country has held since that other momentous one back in 1928, during the Great Prosperity Epidemic or "Black Death." And what do we, the voters, know about the issues of the campaign? *Really* know, I mean. What do we really know of the workings of the machinery by which this great land of ours (a phrase coined during the late Chicago conventions) is governed? What do we really know about politics? What do we really know about anything? I do not like to sound Russian, but isn't it terrible!

I know just what I happen to pick up from a random perusal of the daily papers and some of the weeklies (I caught an interesting story the other day about two cows

which had been struck by lightning so hard that they had ended up by being one cow), but I shall be glad to impart the fruits of my research to those who still feel that they are in the dark on several of the more important points. There are one or two things on which I am not quite clear myself, but they will probably come out as we go along. We might as well all stick together in this thing, and if there are some things I don't understand I will ask *you*.

The Issues

1. ECONOMIC REHABILITATION. This, I take it, is the most important issue of the campaign, although a lot of people feel that Prohibition is. But what good is it going to do to get beer back to five cents a glass if we haven't got the five cents? I still hold out for Economic Rehabilitation, especially up in that little corner of a certain bank where a bronze tablet now marks the site of what used to be called my "drawing account." I want that fixed up first. And the bank does too, so the officials tell me. At present, they say, it is just a plague spot, contaminating the other accounts.

Now, as I understand it, Economic Rehabilitation depends upon a number of things, such as Overproduction, Underproduction, the Gold Supply, the Tariff, Taxation, Public Confidence, and plenty of Vitamin B. Then, too, there is Currency Inflation. If I have diagnosed Currency Inflation correctly, the same thing if practiced in an attic by a little group of private citizens is called "counterfeiting," and is punishable by, or both. If an inflation of the currency is agreed upon, I, personally, am sitting pretty, for I have at this minute a pile of gold-papered chocolate dollars in my drawer which ought to be good for a half million if there were any equitable system of exchange in the world. So don't worry about *me* if we have Currency Inflation, and don't come sniveling around for any of my chocolate dollars.

The problem of Taxation is a difficult one, owing to the necessity of thinking up different names for the one process of milking the consumer. It would be much simpler if the consumer, whenever he earned a dollar (march music, please!) could put it right into a little basket, cover it over with a napkin, and leave it immediately on the steps of the nearest government office. Then we wouldn't have to bother with the different designations, such as Sales Tax, Manufacturer's Tax, Middleman's Tax, or Licensed Pilot's Tax.

There seems to be quite a lot of opposition to the so-called "soak the rich" policy of taxation, but this system would seem right now to be in a class with a "soak the dodo" or "soak the dinosaur" policy, the first problem of which would be first to find your dodo or dinosaur.

I am afraid that I can't be of much help to you on the question of Gold Supply, as I myself am more than a little hazy on the subject. The United States and France are said to have most of the gold in the world (except for those gold-covered chocolates in my drawer which nobody knows about), and they keep shuttling it back and forth across the ocean until anyone trying to follow it with his eyes would grow dizzy. But then, what? When you have got all the gold, what do you do? Do you count up to 100 by tens and cry, "All 'round my goal are It!" and then run like everything? To be perfectly frank, I don't believe there *is* any gold at all. If Germany can pay $100,000,000,000 without even one actual dollar changing hands, what is to prevent a shipload of "gold" from going to France from America, or vice versa, with nothing in it but 500 bales of herring? I don't want to start any financial panic. I am just asking.

The question of Prohibition is a peculiar one, owing to its having been taken up by the funny papers. One minute the whole nation seems to be up in arms for a repeal of the eighteenth amendment, and it looks like a question of only a few hours before Martinis will be on sale at the stands now devoted to pineapple juice. Then, the next minute, Congress votes on a proposition to allow one extra inch of foam on near-beer, and it is defeated 389-6. There must be a slip-up somewhere.

One of the things which complicate the issue of changing the Constitution is the Constitution itself. According to the provisions in this noble document (another good line from the Chicago conventions) the process of repealing an amendment is second in difficulty only to the process of carving George Washington's face on Stone Mountain. As I understand it, in order to repeal the eighteenth amendment, no matter *which* party wins, the

I have at this minute a pile of gold-papered chocolate dollars in my drawer

GW

following formalities will have to be gone through with:

Each family will have to select a blond member to pack up and attend a convention at the State Capital. After an invocation and a reading of the minutes of the last meeting (if there happens to have been no last meeting, a last meeting will have to be held) a rising vote will be taken as to whether or not a quorum has been constituted. If it turns out that there is a quorum and a sufficient number of people who can sing bass, there will be another invocation and a singing of *The Star Spangled Banner* by a large soprano. Delegates will then be elected, *viva voce*, who are to attend another convention to be held at the State Fair Grounds on the second Tuesday following the first Monday of the next month without an "R" in it. Everybody will then go home and wait until that date.

At this second convention, after the invocation and a singing of *The Star Spangled Banner* by two large sopranos, a vote will be taken, *sotto voce*, on the question of whether or not the amendment will be repealed. There will be considerable confusion, owing to several of the delegates thinking that it is the fifteenth amendment which is up for consideration, and three or four of the conventions will turn in a vote favoring taking the franchise away from the colored people. But this will be all straightened out in the course of six or eight months, and an embossed record of the various resolutions will be forwarded to Congress, with the photographs of each delegate attached and a copy of the state song.

As soon as every state in the Union has gone through with this formality (a process which took something like fifty years for the *passage* of the eighteenth amendment), *then* the actual work of repeal may be said to have been begun. So it will be all right if you don't start cracking the ice quite yet for those legal Martinis. There is nothing worse than a warm Martini full of melted ice water.

The candidates of the two leading parties are named Hoover (Rep.) and Roosevelt (Dem.). Mr. Roosevelt wears glasses most of the time and Mr. Hoover does not.

A singing of "The Star Spangled Banner" by a large soprano

GWYAS
WILLIAMS
drew the pictures

THE ROBERT BENCHLEY SOCIETY

155 24922

(GARBLED FAVORITES)

"Frau Be

Founded in 2003 by some people of taste, wit, and several extra bottles of wine and some old bitters, the Robert Benchley Society is dedicated to the study and appreciation of America's Greatest Humorist Robert Benchley. In Benchley's articles, books, and movies lurks the master of nonsense and fun.

We are perpetuating Benchley's work and his laughter.

To be a part of the Annual Robert Benchley Writing Contest, or join a local chapter you need to send large quantities of cash or if that is a problem, just your email.

To join simply contact:

Benchley.blogspot.com or Robertbenchley.org
Enter your email and you are in.